# Universal Human Rights in a World of Difference

BROOKE A. ACKERLY
*Vanderbilt University*
*Political Science*
*brooke.ackerly@vanderbilt.edu*

CAMBRIDGE UNIVERSITY PRESS
Cambridge, New York, Melbourne, Madrid, Cape Town, Singapore, São Paulo, Delhi

Cambridge University Press
The Edinburgh Building, Cambridge CB2 8RU, UK

Published in the United States of America by Cambridge University Press, New York

www.cambridge.org
Information on this title: www.cambridge.org/9780521707558



First published 2008

Printed in the United Kingdom at the University Press, Cambridge

*A catalogue record for this publication is available from the British Library*

*Library of Congress Cataloguing in Publication data*
Ackerly, Brooke A.
Universal human rights in a world of difference / Brooke A. Ackerly.
p. cm.
Includes bibliographical references.
ISBN-13: 978-0-521-88126-5
1. Human rights. 2. Feminist theory. I. Title.
JC571.A136 2008
323–dc22

2007051567

ISBN 978-0-521-88126-5 hardback
ISBN 978-0-521-70755-8 paperback

# *Universal Human Rights in a World of Difference*

From the diverse work and often competing insights of women's human rights activists, Brooke Ackerly has written a feminist *and* a universal theory of human rights that bridges the relativists' concerns about universalizing from particulars and the activists' commitment to justice. Unlike universal theories that rely on shared commitments to divine authority or to an "enlightened" way of reasoning, Ackerly's theory relies on rigorous methodological attention to difference and disagreement. She sets out human rights as at once a research ethic, a tool for criticism of injustice, and a call to recognize our obligations to promote justice through our actions. This book will be of great interest to political theorists, feminist and gender studies scholars, and researchers of social movements.

BROOKE A. ACKERLY is Associate Professor of Political Science at Vanderbilt University. She is the author of *Political Theory and Feminist Social Criticism* (Cambridge, 2000) and co-editor of *Feminist Methodologies for International Relations* (Cambridge, 2006).

*For Aasha*

# *Contents*

# *Acknowledgments*

Writing is a privilege. Writing acknowledgments is a challenging privilege. How do I appreciatively bring to light the collective effort that this project has been *and* take single authorship of the ideas it generated?

My first thanks goes to Marie and her family for asking for help, instilling their trust, and (much later) allowing me to tell their story. Despite our challenges of communication and their accumulation of unbelievable misfortunes, they were continually courageous. I appreciate their renewable faith in the possibility of a better world and better life for the children. I am also grateful to the host of people who helped me understand their life situation and support their case. At times it was unreal to me; by listening to me retell their story and offering constructive advice or direct help, many friends sustained my commitment to Marie's family. These include Catia Confortini, Sarah Park, Klint Alexander, and Bina D'Costa. Holly Tucker and Anne Marie Goetz showed true friendship by helping me understand, fulfill, and find the boundaries of my obligations to Marie and her family.

During the beginning and middle of this project, I have had the privilege of being hosted away from home. I owe a special debt to the University of Southern California's Center for International Studies (CIS), in particular its then Director, Ann Tickner, and an enthusiastic graduate student, Catia Confortini, for encouraging the first workshop. Like the CIS, the Robert Penn Warren Center for the Humanities at Vanderbilt University created the ideal work environment for an academic – great colleagues, administrative smoothness, and tea. Thank you Marisela Schaffer, Mona Frederick, Galyn Martin, Lacey Galbraith, Tonya Mills, Tommy Womack, and Darlene Davidson, whose efficient administration enables so many to focus on ideas. And, though it wasn't home for long, thank you to Richa, Mrinalini, and Sonalini Sapra for giving me a home and family in Mumbai that was rich in food and conversation.

I am also appreciative of the opportunity to participate in two interdisciplinary groups sponsored by the Center for the Study of Religion and Culture at Vanderbilt University. These groups, one on *Spirituality and Ecology* and one on *Poverty and Religion*, supported my individual work on human rights as an assistant professor with faith that ultimately my scholarship on global social justice and my tenure would enable me to make a contribution to collaborative scholarship on poverty, the environment, and religion. This faith is an essential ingredient of transdisciplinary collaboration that is inclusive of pre-tenure colleagues.

I am particularly privileged to have worked with Bina D'Costa – co-researcher, co-author, and co-traveler. I am grateful to her for collaborating on a related project through which much of the interview data in this book were generated. During our work together we explored many of the meanings and challenges of collaboration. These challenges and their fruit continue to inspire as does Bina through her scholarship, activism, and teaching.

*Universal Human Rights in a World of Difference* has benefited from critical engagement with so many. I include among these Vanderbilt colleagues who have stretched my disciplinary boundaries by sharing their own work: Ed Rubin, Lenn Goodman, Melissa Snarr, Monica Casper, and Jaya Kasibhatla.

Uma Narayan, Moira Gatens, Ted Fischer, Beth Conklin, and Jaya Kasibhatla were always looking over my shoulder reminding me that I too am claiming an epistemological authority. I particularly appreciate Ted and Moira reading my first chapter so reflectively (and quickly). I was holding my breath. By thanking them, I don't mean to indicate that they approve of my methodological solution to the always present challenge of making the exercise of the power of epistemology visible.

A number of specific conversations along the way had greater impacts on my work than perhaps the interlocutors realized. Many of these were with one person: the creative and generous Mona Frederick. Others, while not ongoing, had significant impact. Hayward Alker and Ted Slingerland led me to reflect on the work of Lakoff and Johnson and on the importance of metaphor. This influence is visible in the central role that the "right of way" metaphor plays in my view of human rights.

For discussions about justification and legitimacy, I am grateful to Michael Goodhart, Josh Cohen, and Moira Gatens. I am particularly grateful to Michael for being the person I can call on a rainy day and to Moira for that great conversation underneath the L in Chicago.

For keeping me reflective about methodological challenges, I am privileged to have had ongoing and fruitful discussions with Bina D'Costa, Maria Stern, Jacqui True, Carol Cohn, Lyndi Hewitt, Sonalini Sapra, all of the participants in the edited volume *Feminist Methodologies for International Relations*, and my collaborators in the Global Feminisms Collaborative at Vanderbilt.

For great conversations and for hosting those conversations during the formative year of this project I thank Sarah Song and colleagues at the Gender and Political Thought seminar at the Massachusetts Institute of Technology. I am particularly appreciative of Jane Mansbridge, Josh Cohen, Sarah Song, and Sally Haslinger for making me consider the normative power I claim to be drawing from the study of activism. I am particularly grateful to Josh, forever the promoter of deliberation, for encouraging my criticism of his work.

For being a great discussant and host at University of North Carolina Chapel Hill's Political Theory Workshop, I thank Jeff Spinner-Halev for giving me a chance to reflect in public on human rights as a non-ideal theory. The influence of the faculty and graduate students' reflections are visible mostly in chapter 2. In addition, Susan Bickford had a profound affect on my thinking about the role of listening in human rights praxis and her work is central to my exposition of immanent universal human rights theory in chapter 7.

At University of Pennsylvania Women's Studies Program, the Alice Paul Center for Research on Women, Gender, and Sexuality, and Political Science Department, I received generous feedback from Nancy Hirschmann, Rogers Smith, and their colleagues. Also thanks to Jim Bohman for inviting me to the Democracy and Global Justice Conference. Special thanks to Larry May and Marilyn Friedman for pushing me to clarify that one could hold deep religious convictions and a commitment to immanent universal human rights.

For important nudges here and there thanks to Michael, Bina, Don Herzog, Joanna Kerr, and Audie Klotz. For generously reading through the entire manuscript, Bina, Jessica Kruetter, Umi Lasmina, Ali Sevilla, and two anonymous reviewers, thank you so much. Special thanks to Adrian Stenton for attention to detail.

I am grateful for all of my colleagues at Vanderbilt, particularly James Booth and Neal Tate. George Graham, after reading the entire manuscript, offered suggestions for where else I could go with this project. He never showed evidence of "chemobrain" and was an engaging colleague throughout his life and illness.

I am still grateful to Susan Okin, who was supportive, always engaging, and always insightful. I am grateful for the conversation that opens chapter 5 – and for so many other conversations.

For research assistant work at various points throughout this project, thanks to Katy Attanasi, Lyndi Hewitt, Jessica Kruetter, Sonalini Sapra, Ali Sevilla, Sarah VanHooser, and Sasha Zheng. And thanks to Chris DeSante for doing research for another project so that I could finish this one. Thanks to Vicky Abernathy for handling the repetitive bibliography entry work and to Stacy Clifford for editorial typing that I was unable to do due to a repetitive strain. For translation thanks to Guilherme de Araujo Silva, Maria Clara Bertini, Julie Huntington, Mingyan Li, Ararat Osipian, Fabrice Francois Alain Picon, and Sonalini Sapra.

For funding my work, I thank the United Nations Research Institute for Social Development, Vanderbilt's Center for the Study of Religion and Culture, the Center for the Americas, the Graduate School, the College of Arts and Science, and the Warren Center. For funding the meetings that made my participant observation possible, thanks to the Association of Women's Rights and Development, Women's World Congress, the World Social Forum, the Center for International Studies at the University of Southern California, and the Ford Foundation. Thanks particularly to all those admininstrators and service people whose excellence at their work is often best recognized by its invisibility.

Finally, in case sprinkling their names throughout these acknowledgments is seen to dilute their influence, to Bina D'Costa, Sonalini Sapra, and Lyndi Hewitt for being engaged colleagues throughout the research phase of this and related projects, this project owes a huge intellectual debt. Working with them is a privilege.

My greatest privilege is my near and far family who care for and complement each other. Not living in a feminist world, it is hard to live a feminist life in community. Yet, Aasha, Annlyn, and Bill Zinke, Beth Gaddes, Katherine Stevenson, Barbara Zinke, Rick Ackerly, and I have thoughtfully created a dynamic, supportive, and wonderful life. I appreciate the joy they bring to this way of living and working and the fun they create in the process!

Perhaps, despite all of its influences, a piece of feminist scholarship can be understood to be single-authored. (Certainly, I wouldn't want the reader to hold anyone other than me responsible for the mistakes herein.) However, with apologies to Mary Catherine Bateson, the project shows again that a feminist cannot compose her life or her scholarship alone. My particular circumstances and relationships have enabled me to compose *this* feminist life, and *this* feminist work on immanent universal human rights. At the center of this project are all of the contributors who generously gave of their time and reflection in public venues and in private. I hope that each is strengthened in her attempt to make it possible for others to live a feminist life in their not-so-feminist worlds.

# 1 *Universal human rights in a world of difference: challenging our thinking*

Feminist activists have done the apparently impossible: they've shown us how to think about human rights as local, universal, *and* contested. They have shown us that contestation over human rights is not evidence that rights do not exist. Rather, contestation provides a basis for understanding their universal meaning. Or so I argue here.

Before we get to that argument, let us consider why we need a political theorist to argue that there are human rights and human rights violations. Do we need a theorist to tell us that our moral intuitions are universal? That sounds like the basis for imperialism.[1] Can a political theorist offer any argument that would persuade a torturer that torture is wrong? That seems like a waste of time, light, and ink. When even the well-intended can go wrong and the ill-intended cannot be convinced, why do scholars, why do feminist activists, keep at it? What can we learn from them about human rights? And what would it mean for these activists to be accountable in *practice* to their own *theory* of human rights?

As the research leave during which most of this book was drafted came to an end, Marie sent me her latest plan. Marie is trying to get her children out of Rwanda. She had two with Jean-Paul, her husband, three more, orphaned in Burundi, whom Jean-Paul and she adopted in 1992, and a sixth child whose parents were recently killed. Her country did not demilitarize after the Rwandan Liberation Front and

[1] Jon Sobrino SJ notes the ironic juxtaposition of the theoretical advance and formal spread of universal human rights against "considering life for the vast majorities, the actional condition of this life does not improve in line with theoretical advances" (2001: 135). Sobrino cites Father Ignacio Ellacuría, who was one of eight defenders of human rights who were executed in El Salvador, November 16, 1989: "The problem of human rights is not only complex but also ambiguous, because within it not only does the universal dimension of man meet with the actual situation in which men's lives are lived, but it tends to be used ideologically in the service not of man and his rights, but rather in the interests of one group or another" (Ellacuría 1990: 590).

paramilitaries ended the 1994 genocide.[2] When her family returned from a refugee camp in Uganda, though he had not participated in the genocide, her husband was killed by paramilitaries in post-genocide violence. Over the next ten years she worked in a pharmacy, aspiring to start her own, but eventually started a photocopy shop which required less start-up funds. Her efforts to rebuild her life were stymied by her own ill-health, recurring mental illness, and bleeding ulcers. In renewed violence in 2004, her children were explicitly threatened. A relative and the parents of the baby she now cares for were killed. Government efforts to deal with this growing violence were not obvious. Living in fear, they left the house at night to sleep. Now, she has hidden her children in a neighboring country and is trying to figure out how to keep them safe. She has even considered putting her children up for international adoption. While she is hiding her children, she has no economic means to support them. Under this kind of stress, she has difficulty thinking clearly, assessing proposals that others make to her, or designing a plan of her own.

Is Marie's situation unique? In what sense? Of course, the life she had with Jean-Paul was their own: their hard work in the early years of their marriage when they were both thin from physical work, the later success at their farm by getting cows to produce more milk through improving diet, their sharing that success through a non-government organization (NGO), their adoption of the children from Burundi. Certainly, they had a unique marriage and life together. However, the 1994 genocide, retributive violence, health problems, and limited economic opportunity are not unique to Marie and Jean-Paul. Sadly, in Rwanda they are not unique to their family, to a particular ethnic group, or to people from certain regions.

Further, the complicated context of post-conflict insecurity – conflict, inadequate civilian rule of law, difficult health conditions, and economic uncertainty – is not unique to Rwanda. In 2005, Amnesty International reports from Afghanistan, Colombia, Democratic Republic of the Congo, Côte D'Ivoire, Haiti, Iraq, Israel and the Occupied Territories, Sierra Leone, and Sudan describe these conditions.[3] Even when the

[2] On one reading, demilitarization in Rwanda was a difficult project because militants and population could not be distinguished. Moreover, disarmament had a different meaning in Rwanda because the primary weapon of the genocide was an agricultural tool (Waters 1997).

[3] Amnesty International 2005: 36, 80, 86, 134, 139, 221, 235.

violence is not imminent, fear creates an environment where basic health, education, and opportunity for livelihood are conditional. For example, in Israeli Occupied Territories, Palestinians' mobility is constrained with checkpoints and barriers such that getting adequate health care, seeing and supporting their family members, going to school, and getting to work are severely curtailed.

Images from Hebron before the 2006 violence between Israel and Hezbollah reveal the constrained conditions of daily life. A man walks down a street; wire mesh prevents trash from Israeli settlements from falling on the Palestinians in the old city. A woman takes her daughters to school, her younger son in tow.[4]

[4] Tone Andersen, photographer.

The complexity of insecurity – political, social, and economic – is not unique to post-conflict contexts. For example, in Bangladesh violent crimes against women – rape, dowry death, domestic violence, acid burning, and suicide – go under-reported; when reported, women are discouraged from filing their cases; when filed, cases are pursued slowly. Although these crimes are illegal, the police's willingness and ability to enforce these laws, and the judiciary's uneven record at carrying out the law, mean that women live in a context of insecurity.[5] Of course the police failure to ensure women's safety is an important element of the human rights context for women in Bangladesh; however, the human rights violating social practices are inextricably linked to these legal failures. The practices of dowry, of integrating a new bride into the domestic hierarchy of her husband's family, of domestic violence in order to gain a first wife's assent to a second wife, of forced marriage, of local religious and community leaders issuing *fatwas* or community-authorized punishments all contribute to the context of

[5] Women aged thirteen to eighteen are most often victims of rape and acid burning; women over nineteen are most often victims of domestic violence and dowry death (Ain o Salish Kendra 1999; 2000).

human rights violations.[6] Further, the economic context of poverty and increasing local class inequality influence the evolution of these practices such that dowry amounts have risen; the period over which they are paid now extends after the marriage, often years after the marriage; and new dowry demands made after marriage are increasingly common.

The complexity of insecurity – political, social, and economic – is not confined to so-called developing countries. In parts of the United States, lack of economic development creates a different but equally distressing context. Often concerns about these forms of insecurity are brought to our attention through statistics. According to 2001 statistics, in the US 18.2% of children under six live in poverty and 48.9% of children living in female-headed households live below the poverty level.[7] Nearly half of all US children aged one to four live so close to poverty that their families need federal assistance in order to afford adequate nutrition.[8] Of the 11.1% of the US population who experience food insecurity, 3.5% were not caught in either government or private safety nets and experienced hunger during the year.[9] In the United States, the infant mortality rate is about 7 per 1,000, and almost 15 per 1,000 among children born to African American mothers.[10] In the United States 20.7% of the population lacks functional literacy.[11]

Because of familiar media images in the United States, these statistics evoke images of poor urban minority children.[12] However, these statistics are as bad or worse among certain regional and ethnic subsets of

[6] Government of Bangladesh 2001. [7] Proctor and Dalaker 2001: 4.

[8] The Special Supplemental Nutrition Program for Women, Infants and Children (WIC) was started in 1972 and catered to an average of 88,000 participants per month. That number has now risen to an average of 7.2 million in 2000. Almost half of all infants and all children of one to four years of age participate in the program. WIC accounts for almost 12% of total federal expenditure for food and nutrition assistance (Oliveira 2002).

[9] On any given day in 2003 that number was between 490,000 and 698,000 (Nord 2004).

[10] MacDorman 1999.

[11] The National Adult Literacy Survey (reported in 1993) found a total of 21–23% (40–44 million) of American adults (defined as age 16 or older) functioned at the lowest literacy level, i.e. they had difficulty using certain reading, writing, and computational skills considered necessary for functioning in everyday life (South Carolina Department of Education 1998).

[12] For a critique of the politics of poverty see Kimberle Crenshaw on the Monyihan Report (1965) (Crenshaw 1989).

the population who live in some persistently poor and economically depressed rural areas, such as in the Mississippi Delta, Appalachia, and the lower Rio Grande Valley.[13] In the US, 20% (55.4 million people) of the population is rural[14] and the rural poverty rate has always been higher than the urban rate (2.1% higher in 2003) though the gap has been closing due to increases in urban povety. In 2003, 7.5 million people, or 14.2% of the population who lived in non-metropolitan areas, were poor.[15]

These statistics, while shocking, and while they may stir us to action, are measures of symptoms: symptoms of political, social, and economic institutions and practices that perpetuate these conditions. These social, political, and economic conditions limit the opportunities for composing a life. Consider the child born into each of these contexts. From birth she experiences constrained health and education. Her opportunities for developing herself and her economic prospects are constrained. In each context for developing a life – in Rwanda, in Israel and the Occupied Territories, in Bangladesh, in the United States – we should ask if human rights are being violated.

In the case of Marie, the answer must be "yes." The lives of her children have been explicitly threatened; the police are not a reliable resource and to her knowledge have perpetrated or condoned some of the acts of violence she has witnessed. Due to this fear she is prevented from living in her home, her health is unstable, and she cannot support her family despite her ability and willingness to work. Even though she cannot name the government officials who are failing to secure her children, even before her own children were explicitly threatened, the environment of fear perpetuated by the sight of murdered neighbors in the street itself constitutes a human rights violation. The destructive impact on economic and social systems of an "environment of fear" makes the human rights impact more complicated to understand and address.[16] More generally, consider the life chances of a child born and raised in this context. Can we think of the *lack* of opportunities – that

[13] Lichter and Leif 2002. [14] Hobbs and Stoops 2002.
[15] Economic Research Service 2004.
[16] Some scholars have been developing different methods for identifying and studying insecurity that do a better job than the study of war alone at making visible the insecurity of marginalized populations (Ackerly, Stern, and True 2006; Derriennic 1972; Galtung 1969; Krause and Williams 1996).

is, her *lack* of possibility to develop as she might choose to if the possibility existed – as a human rights violation?[17]

Familiar accounts of human rights treat rights as "entitlements" with corresponding "duty-bearers."[18] Is there no rights violation if there is no identifiable collective or individual duty-bearer? Does society bear responsibility for the contexts it creates? Do individuals bear responsibility for the contexts their society creates? What are the boundaries of the society that bears that responsibility? Are they local or global boundaries? Geopolitical or geographic boundaries? Are they economic or moral boundaries? These questions are hard to answer and raise doubts about the usefulness of the thinking about human rights as entitlements with duty-bearers in the familiar senses.

In the examples I have been offering, there are sometimes identifiable actors, but their actions would not be characterized as human rights violations but for the collective failure of social, political, and economic institutions and the habits and practices that sustain them. While it is important for a theory of human rights to enable us to be critical of

[17] While some proponents of the capability ethic hesitate to equate human rights with human capabilities, the view of human rights presented here treats these as very similar. Institutions and practices that create and foster conditions in which human rights are violated are the same that make human capabilities unrealizable. Sen (1999a) argues we would do well to think of human rights violations as unfreedoms. Sen (2004) and Nussbaum (1997) tentatively suggest that human rights concerns are a subset of human capabilities concerns. But Sen's 1999 argument does not require this interpretation. Even his later argument does not argue that rights are not capabilities (2004).

[18] "A claim about rights generally involves a fourfold assertion about the *subject* of entitlement, the *substance* of entitlement, the *basis* for entitlement, and the *purpose* of entitlement" (Shapiro 1986: 14). "A right in this sense can be thought of as consisting of five main elements: a right-holder (the subject of a right) has a claim to some substance (the object of a right), which he or she might assert, or demand, or enjoy, or enforce (exercising a right) against some individual or group (the bearer of the correlative duty), citing in support of his or her claim some particular ground (the justification of a right)" (Vincent 1986: 8). "Historically, the idea of rights has embodied two foundational claims. First, that there is an identifiable subject who has entitlements; and secondly, that to possess a right presupposes the existence of a duty-bearer against whom the right is claimed" (Dunne and Wheeler 1999: 3–4). Though freedom is important to Benhabib's account of rights, she uses the language of entitlement (2004b: 140). I think the constraint of this metaphor on the theoretical imaginary is in part to blame for the difficultly she takes in explaning why membership is a right. As we will see, in an immanent theory of human rights what Benhabib conceives of as "membership rights" can be easily understood in their social, political, economic, and civil indivisibility.

human rights violations by a single actor, a theory of human rights cannot be limited in application to such examples. A theory of human rights can also be a critical tool of macro political forces, such as state and global politics, that create exploitable hierarchies. Further, it can be a critical tool of micro political forces, such as the patterns created by language, ethical decisions, habits of consumption and expenditure, and aspirations that create exploitable hierarchies.[19] Importantly, activists and the oppressed use human rights to make their own claims. In the process, while struggling against their oppression – or rather the sources of oppression that their analysis has indicated are those against which they might be most effective – they are not reifying either the source of their domination *or* themselves as victims. Rather, they are realizing an identity as a political actor and, to the extent that their struggle is against some subset of their sources of oppression, as a strategically minded political actor at that. Though one identity or another may be strategically useful (mother, citizen, survivor . . .), the malleable identity forged through human rights activism is that of strategic political actor with all of the ambiguity that such an identity entails in any place and time and across space and time.

The remoteness of the impact of our habits of daily life, institutions, practices, and global interactions conceal their rights-violating implications. We need tools for revealing these, not definitions of "rights" and "duty-bearer" that obscure them. Further, the meanings of "society" and the boundaries of "obligation" they suggest need to be examined if they are to be resources in our reflections on human rights violations.[20] We cannot assume that boundaries are geopolitical or that obligations are bounded. These need to be a part of a theory of human rights.

In this book, I mean to confront well-reasoned theories of human rights with the reality of human experience, some of which might be invisible to the human rights theorist. The epistemological challenge for human rights theorists has always been not to bias our understanding of human rights as a theoretical inquiry by our comfortable but limited exposure to the experiences of human rights violation most often referenced by global politicians. Because a room, a pencil, paper,

[19] As Wendy Brown puts it in summarizing what we learn from Nietzsche and Foucault about "the atomic powers of history": power is constructed and manifest "in the very making of bodily subjects and socio-political desire" (1995: xii).

[20] See Galtung 1969; 1985; 1990. See also Brown 1995: 113.

and a cup of tea afford the luxury of reflection, the academic needs methodological tools for revealing the invisible to herself, to her theory, to her interlocutors, and to "us."

In this book I use many "we"s. Sometimes, I mean the reader and I on a journey together, having covered one argument and moving on to the next. Sometimes, I mean my informants and I, or those who participated in the online groups and meetings that are part of the context of this study. Sometimes, I mean my research partners and I. Sometimes I mean human rights scholars more generally. I have tried to be careful. History (including the history of feminist thinking) includes lots of examples of political thought that over-determines (that is, assumes that the knowledge from one perspective applies to all, such that the differences of some are invisible) or under-determines (that is, assumes that the knowledge from one perspective doesn't apply to all, such that some people are left out). Before we are done, I will have a lot more to say about invisibility and exclusion *and* I will likely have said things that cause both. The occasionally ambiguous use of "we" in this text is meant to provoke, not just the question, "Just who does she think 'we' is?" but also, "Who do *I* think 'we' is?" We cannot know who "we" are if we confine our self-understanding to engagement with the visible.[21] Some of "us" are invisible and some of who "we" are we can come to know only by reflecting on the invisibility within "us."

## Invisibility

Now let's take the inquiry one level further. What if we couldn't see Marie and her children? What if the conditions of their lives were unknown to us. Would these conditions still constitute rights violations? Certainly, if they do when we know about them, they do even if we do not know about them. Thus, to be fully attentive to human rights, we need to be attentive to human rights violations beyond our sights.

There are many ways in which human rights violations may be invisible. Women's human rights activism and scholarship have tried

[21] A common concern about who "we" are is at once a concern about when and why we group ourselves as "moral beings, citizens, and members of an ethical community" (Benhabib 2002: 147). In addition, my concern about the use of the first person plural is as an exercise of power.

to expose many of these: trafficking for sex work,[22] slavery as domestic servants,[23] bonded sweatshop work,[24] death due to botched illegal abortion,[25] and domestic violence,[26] to name a few.[27] Health, labor, homeless, and indigenous activists similarly attempt to make the invisible visible. In each of these cases there are particular individuals who have violated particular individuals' human rights.[28] However, social, political, and economic conditions in particular contexts and *relative* conditions between contexts are particularly conducive to these violations. Global social, political, and economic factors – not fate or karma which influence the accident of birth – determine which children are most likely to grow up to be able to take advantage of social, political, and economic conditions and which will grow up with their opportunities constrained by those same conditions.

Consider women trafficked from Nigeria to Italy for prostitution. Illegal but well-established paths, particularly from the Ebo state and Benin City, create conditions of vulnerability, in which women choose to engage because of the economic landscape in Nigeria and in which they are kept to work in a form of bondage due to the immigration laws of Italy.[29] The relative economic prospects in Italy and Nigeria combine with the familial and legal context of Nigeria to generate an economic opportunity for these mostly young women, but that opportunity is constrained by exploitable hierarchies.[30] Like Marie, trafficked

[22] Orhant 2001. [23] Chin 1998; Human Rights Watch 2002.

[24] Bender and Greenwald 2003; Brooks 2003; Elson and Pearson 1997.

[25] Jen Ross 2005.

[26] Agnew 1998; Coomaraswamy 2002; Milwertz 2003; Pence and Shepard 1988; Schechter 1998; Vickers 2002.

[27] Bunch 1990; 1995; Mayer 1995a; [1991]1999.

[28] The Committee Against Slavery and Trafficking (CAST) cases and Tahari Justice Center are two among many organizations worldwide whose work documents cases of individuals violating the human rights of other individuals in a context of domestic servitude or marital violence that is not publicly visible.

[29] A new European agreement regarding trafficking could potentially mitigate some aspects of vulnerability (Council of Europe Convention on Action against Trafficking in Human Beings 2005).

[30] Is every instance of exploitable hierarchy (MacKinnon 1993), domination (Pettit 1997), or capability failure a human rights violation? Some people want to save "rights" for some subset of these conditions. I argue with women's human rights activists that without attention to the broader context, no subset is secure. And so at a minimum every instance of exploitable hierarchy, domination, or capability failure is cause for skeptical scrutiny of the prospect that human rights have been or may be violated.

women make important life choices that may lead them into ever more exploitable contexts. Because legal immigration is constrained, the trafficked woman is subject to manipulation by the trafficker. Although she knew she was immigrating for prostitution, she may not have anticipated the working conditions, including exposure to AIDS and other STDs and the preferences of her Italian clients, that she met in Italy. Her trafficker kept her passport and forged her visa so her trafficker's threat of deportation if she doesn't pay her bond is credible. Like the conditions of Marie in Rwanda, these are structural conditions of human rights violations. Yet sometimes the very agency of these women renders the exploitable conditions of their contexts invisible.[31]

Similarly, in the US, low wage workers work multiple part-time jobs but are eligible for health insurance at none.[32] Or low wage workers work full time, receiving health benefits but supplementing their family nutrition with foodstamps. Their lack of health care and nutrition are invisible to the broader society and even to some of those beside whom they work. These conditions may be understood as the result of the proper functioning of the market.[33]

Still other rights violations are invisible because their cultural context treats the practices that sustain them as socially appropriate and culturally important or as social manifestations of men's and women's natures. These might include a decision of a *shalish* (a local informal court of elites in Bengali villages) to deny a divorced woman sufficient financial maintenance, of parents to marry their daughter at a young age in Kenya, or of parents to force an arranged marriage in Pakistan. The acceptance of some rights violations as natural or socially appropriate may come from some people within the cultural context in question.[34] Further, others from outside the cultural context may

[31] Jaggar 1994; Kinoti 2006; Marcus 1992.

[32] For example, the HRSA Household Survey 2004 noted that 41% of uninsured adults in New Mexico work multiple part-time jobs (New Mexico Human Services Department 2005). Coverage is declining even for those with full-time employment: "the number of uninsured people in the United States has risen by nearly 4 million since 2001 to 45 million people in 2003 with nearly the entire increase accounted for by a decline in employer-sponsored health insurance coverage" (Collins *et al.* 2004; see also DeNavas-Walt, Proctor, and Mills 2004).

[33] Adams and Neumark 2005; Bartik 2004; Sander and Williams 1997; Sander, Williams, and Doherty 2000.

[34] Bangladesh and Algeria had reservations about Article 2 of the Convention on the Elimination of All Forms of Discrimination Against Women (CEDAW)

accept such violations as culturally appropriate either as a form of cultural relativism or due to their resonance with similarly oppressive conditions in their own context.[35]

Once made visible, some may be able to see these as human rights violations. However, such human rights violations may be invisible to others, particularly (but not exclusively) to those with certain forms of privilege or to those willing to respect cultural norms without critically reflecting on their historical and social construction.

To help illustrate this form of acculturated human rights violation, I adapt a concept put forward by Joyce King, a teacher educator who focuses on ways that US schooling "contributes to unequal educational outcomes that reinforce societal inequity and oppression."[36] King seeks to reveal to her students the habits of racism that they have internalized and that they replicate. She calls these repressive habits "dysconsiousness":

> Dysconsciousness is an uncritical habit of mind (including perceptions, attitudes, and beliefs) that justifies inequity and exploitation by accepting the existing order of things as given. If, as Heaney (1984) suggests, critical consciousness "involves an ethical judgement" [*sic*] about the social order, dysconsciousness accepts it uncritically. This lack of critical judgment against society reflects an absence of what Cox (1974) refers to as "social ethics"; it involves a subjective identification with an ideological viewpoint that admits no fundamentally alternative vision of society.[37]

Not all dyconsciousness rises to the level of human rights violation, but dysconsciousness is what enables us to partake uncritically in practices that are human rights violating or to leave certain human rights violating practices unexamined. It is even possible to examine human rights violating practices in a dysconscious way. For example, William Talbott's examination of women's rights and female genital cutting practices is dysconscious, uncritical about the neo-colonial, political, social, and economic oppressive habits that his criticism of

treaty, which mandates state parties to condemn discrimination in all its forms and to ensure a legal framework, including all laws, policies, and practices that provide protection against discrimination and embody the principles of equality. Egypt had reservations about Articles 2, 9, 16, and 29 (see United Nations 1979).

35 Marglin 1990; Song 2005.

36 King 1991: 134. Thanks to Jennifer Obidah for introducing me to King's concept.

37 King 1991: 135.

certain human rights violations itself reinforces.[38] When Talbott seeks to answer the important question, "What *Do* Women Want?," he does not refer to primary or secondary research that asks women the answer to that question.[39] By answering this question about women's demands for justice based on Amartya Sen's *Development as Freedom* and Steve Kelley's article in the *Seattle Times* rather than drawing on any women's insights directly, he deploys a privileged methodology that dysconsciously "admits no fundamentally alternative vision of society" than the one that supports the forms of gender hierarchy his question may have led us to criticize. Although not all dysconscious action rises to the level of human rights violation, dysconscious actions and arguments cannot be liberatory because they do not take on the fundamental hierarchies of injustice.

In sum, human rights violations may be invisible because they are remote and not covered by localized news. They may be invisible because they are illegal and concealed, as in the case of slavery, indentured servitude, and bondage. Invisibility may be the byproduct of our observing people making choices; that is, because we witness people making choices, the structural constraints of those choices may not be visible. Further, human rights violations may become invisible through habituation in the daily practices of cultural and economic life. Finally, dysconscious individual behavior can perpetuate the invisibility of rights violating acts, habits, and practices.

Which nearly invisible insecurities constitute human rights violations? What kind of theory of human rights would enable us to notice, assess, and address all of these rights violations? In this book, I develop an account of universal human rights that enables us to see violations of human rights regardless of the relative degree to which perpetrator action and structural factors function to create the human rights violation. Of course, there may always be individuals, groups, and networks who try to violate human rights. The argument is that our efforts to expose, end, and ameliorate human rights violations will not be complete if they focus only on political institutions. The need to focus on the entire apparatus of *civil society*[40] – social, cultural, familial,

[38] Talbott 2005. [39] Talbott 2005: 101–102.

[40] Note, whenever I refer to "civil society," I mean to avoid listing the entire social, cultural, familial, religious, economic, and political infrastructure of institutions, values, practices, and norms, including those we understand as public and those some are inclined to treat as private.

religious, economic, and political – and to encourage a way to take individual responsibility for social ills by expecting a social ethics that willingly considers that there may be fundamentally alternative visions of society.

To see the implications of our local and global civil society institutions *and* practices we need to see *differently*. Seeing in this way requires that we take individual responsibility not only for how we act toward others (we don't murder), but also for how we see others (we *see* their experience and the ways in which it is conditioned by macro and micro political factors).[41] Seeing with our new sense of what human rights violations look like expands the scope not only of our sense of social responsibility but also of what it means to think responsibly about the world. The suppression of rights is not always the result of direct individual action, but rather provides the context for individual and collective actions and patterns of behavior that (1) violate rights, (2) institutionalize the suppression of rights, and (3) perpetuate the norms that support that institutionalization.

The difference between murder as a crime and murder as a human rights violation is the failure of society to identify, prosecute, and prevent patterns of murder. The "disappeared" during the Pinochet regime in Chile, the unsolved murders of many young women from Juárez, Mexico, since 1993, and the 50 million missing women around the world[42] are all victims of human rights violations. Human rights violations need not be attributed to individual or institutional duty-bearers in order for the pattern to be recognized as a human rights violation. The suppression of rights may be most "visible" in the disappeared, but the rights violations are against not only those who experience the act (the disappeared and their loved ones) but against the whole of society, including those who fear being the next to disappear, those who mourn the loss of the disappeared, and those who are intimidated from demanding the terms of their inclusion in the subsequent democratic government because the threat of chaos or a return to authoritarianism is credible. Suppression of rights is the

[41] This argument is consistent with the social ontology of Carol Gould and its foundation in equal positive freedom (1988; 2004). But one can adopt the view of human rights described here without adopting Gould's social ontology.

[42] Sen 1990c. Oster argues that Sen's "More Than 100 Million Women Are Missing" is an overestimate because in places where Hepatitis B is high, more boy fetuses are born (2005).

existence ("always already")[43] of power – perpetuated through our relationships. The greatest challenge of human rights activism is moving our attention beyond the individual actions we see so that we see the rights violations in their context of power relations. The most challenging reconceptualizations take us beyond these observations of (1) others and (2) conditions in order to see (3) our own position in the relationships of power that enable such conditions to continue and therefore such individual acts to be politically sustainable.

For example, the structures of patriarchy enable the rapist and the abusive husband. The habits of my daily life and discourse enact patriarchal norms. For example, my husband takes our daughters to do our grocery shopping Saturday mornings so that I can work. Though the gender roles are reversed (the man doing the care-giving, the woman working), the roles of child care and shopping are linked in a traditionally gendered way. Similarly, when a friend comments that her family has a similar inversion of traditional gender roles – she with a primary breadwinning income, her husband with a job that lets him be the primary care-giver – she is reifying a conventional way of understanding of income-earning work and care-giving work. Certainly, we wouldn't say that by our daily practices we were violating the human rights of a woman on the phone with a domestic violence shelter trying to decide if she should leave her husband, go to a shelter, and begin a long process of education and training that might lead her to be able to earn a family-sustaining wage. But neither does our working within these roles (reversed as they may be) help us as a society to consider why we organize work and care such that "work" requires seventeen-hour days and weekends and "care" means going shopping. Why aren't I at the park with my children while my husband shops? Why are there kinds of work ("breadwinning" jobs) that require someone else to care for children, shop for groceries, or the worker's double shift to do these things? If work and care were differently organized – with the hours required for success more closely matched with the number of hours that it is reasonable for a child to be in institutionalized care[44] – the

[43] Foucault 1978.

[44] States limit the number of hours a child may be in institutionalized care. For example, The State of Tennessee (Rule 1240-4-3.06) "Children shall not be in care for more than twelve (12) hours in a twenty-four (24) hour period except in special circumstances (e.g. acute illness of or injury to parents, natural disaster, unusual work hours)" (Tennessee [1974] 1998).

woman on the phone with the domestic violence hotline would be facing a different decision. Even if the abusive patterns in which abusers discourage their spouses from furthering their education or from having jobs that enable their economic independence remained the same, the context of her decision would be different if work and care were not as opposed as they are in the US economy.[45]

Local and global, political, economic, social, religious, and cultural institutions, practices, *and ways of thinking and not thinking* need to be transformed so that social institutions, contexts, and norms are the subjects of human rights inquiry around the world. Identifying the theoretical demands and methodological implications of this task is one of the purposes of this book.

## Universal justification

Though attention to invisibility and structural rights violations is important to the activists' theory and therefore will be important to my argument, the turn that *distinguishes* my approach to theorizing about human rights is not the focus on structural and invisible violations. Feminist theorists and other critical scholars have worked with great pedagogical ingenuity to try to break down the conceptual, ontological, and epistemological barriers of our disciplines that make questions about structural and micro politics fall on deaf ears.[46] Specifically, feminists, colonized, ethnically marginalized, and indigenous people among others have worked for decades to bring marginalization and civil society structures under consideration by human rights theorists and activists.

What distinguishes my approach is that I seek an account of human rights that has *normative* legitimacy from the perspective of those who have been working to make marginalized people and marginalizing structures visible. In addition to taking seriously the theoretical criticism of human rights theory coming from post-modern and post-colonial

[45] Vickers 2002.

[46] Hirschmann develops a critique of individualistic freedom. She interrogates the familiar metaphor of freedom as a property right that an individual "has," that a state "secures," and that a villain can "violate." Freedom that is not epistemologically used to individualism requires a "social understanding of power" (2003: 26). See also Gould's social understanding of equal positive freedom (2004; see also Ackerly, Stern, and True 2006; cf. Mansbridge 1993).

theorists, I take seriously the activists' criticism of academic theory in its mainstream and critical forms for reifying a political perspective that privileges the knowledge claims of the academic over the knowledge claims of the less educated.[47] The post-modern and post-colonial perspectives make us suspicious of theoretical claims to legitimacy because so often such claims privilege already privileged voices and therefore are a mask for an exercise of political power. By contrast, the activist perspective makes us suspicious of theoretical claims whose implications for political action are withheld.[48] A human rights theory needs to do both.[49]

Weber left an indelible mark on the study of legitimacy with his descriptive account of three kinds of authority: legal authority, traditional authority, and charismatic authority.[50] Rawls and Habermas offer an alterative to Weber's empirical description of kinds of authority that rests instead on a normative claim about what kind of authority has political legitimacy. In their view, political authority derives from consensus. First Rawls states the question:

> in light of what principles and ideals must we, as free and equal citizens, be able to view ourselves as exercising that power if our exercise of it is to be justifiable to other citizens and to respect their being reasonable and rational?
>
> To this political liberalism says: our exercise of political power is fully proper only when it is exercised in accordance with a constitution the essentials of which all citizens as free and equal may reasonably be expected to endorse in the light of principles and ideals acceptable to their common human reason. This is the liberal principle of legitimacy . . . Only a political conception of justice that all citizens might be reasonably expected to endorse can serve as a basis of public reason and justification.[51]

Habermas shares Rawls's commitment to democratic inclusion, but authors an account of legitimacy that is more dynamic yet still committed to consensus and the use of reason:[52]

47 Sonalini Sapra (I9 2004) and the Feminist Dialogue small group meetings described in greater detail in chapter 6.

48 For example, in an interview with Vicky Bell cited in chapter 3, Judith Butler says that she leaves to activists the responsibility of determining the political action inspired by her scholarship (1999) .

49 Sen 2004: esp. 356; Sobrino SJ 2001.

50 Weber 1947: 328ff. In what follows, I mean to respect that for many people Weber is the point of departure for the study of authority and legitimacy. I do not mean to be constrained by his point of departure.

51 Rawls 1993: 137.

52 Habermas 1979; 1984; 1996a.

we can say that actions regulated by norms, expressive self-presentations, and also evaluative expressions, supplement constative speech acts in constituting a communicative practice which, against the background of a lifeworld, is oriented to achieving, sustaining, and renewing consensus – and indeed a consensus that rests on the intersubjective recognition of criticizable validity claims. The rationality inherent in this practice is seen in the fact that a communicatively achieved agreement must be based *in the end* on reasons.[53]

In the Rawlsian and the Habermasian theories, consensus is possible and everyone is committed to achieving consensus *and* to achieving consensus through the use of shared understandings of what constitute reasonable claims and reasons. In chapter 2, I trade on Rawls's distinction between an ideal and non-ideal theory and argue that human rights theory is non-ideal theory. To anticipate, in non-ideal theorizing the theorist recognizes that the conditions necessary to bring about her theoretical objectives are lacking. In fact, they are so lacking that she lacks the ability to see clearly all that the theory should entail once fully articulated. Non-ideal human rights theory does not require that the conditions necessary to bring it about be in place in order to be a useful guide for political decision making. Nor does it merely describe authority (following Weber) without normative assessment of the political conditions that at any given time give a voice of political legitimacy.

So what kind of claim is a claim that human rights have legitimacy? Can a claim have no decisive source of political power and no decisive normative power and yet have political authority to guide and even compel criticism not only of individual and group actions but also of civil society institutions, values, practices, and norms?[54] Most accounts of legitimacy proceed as if the answer must be "no." I want to proceed as if the answer might be "yes."

To do that I will need to develop a theory by engaging with activists who challenge both political authority and normative authority in their work for women's rights, women's human rights, gender equality, women's empowerment, and a host of issues that fall within and around these ways of describing activist work. These activists are diverse and may or may not describe themselves as feminist (though in the era of gender mainstreaming, they are increasingly aware of the

[53] Habermas 1984: 17. [54] Cf. Bentham 1823.

need to politicize their work so that local, national, and transnational institutions are accountable to women). These activists are particularly instructive for this project because of their two-pronged critical engagement with authority – with the authority to claim the "truth" and with the authority to enforce that truth.

What would it mean to theorize in partnered engagement with activists?[55] As I explain in Part II, my own methodology is not designed to find generalizations or representations of activists as a group, but rather to reveal differences. Differences among them make generalizations misleading.[56] Yet, we can say that the activist's perspective is that of the social critic. Furthermore, the human rights activist is particularly critical of materially and physically exploitable hierarchies that may not be visible to other victims, survivors, and humanitarians.[57] Some human rights activists are able to think through the relationships between different manifestations of hierarchy. Those who cannot do that have the ability to maintain dichotomies between different kinds of hierarchy, noticing one hierarchy, but seeing it as separable from another. In the meetings of feminist activists I attended while researching this book, those who saw the relationships between multiple forms of inequality seemed to outnumber those who did not. But as is revealed in my interviews and in less formal conversations with other activists, human rights activists sometimes exhibit unexamined dichotomous thinking that results in a cognitive dissonance. As we will see, some activists want to support *one* kind of human rights, or the human rights of *some* people, but their way of life or their social,

[55] I have argued elsewhere that activist-informed theory requires a theory and method of social criticism (Ackerly 2000; cf. Fonow and Cook 2005). In chapter 5 I discuss other feminist perspectives that inform this inquiry.

[56] For example, in *Fields of Protest* Raka Ray explores the way in which the political field in each of two cities in India affects the ways in which women identify and mobilize around their interests. For example, Bombay-based women's activists are centrally concerned with issues of patriarchal hierarchy such as domestic violence, whereas Calcutta-based women's activists are more centrally concerned with issues of economic inequality. Working in different political environments – West Bengal has traditionally been Communist-governed, Maharashtra ruled by the more right-wing Shiv Sena – affects the focus of their activism (1999).

[57] For example, the humanitarians to which David Kennedy refers in *The Dark Sides of Virtue* do not see many of the forms of human rights violations that are the subject of activists studied in this book (2004; cf. MacKinnon 2006: chapter 5).

cultural, or religious values make it difficult to see that it is incoherent and even destructive to support some rights but not all rights, or some people's rights, but not all people's rights. Such cognitive dissonance is supported by unexamined dichotomous thinking that enables people to disaggregate political and economic rights or women's and human rights for example. Such cognitive dissonance and unexamined dichotomous thinking can be attributed to activist and scholar alike, often a result of dysconscious, uncritically examined, or unexamined social habituation.

However, it is not enough to want to learn from activists. Theorists need a method for doing so, a method that guides our work and enables others to follow and assess our work.[58] It is not enough to have an epistemology – a "theory of knowledge"[59] – that values activists as knowers. It is not enough to have a theoretical methodology – that is, "a theory and analysis of how [theoretical] research does or should proceed"[60] – a methodology that requires us to learn from activists themselves as opposed to learning from social science research on or about activists. As all research, political theory of activism needs a theoretical *method* – a "technique for (or way of proceeding in) gathering evidence."[61] However, for normative inquiry, a method gives us specific tools not only for gathering data, but also for translating, interpreting, and analyzing that data. For example, it not only specifies our methods for identifying whose insights and experiences we should draw upon, but also gives an account of the steps we take to mitigate the potential for reading our theoretical views into our observations.[62] A method enables others to assess and contribute to our research

[58] The method as I used it was very expensive and was successful only with generous research support from Vanderbilt University, the University of Southern California, the Ford Foundation, and United Nations Research Institute for Social Development (UNRISD), some of which was specific to my project, some of which was possible by coordinating my project with other projects under way. However, depending on research design, similar research can be done with different resources. Thus, while my project was expensive, the expense was a function of my research question and research design. Field-based inquiry supported by opportunities for deliberation may in fact often be expensive, but the general approach set out in Part II *need not* be.

[59] Harding 1987: 3. [60] Harding 1987: 3. [61] Harding 1987: 2.

[62] A method may also specify how power dynamics in the relationship between the researcher and her interlocutors are to be navigated. For discussion of these and other ethical dimensions of methodological choice see Ackerly, Stern, and True (2006) and Smith (1999).

agenda, putting into practice the insight that the struggles and wishes of the age are important problems for us to work on *together*.

Regardless of the differences among activists, it makes sense to theorize about universal human rights by *assuming* that making a human rights argument is an exercise of power. Whatever else is required to theorize in engagement with the perspectives of activists, engaged theorizing requires assuming that, just as any theoretical argument is an exercise of power, the argument of a human rights defender is an exercise of power in the interest of those whose rights are violated[63] (or an attempt to mask an exercise of power as being in the interests of those whose rights are violated).[64] What is wrong with exercising power in the interests of the vulnerable or violated? Often, nothing. However, exercising that power responsibly means being attentive to all human rights violations, even those that are invisible or marginal, and doing so without dysconsciousness, without reifying certain social hierarchies. This feminist view of theoretical argument itself requires the theorist to feel "the possibility of incompleteness."[65] In this feminist view, the power to go unchallenged (Weberian legal, traditional, or charismatic authority) is an exploitable hierarchy.[66]

Because it does not rely on common philosophical epistemological assumptions about what constitutes a convincing argument or a philosophical justification, the theory I present is not strictly a philosophical account. Such agreement would require a prior agreement – itself an exercise of power – about what constitutes good argument that would suggest ignoring the arguments of activists because, as we will see, many exhibit cognitive dissonance, unexamined dichotomies, and disagreement as to what constitutes a convincing argument or justification.[67]

Likewise, this account of human rights is not a transcendental account, relying on a prior agreement about what constitutes transcendental or religious authority and who is qualified to recognize and interpret such authority. While many human rights activists are sustained by their faith and understand human rights in theological terms, religious and all transcendental beliefs are an exercise of power or they authorize one, in

[63] Barsa 2005. [64] Klinghoffer 1998. [65] Bickford 1996: 151.

[66] Susan Okin offers one such argument utilizing the social theory of Robert Goodin in *Protecting the Vulnerable*: "While we should always strive to protect the vulnerable, we should also strive to reduce . . . vulnerabilities insofar as they render the vulnerable liable to exploitation" (Goodin 1985: xi, cited by Okin 1989: 137).

[67] Cf. Young's work on activism and deliberation (2001a).

the same way that philosophical arguments are. They depend on agreement about, but are subject to disagreement about, truth claims.

Instead, human rights theory needs to assume the challenge of agreement despite disagreement. The challenge itself is its foundation. This book offers an immanent account of human rights, developed through engagement with what people do and say in their activism against exploited hierarchies. I will argue that this approach gives us an account of human rights that is universal in the sense of being an account that is engaged with the rights and struggles of *all*, visible and invisible.[68] I will argue that this immanent account of universal human rights is available to all for criticism directed both across and within cultural boundaries. And, in the spirit of critical theory, its claim to universalizability is partially empirically demonstrated in the actions and the insights of activists.

*Immanent* knowledge is knowledge that comes from within – in this case, from within the experiences of human rights violations and the experience of working against human rights violations. An *immanent human rights* theory is a theory of human rights that comes from contextually specific human rights activism and social criticism. An *immanent universal* theory of human rights is a theoretical account of human rights whose source of justification is an immanent methodology and whose application is universal within and across cultures.[69]

Immanent universal human rights are universal in the sense that underwear is universal. Not everywhere in the world do people wear cotton or linen undergarments, but where they wear wool (which itches the skin of most humans), they wear undergarments.[70] Likewise, not everywhere and at all times have people made rights claims and called them "human rights" when doing so, but around the world, when they face oppression they have made claims through their words and actions that can contribute to our understanding of universal human rights.[71]

[68] Human rights from the perspective of the victims, not the humanitarians, and not the political and intellectual elites (see Ishay 2004; Kennedy 2004).

[69] Cf. Seyla Benhabib's "interactive universalism" (1986: 81) and Carol Gould's "concrete universality" (2004: chapter 2).

[70] Barber 1994: 133.

[71] Anna Wierzcbicka and colleagues have developed an empirically tested theory of universals in language (Goddard and Wierzbicka 2002a; 2002b; Wierzbicka 1996; 2005). Even her critics have identified the value of her approach to identifying universal grammar (Palmer 2001).

In the manner of immanent critique,[72] I develop here an account of universal human rights based on these claims and the actions people take to realize them.[73]

In their critical evaluations of their own contexts, activists show us that what it means to be "human" and what constitute "rights" are socially constructed such that promoting universal human rights requires *institutional* and *social* change. Changing political, social, and economic contexts requires not only changing laws and institutions so that the police can be reliable sources of security rather than sources of insecurity, but also changing social practices so that community members exhibit and practice habits of community building. Human rights respecting contexts will differ from each other but they will be sustained through institutions *and* practices. For example, activists in Turkey asked for laws that change the patterns of practice associated with domestic violence rather than a law that raises the punishment for domestic violence.[74] Activists in rural Bangladesh use street theater to change the practices of local informal courts (*shalish*) by getting the most powerful in a community to role play the circumstances of women and the poor.[75]

Through their work, women's human rights activists give us the sketch of a theory of universal human rights:

- the human rights of all humans are related to those of others,
- all human rights are indivisible, and
- all human rights are a function of normative and institutional contexts.

72 Compare my approach to Walzer's immanent criticism (1987), Gould's continentally informed analytical philosophical justification (2004), and Benhabib's Habermasian-informed deliberative justification (2002: chapter 5).

73 Criticisms of the universalizability of human rights based on linguistic claims about the word "rights" include Pollis (and Schwab 1979; see also Bell 2000). By contrast, Brown studies human universals that do not rely on shared language (1991). David Beetham argues that while the institutionalization of legitimacy varies by time and place, each society will have three criteria of legitimacy: following established rules, consistent with shared beliefs, and consistent with the expressed consent of those qualified to give it (1991; 1993).

74 Women for Women's Human Rights (WWHR) Istanbul 1998. In Bangladesh, India, and Russia, activists continually argue that increasing punishments for crimes against women (particularly crimes in which the assailant and victim are related) is not effective at deterring violence against women. Rather, they argue, governments should focus on preventing that violence by enforcing civil protection or restraining orders and facilitating women's ability to function in everyday life.

75 Ain o Salish Kendra 1997; 1999; 2000.

Each of these views has been supported by a range of academics and activists. They are in fact foundationally important to the Universal Declaration of Human Rights itself.[76] However, securing them in international institutions is insufficient for their global recognition and realization. Some will dismiss them as moral values unsustainable by political institutions.[77] Some will see them as institutions conditioned by cultural values, that is, where the implications of the institutions and values conflict, the cultural values trump.[78]

If we see human rights as either a system of values or a system of institutions we miss what human rights has in common with law. Human rights is, as Habermas characterizes law, "two things at once: a system of knowledge and a system of action."[79] These two systems are importantly interrelated. Human rights are a dynamic system of action because they have been and will continue to be incompletely, and in fact unsystematically, developed. Not only have "human rights" been developing within and between states, in treaties, in national legislatures, in international courts, in United Nations sponsored meetings, and in activists networks, but also, because they have been developing institutionally, they have been developing as a system of knowledge and values. Because women's human rights activists ask *more* of these systems of institutions and knowledge, because these activists are particularly attentive to marginalization and invisibility, I focus on these activists. However, in many realms in which human rights have become important, the same phenomenon of human rights as an evolving system of knowledge and tool for guiding action has been observed.[80]

If we appreciate context as characterized by systems of knowledge, values, practices, norms, and institutions, then when we distinguish between social values and political institutions, we construct a false dichotomy. The dichotomy between institutions and values may be rhetorically useful for dismissing the universal aspiration of human rights, but it is not substantively meaningful among people of religious communities where, for many, institutions are the context and the structure of moral value systems.[81] Moreover, even secular society is

[76] Universal Declaration of Human Rights 1948.
[77] Bentham 1823; cf. Sen 2004: 319.
[78] Shea 2003. See also many countries' reservations to CEDAW.
[79] Habermas 1996a: 79. [80] Bellah 1992.
[81] Hauerwas [1988] 2001; Niebuhr 1951; Vandenbergh 2001; 2005; cf. Rubin 2005: chapter 8 and 332–333.

filled with institutions whose meaning and substance are realized through practices that affirm espoused values. In families, public school systems, libraries, wage practices, environmental use and management, and housing patterns, institutions enact community values, functioning to affirm or transform them. The attempt to dichotomize institutions and values may be an enlightenment artifact or more specifically a byproduct of the disciplinary norms of law, International Relations, and Political Science, where so much human rights work is done.[82] The human rights theory of activists does not practice this dichotomization.

Why should political theorists work in ways that take seriously the theoretical insights of women's human rights activists? Beyond any normative reason why we should think that the views of women's human rights activists are important, purely on the merits of the account, we should pay attention to activists. The theory of immanent universal human rights to which their insights lead offers us a way of understanding human rights such that the issues that usually curtail the critical ambitions of human rights theorists can be reframed and redressed. They offer a coherent theory in practice.[83]

The work of women's human rights activists reveals that principal philosophical objections to universal human rights are best understood as empirical or practical challenges. Political theorists of human rights can interrogate the philosophical masks of their politics. *Not* to confront these challenges philosophically is to treat a political challenge as a philosophical justification for inaction. Consider the following objections.

(1) Human rights cannot be a legitimate basis of claims because they rely on pre-legal principles.[84]
(2) Even if we were convinced that pre-legal ethical principles could be the basis of political demands, there can be no universal pre-legal or pre-political principles because there are no culturally universal foundations.[85]
(3) Even if we could agree that there were universal human rights despite lacking universal moral foundations, we could not agree

[82] Dunne and Wheeler 1999.
[83] Donnelly is suspicious of whether the cacophony of activists can be read as offering a theory (1989: 44–45).
[84] Sen 1999b. [85] Pollis and Schwab 1979.

on what they were because we cannot agree on what their foundations are.[86]

(4) Even if we could agree on what rights were, in order to realize them, we need to be able to assign correlative duties and obliged agents to each right.[87]

Of course, these political objections to universal human rights cannot be met with philosophical argument,[88] ... unless such argument begins with the *politics* at stake in each question. My approach is to treat the politics of human rights as foundational to a theory of human rights.

The observed sources of legitimacy outlined by Weber may be normatively illegitimate from Rawls's or Habermas's perspective. However, is a Rawlsian or Habermasian *normative ideal* the best tool for interrogating the existing legal, traditional, and charismatic authorities in the world? With attention to the politics of knowledge (to the power of epistemology[89]), the account of immanent universal human rights I present lays bare the politics of *any* account of human rights. Accepting that all accounts of human rights (especially those that argue that there are no universal human rights) are accounts of power, I offer an account of universal human rights that is the basis of an always ongoing criticism of marginalization, silencing, and exploitable hierarchies.

I offer a theory of human rights whose universal justification is based on a dynamic understanding of political legitimacy where the authority of human rights as a tool for criticism is not undermined by a commitment to interrogate that authority. Nor is it undermined by its lack of legal, traditional, or charismatic authority at any given time in any given context. If we cannot build this critical architecture on foundational authority or principles, on what can we build it? This is political theory in the non-ideal world.[90]

[86] Pollis and Schwab 2000; cf. Appiah 2001; Ignatieff 2001.

[87] Dunne and Wheeler 1999.

[88] Cf. Goodhart 2005.

[89] An epistemology is a philosophy of knowledge, including its methods, validation, scope, and the distinction between belief and opinion.

[90] I am referring here to the Rawlsian distinction between ideal and non-ideal theory in his A *Theory of Justice* discussed in chapter 2.

## Critical theory and methodology

The key to my identification and articulation of the activists' argument is methodological. In different ways Foucault, post-modernists, post-colonialists, transgender theorists, and Third World feminists ask us to subject knowledge claims – any claims to have identified any truth or fact – to scrutiny.[91] These theorists seek to challenge unreflective ways of knowing in order to reveal forms of power concealed in institutions and habituated practices. Taking the insights of critical, post-modern, post-colonial, and Third World feminists as having foundationally epistemological importance, I build a methodology of inquiry that seeks out different and even competing accounts of human rights. The methodology requires sustained self-reflection which is facilitated by a *destabilizing epistemology*, perpetually attentive to the power dynamics manifested in any account that is likely to be interpreted as in any way definitive.[92] Consequently, with the activists, I build a political account of immanent universal human rights from the perspective of those fighting for their rights. Rather than assumed away prior to the exercise of theory building, the politics of being a source for this account, the politics of non-transcendence, and the politics of argument are all *part* of this account of universal human rights.

Whatever account of universal human rights theorists offer, and whatever their predisposition toward critical theory, by taking up the question of human rights itself, political theorists are somewhat obligated to test out their theories in practice as critical theorists inspire us to do.[93] Interestingly, in this case, with so much diversity on the ground, the critical theorist is equally challenged. How can she be expected to author a theory coherent with social action when so

[91] Ackerly 2000. See Harding, "Only in this way can we hope to produce understandings and explanations which are free of distortion from the unexamined beliefs of social scientists themselves" (1987: 9). Habermas shares the feminist focus on theoretical methodology, and yet feminists find *his* methodology is not sufficiently critical (Fraser 1991; Habermas 1984; Mies 1983).

[92] Talbott calls on human rights theory to be "epistemically modest" (2005).

[93] Marx defines the role of criticism as promoting the "self-understanding of the age concerning its struggles and wishes. This is the task for the world and for us" ([1843] 1967). Gramsci writes in a letter to Tatiana, "thinking 'disinterestedly' or study for its own sake is difficult for me . . . I do not like throwing stones in the dark; I like to have a concrete interlocutor or adversary" (December 15, 1930) (1971: x).

much of that action is incoherent at a certain level? I have not illustrated this point yet, but as the argument proceeds, we will see that one of the challenges of a methodological approach inspired by a destabilizing epistemology is that we have to confront competing, even irreconcilable, views among activists. Some prioritize redistributive claims, some recognition claims, some sexuality claims, and some political claims. Importantly then, this form of immanent human rights theory requires both immanent sources of insight *and* immanent processes for revealing and considering conflicting insights.

To develop this theory – as either author or reader – we will need to move between many worlds, including the worlds of the philosopher, the activist, the feminist methodologist, and the comparative political theorist. Like literal world-traveling, intellectual world-traveling requires transcription, translation, interpretation, conversation, and orchestration.[94] Such traveling is made all the more uncomfortable because the challenges we face are so important and daunting at once. And perhaps most importantly, my repeated attempts to itch our skin with my destabilizing epistemology will make us long for underwear.

I am going to argue that immanent universal human rights enables us to consider the most profound and important political questions of the day and to consider them in ways that respect all of the cultural diversity and intra-cultural conflict that make the world such an exciting and scary place to be. We don't avoid our cultural contexts, our ways of life in which we find so much value, but we do need to shield ourselves from the ways in which the habits of our daily lives can threaten us. Human rights is that protective layer.

The rights expected by our activists are not offered as an inclusive account of universal *values*, rather they are offered as a list of *prerequisites* to a right of way. One cannot pursue one's individual or collective objectives if the rights of way of life are not secure. Carol Gould describes the social dimension of human rights in less metaphorical language:

> Human rights are always rights of individuals, based on their valid claims to conditions for their activity, but individuals bear these rights only in relation

[94] Ackerly 2000; Alexander 2005; Berman 1984; Dallmayr 1999; Euben 2004; Gunning 1992; Lâm 1994; Lugones 1990.

> to other individuals and to social institutions. Right is in this sense an intrinsically relational concept. Furthermore, although these rights are in principle claims by each on all the others, yet since most of these rights cannot be satisfied by each human being acting separately, and since the conditions for the self-transformation of any individual are most often social ones that can be met only by a community or society, then it can be said that individuals hold these rights against society in general.[95]

Gould is describing a notion of human rights based on the "concrete universality" of human rights as a philosophical extension of the universal human experience of positive freedom as the "self-transforming activity" of making choices unconstrained by "means or access to the conditions necessary for making these choices effective."[96] Human rights provide the context for the effective exercise of positive freedom. They are not on Gould's view metaphorically analogous to entitlements.

As I have been researching this project I have developed the personal hobby of collecting universals of this sort.[97] Not everywhere in the world do people wear pants, but everywhere they ride horses, they wear pants.[98] Not everywhere in the world are treats very sweet, but everywhere that they eat spicy food, they have relatively sweet sweets. Not everywhere are the rules of yielding the same, but everywhere in the world, whether on land or sea, whether for bike, boat, or bus, there are rules for yielding. Some are legal; some are rites; they are generally logistical, sometimes quite hierarchical, rarely egalitarian, but universally there are norms of yielding.

When looking specifically at women's human rights violations we see that legal mechanisms for protecting rights vary and are generally insufficient for securing women's human rights. Changing some of the habits and practices of the daily lives that we value is universally necessary for securing women's human rights. What the patterns are and what they need to become may vary greatly or not so much depending on the contexts being compared, but the need to

95 Gould 2004: 37. 96 Gould 2004: 32–33.

97 For an anthropologist's approach to identifying human universals see Brown (1991: esp. chapter 6). Matilal shares my approach of drawing universal principles from the universals of human experience and offers an account of this view of universality by reference to the "basic values concordant with the value-experiences of the 'naked man'" (1989: 357).

98 Barber 1994.

redress women's rights violations with changes in social habits, not just institutional changes, is universal.[99]

Because all human societies are hierarchical,[100] the political attempt to mitigate the abuse of hierarchy is universalizable. Given the power dynamics of some contexts in which these claims arise, an appeal to a transcendental moral justification of such claims is common.[101] This observation has empirical and normative implications. A correlated empirically testable hypothesis might be: the more totalitarian (complete) the political authority, the more likely a moral claim will be couched in transcendental terms. If the particularity of each context in which such claims are made can likewise be taken as given, then a second, empirically testable hypothesis is that the language and theoretical resources of transcendental claims will vary quite significantly.[102] Mine is not an empirical argument about when, and under what conditions, human rights claims will emerge as "human rights" claims. Nor is it an argument about when human rights claims will have political legitimacy in the Weberian sense. Political Science, History, Sociology, and Anthropology can research these observable phenomena. I am interested in a normative argument that can interpret a range of particular claims[103] as *not* particular but rather based on the *substance* of the claims as immanent and universal. These claims emerge in particular contexts and yet have a political basis for being universalizable.

As was suggested at the outset of this chapter, exploring these questions with an epistemological uncertainty means that even the definitions of society, obligations, and rights should be interrogated. The notion of rights as entitlements with corresponding duty-bearers is common in Western social contract framing of rights.[104] George

[99] After studying 15,000 proverbs originating in 245 languages, Mineke Schipper argues that there are general categories of proverbs, one of which is "Female power (... mentioned in terms of verbal talents, work, knowledge, witchcraft and so forth), and the countermeasures invented to restrict all that female power (such as numerous prescriptions and proscriptions for female behaviour, and, of course the recommendation of violence as a last means of utter helplessness)" (Association for Women's Rights In Development 2005; cf. Schipper 2003).

[100] Diamond [1997] 2003.

[101] I will discuss examples of these in chapters 2 and 3.

[102] This work is being done in linguistics (Goddard and Wierzbicka 2002a; 2002b).

[103] As we will discuss in chapter 3, many claimants ground their particular claims on a particular interpretation of transcendental authority.

[104] See also Ackerly (forthcoming-b).

Lakoff and Mark Johnson argue that philosophical ideas have structural forms that make metaphorical use of humans' physical experience of the world.[105] These need not correspond, therefore, to particular cultural or historical contexts. For example:

> When actions are understood metaphorically as motions along paths, then anything that blocks that motion is a constraint on one's freedom. Accordingly, a right becomes a *right-of-way*, an area through which one can move freely without interference from other people or institutions.[106]

The metaphor of physical movement is used to describe the moral idea of freedom. Lakoff and Johnson generally and Edward Slingerland more specifically offer evidence that the metaphor of right-of-way is a universal language.[107] This metaphor can be used to describe the political dimension of human experience, that is, the politics of inequality and hierarchy experienced by humans in human society. The understanding of "rights" that is revealed in the work and thoughts of the activists I study is well captured by this metaphor. More importantly, the methodology of looking to that which is universal in human experience by looking at the specifics of human experience across contexts and histories describes my approach as well.

## What you see is what you get

I am beginning this book about universal human rights with a family's everyday struggle in a post-genocidal region, some images, some statistics about health and well-being, and the universality of undergarments. Let us consider some other ways of setting the stage for a discussion of universal human rights. Mary Ann Glendon begins with the image of power – the military power of fifth-century Athens and of the post World War II "Big Three" (Britain, the Soviet Union, and the United States).[108] Michael Perry begins with a vivid image from Mark Danner's book *The Massacre at El Mozote*, of a girl singing "strange evangelical songs" while she is raped, shot, and shot again, ceasing to sing only when her throat is cut.[109] Micheline Ishay inspires us to think about the history of the victims of conquerors, not that of the

[105] Lakoff and Johnson 1999. [106] Lakoff and Johnson 1999: 305.
[107] Lakoff and Johnson 1999; Slingerland 2004.
[108] Glendon 2001. [109] Perry 1998.

conquering authors of history.[110] Michael Ignatieff begins with the image of a man whose fate – the gas chamber or the chemistry lab – is about to be decided.[111] Johan Galtung starts off with definitions.[112] Seyla Benhabib, Carol Gould, Katerina Dalacoura, and Michael Goodhart begin with theoretical puzzles raised by considering politics as it has been changed by globalization.[113]

Each of these beginnings signals the central issue of the author: the post World War II political context from which the present human rights institutions evolved, the challenge of being moved to a sense of urgency about human rights, the story of the victims in history, the defining boundaries of humanity, and the present political context in which culture, politics, and economics are not confined by geographic or geopolitical boundaries. Beginnings matter.

All of these – power, urgency, history, cultural meanings, and global politics – are important to a theory of universal human rights. Taken together they illustrate both the timelessness and the context-specific dimensions of the exercise of power. In this project on universal human rights I explore these same questions by giving particular attention to the timelessness and particularity of human experience made marginal or invisible by the exercise of power.

Beginning as I do, I mean to signal my epistemological assumption that human rights pertain to all of humanity. By beginning with Marie, I mean to signal that human rights promotion is about changing contexts so that with all of humanity, Marie and her family can enjoy the full range of human capabilities. Marie's example makes us wonder whether it is appropriate to think of genocidal violence as creating qualitatively different responsibilities than pre- or post-genocidal violence.[114] Marie's case makes us curious about the roles of colonialism, decolonization, nation-building, economic development, poverty, class stratification, gender, race, and disability in human rights violating contexts. Most challenging, Marie's story signals where the boundaries of responsibility for human rights violations must extend. Importantly, there is no coincidence between those boundaries and our individual abilities to effect change. However, the difficulty in effecting change,

[110] Ishay 2004. [111] Ignatieff 2001. [112] Galtung 1994.
[113] Benhabib 2004b; Dalacoura 1998; Goodhart 2005; Gould 2004.
[114] Adelman and Suhrke 1999; Eltringham 2004; Rusesabagina with Zoellner 2006; Uvin 1998.

just like the difficulty in seeing the need for change, does not allow us to dismiss our global social ethical obligations.

I aspire to offer a theoretical argument whose politics are transparent and democratic. One long-standing theme in contemporary feminist theory has been the politics of knowledge.[115] From this huge body of literature, I understand feminist theoretical inquiry to require (1) a commitment to ongoing interrogation of epistemological assumptions (articulated and masked), (2) a commitment to methodological innovation in seeking insights in which we make use of the multiple perspectives we can know, seek out others, and be aware that there are many more we cannot know, and (3) a commitment to theoretical work that is inspired by and relevant to contemporary political struggles.[116] I am not confident in the political legitimacy of this argument in the way that Rawls, Habermas, and others are confident in the political legitimacy of theirs,[117] but rather I am interested in assessing the political legitimacy of the argument presented in this book.

I offer a theory of universal human rights whose political legitimacy, such as it is, comes from the epistemological obligation to challenge the unexamined, the absent, and the silent. Because the theory is attentive to cross-cultural and intra-cultural differences and dynamics, the political legitimacy of this theory of universal human rights does not come from singular contested cultural resources but rather from intra-cultural and cross-cutural contestations.[118] Concerned about marginalization, I have sought a theory that is informed by (and potentially critical of) political, social, cultural, and economic institutions *and practices* that provide the contexts of human lives. To the extent that the theory of human rights presented here is a definition of politically legitimate universal human rights, it is not a static definition.

In order for us to "see" why this immanent account of universal human rights is necessary, I need to offer the reader illustrative

[115] In International Relations see for example Tickner (1992; 1997). In Black Feminist Thought see for example Crenshaw (1989) and Collins ([1990] 1991). In Sociology see for example Reinharz (1992). In Political Theory see for example Benhabib (1987) and Hawkesworth (2006a).

[116] Ackerly 2000.

[117] See Habermas (1984: especially the last chapter), Rawls (1993), Nussbaum (2001), and my discussion of Rawls in chapters 2 and 4. See also Hampton 1989.

[118] On my reading both Weberian traditional authority and Rawls's account of free and equal citizenship are contested cultural resources as we will see in chapter 3.

examples of people whose rights are violated. However, for the reasons discussed above these violations might be invisible to some or seem appropriately acceptable to others.

After setting up the problem of epistemology in chapter 2, in chapter 3 I discuss a range of accounts of universal human rights. Each affirms human rights, but does so in a way that conceals a logically prior political decision. The concealed politics may be in the form of either the power to interpret transcendental claims or the power to adjudicate between philosophical claims. Both theological and philosophical arguments that claim to be offering an account of universal morality in fact conceal a politics of authority.

One response to the revealed mask of such authority is to reject human rights altogether. This approach, also discussed in chapter 3, looms in the background of the entire book. The impetus to reject universal human rights altogether is based on a *philosophical* claim about the cultural embeddedness of moral values and a *political* claim about the authority to interpret such values on behalf of a collective. When the contestation over the political claim is itself unmasked, we see that even where moral values are culturally embedded, their meaning is multiple. Therefore, the rejection of human rights on this basis is not philosophical but rather a political rejection of the claims of those lacking political authority in a given context. While responsive to some forms of concealed power, relativist approaches conceal power by other means.

The concerns raised in chapter 3 can be addressed by an immanent approach to universal human rights. An immanent approach draws on the normative resources within a given context. An immanent approach to *universal* human rights compares these immanent norms across differing accounts and finds an account of human rights that is universally justified though perhaps based on different normative resources. In chapter 4 I look closely at four theorists' accounts of immanent universal human rights. I argue that each illustrates that immanent universal human rights theory is possible but that, as with the two previously considered approaches, immanent human rights theory can mask the power of knowledge claims. Each of these authors is inadequately reflective on her or his epistemological assumptions. Consequently, each masks, rather than exposes, the *political* challenges of an immanent theory about universal norms.

In the heart of the book, the politics of knowledge and of disagreement are placed at the center of my account of immanent and universal human rights. First, in chapter 5, I lay out an epistemological perspective – which I call "curb cut feminism." Curb cut feminism is a destabilizing epistemological perspective, familiar to feminists, that requires the theorist to be especially attentive to oppression and to the possibility of exclusion, exploitation, powerlessness, value imperialism, marginalization, invisibility, violence, ignorance, silencing, domination, and hegemony.[119] Also in chapter 5 I describe my methods of data collection which are (among other things) attentive to the potential for these practices to prevent an immanent account of human rights from being broadly informed. In chapter 6 I discuss my analytical methods that allow an account of immanent human rights to be informed by the full range of views. This requires being attentive to, but not rendered incapable of theorizing by, the prospect that certain accounts of human rights delegitimate the rights claims of others.

In chapter 7 I provide an account of the immanent and universal theory of human rights emergent in women's and feminist activisms. This account is respectful of the differences among feminists but treats these differences as resources for reasoning more fully about human rights. Taken together, activists voice the cacophony of inclusive accountability. The result is a theory of human rights that is able to work through profound differences without undermining the political legitimacy of human rights as a basis for social criticism. I try to show how feminists have and might work through their profound differences in chapter 8. Finally, in chapter 9 I demonstrate the implications of the immanent and universal theory of human rights for assessing women's human rights activists' local and global strategies.

In the latter part of the book, I cite at length from my interview sources and I reveal many of the difficult differences among women and feminist activists. While these differences are not often part of the public face of feminism, as my research shows, these differences and others are in fact important to women's and feminist activism.[120] I worry that by revealing these differences, I have violated a trust of feminist activists – not just the feminists whose words I cite, but of all

[119] See Gramsci (1971: 57ff). See also Young's five faces of oppression (1990: chapter 2). See Walzer's discussion of domination and monopoly (1983). See also Ackerly 2007a; Harding and Norberg 2005; Hawkesworth 2006a; Riles 2002.

[120] Loretta Ross discusses some aspects of the racial dynamics in US feminist work (IB13 2005).

feminists who find strength in the unity of the movement. But more is at risk here, the trust of activists and academics who share a commitment to a movement, who are overworked, under-recognized, and fragmented by our own doing and by the ways in which political forces work against us. Considering this risk, I proceed, confident in the strength of the movement, confident that I am continuing an established tradition of collective self-reflection among feminists.

## Conclusion

What does the activist-informed immanent theory of universal human rights offer? To philosophers, it offers an opportunity to consider the normative questions that get tabled when we bracket the politics of knowledge. To activists, it offers not only a guide for strategizing as discussed in chapter 9 but also a guide for engaging with questions and people outside of familiar contexts. Immanent and universal human rights offers scholars and activists a way of asking questions about human rights together, privileging neither philosophy nor practice.

Having witnessed human rights violations – coming across the concentration camps at the close of World War II, finding the bodies of victims after the 1994 genocide in Rwanda, watching a woman bleeding to death from an illegal abortion, seeing a woman permanently scarred and ostracized due to dowry violence – humanity needs to ask not "Do we know what universal human rights are?" but rather, "Do we have the political will to do anything about their violations?"[121] Samantha Power argues movingly that the collective will to stop genocide is often stymied by politically motivated manipulation of information.[122] Her audience is those who might be moved by increased awareness. Rorty too thinks that developing our awareness of and sentimental attachments to others is a "more efficient" way to promote human rights.[123] However, in her imploring each reader to join the political voices against genocide, Power makes us aware that neither ignorance nor adherence to culturally relativist ethical schema are viable explanations for why such political will has not formed in the past.[124]

[121] Paul Wolfensohn asks a similar question with regard to the conditions in Africa at the end of his ten-year term as President of the World Bank (Wolfensohn 2005).
[122] Power 2002. [123] Rorty 1993. [124] Power 2002; cf. Roy 2004.

In contrast, this book is not written for those who lack the interest necessary to care about human rights violations around the world.[125] Of course, I mean to deprive them of their normative justification for ignoring the full range of human rights violations. However, I do not hope to change their political behavior.[126]

Rather, we need to empower *normatively* those who would otherwise believe that toleration and respect require relativistic *laissez-faire*. To "leave" some "to do" is to leave others *to struggle*. Moreover, by participating in the structures and norms that create the contexts that enable the rights-violator to commit individual acts, we are not innocently leaving others to do as they will. Rather, we are complicit in the structures that enable them "to do." However we would like to define the boundaries of "society" – geopolitically, morally, economically – our actions transgress those boundaries through the structures and norms in which they operate such that there is no normative basis for shirking individual or collective obligation.

Parenthetically, those with morally or philosophically based *transcendental* beliefs against the possibility of universal human rights cannot be convinced by the argument in this book. The argument in this book requires a willingness to suspend such transcendental commitments. It does not require suspending all transcendental commitments; it certainly does not require suspending those ethical values that are sustained for many by their transcendental commitments. However, it does require suspending a transcendentally based belief that human rights are not universal. Some hold such transcendental commitments as immutable aspects of their belief systems; others have become habituated to this transcendental commitment. Whether belief

125 Rorty, like Aristotle, worries less about how to argue with Thrasymachus and Callicles and more about educating our children so they don't grow up like them (1993: 123).

126 On the possibility of motivating people unmoved by human rights violations, Samantha Power's *A Problem from Hell* is cynical (2002), but Arunadhati Roy's *An Ordinary Persons Guide to Empire* is more optimistic about the potential of the United States citizenry to develop a political will to criticize genocide and other human rights violations (2004). Louise Antony concludes her essay "Natures and Norms" with the following: "Moral community might not be impossible without powerful resemblances to facilitate our knowing and identifying with each other, but it would be vastly more difficult. The very happy fact is that our commonalities make it, if not easy, at least something well within our grasp, to figure out what we ought to do with respect to each other. All that's left is to do it" (2000: 36; see also Held 1987).

or habit has rendered these commitments unable to be suspended, such commitments may make the argument presented here difficult to embrace. However, the theory can fruitfully engage with most transcendental commitments *except* a transcendentally committed belief that the question of whether there are universal human rights has been answered definitively in the negative.

For those moved by human rights violations, the book offers three things. First, I offer them a philosophical justification for the political legitimacy of their moral intuitions. Regardless of the spiritual, religious, and personal resources that motivate them to think about the rights of all of humanity, whether their own moral system is grounded in a transcendental divine power, in the power of a good argument, or in the power of human relationships, the concern for human rights has universal authority to guide criticism. Second, I offer those working for the human rights of all of humanity a way to think about human rights that is dictated neither by a cultural nor by a political tradition, but that has nevertheless a universal authority to guide criticism. Third, this book offers guidance in thinking about universal human rights so that human rights activism continues in ways that support the human rights of all of humanity by transforming the institutions and practices that condition the lives of all of humanity.

This view of immanent universal human rights requires rethinking rights, obligation, and society. Feminist and comparative political thought on obligation can help us rethink the view of agency that has constrained so many human rights theorists from considering the full range of human rights because correlative obligations and duty-bearers cannot be found.[127] Of course, the state has significant power to influence the human rights context within its borders. Further, many states can design institutions and support practices that are conducive to human rights conditions in other states. But because of the social and economic dimensions of the human rights context, neither states nor individuals nor groups of individuals can bear responsibility for the human rights context alone. In exploring these implications of

[127] Hirschmann 1992; Jaggar 1992: 361–370; O'Neill 2000: 97–111. A brief interrogation from a Confucian perspective suggests that rethinking obligation will require thinking through the relationships of people within the state, not just the relationship of the state to the individual, such that a full exploration is well beyond the scope of this project. My thought on this thus far is captured in Ackerly (2005a).

human rights for responsibility, we will raise many questions that are familiar themes for theorists of democracy, justice, and freedom.[128] For activists, the interdependence of human rights, democracy, freedom, and justice mean that in order for our strategies for promoting human rights to be long-term effective, we need to be attentive to the ways in which our short-term human rights strategies affect long-term human rights conditions.

128 Ackerly 2005a; Goodhart 2003: 935–964; Gould 1988; Pettit 1997; Sen 1999b; Shapiro 1990; 1999.

PART I

# *Epistemology, diversity, and disagreement in theory and practice*

In Part I, we consider the field of human rights theory in order to determine what a political theory of human rights as a tool for criticism of injustices is and is not. We begin in chapter 2 with the debate over whether a universal theory of human rights is possible. I conclude that all human rights theories must be attentive to the political power of epistemology, to the fact of diversity, and to the prospect of disagreement about important moral issues such as human rights among those who would respect human rights and among those who would limit the scope of human rights in order to undermine the political legitimacy of certain criticisms of injustice.

In chapter 3 we turn to a criticism of the ways in which most universal theories of human rights rely on a political authority. In one set of approaches, the power of interpretation of a transcendental moral authority exposes human rights to political exploitation by an elite able to claim the appropriate application of human rights or whether to recognize them at all. Another set of approaches gives authority to a principle, a foundational principle. Like the first, such approaches give the power of interpretation to those better capable of wielding an argument. Even if such theories were more democratic in their notion of interpretive authority than they generally are (as in some cosmopolitan republican arguments), the form of theory that relies on a principle leaves the epistemological basis of that principle uninterrogated and thus such theories have the potential to support exploitative hierarchy as well.

From the discussions in chapters 2 and 3 we see that a universal theory must be immanent if its critical capacity is to be politically legitimate. Consequently, in chapter 4 we consider those theorists who have offered a form of immanent universal argument. However, in considering these arguments, we realize not only that a theory must be immanent, but also that, in order to be used for social criticism, an immanent theory must have an explicit methodology that includes the *methods* of its own criticism (and not just self-criticism). For a theory to be a legitimate guide for social criticism it must have an immanent source of authority and a methodological source of legitimacy.

In this approach to human rights, human rights are not individual in the tradition of natural law theory or liberal constitutional theory. Human rights are sociological. In both the empirical study of rights and the normative theorizing about human rights, human rights need to be understood *sociologically*. Those who work in the positive theory of human rights generally do understand human rights sociologically.[1] In Part I, we consider many normative theories of human rights (those of both advocates and critics) that do not understand normative theory sociologically, but rather as knowable through analytical thought.

Sometimes in this argument I refer to language that may be more familiar to some readers than to others. When I deem such language necessary (as in the distinction between positive and normative theory, discussions of epistemology, non-ideal theory, etc.), particularly necessary for a political theorist to be able to follow the nuance of an argument, I will also use non-theory language to explain the concept. These moments are cross-referenced in the index so that a reader with growing interest in the more theoretical aspects of the argument may refer back to them, but none of this jargon is required for understanding the basics of the argument.

Following the exposition in chapter 1, the reader may be anticipating the argument in the following chapters to be illustrated with citations from my interviews and other sources. However, while my argument depends on our willingness and ability to listen to the arguments of those struggling against injustice, as we will see in chapter 4, such listening needs to be guided by a critical methodology. Once I have argued in Part I why such a methodology is necessary, in Part II I will describe such a methodology that enables us to reflect upon the politics of epistemology, diversity, and disagreement among informants, and in Part III draw on that methodology to lay out the theory.

[1] See for example Cingranelli and Richards 1999; Keith and Poe 2004; Milner, Poe, and Leblang 1999; Poe, Carey, and Vazquez 2001; Poe and Tate 1994; Poe, Tate, and Keith 1999; Poe, Wendel-Blunt, and Ho 1997; Richards 1999; Walker and Poe 2002.

# 2 *Universal human rights?*

## Introduction

Because human rights are a matter of life and death, a theory of universal human rights for cross-cultural and intra-cultural criticism needs to be sustained when ideal conditions are lacking. Philosophical questions of global injustice and human rights have been pursued as questions of ideal or non-ideal theory. I argue that they should be pursued as a form of non-ideal theory.

Ideal theory is the project of determining the nature and aims of the "perfectly just," "well-ordered" society in which "Everyone is presumed to act justly and to do his part in upholding just institutions."[1] Rawls is describing ideal theorizing about a *society* which he understands to be roughly similar to a contemporary state. But the same expectations of institutional justice and individual behavior would be expected of ideal theory globally.

However, are the expectations of ideal theory appropriate for theories of global justice and human rights? I argue no. Because these injustices are a function of a historical legacy that causes as well as characterizes the problems of global injustice including human rights violations and because this historical legacy likewise delimits solutions that might be in the offing, non-ideal theory is a better tool for theorizing about human rights. Non-ideal theorizing offers mechanisms for considering how to move from unjust arrangements to more just arrangements, not just for theorizing about what just arrangements might look like.

Furthermore, for the same reasons, the Rawlsian justificatory scheme is an inadequate scheme for a politically legitimate justification of a non-ideal theoretical argument. Instead we need theoretical methodologies for asking the critical questions that post-modern, feminist,

[1] Rawls [1971]1999: 8.

post-colonial, and other critical theorists have been asking. In this chapter I outline the concerns about the politics of knowledge, difference, and dissent which our theoretical methods need to address in order that our theory of human rights reveals the silences and absences of justice.[2]

While I was polishing this chapter to present at the University of North Carolina, Chapel Hill, Marie and the three youngest children arrived in Uganda and were reunited with the three older children who had come over the border from Rwanda earlier that month. They were tired, hungry, and had no plan for what to do next. Fortunately, two former students and one current graduate student of an institute in the United States had experience with helping refugees from Rwanda and offered to help her. From their job titles and organizations it was unclear if they would be friends to Marie, offer NGO support, or be her first contact with authorities. Each wanted to know her story. She didn't want to tell her story over the telephone. And she was afraid of whether the story she told would extend or close off these prospective offers of guidance and help. As the days passed, the communication from each of the three volunteers and from Marie became worrisome. Would she be able to describe her particular experience in a way that illustrated both that she has genuine reason to flee, particular to herself and her family, and that this experience corresponded to a recognizable pattern of threat familiar to those working with Rwandan refugees in Uganda? The success of her claim would be predicated on the preconceived political legitimacy of her claim. Those making the assessment would evaluate her claim against the experiences with which they were familiar; later an official would determine the legal merit of her claim.

Before we survey human rights theory for insights about what a theory of universal human rights needs to consider, we need to determine what kind of theory a human rights theory is and what are appropriate modes of justifying a particular human rights theory. Then, we will have a basis from which to assess those theories. Such assessment, as I will illustrate in chapter 3, needs to reflect our understandings of what a theory of human rights needs to be generally. Therefore, rather than beginning with a survey of other human rights theories, I begin with the political struggles for human rights. For, we

[2] James Booth describes poignantly the relationship between silence and injustice (2006: chapter 3, esp. 73–79).

need a point – or several points – from which we can assess not whether Marie's experience or any particular claim of human rights violation corresponds to our understanding of human rights violations or more narrowly to our understandings of present patterns of human rights violations in the Great Lakes region of Africa. Rather, we need to be able to ask what Marie's particular story tells us about human rights violations generally, and the patterns of human rights violations generally. It should not matter *at the outset* if our theory conforms to *other* theories of human rights with which we are familiar or comfortable.

What kind of theory is human rights theory? A non-ideal theory of justice.[3] Human rights theory is best understood as a non-ideal theory, that is, a political theory of a concept that needs an understanding of past exercises of power, both oppression and resistance. A human rights theory cannot be an ideal theory in the sense of John Rawls's *justice as fairness*, that is, a theory with no history.[4] Human rights theory inherently has a past – the past struggles of individuals, communities, and peoples against their oppressions.

Because non-ideal theorizing gets its boundaries from the historical injustices that make justice as much a matter of *setting* things right as of *getting* them right, non-ideal theory needs to be informed by the injustices that got things wrong. In addition to identifying those injustices, we would need to determine if they were a historical aberration or if they were always a potential concern. If they were a historical aberration, we could hope that a measure of what Aristotle calls "rectificatory" justice could set things right and that, after such a correction, we could expect ideal theory to be able to inspire our reflections on justice most closely. However, if the injustices that caused our history were always a potential concern, then non-ideal theory would be used, not just to set right a past problem, but always to

[3] I follow Rawls in his understanding of ideal theory which "assumes strict compliance and works out the principles that characterize a well-ordered society under favorable circumstances. It develops the conception of a perfectly just basic structure and the corresponding duties and obligations of persons under the fixed constraints of human life" ([1971]1999: 212, also 217–218, 216, 277). I could also argue that the immanent and universal theory of human rights is a *democratic* theory of justice. But for now, I will confine the argument to an exposition of human rights theory as non-ideal theory.

[4] Rawls [1971]1999: §16; Rawls and Kelly 2001: 64–65.

guide our critical reflection on the *potential* for injustices to recur.[5] On this reading, non-ideal theory is a better tool than ideal theory for setting the background conditions of a society, what Rawls calls the "basic structure."

Thus, the chapter proceeds in two ways: first I argue that theoretical accounts of the content and function of human rights should be a form of non-ideal theory and second I develop the methodological questions to which a theorist of non-ideal theory needs to be attentive.

## Human rights as a non-ideal theory

In *A Theory of Justice* Rawls makes an important distinction between ideal and non-ideal theory.[6] The distinction is important for his argument and for our reading of his work. This distinction is different from the distinctions that Aristotle offers in the *Nicomachean Ethics*, Book V, between complete and partial justice, between distributive and rectificatory, and between natural and conventional justice. For Rawls, ideal theory derives a "realistic utopia,"[7] a theory of justice from assumptions we all share. Despite value pluralism, there is political agreement on norms of justice after a thorough discussion of our different views.[8] A non-ideal theory of justice would be a theory of justice that did not assume full agreement on, and adherence to, the theory of justice. Ideal theory begins with a methodological assumption of universal agreement, political consensus despite value pluralism, and shared standards for justification. Non-ideal theory proceeds from an assumption of disagreement, value *and* political pluralism, and epistemological dissensus. Both include suggestions for dealing with occasional noncompliance.[9] Ideal theory sets out ideal background conditions. Only

[5] By contrast, Rawls works analytically: while we know some "facts of social science," we do not know the history of "various democratic regimes and . . . [the] rights and liberties that seem basic and are securely protected in what seem to be historically the more successful regimes" (2001: 45). Because of the nature of our diagnoses of the political problems related to diversity, disagreement, and the politics of knowledge, discussed shortly, I caution that we remain vigilant against recurring injustice even in a world that is well-ordered.

[6] The distinction is reiterated in Rawls ([1971]1999: §16) and Rawls and Kelly (2001: 64–65).

[7] Rawls 1999b: 5–6. [8] Rawls [1971]1999: esp. 508–509.

[9] Rawls [1971]1999: 7–8, 212, 216, 277.

non-ideal theory guides our reflections on the *modification* of unjust background conditions.[10]

We can use ideal theory to think about non-compliance to a limited extent. To do this we assess injustice against the characterization of justice spelled out by the ideal theory. When we do so we see that we have "partial compliance" according to which either part of "us" are not complying or are complying only partly.[11] Partial compliance theory "includes among other things, the theory of punishment and compensatory justice, just war and conscientious objection, civil disobedience and militant resistance."[12] Liberal and decent societies are conforming, but rogue ("outlaw") states are not.[13]

While each of these questions have been explored within the realm of ideal theory, these questions of justice sometimes reflect political challenges, often cued by the politics of knowledge, diversity, and dissent that are assumed away in the methodological assumptions of ideal theory. These assumptions – that society is well-ordered, that value pluralism does not inhibit sharing norms of justice, and that dissensus can be resolved though norms of public reason – do not need to hold for non-ideal theoretical inquiry. Because human rights are violated in contexts where these assumptions do not hold, a human rights theory needs to be at least in part a non-ideal theory. Further, even if one thought that background conditions could be consistent with ideal theory sometimes,[14] because background conditions *can become* inconsistent with ideal theory, a human rights theory always needs to be at least in part a non-ideal theory.[15] Whatever else we know, History, Sociology, Anthropology, and Political Science have taught us that economic, social, and political processes can bring about

[10] Mills and Pateman forthcoming; Rosenfeld 1991. Like Rawls, Robert Nozick offers an ideal theory. The justness of the holdings and the minimal state that recognizes entitlement depend *entirely* on the justness of acquisition (1974). Non-ideal theory reveals the ways in which power inequalities portray unjust acquisition by choice.

[11] Rawls [1971]1999: 216, 267, 308–219, 343; [1993] 1999: 537.

[12] Rawls [1971]1999: 309.

[13] Rawls 1999b: 5; [1993] 1999: 537.

[14] For example see Benhabib's discussions of deliberative democratic theory (2002).

[15] From a critical perspective, we can never be confident that we can characterize the background conditions as just in any place at any time. In chapter 3 I will argue that the methods of ideal theories make them transcendental theories and therefore they are theories without the universalizable political legitimacy of non-transcendental theories.

injustice.[16] Non-compliance has to be explored within the context of non-ideal theory because what is at issue with non-compliance may also be the failure of the background conditions that make compliance possible.[17] Non-ideal theory is necessary for assessing these possibilities because it does not have the strong epistemological assumptions of ideal theory.

In human rights theory we might be concerned with the problem of non-compliance with ideal theory. We might require "principles for governing adjustments to natural limitations and historical contingencies."[18] However, if "natural limitations and historical contingencies" are always potentially a problem, we would do better to think of human rights theory as *always* a non-ideal theory. Further, theoretical solutions to non-compliance may be a matter of "principles for meeting injustices."[19] Again, if these injustices are going to be chronically occurring as a result of natural and social contingencies, it is better to understand human rights theory as needing to be reasoned using the methodological tools of non-ideal theory.

Of course, Rawls says that we should work out an ideal theory of justice and then, with the ideal in our sights, derive the non-ideal theory. However, human rights theory cannot be an amendment to an *ideal* theory of justice in this way. When human rights abuses occur, the deviation from justice is both a failure of background conditions *and* a failure of one or many actors. The characterization of human rights violations as non-compliance with an ideal is inconsistent with our considered judgments about human rights. These considered judgments include an understanding that human rights are a basis from which to make pleas for change. Tautologically, a human rights theory would be unnecessary if everyone were compliant with an ideal theory of justice, or even if all background conditions and most behavior were

[16] Agreement with this account of social processes depends on your view of justice. Robert Nozick would argue that within ideal theory just initial acquisition and subsequent just transfer of entitlements yield just distributions (1974). Because by his stipulation transfers of entitlements are a function of the exercise of individual free choice, the social science describing the structural processes of those choices which might enrich the understanding of transfers of entitlement are not relevant to a theory of justice.

[17] Rawls 1999b: 5; [1993] 1999: 537.

[18] Rawls [1971]1999: 216.

[19] Rawls [1971]1999: 216.

compliant. Dealing with human rights violations requires more than rectificatory justice.

If human rights theory needs to be developed as a non-ideal theory, what does that mean for *how* we theorize about human rights? Again, turning to Rawls, ideal theory can guide social reform,[20] but as he argues in his discussion of the priority of liberty, in his project, "The principles and their lexical order were not acknowledged with these situations [of non-compliance] in mind and so it is possible that [the principles and their lexical order] no longer hold."[21] Though he does not labor over the point, he does acknowledge that non-ideal theory may require us to reason differently and may in fact lead us to different conclusions. Though he gives little attention to the appropriate methodology for non-ideal theory, he acknowledges that the justification scheme for non-ideal theory would differ from the justificatory scheme of ideal theory.

## Rawlsian methodology and non-ideal theory

In contrast with Rawls, who argues that ideal theory is necessary for non-ideal theory, I am going to argue that non-ideal theory needs to be reasoned differently than Rawlsian ideal theory. Reasoned following my methodology, I propose the argument for human rights is better theory *and* a basis for the political legitimacy of human rights. Because the politics it needs to address are not born of ideal circumstances, non-ideal theory may not most constructively be understood as a derivative of ideal theory. However, before starting from scratch, let's consider the Rawlsian methodology of justification in part because this method has been deployed by Charles Taylor, Martha Nussbaum, and Joshua Cohen, three theorists whose attempts to articulate an immanent account of universal human rights I discuss in chapter 4.

The attention that a political theorist should pay to the political legitimacy of her argument became part of mainstream contemporary political liberalism itself with Rawls's turn in "Justice as Fairness: Political not Metaphysical"(1985) and "The Idea of an Overlapping Consensus"(1987), and reiterated in *Political Liberalism* and *Justice as*

[20] Rawls [1971]1999: 215. [21] Rawls [1971]1999: 216.

*Fairness.*[22] Rather than arguing that political liberalism generally, and justice as fairness particularly, has a universalizable metaphysical justification, he argues that political liberalism characterized by justice as fairness is a politically legitimate proposal for a context of pluralism. Rawls argues that in a politically liberal society, despite a range of metaphysical justifications for political liberalism, people will hold political liberalism as the best manifestation of their values even metaphysically understood.[23]

In the Rawlsian model, the political legitimacy of the justificatory scheme is important. In this sense, mine is a Rawlsian project. However, in my view, the Rawlsian justificatory scheme offers an inadequate methodology for universal human rights theory because it applies only under norms of consensus and because it does not interrogate the politics implicit in any system of acquiring evidence, evaluating evidence, and making arguments.[24]

The basis of political legitimacy in the Rawlsian view is:

> When citizens share a reasonable political conception of justice, they share common ground on which public discussion of fundamental questions can proceed.[25]

This is deliberation under norms of consensus.[26] All pieces have to hold in place for political legitimacy: (1) the justification is "open and public"; (2) the justification relies on "mutually recognizable reasons and evidence"; (3) the justification is "supported by the preponderance of reasons as given by an appropriate procedure"; (4) the justification

[22] In a 1989 article, "Should Political Philosophy be Done without Metaphysics," Jean Hampton looks at Rawls's turn in these first two articles (1989). See also Erin Kelly's "Editor's Forward" to *Justice as Fairness: A Restatement* (2001). Habermas (2001b: 59) traces the turn to "Kantian Constructivism in Moral Theory" ([1980] 1999). See also Benhabib 2002; Cohen 1996; Estlund 1998a; 1998b; Gaus 1990; 1996; 1999; 2003.

[23] Most deliberative theory can be understood as developing this approach (see e.g. Benhabib 1996; 2002; Cohen 1996; Elster 1998).

[24] Likewise the Rawlsian justificatory scheme offers an inadequate methodology for any theory of democracy applicable in a context of dissent, inequality, and constraints on freedom. The theory of human rights in this book is part of a theory of democracy not set out here.

[25] Rawls 1993: 115.

[26] See also Shiffman (2002). In chapter 7 I take great inspiration from Susan Bickford's move away from consensus toward listening as a better characterization of the democratic impulse (1996: esp. 141).

relies on "reasons given by ... [the] principles" of the justificatory scheme and not on reasons that are convincing to oneself; (5) the appeal of the justificatory scheme is such that I bring my own view of what constitute good reasons in line with the "objective point of view" that is the "shared public basis of justification"; and (6) all members of a society are free and equal with respect to (1)–(5).[27] This means that the justification is open and public *to all*, that all members are equally able to recognize reasons and evidence, and that all members are freely and equally convinced of the same conclusion by the preponderance of reasons.

There are three problems with the Rawlsian justificatory scheme that undermine its claim to political legitimacy: (1) the assumption of free and equal participants (that is, the politics of dissent and inattention to the legitimate claims of the silent); (2) its inattention to structures (that is, the politics of diversity and micro-structures as opposed to the basic structure that make opening justification processes to the public insufficient means for interrogating processes of exclusion);[28] and (3) its account of evidence (that is, its *un*deconstructed epistemology and inattention to the politics of knowledge).

The first problem with the Rawlsian justificatory scheme is the assumption or assertion that citizens are free and equal – or free enough and equal enough that they can participate in internal politics using reasonable arguments to convince others of their views.[29] In *A Theory of Justice*, we were asked to reason *as if* we were free and equal, from behind the "veil of ignorance" where we knew nothing of our particular circumstances. For justice as fairness to have political legitimacy, the expectation is even higher: again, "citizens share a reasonable political conception of justice."[30]

However, what if, as in the non-ideal case, we are not free enough and equal enough within our society to trust reasonable argument to reflect our interests? Then, we are in a moment of "constitutional" debate, when dissensus is the practice and consensus the dream.[31]

[27] Rawls 1993: 115. [28] Ackerly 2000; Young 2001a.

[29] See David Lyons (1972) for an early discussion of Rawlsian methodology and justificatory scheme. Compare Rawls's assumption of free and equal citizens with Gould's argument for securing equally effective positive liberty for all (2004).

[30] Rawls 1993: 115.

[31] Shiffman argues that, characterized by high salience and long-term impact, the constitutional moment requires consensus (2002; cf. King 1963[2007]).

Within a polity, when some are making claims regarding their freedom, equality, rights, and inclusion, norms of consensus are conservative.

Further, given that polities are dynamic, norms of deliberative democracy are best secured when we assume that norms of consensus *do not* hold. If we want people to be free and equal in our politically liberal society we have to assume that they may not always be so and use social criticism to identify and mitigate forms of marginalization that undermine freedom and equality.[32] So, while I agree with Rawls that our political philosophy needs to be politically legitimate, I disagree that norms of consensus are likely to make it so, given a non-ideal context.

Rawls is aware that his assumption that a liberal people shares common sympathies is very strong:

> As for a liberal people being united by common sympathies and a desire to be under the same democratic government, if those sympathies were entirely dependent upon a common language, history, and political culture, with a shared historical consciousness, this feature would rarely, if ever, be fully satisfied. *Historical conquests* and *immigration* have caused the intermingling of groups with *different cultures and historical memories* who now reside within the territory of most contemporary democratic governments.[33] [*Emphasis added.*]

Some have gained and others have lost in the disagreements and the processes of resolution that have brought them to the moment of defining themselves as a people. For Rawls, inequality and the micro-structural support for inequality in the micro-structures of society can be assumed away so as not to be an obstacle to their conceiving of themselves as a people and agreeing to settle constitutional matters by norms of consensus.

Consider three reflections on discursive argument: one by Jean Hampton, one from the Melians in the exchange that preceded

[32] Ackerly 2000.

[33] Rawls 1999b: 24–25. See all of *Law of Peoples* section 2.1 for greater detail. See also *Law of Peoples* pages 44 and 62 in which Rawls asserts that a people's sense of honor comes from its history and achievements. Despite the qualifications in the passage I quote, this definition is important to Rawls's argument about both liberal and decent peoples. Rawls argues that his *Law of Peoples* argument proceds in two stages, first the ideal and second the non-ideal. However, the characteristics of ideal theory that he offers in *A Theory of Justice* and *Justice as Fairness* do not apply in his discussion of a law of peoples.

their being conquered by the Athenians, and the third by Frederick Douglass. Jean Hampton is sympathetic to Rawls's reframing of political liberalism as a challenge of political legitimacy:

> implicit in genuine philosophical argumentation is respect for one's opponent. One might not respect his ideas, but when one argues with him (as opposed to, say, fighting with him), one respects him and seeks to win him over to one's side.[34]

Hampton applauds the mutually respectful terms of philosophical debate. The philosopher is not oppressed by her interlocutor and neither apparently is the interlocutor oppressed by the philosopher. Politics is the exercise of discursive, not coercive, power. Force appears only in parentheses and then only to indicate that it is not present here.

But many discursive opportunities take place in more coercive contexts. Consider a second argument. With a force of "thirty of their own ships, six from Chios, and two from Lesbos; 1,200 hoplites, 300 archers, and twenty mounted archers, all from Athens; and about 1,500 hoplites from the allies and the islanders"[35] poised to invade, the Athenians met with the Melians (Melos was a colony from Sparta that had until recently been neutral). The Athenians ask (I paraphrase), "why don't you let us address the entire population? Oh, because you think that we would convince them. We get it, and why won't you let us speak to you without constantly being interrupted?" The Council of the Melians responds:

> No one can object to each of us putting forward our own views in a calm atmosphere. That is perfectly reasonable. What is scarcely consistent with such a proposal is the present threat, indeed the certainty, of your making war on us. We see that you have come prepared to judge the argument yourselves, and that the likely end of it all will be either war, if we prove that we are in the right, and so refuse to surrender, or else slavery.[36]

As both the Athenians and the Melians recognized, the question of how we should judge an argument is *political*. Any assessment of a human rights theory ought to acknowledge the political struggles that call for human rights.[37]

[34] Hampton 1989: 811. [35] Thucydides 1954: 358.
[36] Thucydides 1954: 359. [37] See for example Ishay (2004).

To be inattentive to those power politics, to theorize as if the justificatory scheme and the mode of discourse itself are not a product and practice of politics, is to ignore the history of power.[38] By contrast, Frederick Douglass is incensed by the requirement that he offer an argument bound by the discursive norms of political justification set out by his interlocutors:

> Would you have me argue that man is entitled to liberty? . . . To do so, would be to make myself ridiculous, and to offer an insult to your understanding. There is not a man beneath the canopy of heaven, that does not know that slavery is wrong for him.
>
> What, am I to argue that it is wrong to make men brutes, to rob them of their liberty, to work them without wages, to keep them ignorant of their relations to their fellow men, to beat them with sticks, to flay their flesh with the lash, to load their limbs with irons, to hunt them with dogs, to sell them at auction, to sunder their families, to knock out their teeth, to burn their flesh, to starve them into obedience and submission to their masters? Must I argue that a system thus marked with blood, and stained with pollution, is wrong? No! I will not. I have better employments for my time and strength, than such arguments would imply.
>
> What, then, remains to be argued? Is it that slavery is not divine; that God did not establish it; that our doctors of divinity are mistaken? There is blasphemy in the thought. That which is inhuman, cannot be divine! Who can reason on such a proposition? They that can, may; I cannot. The time for such argument is past.
>
> At a time like this, scorching irony, not convincing argument, is needed.[39]

Together, these passages expose the *political* problem with Rawlsian justification or Rawlsian political legitimacy.

In the first passage, Jean Hampton is defending Rawlsian deliberation as appropriate for philosophizing under Rawlsian conditions.[40] The subject of such debate within a politically liberal state might be free health services; and we could assume that all deliberants were free enough and equal enough to deliberate, even though the outcome of the deliberations might affect them differently. The passage from Frederick Douglass reminds us that often (and precisely when we need them) these Rawlsian ideal conditions are lacking. We can not assume that deliberants were free enough or equal enough to debate health care let alone slavery; the outcome of the deliberations is a

[38] Foucault 1978. [39] Douglass 1852. [40] Hampton 1989: 810.

matter of life or death for some. From the perspective of the enslaved or those threatened with slavery or afraid of their interlocutor (like the Melians and Marie), open deliberation guided by public reason is an oppressive norm.

In short, a non-ideal theory needs methods for exploring the sources and meaning of dissent. As problematic as norms of consensus are for a people or a state,[41] such norms are even more problematic when taking up the subject of universal human rights which must function critically within states *and* internationally. Transnationally, when some are making claims regarding their freedom, equality, rights, or inclusion, norms of consensus are conservative. We need a non-ideal theory of human rights in order to evaluate those claims in a context of dissention. The basis of that theory must not be norms of consensus as in ideal theory. The assumption of free and equal members is *very* strong for any state with a past and an inappropriate basis for political legitimacy for any theory, ideal or non-ideal. Of course, if we assume consensus, political legitimacy is a function of argument not politics, but only in a tautological sense. In order for the claim to political legitimacy to mean anything *politically*, as Rawls surely intends it too, ideal theory needs to abandon its epistemological assumption of consensus.

This is not an indictment of Rawls's justificatory scheme, but rather an argument for its limits. Political legitimacy is a fairly unchallenging aspiration for an ideal theory. By contrast, political legitimacy is an important aspiration for non-ideal theory.

The second problem with the Rawlsian justificatory scheme is that despite his claim that the basic structure is the subject of justice, structural causes of non-compliance are invisible to his methodology. The argument here could just rehearse the arguments related to the first problem – the presumption of free and equal participants – because both are related to the social contract nature of Rawls's justificatory scheme. Instead, here I want to push the critique further and emphasize the structural causes of non-compliance. How have international politics and local politics created the conditions of injustice (and eminent threat to human rights) with which Marie and her family have been living?[42]

[41] See Buchanan's review of *Law of Peoples* (2000) in which he argues that by "people" Rawls meant "state."

[42] Klinghoffer 1998; Reyntjiens 2004; Uvin 1998.

As Michel Rosenfeld argues in *Affirmative Action and Justice* with regard to Rawls, ideal theories have no history.[43] Questions of human rights related injustice have a past and a future, further they have *structures* as well as actors and they may be institutionalized through the habits and roles of actors. Thus, the meaningful discussion of human rights injustices that can be conducted within the intellectual bounds of ideal theorizing is limited. Human rights are a meaningful global norm not because they sprung forth fully formed – as Athena from Zeus's skull – from global reasoning, disconnected from each other, other global norms, and the global struggles that produce these. Rather human rights are meaningful because they emerge out of local and global struggles and because they reflect the norm-generating processes of political life, civil society, and individual conscience,[44] each of which is a terrain of dissent and epistemological uncertainty.

The third problem with the Rawlsian justificatory scheme is its politics of knowledge, which does not require that we look for that which is invisible. By relying on "mutually recognizable reasons and evidence" the Rawlsian justificatory scheme challenges those whose reasons and evidence are non-conforming. What kind of evidence that Marie offers will be recognized? Who assesses whether the preponderance of reasons are on her side? What is the process of being educated to be able to offer reasons acceptable to others? Whose view represents the objective point of view when human rights are violated? The justificatory scheme for non-ideal theory needs methods for asking and answering these questions.

Whether or not ideal theorists are willing, the non-ideal theorists need to be concerned both with the political legitimacy of our arguments and with the challenges to that legitimacy posed by the politics of knowledge, diversity, and dissent. That is, human rights are better understood as a part of non-ideal theory.

What, then, should be our theoretical methods for developing a politically legitimate justificatory scheme for a non-ideal theory?

[43] Rosenfeld 1991. Charles Mills draws our attention to this interpretation (forthcoming; see also Mills 2005). In the context of his discussion of transitional justice, Rosenfeld also reminds us of the limiting scope of Rawlsian reflection on questions of justice that are the result of framing his project as one of ideal theory.

[44] Rubin 2005: chapter 8, 332–333.

## Methodologies for non-ideal theoretical arguments

The obvious theorists to turn to for theoretical insights into politically legitimate arguments for non-ideal theory are those who have criticized the political legitimacy of ideal theoretical arguments. Such criticisms have been variously raised by critical perspectives including strands of Feminism,[45] Queer Theory,[46] Cultural Studies,[47] Critical Race Theory,[48] Bioethics,[49] Post-colonial Theory,[50] Anthropology,[51] Critical Theory,[52] Multiculturalism,[53] Post-modern Theory,[54] and Comparative Political Thought.[55] Each of these (obviously overlapping) critical perspectives draws our attention both to *patterns* of oppression and to the *particulars* of oppression.[56] Each critical perspective seeks to make us attentive to the particulars of the excluded, marginalized, and otherwise oppressed and in so doing makes us aware of the patterns of exclusion, marginalization, and oppression sustained by insufficiently critical perspectives. But further, each cautions us against ignoring unimagined, invisible, or silent particulars while being attentive to certain patterns of oppression. From these perspectives, to have political legitimacy a theoretical argument needs to be

[45] Ackerly 2000; Gatens 2004; Harding 2000; Okin 1999.
[46] Sedgwick 1990.
[47] Basu and McGrory 1995; Kempadoo and Doezema 1998; Moghadam 1994; Suthrell 2004.
[48] Bybee 1997; Crenshaw 1989; 2000; Harris 2000; Williams 1993.
[49] Donchin 2003; Silliman and King 1999.
[50] Badiou 2001; Gandhi 1998; Gordon 2004; Mohanty 2003; [1984] 1991; Mohanty, Russo, and Torres 1991; Narayan 1997; Nash 2002; Said [1978] 1979; Sandoval 2000; Scott 1999.
[51] Abeysekara 2002; Benson and Nagar 2006; dé Ishtar 2005; Liamputtong, Yimyam, Parisunyakul, Baosoung, and Sarsiriphan 2004; Tsing 2005; Williams 1996.
[52] Bohman 2004; Cox 2001; Fraser 1997; Geuss 1981; Jones 2001; Landes 1992; Morgan 2003.
[53] Appiah 1994b; Benhabib 2002; Harris 1995; Kymlicka 1995; Shachar 2001; Taylor, Gutmann, and Taylor [1992]1994.
[54] Butler 1995; Di Leonardo 1991; Nicholson and Seidman 1995; Sylvester 1994; Wolf 1992; Zalewski 2000.
[55] An-Na'im 1990; 1992a; 1992b; Dallmayr 2004; 1998; 1999; 2001; Euben 2004; 1999; Falk 2000; Geertz 2000; Muzaffar 2002; Said [1978] 1979.
[56] In this chapter I refer to these as "critical perspectives" or "critical theories." When I mean Critical Theory as an intellectual school inspired by Marx and Gramsci, including scholars of the Frankfurt School and contemporary International Relations Critical Theorists, I will capitalize "Critical."

attentive to the politics of knowledge, to cross-cultural and intra-cultural diversity, and to the politics of disagreement.

## *The politics of knowledge*

Critical interlocutors are engaged with perspectives that do not always share their epistemological uncertainty.[57] In a 2004 interview with Ron Suskind published in *The New York Times Magazine*, an unnamed senior adviser to the President of the United States exhibits the form of certainty with which the critical perspective is uncomfortable. He explains the relationship between the leaders of the US empire and the reporter with complete confidence in the epistemological power of empire.

> We're an empire now, and when we act, we create our own reality. And while you're studying that reality – judiciously, as you [the reporter] will – we'll act again, creating other new realities, which you can study too ...[58]

The speaker is inattentive to diversity in any concrete sense, but he is conscious of the power of knowledge and its role in constructing a political reality that ignores disagreement or dissent.

Responding to the political impetus to use empire to craft a political reality for the elite of the empire, in *An Ordinary Person's Guide to Empire*, Arundhati Roy calls on American citizens to be a great people by challenging the use of imperial power to contribute to an oppressive political reality for most of the world's population.

> I hate to disagree with your president: yours is by no means a great nation. But you could be a great people.[59]

[57] For a discussion of the political authority vested in preachers by fundamentalists of various "Bible Believer" stripes, see Harding (2000).

[58] Suskind 2004. Suskind's article was cited by Mark Danner in a graduation speech delivered at Berkeley's English Department graduation and published in *The New York Review of Books* (Danner 2005). Mark Danner is the author of *The Massacre at El Mozote*, which describes horrific human rights violations in a massacre by US trained Salvadoran forces during the Cold War (1994). This is the book I referred to in chapter 1 as it offers the opening images of Michael Perry's *The Idea of Human Rights* (1998).

[59] Roy 2004: 68.

A great people would not delegate to its leaders the authority over knowledge when it delegated to them the responsibility of political authority.

Theorists with a broad range of intellectual backgrounds have thought about possibilities for global justice despite the politics of knowledge, diversity, and dissent. Thinkers as different from one another as Fred Dallmayr, David Held, Carol Gould, Michael Goodhart, Samuel Huntington, Francis Fukuyama, Benjamin Barber, Richard Falk, John Rawls, Amartya Sen, Ernesto Laclau, Slavoj Žižek, Judith Butler, Tariq Ramadan, Richard Rorty, and Charles Mills reflect on hegemony, globalization, and cultures.[60] The theoretical approaches of some exhibit more confidence than others in the appropriateness of attempts to interrogate epistemological politics.

Without taking up the question of global justice, in his criticism of social contract theory, Charles Mills offers a helpful device for considering the politics of knowledge. He argues that there are three parts to the social contract in ideal theories: the epistemological, the moral, and the social.[61] A non-ideal theory needs to offer a criticism of the epistemological contract that silences dissenting knowledge or renders experiential evidence to the contrary invisible.

Given the political power of epistemology, a theoretical methodology for non-ideal theory should not assume any agreement nor should it base its confidence in its own account on its consistency with "our considered judgments in reflective equilibrium,"[62] nor should it be expected to be perfectly coherent.[63] Rather, it should begin with the social and political fact that epistemology can be used consciously or inadvertently to cast political inequality as apolitical difference.

Attentive to knowledge as a source of political power, we cannot begin non-ideal theorizing with confidence that our intuitions about justice are shared. Rather we should submit our intuitions to skeptical scrutiny.[64] We should not be confident in an account of justice that

[60] Barber 1995; Butler, Laclau, and Žižek 2000; Dallmayr 2001; Falk 2000; Fukuyama 1992; Goodhart 2005; Gould 2004; Held 1995; 2003; Huntington 1996; Mills forthcoming; Ramadan 2004; Rawls 1999b; Rorty 1991; 1993; Sen 2004.

[61] Mills 1997.

[62] Rawlsian fixed points assume that some values of justices are shared and fixed (Rawls [1971]1999: 507).

[63] Rawls [1971]1999: 507 and 504. [64] Ackerly 2000.

seems to fit all of our considered judgments in reflective equilibrium, but rather we should wonder what views were not represented in the list of considered judgments upon which we reflected. Finally, we should be suspicious of an account that is perfectly coherent. It is possible that that coherence was achieved at the expense of the consideration of some insight or as a result of applying norms of argumentation and consensus building that suppressed certain interpretations or ways of arguing. Each of these considerations – about our beginning point, procedures, and outcomes of theoretical argument – suggests that for a non-ideal theory to have political legitimacy it must deploy a multifaceted destabilizing epistemology that enables each aspect of a justificatory scheme to be interrogated for its hidden epistemological assumptions.

Of course, we wouldn't want to impede the political project of coming up with solutions to lived world crises in human rights violations. Yet, we would also not like to allow non-ideal theory to become the tool of the powerful. While appreciating the usefulness to the privileged of "Master's Tools" of contract theory,[65] ideal justification, and dependent political legitimacy for the ideal theory project that Rawls and other ideal theorists deploy, we must not deploy these in unreconstructed ways as the tools of non-ideal theory. With apologies to Audre Lorde, the Master's Tools are as well-suited in theoretical metaphor as they are in construction practice for dismantling the Master's house. Immanent criticism, criticism that shows that the argument as constructed by the theorist is absurd or unable to achieve its own objectives is some of the most effective theoretical criticism. However, to build a new theory and a different kind of house, we need tools and resources that the master never deployed or even imagined. A destabilizing epistemology can be a valuable methodological starting place for developing the methodological tools of non-ideal theory.

## *The politics of diversity*

In addition to a destabilizing epistemology, a theoretical method for non-ideal theory also needs to interrogate the research subject. Rawls

[65] Charles Mills criticizes the use of social contract theory as an ideal theory, but argues that within non-ideal theory one can constructively use the patterns of domination that contracts reinforce to criticize those same contracts and to argue for redress for historical wrongs (forthcoming; 1997).

sets out that the subject of justice is the basic structure or the basic social, political, and economic institutions of society. The theoretical method for non-ideal theory needs to ask what should be the subject of a theory of human rights and injustice globally.

In *Justice and the Politics of Difference* Iris Marion Young sets out a challenge to the discussion of justice as discussed by distributive theories of justice which warrants citation at length:

> The logic of distribution treats nonmaterial goods as identifiable things or bundles distributed in a static pattern among identifiable, separate individuals. The reification, individualism, and pattern orientation assumed in the distributive paradigm, moreover, often obscure issues of domination and oppression, which require a more process-oriented and relational conceptualization.
>
> Distributive issues are certainly important, but the scope of justice extends beyond them to include the political as such, that is, all aspects of *institutional organization* insofar as they are potentially subject to *collective decision* ... [O]ther important aspects of justice include *decision-making procedures, the social division of labor, and culture.* Oppression and domination, I argue, should be the primary terms for conceptualizing injustice.[66] [*Emphasis added.*]

Though her inquiry is not cross-cultural (as a theory of human rights needs to be), Young puts on the table all of the questions of justice to which we should be attuned with regard to injustice and oppression cross-culturally and intra-culturally and these help us think about the scope of a non-ideal theory of justice:[67]

(1) Differences are social, economic, and political and a source of injustice when they become a means for oppression.
(2) The social division of labor and other social patterns created and perpetuated by individual habits which are endorsed by dominant cultural norms can be vehicles for oppression.
(3) Decision-making procedures that make social differences into political differences are sources of oppression and, following Gramsci I would add that such oppression may function hegemonically such that the "decision-making" procedure hardly warrants characterization as such.[68] That is, habituated social practices function to treat many political decisions as *not political, but rather social*, determined by roles, not authority. Such habituation is a form of masking politics.

[66] Young 1990: 8–9.
[67] Her later writing makes clear that this is what Young intends (2006).
[68] See also Gould 1988; 2004; Hirschmann 2003.

(4) Consequently, culture is rightly the subject of inquiries about justice.[69]
(5) Further, distributional forms of oppression should be understood as part of the many faces of oppression, including exploitation, marginalization, powerlessness, cultural imperialism, and violence.[70]

In order to put culture at the center of inquiries about justice, we need to examine the relationship between culture and social, economic, and political institutions, between culture and the patterns of social life, and between culture and decision making. The key to this cultural turn is to see culture as dynamic, internally heterogeneous, and a terrain of political contestation.[71] Furthermore, we need to understand social, political, and economic mechanisms of oppression working through culture in this dynamic way.[72]

While this may seem an obvious characterization of culture and many others endorse it, the tendency, even for critical scholars, is to ossify an account of culture at a particular moment – the moment of the author's reflection. In *Achieving Our World*, Fred Dallmayr discusses a range of critical theorists – including Edward Said – who make that slip, a momentary lapse in their attentiveness to diversity and its potential as a source of oppression.[73]

Feminists, some inspired by the critical theorists whom Dallmayr discusses, have theorized about culture as a dynamic, internally heterogeneous, and contested terrain. From political theorists Seyla Benhabib and Ayelet Shachar to activists for women's human rights, the contested and dynamic character of culture has been central to claims

[69] Cf. Benhabib 2002; Shachar 2001; Song 2005; Spinner-Halev 2000.

[70] Young 1990: chapter 2.

[71] The tendency to see modern, secular, and Western cultures as plural and dynamic and correspondingly to see traditional, religious, and non-Western cultures as homogeneous and static can be seen in discussions whose subjects differ significantly (Harding 2000; Said [1978] 1979).

[72] Appiah 1994b; Benhabib 2002; Dallmayr 2004; Mills forthcoming; Mills and Pateman forthcoming; Mohanty 2003; Said [1978] 1979; Shachar 2001; Smith 2003; Spinner-Halev 2000. For an enriching example see Anna Tsing, whose ethnography of global connections among Meratus Dayaks, whose livelihood depends on forest foraging, transmigration, government, national business interests, international business interests, global capital markets, etc., breaks down the tenacious conventional dichotomy and rearticulates it as "friction" (2005).

[73] Dallmayr 2001. Song is particularly good at thinking through the interstices of multicultural societies and the ways in which these are dynamic (2005).

about social justice. Around the world women's social movements often exhibit the feature of immanent critique – that is, of working within local social norms to transform those same local social norms.[74] However, sometimes, when a political elite deploys its political power as cultural authority, the voices of those who would transform local norms are inaudible or treated as corrupted by outsiders.[75] Consequently, some social activists seek to justify their claims with reference to a universal moral source that transcends the particulars of one moment in a cultural political history.

Observing social struggle, Butler writes:

> Indeed, it seems to me that most minority rights struggles employ both particularist and universalist strategies at once, producing a political discourse that sustains an ambiguous relation to Enlightenment notions of universality.[76]

Butler's characterization of all "universalist strategies" offers a sleight of hand that might suggest to a reader that all forms of universality come from the Enlightenment, or stated less absolutely, every form of universality is contaminated by the Enlightenment.[77] In either, she is mistaken. Butler is right to urge the social critic to be attentive to the *possibility* that a universalist discourse has an unreflective relationship to Enlightenment ideas and thus may reify some hierarchies even as its authors seek to break down others. However, the possible characterization of all universalizations as necessarily in relationship to the Enlightenment supports an alignment of dichotomies modern and other, universal and particular. Though some activists may appeal to universalist strategies that are Enlightenment inspired (or contaminated), as we shall see in considering many activists' social criticisms, the hegemonic move may be the critical perspective that *requires* that all struggles be understood in relation to the Enlightenment. Such a

74 Ackerly 2001a; Basu and McGrory 1995.

75 Importantly, outsiders are not necessarily Westerners. At the Women's World Congress 2005, Leehan Jieun illustrated the point during the discussion of her paper (2005). In responding to a question about foreign influence she said: young Korean lesbians are criticized for being manipulated by a foreign culture, "oh, you get that from Taiwan" say the parents of a lesbian ("iban") teenager (cf. Narayan 1997: chapter 1).

76 Butler, Laclau, and Žižek 2000: 42, fn15.

77 Dalacoura 1998; cf. Gatens 2004.

move also conceals other ways in which the epistemological mask of power, which I take to be Butler's ongoing concern, can go undetected.

Feminists from liberal, post-modern, and post-colonial theoretical perspectives disagree about how to interpret the social struggles of women activists.[78] By their example, these theorists put on the table our primary methodological concern regarding diversity, universality, and particularity: to be attentive to the possibility that even as we theorize about these, we may contribute to a dichotomization that subtly (or not so subtly) undermines our normative objective, in part by characterizing the subject of justice too narrowly. The normative object itself becomes more clear when we reflect carefully about ways that others have theorized about difference, by observing the ways in which activists with many differences among them have analyzed their own challenges, and by witnessing Marie's struggle to articulate her own challenges. There is no other way to deal with the crises of the world but to try to develop the political will and means to respect differences across and within cultures while integrating particular contexts into global social, political, and economic structures in a way that undermines rather than strengthens global hierarchies.

I began this discussion by citing at length a passage from Young, who invites us to reflect upon the ways in which politics – potential sources of oppression – gets concealed in institutions and decision-making procedures. I ask us to understand her invitation in the broadest possible sense: many forms of power get concealed in the habits of everyday life – political decisions get made by our unreflective actions. They may even be made by our reflective political actions that are inadequately reflective or that are based on an incomplete range of perspectives. Often the dissenting perspectives are outside that range. In the preceding section, we saw that the authority of knowledge can be treated as an apolitical authority even by a political theorist. These reflections reveal that the authority of knowledge is actually a very powerful political authority, powerful enough to conceal its power as it silences dissent or renders it inaudible. In non-ideal theory our subjects are the invisible and visible, the legal and habitual outcomes and institutions of the basic structure.

[78] See the exchange between Flax and Okin (Flax 1995; Okin 1994; 1995) and critical discussions of Okin (1999), including Honig (1999).

## *The politics of dissent*

The challenge for the kind of normative political theorizing I am proposing is to make the *political* legitimacy of argument and theoretical justification methodologically prior to other normative questions. We can see the problem with the justificatory scheme for ideal theory when applied to non-ideal theory even if we are not distracted by the obvious fact that in no context are all people free and equal in the Rawlsian respects. Since we know that one of the features of the realm of non-ideal theory is dissent, a third methodological reflection for non-ideal theorizing about justice needs to be about *how* we interpret dissent. Is the person whose rights are violated a dissenter? A dissenter worthy of more or less consideration than the person accused of violating her rights? Are these insights worthy of more or less consideration than those of a person confronted with the challenge of determining whether or not human rights violations have occurred in a particular instance? Is there a role for public reason – the methodological tool for the Rawlsian ideal theorists – in drafting a non-ideal theory of justice?

To answer this question, we first need to explore the role of public reason in ideal theorizing. Because of the politics of epistemology, arguments, including arguments for an account of ideal theory, are political.[79] Even if we understand Rawls's standard of public reason as an idealized standard by which to assess the objectivity of actual situated arguments, that is, even if we can accept the purpose of an assumption of free and equal members, Rawls's account of political neutrality still contains a form of power politics that cannot be mitigated by the scheme as articulated.

The key to seeing the problem with this otherwise compelling account of an objectivity that is politically neutral is an appreciation that it requires us to bring our views in line with the shared view – the principles taken as a whole – and our tools for doing this are public reasons. What constitutes "public reasons" cannot be assumed to be prior to politics (or prior to our account of ideal theory), but rather as

[79] Others are confident that people may be free and equal *enough* for deliberation given a certain institutional design (Benhabib 1996; Cohen 1996). Due to my understanding of the power of epistemology, I am suspicious of confidence in the freedom and equality of any venue. Benhabib (2002) is attentive to this problem (cf. Gould 2004).

part of an ideal theory of justice just as our considered judgments are. However, while Rawls is quite clear that justice as fairness and the first two stages of the Law of Peoples are ideal theories that make use of public reason,[80] his view of the role of public reason in the non-ideal context is less clear:

> it is often thought that the task of philosophy is to uncover a form of argument that will always prove convincing against all other arguments. There is, however, no such argument. Peoples may often have final ends that require them to oppose one another without compromise. And if these ends are regarded as fundamental enough, and if one or more societies should refuse to accept the idea of the politically reasonable and the family of ideas that go with it, an impasse may arise between them, and war comes.[81]

In assessing the role of public reason as a theoretical methodology for non-ideal theory, we should consider the constraint on the use of public reason that worries Rawls: final ends that require people to oppose one another without compromise. However, competing interests are not the only constraints on the exercise of public reason. We should consider other limitations as well.

Three cognitive differences – in thought processes, argumentation, and evidence – make determining public reasons *political*.[82] There are cognitive, sociological, and political differences in how people think about social and political life. Further, public reasons, while public, are not fixed in their ranking or value for making every argument. No single reason can be mistaken for the whole view. We need to use our reasons, with evidence and arguments, to develop a reasonable argument. With some evidence certain reasons might be important. Without that evidence, other reasons may be convincing. How do we know if we have all of the evidence?

Methods need to respond to these cognitive differences, because the meaning of human rights itself is at stake in these differences. For example, as Marie prepares to report her experience to the police in Uganda and then to refugee lawyers, NGOs, and government administrators, what evidence and reasons should she report? In chapters 5 and 6, in the exposition of my own methodology for immanent human rights theorizing, I give an account of women's human rights activists who do not agree as to which rights are *human* rights (political rights in

[80] Rawls 1999b; [1971]1999: §87. [81] Rawls 1999b: 123. [82] Rosenberg 2002.

some places, yes, but not universal *human* rights). From Burkina Faso and elsewhere some feminists argue that sexual rights are not human rights because some sexuality is not "normal," whereas land rights and political participation are human rights because they are universal. From India and elsewhere others argue that basic needs are fundamental economic rights and are more important, because they affect more people, than cultural rights. What evidence or arguments could be used to justify either claim or to treat either view of human rights as universal?

## Conclusion

Interestingly, the Rawlsian scheme of justification could mitigate the form of inequality it reifies if it didn't treat the epistemological assumptions of the justificatory scheme as settled. What if we understand that the questions – What is knowledge? Who is a source of knowledge? What kinds of experience can convey knowledge? – are always political such that we could *never* settle epistemological questions prior to engaging in a theoretical research project? What would it mean for a project of political justification if we assumed that questions of what constitute evidence and argument would always be political? Asking these questions we exhibit a different understanding of the political legitimacy of philosophical argument than that exhibited in the Rawlsian justificatory scheme for ideal theory. The Rawlsian justification really could be articulated by one representative person.[83] The political legitimacy of a non-ideal theory of human rights depends on broader participation and the methodological exposition of the politics of knowledge, diversity, and dissent.

Whether we know personally Marie, the Melians, or Frederick Douglass, or anyone like them, political life constantly reminds us that the weak and the strong have different accounts of injustice. And as Aristotle reminds us, they are not similarly interested in justice and equality:

> although it may be difficult in theory to know what is just and equal, the practical difficulty of inducing those to forbear who can, if they like, encroach, is far greater, for the weaker are always asking for equality and justice, but the stronger care for none of these.[84]

[83] Rawls [1971]1999: 56. [84] Aristotle 1996: VI, 3, 1318b, 1312–1316.

Although I have criticized the Rawlsian justificatory scheme, I share Rawls's ambition for a theoretical argument to be politically legitimate and reasonable. I propose a norm of *a priori* and ongoing epistemological reflection combined with perpetual attention to the possibilities for differences to be deployed as power inequalities and for dissent to be made visible behind implausibly apolitical devices. My focus is on epistemological sources of power and on the practices and processes of marginalization as the mechanisms for masking and legitimating the power of knowledge. In chapter 4, through critical readings of Charles Taylor, Joshua Cohen, and Martha Nussbaum (who are political theorists who likewise seek an immanent theory of universal human rights), I argue that with the *methodological* norms of epistemological reflection and of attention to exploitable hierarchies, a theory of human rights can be derived from particular context-situated understandings *and* be universally understood as politically legitimate.

The question is: can non-ideal normative theorizing be universalist, and if so, in what sense? Over the course of the next five chapters, I argue that such normative theorizing need not take the form of transcendental or essentializing universalization. It is possible to identify universal human rights that can take the form of a non-transcendent universal. A non-transcendent universal does not defy the challenges raised by critical attention to the politics of knowledge, cross-cultural and intra-cultural diversity, and dissent, but it does offer a methodological tool that puts the *politics* of diversity at the center of the engagement with diversity. This politics of diversity is dynamically conceived. It does not rely on assumptions of homogeneity – homogeneity of historical materialism, of values, or of public reason – as transcendental universals do. Nor does it rely on assumptions of collective distinctiveness – based on shared languages, shared history, shared understandings – as other forms of immanent critique do.[85]

Reflecting on the broader challenge of global politics (rather than the more narrow question of a role for a universal theory of human rights in global and local politics), Fred Dallmayr writes:

> In my view our contemporary world cannot be "achieved" in any significant way unless serious attention is given both to the vertical thrust of current developments – the (potential) integration of localities into an emerging

[85] Walzer 1987.

cosmopolis – and to the cultivation of lateral, cross-cultural, or cross-societal sensibilities (discussed here under the label of "self–other" relations). In large measure, the achievement of the former integration depends or is predicated on advances in the latter domain – in the sense that genuine "universalism" or universality is possible only through the interaction and mutual transformation of sedimented particularities.[86]

Sharing critical scholars' concerns with the theoretical and practical problems associated with communication, language, translation, transcription, interpretation, mitigation, maneuvering, essentializing, deconstructing invisible constructions, and making audible the silent and silenced, Dallmayr and I see the challenge of universalizing and respecting particularity as *both* a normative and a methodological challenge.

Inspired by the work of activists, I am continually reminded that the challenge is also practical. Human rights are a tool of social criticism. The theoretical challenge set out by attentiveness to the politics of epistemology, diversity, and dissensus is to offer a normative account of universal human rights derived using a methodology that supports the *political* legitimacy of the account.

Marie's situation exhibits the political crises in each of these concerns. To whom does she tell what? Who will help her secure a safe place to live for her family? Who will intervene to get her children sent back to Rwanda? What about her experience has been particular and what is part of a recognizable pattern of oppression? What facts should she tell? Should she leave any out? Who will decide if her human rights and those of her children have been violated? She will have no opportunity to dissent from the decision made ultimately by judges with only knowledge of her circumstances based on what she says and their prior understandings of the patterns of oppression faced by people like her. For Marie and six dependent children the politics of knowledge, diversity, and dissent are a matter of life or death.

[86] Dallmayr 2001: xiv.

# 3 *Universalisms and differences*

## Introduction

In this chapter I argue that normative arguments that make or rely on explicitly transcendental claims about justice (like some religious arguments) and normative arguments that use formal rules to derive claims about justice (like some philosophical arguments) exhibit a form of reasoning that conceals a particular politics, often defining that politics as apolitical or prior to politics. The first vests truth in a transcendental source and vests authority in those philosophers, theologians, and spiritual leaders who interpret the transcendental source. The second vests truth in particular ways of reasoning about truth and vests authority in those philosophers, theologians, and other leaders who are most adept at following those norms. They both have an undemocratic basis for the authority to define the norms of argument. Both approaches vest authority in intermediaries or interpreters. Each intermediary or interpreter has a potentially exploitable authority to make universalist arguments about justice. Such authority is subject to manipulation by the politics of epistemology, diversity, and dissent discussed in chapter 2. Thus, they both mask political authority as authoritative interpretation. Their political universalisms are problematic not because they are universalist but because they portend to be apolitical universals. This criticism, applicable to many approaches to human rights theory as revealed in its elaboration in this chapter, sets up the proposition explored in the following four chapters: the possibility of theorizing about universality without assuming a falsely apolitical stance.

When we turn to human rights as a basis for political criticism within and across national and cultural boundaries, we deploy a rhetorical tool whose political weight is proposed to rest on its moral legitimacy. Most argue that the foundations of human rights are the source of the moral *and therefore* political legitimacy of human rights. And yet while international consensus that there are universal human rights is growing, there appears to be no growing consensus on their foundations, nor on when their violation constitutes a political imperative.[1] In the preceding chapter I argued that the politics of epistemology, diversity, and dissent make universalizing political theory *politically* problematic.

The question for this chapter is: does our reflection on these politics lead us to conclude that there can be no universal theory of human rights? Briefly, no. Considering a range of universal theories, I argue that not their universalism, but rather their founding of that universalism on a narrowly accessible interpretive authority, is a politically problematic but surmountable obstacle to universal theorizing about human rights.

In this chapter, we look at approaches to universal human rights that, despite their claims to universality, offer instead an ethical, or situated, understanding of human rights, not one that could transcend time, place, material conditions, or politics. To anticipate, I argue that no rights claims that are based on a transcendental source of justification can be universally politically legitimate. Transcendental justificatory schemes rely on interpretation and intermediaries with the authority to interpret. This authority is politically legitimate if and only if it includes politically legitimate means for resolving the politics of epistemology, diversity, and dissent. However, most interpretive and intermediary schemes put the power of knowledge of the transcendent into particular hands whose source of legitimacy is metaphysical[2] and not political. Consequently, because people cannot distinguish the interpretive authority of a transcendental source from the political abuse of that authority without shared interpretation of the transcendental authority, and because no such interpretation is universally shared (in either a faithful or political sense),[3] the political justificatory

1 See Power (2002) and Rorty (1993) and Rabossi cited by Rorty.

2 For simplicity of my initial exposition of the subject, here I discuss only the notion of transcendental authority, which is an argument that readers might anticipate. In the text that follows, using the political concerns raised in chapter 2, I extend the argument to the norms of argument, thereby including those intermediaries whose source of legitimacy is conformity with secular norms of justification.

3 See Ramadan's discussion of differences in faithful belief among Muslims and Susan Friend Harding's discussion of faithful and political differences among US Christian fundamentalists (Harding 2000; Ramadan 2004).

scheme of universal human rights cannot rely on a transcendental universal source of legitimacy.[4]

This chapter considers three forms of transcendental argument: metaphysical transcendental universalism, secular transcendental universalism, and the universalism of anti-liberalism and relativism. The next chapter considers a fourth: the universalism of some forms of immanent critique. The first two are commonly understood among their proponents and critics to be forms of universalism. The other two are critical perspectives from which the first two are often criticized, and yet these, too, exhibit a certain dimension of transcendent universalism as well. We can learn a lot about human rights, universalistic theories, and critical methodologies for unmasking universalisms from reflecting on these theoretical perspectives. We also learn that it is hard to theorize universally, but I don't think we learn that it is impossible. We learn instead that we need to think very hard and often about *how* we do so. While our specific question is human rights, this book is also about *how* to do political theory in a world where we are now aware of so much difference and even aware that there are differences, dissent, and epistemologies we do not yet perceive. One dimension of our blindness (of which we can be aware) is that our epistemologies are not our own. While we may work very hard to be aware of the forces that condition our development and uses of our conceptual frameworks as the work of feminists, post-modernists, and other critical thinkers encourages us to do, their work and our own reflection reveal to us that we are likely to do an incomplete job.[5]

## Transcendental universalisms

In the following sections, I review a range of universalist thinking – some of it specifically about rights, but all of it related to trans-contextual normative theorizing. Each offers a political model of universalizing, one that masks its particularism behind a universalist assumption or discourse. However, I do not assume that the repeated

[4] A further critique of rights offered by Wendy Brown, which we will consider in the body of the chapter, is that rights constructed in opposition to a particular form of power discursively and conceptually mirror that power while struggling against it (1995). I will argue that this criticism should be understood as a reason for skeptical consideration of each rights theory, not as a reason to dismiss all of them.

[5] See Wendy Brown on Nietzsche, Marx, and Foucault (Brown 1995).

tendency to make our particularities invisible behind a veil of universality or abstraction is itself evidence that it is not possible to deal *methodologically* with the political challenges of trans-contextual normative theorizing. Rather, I demonstrate by this brief survey that a politically legitimate universalism must engage with the always present or looming politics of diversity, dissent, and epistemology.

## *Metaphysical transcendental universalism: faith and other metaphysics*

Some theorists seek transcendental moral justifications for universal human rights. These theorists justify the political use of human rights for social criticism on transcendental grounds that may or may not have universal appeal. However, scholars who share this approach offer different arguments as to which quality of the human species transcends national and cultural boundaries enough to legitimate social criticism across and within them. Some bases that have been put forward are individual moral standing of the person,[6] individual autonomy,[7] human agency,[8] human dignity,[9] equal creation by a divinity,[10] membership in the human family,[11] membership in political society,[12] well-being,[13] and human functioning.[14] On this view, as international law develops, it puts these transcendent moral dictates into an internationally politically legitimate contemporary language and creates the political institutions for realizing human rights.[15]

6 Goodman 1998.

7 Nagel 1979; Talbott 2005; Benhabib 2004b: 133. Benhabib also says that reciprocity is foundational (2004b: 130).

8 Ignatieff 2001. Cf. Gould, who grounds norms in human agency and interaction (1988; 2004).

9 Donnelly 1989: 17, 28–37; Goodman 1998; Muzaffar 2002; Nino 1991. Note that Rorty argues that the universality of human dignity does *not* rest on their being any "distinctively human attribute" (1993: 116).

10 Locke [1688] 1988. 11 Sobrino SJ 2001: 153.

12 Cohen 2004: 197. Compare this to Benhabib, for whom membership is the right and personal autonomy the foundational principle (2004b: chapter 4).

13 Bruton 1997; Yasuaki 1999.

14 Nussbaum 1997; 2000a; 2000b; Sen 1999a; 2004. In chapter 7, I will discuss Carol Gould's notion of effective positive freedom which shares, in a more generic sense, Nussbaum and Sen's notion of what it means to live a fulfilling human life (Gould 2004).

15 Donnelly 1989; Ignatieff 2001; Ishay 2004.

The possibility of differing and disagreeing interpretations of these metrics makes us aware of the potential ways for the politics of difference and dissent to threaten the political legitimacy of a human rights argument based on these transcendental justifications. Each of these rests on an essentialist characterization of human beings and their relationship to transcendental authority. As we saw in the preceding chapter, essentialist characterizations of humanity obscure the ways in which some humans do not conform to the essentializing norm.

Such a discussion generally brings to mind an example such as the reference to the "Creator" in the US Declaration of Independence:

> We hold these truths to be self-evident that all men are created equal, that they are endowed by their Creator with certain inalienable rights, that among these are life, liberty and the pursuit of happiness.

The Creator is a transcendental authority. On earth, interpreters of the Creator's intent, such as the authors of the Declaration, theologians, and spiritual leaders, rely on others to vest them with the authority to interpret the transcendental authority. That authority is both metaphysical and political, as the use of the Creator in the Declaration of Independence makes clear. The politics of the US Declaration of Independence exhibits a politics of diversity (not everyone would be similarly impacted by independence from Great Britain),[16] a politics of dissent (not everyone wanted to be independent from Great Britain), and a politics of epistemology (not everyone understood "rights" as having a transcendental source).[17] Most obviously, in asserting their rights claim, the authors of the US Declaration of Independence masked their own diversity and dissent, and concealed from themselves their own politics of exclusion behind a language of universality.

It is politically problematic to base an account of universal justice on a transcendent source as, for example, Locke bases rights on the essence of human as created by God. As Locke interprets the transcendental authority of God, he argues that God gave the world to "the Children of Men *in common*," but through the industriousness of some and the agreement of all to use money, men gain "distinct titles to several parcels of it, for their private uses; wherein there could be no

[16] Schama 2006.

[17] For example, think of Bentham's famous reference to rights as "nonsense" (1823).

doubt of Right, no room for quarrel."[18] Because, Locke argues, God gave the world to "the Children of Men *in common*," the right to property is not handed down from Adam. Locke uses this interpretation of divine intent politically, to argue that setting up states is the project of propertied men, not of God, and therefore political authority within states rests with propertied men, not in the divine right of kings.[19]

In his criticism of Filmer's claim that "*Most of the civillest Nations of the Earth, labour to fetch their Original from some of the Sons or Nephews of* Noah," Locke discusses the diversity of the world. The resting of political power in Noah's having divided up the world among his sons is absurd, Locke suggests. Aware of cross-cultural differences, Locke argues:

> the *Chineses*, a very great and civil People, as well as several other People of the *East, West, North* and *South*; trouble not themselves much about this matter. All that believe the Bible, which I believe are [Filmer's] *most of the civillest Nations*, must necessarily derive themselves from *Noah*, but for the rest of the World, they think little of his Sons or Nephews.[20] [*Emphasis in original.*]

Locke uses the politics of cross-cultural diversity to criticize Filmer. Within the England of his day and recent history, the relationship between church and state was a subject of political debate. Moreover, people of different religions experienced different political support and persecution during Locke's time, but the politics of these differences are masked by his founding political society on property and consent.

On the politics of dissent, Locke is less open. There is "no room for quarrel" about the right of people to private property if that private property has been acquired through one's labor (or the labor one hires), without wastefulness. Yet, Locke wrote during a time and place of economic transformation that included changes in how land was owned and used.[21]

18 Locke [1688] 1988: 296.

19 In the *First Treatise*, Locke engages in a protracted dispute about Biblical interpretation with Filmer (Locke [1688] 1988).

20 Locke [1688] 1988: 243–244.

21 Bradstock 2000; Goodhart 2003; Winstanley 1652; Winstanley and Sabine 1941; Wood 1984.

We can think of ways in which the Lockean framework can be revised to consider the politics of difference and dissent. In fact, we might think of institutional solutions in the US Constitution as offering some of these. History proves these provisions inadequate in the original constitution. The Bill of Rights proved necessary for the political legitimacy of the constitution and most subsequent amendments have been moves to enhance the political legitimacy of the constitution. Later amendments to the constitution, legislation (such as the Voting Rights Act),[22] and judicial decisions (such as *Brown v. Board of Education* and *Roe v. Wade*)[23] challenge previously held epistemologies. Those changes were hard won; yet, the politics of epistemology in the transcendental approach is not so easily mitigated.

Many accounts of a transcendental universal rely on a metaphysical view that is not shared universally. Since around the globe and within states we do not all share the same god(s), or even when we do share the same god(s) we do not share the same understandings of the god(s)' instruction, this justification for human rights can be a justification for the exploitation of certain power inequalities. Even though a loving god would not condone the misuse of political power, because the authority to interpret the teachings of the loving god gives those with that authority political power, what it means to respect the human rights of all is not actually in the hands of any transcendental deity, but rather in the hands of those who would interpret god(s)' will. Consequently, justifying human rights through a transcendental argument puts the authority to determine when and how human rights can be a tool of social criticism in the hands of those who have religious authority. The transcendental method of justifying moral authority is, through the institutionalization of religion among humans, a method for legitimating the political arguments of those to whom humans give the moral authority to interpret god(s)' meaning. Because there is not a global consensus on who should have that moral authority on earth at any point in time (let alone for all time), transcendental arguments are a mask for political arguments for human rights.[24]

[22] 1965. [23] 1954; 1973.

[24] We need to reveal this mask, I have been arguing, because as women's human rights movements, indigenous rights movements, and the history of genocide and human rights violations have taught us, what constitutes "human" is also socially and politically constructed.

Further, the transcendental arguments ignore the challenges of interpreting the various proposed metrics of human rights. Each of these – individual autonomy, human agency, human dignity, equal creation by a divinity, human functioning – requires interpretation. What does dignity mean? For whom? What kinds of rights claims or obligations follow from such interpretation? Anyone who has done comparative work (or read a novel) recognizes that even while there may be a universal value of dignity exhibited and claimed by people all over the world on their own behalf, what it means to have dignity takes different forms around the world and within contexts. The substance of each of these metrics – what it requires – is understood only contextually and thus is a problematic basis for universal human rights.[25]

## *Secular transcendental universalisms: philosophical and legal arguments*

The politics of diversity, dissent, and epistemology create problems even for arguments that do not rely on a transcendental metaphysical authority. Those arguments that rely on procedural norms, most commonly rules of argument, to justify theoretical claims, are likewise problematic with respect to the politics of diversity, dissent, and epistemology. Many secular philosophical arguments have the same political problem as those with a transcendental spiritual foundation because of the *political* power vested in the interpreter/philosopher who makes the argument that best conforms to the norms of argument.[26] The norms of argument decide which differences, disagreements, and epistemologies will be heard and determine how difference, dissent, and knowledge will be defined and adjudicated.

[25] Dignity is not really an "essentially contested concept" in the way that rights, democracy, community, freedom, and equality (for example) are. But the work in exploring essentially contested concepts is relevant for considering each of the transcendental metrics of human rights. See Connolly 1993; Gallie 1962; Rubin 2005.

[26] In modernity these norms are what Weber called "instrumental rationality," Marcuse called "technical reason," Habermas "means-end rationality," and Rawls calls "public reason." For a rich theoretical discussion of the power masked by the dominance of, and conceptual constraints imposed by, technical reason in our secular discussions see Brown (1995: chapter 2). Compare these to Gould's conditions on which a philosopher might claim her argument is "true" (2004: 63).

Rawls, Habermas, and Putnam can each be accused of seeking to articulate a transcendental universalism in which God is replaced by a device of philosophic invention. To borrow from Thomas McCarthy, their theories of:

> reason, truth, and justice . . . while no longer pretending to a God's-eye point of view, retain something of their transcendent, regulative, critical force.[27]

That force comes less from substantive foundations and more from the terms and patterns of philosophical discussion each authorize.[28]

Secular forms of transcendental universalism are less obvious about their underlying essentialism than explicitly metaphysical forms. In fact, each of these forms of transcendental universality explicitly acknowledges some aspect of pluralism and seeks to avoid appealing to any metaphysical transcendental authority. However, each of these arguments, while appealing to a secular source of legitimacy, has the same form of a transcendentally justified argument as the explicitly transcendental arguments because each relies on *interpretative authority* and is only weakly aware of that authority's political quality. These arguments privilege a way of knowing without sufficient reflection on the politics of knowledge, difference, and dissent. Often these authors are attentive to at least certain aspects of the politics of difference and their insights can be valuable for cross-cultural and intra-cultural normative theorizing. However, where these are insufficiently attentive to the politics of diversity, dissent, and epistemology, these accounts offer a universalist mask for particularist accounts of norms.

Generally, these views *assume* that justice requires treating people neutrally with regard to their differences. This attempt at neutrality allows injustice to creep in through social norms.[29] This form, common in legal and theoretical accounts of neutrality and objectivity, makes much of the human capacity for respect and toleration. Others have furthered the requirements of neutrality to include additional norms of argumentation such as consensus building and protections against the tyranny of the majority.[30] Like the preceding, these forms of

[27] McCarthy 1990: 367. [28] Cf. Ackerman 1994.

[29] For a particularly effective critique of this perspective see Williams (1993) and most writings on women's human rights (including Bunch 1990; 1995; 2003; Charlesworth 1994; Crenshaw 2000; Engle 1992; Fraser 1999; Mayer 1995a; Mayer 1995c).

[30] E.g. Benhabib 1995; Gutmann and Thompson 1996; Habermas 1996b.

universalism ignore difference by treating the quality of one (or some) as the quality of all and ignore dissent by *assuming* that if the procedures of political participation are properly specified, dissenting voices will not merit any political recourse.

This form of universalism manifests itself in individual liberty, deliberative democracy,[31] liberal individualism,[32] heteronormativity,[33] non-discrimination oriented legal activism,[34] single-axis accounts of oppression,[35] and accounts of oppression that fold the range of intersectional experiences into one axis.[36] According to these forms of universalism, while being human requires an essential human quality, not all "humans" have these qualities and therefore all people are not equally human. These essentialist forms of universalism acknowledge differences among people, but they treat these as deficiencies in some people rather than as evidence that the universal they propose is not in fact universal.

Although there is diversity among these views, justice in the context of pluralism requires neutrality. And the political legitimacy of each of these accounts of neutrality depends on the political legitimacy of its substantive account of neutrality or on its procedures for securing neutrality. Because social critics have drawn our attention to the ways in which these secular arguments have failed to secure justice in a range of contexts, we must consider that the politics of epistemology, diversity, and dissent are not adequately addressed by these secular arguments.

Feminists concerned with this form of universalism argue against the claims that these procedures or ways of arguing are neutral. Consider for example, the assumption that all individuals are free. Carole Pateman argues that formal freedom is only mythologically an essential, apolitical feature of man.[37] Drucilla Cornell argues that with

[31] Benhabib 1996; Cohen 1989; 1996; 1993; Dahl 1997; Dewey [1927] 1954; [1932] 1990; [1942] 1989; Dryzek 2000; Elster 1998; Fishkin 1991; 1995; Gutmann and Thompson 1996; Manin 1987; McAfee 2004; O'Neill 1996; Rawls 1996; 1999a.

[32] Nussbaum 1998; 2000b. [33] Chodorow 1978.

[34] See Crenshaw 1989; Jhappan 2002; MacKinnon 1993; Manfredi 1993.

[35] Daly [1978]1990; MacKinnon 1989.

[36] Fraser (1995) does this while she says she does not; Benhabib (2002) accuses Taylor ([1992]1994) of doing this; Eve Sedgwick (1990) accuses some antihomophobic inquiry of taking this form.

[37] Pateman 1988; cf. Butler 1993; [1990]1999; Kant 1997; [1887] 2002.

social and legal constraints on our freedom and equality, we cannot even imagine what we would be if we were free and equal.[38] Critiquing foundational liberal assumptions, Susan Okin argues that humans are not inherently free, but rather inherently dependent.[39] In a slightly different vein Carol Gould argues that negative freedom does not give everyone the same freedom.[40]

Other feminists, particularly during the 1990s, argue that in deconstructing the Enlightenment myths of freedom, equality, rights, citizenship, and other socially constructed concepts, feminists themselves risk essentializing about women's oppression based on the narrowly extendable experiences of white, Western, middle-class, heterosexual women.[41] For example, they argue that differences among women make it impossible to talk of "women" as a meaningful category for social criticism.[42] Thus, these feminists from other critical perspectives accuse liberal feminism of having an essentialist form of universalism. A 1994 essay by Susan Okin typified this view to Jane Flax.[43] By referring to the oppression of women in developing countries as "similar" to that of Western women "but more so," Okin described differences in women's oppression as a matter of degree but as qualitatively similar. Flax argued that while criticizing oppression of women around the world Okin was normalizing a particular way of being a woman. Okin's defense of that account attended to the empirical questions raised by Flax's critique but were not attentive to the political concerns underlying Flax's empirical questions.[44] Okin was inattentive to the politics of difference and epistemology. Her account, reiterated in her response to Flax, was inattentive to the idea that *the way she argued*

[38] Cornell 1998. [39] Okin 1979.

[40] Gould 1988. Gould further explains this critique and develops an alternative proposal, "equal positive freedom" (2004: 46). Pettit's notion of freedom in *Republicanism* could be developed to this purpose as well, but in his own formulation it is inadequately attentive to the politics of diversity (1997; cf. Hirschmann 2003). Consider liberal feminists writing of freedom, equality, or rights in ways that criticize Enlightenment framings (Astell [1694] [1697] 2002; Mill [1869]1998; Pateman 1988; Wollstonecraft 1792[1985]).

[41] Brown 1995; Butler 1993; [1990]1999; Crenshaw 1989; Flax and Okin 1995; Mouffe 1995; Narayan 1997; Nicholson and Seidman 1995; Spelman 1988a.

[42] Fraser calls these scholars anti-essentialists and attributes this view to Judith Butler (see Butler 1995: 180ff). They include Brown 1995: chapter 4; Flax and Okin 1995; Fraser 1997; Mohanty [1984] 1991; Spelman 1988b. See also Benhabib and Cornell 1987.

[43] Flax and Okin 1995; Okin 1994. [44] Okin 1995.

could itself have political import separate from the substance of her argument. Though critical of the contemporary use of secular transcendental universalism for women's rights, Okin herself echoed that universalism in her critique of women's oppressions.

Though individually incompletely reflective on the power of epistemology, collectively feminist theorists have taken up the range of critical perspectives discussed in chapter 2. Iris Young criticizes the characterization of deliberative democratic norms as neutral.[45] Anne Phillips and Seyla Benhabib invite us to rethink equality; Okin, Young, and Fraser, justice; Pateman, contract; Shanley and Okin, family; Hirschmann and Cornell, freedom; Mouffe and Benhabib, democracy; Wendy Brown, the state.[46] To note some particularly influential works is not meant to ignore the influence of other important works or to suggest that this subset represents the collective project of feminism. Rather, my point is to signal the range of feminist political theorists and the questions that they have asked us to consider anew, questions that political theorists have thought pressing throughout history.

Moreover, were we to look within their texts we would see these feminist theorists actively engaged with historical and contemporary political theorists in critical ways that don't necessarily ask us to abandon the theoretical work of those working within the secular norms of argument. For example, Nancy Hirschmann argues that the most familiar Western understandings of freedom ignore the range of experiences that demonstrate the complexity of freedom.[47] Central to her argument is the notion that social context conditions not only our individual freedom, but also our ability to imagine ourselves in a full range of human activity. Hirschmann is attentive to the politics of difference, dissent, and epistemology in both her criticism of other theories of freedom and in her exposition of her theory of freedom. For Hirschmann, confidence in the political legitimacy of her account comes from thinking through a range of political realities that suppress women's freedom and in so doing she exhibits the full complexity of the concept.

[45] Young 2001a. See also Ackerly 2000; Stokes 1998.

[46] Benhabib 2002; Brown 1995; Cornell 1998; Fraser 1997; Hirschmann 2003; Mouffe 2000; Okin 1989; Pateman 1988; Phillips 1993; Shanley, Cohen, and Chasman 2004; Young 1990.

[47] Hirschmann 2003.

Revealing the politics of epistemology, disagreement, and dissent, feminist theorists speak to scholars within this generation and across generations to reveal the bias of false universalism. Yet, each argument is potentially made stronger. For example, Cornell argues that the device of the imaginary domain would enable us to imagine ourselves in a domain in which we are Kantian free and equal persons so that we *can* use the Kantian assumption of free and equal persons to deconstruct the legacy of social and political obstacles to such freedom and equality in political life.[48] Likewise, Okin offers Rawls a restoration of the original position as a device for reasoning about justice.[49] Again, my purpose here is not to celebrate any particular feminist effort to challenge the secular authority of any particular philosopher's reasoning, but rather to illustrate the importance of the feminist enterprise for revealing the politics of the seemingly neutral authority of philosophical discourse when the politics of epistemology are masked.

One of the particularly effective tools for masking the politics of epistemology is distraction. Rawls distracts us from the politics of epistemology by being attentive to pluralism.[50] Philip Pettit distracts us from the politics of epistemology by being attentive to domination.[51] Joshua Cohen distracts us from the politics of epistemology by submitting differences to deliberation.[52]

In general, feminist theory demonstrates that philosophical transcendentalism (like religious or metaphysical transcendentalism) requires an integrated account of social criticism so that the politics of epistemology, diversity, and dissent are the concern of the philosophy, not assumed away prior to construction of a philosophical argument.

Critical assessment of secular transcendentalism does not, however, lead to an end of philosophy.[53] Rather, it pushes us to take our inspiration from one another and from our critical inquires so that we do philosophy differently than our forbears – methodologically attentive to more of the possibilities for being blind to our own politics of knowledge than those who did not have the benefit of critical theories.

Such attentiveness does not undermine the prospects of a universal theory of human rights, but it does focus us on the methodological aspect of the question. We need a way to be attentive to the politics of

[48] Cornell 1998. [49] Okin 1989. [50] Rawls 1993.
[51] Pettit 1997. [52] Cohen 1996. [53] Heidegger 1969.

universality as we theorize about human rights because universal human rights need some *universal* source of legitimacy. Without *a* form of universality, human rights claims have no greater political legitimacy than other justice claims in a particular context and no greater authority cross-culturally than the power of persuasion. Situated understandings of human rights are similarly of limited value to intra-cultural social criticism. Likewise, unmasked, situated understandings of human rights are of limited value to cross-cultural social criticism.

## *The universalism of anti-liberalism and relativism*

Criticisms of the secular universalism of Enlightenment liberal individualism have been mounted from non-feminist perspectives as well. Communitarians like Alasdair MacIntyre, Michael Sandel, and Amatai Etzionni along with more liberal communitarians (or communitarian liberals) including Charles Taylor, Will Kymlicka, and Michael Walzer argue that, even in liberal communities, people value their communities.[54] Therefore, the individualism of Enlightenment liberalism is a false universal. Kymlicka and Walzer offer accounts of liberalism in which the freedom and equality of individuals does not rest on their autonomy.[55] Each of these theorists treats culture as local and particular.

From a different direction, Richard Rorty argues that we can develop a culture of human rights that does not depend on transcendental universalism. For Rorty, a human rights culture rests not on moral knowledge but rather on sentimentality.[56] When we have been moved to act to respect human rights, it has been not because we have been moved by reason, but rather because we have been moved by emotion. It is an interesting idea.

Rorty reasons as a pragmatist:

> We pragmatists argue from the fact that the emergence of the human rights culture seems to owe nothing to increased moral knowledge, and everything to hearing sad and sentimental stories, [leads] to the conclusion that there is probably no knowledge of the sort Plato envisaged.[57]

[54] Etzioni 1996; 2004; Kymlicka 1995; MacIntyre [1981] 1984; Sandel [1982] 1998; Taylor, Gutmann, and Taylor [1992]1994; Walzer 1983.
[55] Cf . Cornell 1998; Dworkin 1977; 1990.
[56] Rorty 1993. [57] Rorty 1993: 118–119.

This sort of knowledge is the sort of knowledge that "a whole community might come to know."[58] The challenge for this pragmatist view is in determining when we – people, individually or collectively – cannot come to know something or cannot come to have a political will to do what we know we should.

To paraphrase Frederick Douglass, we all know what it would mean to respect our human rights, what we lack is the political will to recognize that others have them.[59] Rorty takes our political indecisiveness (on the generous interpretation of our behavior) or our will to dominate (on the less generous interpretation of our behavior) and treats it as evidence of a different sort of transcendental universal: that values are historically embedded.

There is, however, no reason why we should assume that because we *don't* recognize them politically, we *cannot* recognize them morally. Of course rights claims are culturally embedded. What isn't? Food differs, but we all eat food. Reflection differs, but we all reflect. The pragmatist has to be willing to test Douglass's empirical hypothesis that we all know what it means to respect human rights, we just lack the political will to do so. If it is politically advantageous to deny that we have an "ahistorical human nature," behavior resulting from taking that advantage cannot itself be evidence that human rights doesn't have a universal basis. We may not know what that basis is yet, but political opposition to the pursuit of such a basis cannot *itself* be taken as evidence that there is no such basis.

Though they differ from each other in significant ways, the criticisms of liberal universalisms share a form of essentialism in that they rely on seeing homogeneity and cultural embeddedness of shared history, language, and culture as the source of community values. The dependence of these views of community on a coherence that denies the different ways in which members of communities experience their membership is problematic.[60] The willingness to ignore intra-cultural politics of epistemology even while being attentive to intercultural politics of epistemology is worrisome.[61]

[58] Rorty 1993: 118. [59] See my discussion of Frederick Douglass in chapter 2.

[60] Cf. Ackerly 2000; Benhabib 2002; Okin 1989; Shachar 2001.

[61] Benhabib, Fraser, Okin, and Shachar criticize multiculturalists for doing this (Benhabib 2002; Fraser 1995: 180ff; Okin 1999; Shachar 2001). According to Fraser's misreading of Young, *Justice and the Politics of Difference* also has this problem (1990). However, as I will argue in discussing the importance of

Such a stance – the stance that beliefs are universally culturally embedded or that beliefs are shared within community – has a politics of epistemology, difference, and dissent that, like the transcendental univeralisms just discussed, is of interest to us. These politics are important to the *meaning* of these values to the community. Members have these values because they have developed them through reflection and socialization, through discussion and dissent.

Treating values as embedded and apolitical undermines the meaning of "values." They are *valued* values. Treating values as relative ignores that which is *valuable* to those who value them. As Tariq Ramadan, a contemporary Islamic theorist, argues:

> it is one thing to relativize what I believe and another to respect fully the convictions of the Other. The post-modernist spirit would like to lead us unconsciously to confuse the second proposition with the first. I refuse: it is in the very name of the universality of my principles that my conscience is summoned to respect diversity and the relative[62]

Ramadan makes an important distinction between relativism and respect, arguing that relativism undermines the basis of respect. On Ramadan's view, one cannot both think relatively about commitments *and* respect the universalizing claim of another. Those claims are a function not only of individual reflection (as in Ramadan's reference here), but also of collective reflection.[63]

Further, ignoring the epistemology, diversity, and dissent is one way in which relativists essentialize about communities. As Pollis and Schwab exhibit discovering over the course of two decades,[64] both cultural relativism and Western liberal universalism essentialize about political communities. Such essentializing ignores internal differences that can be politically salient and the ways in which internal differences can be sources of oppression. Having recognized that the mistake of essentializing about culture invites us to ignore differences within cultures,

distinguishing processes and outcomes in chapter 6, Young's framework relies on an intersectional view of oppressions and her five faces of oppression are the outcomes of processes subject to scrutiny, not themselves the basis on which groups should be identified and their injustices addressed. Rather, she argues that the basic structure and the visible and invisible practices that sustain it should be the subject of criticism (2006).

[62] Ramadan 2004: 6. [63] See also Khan 1967 [1970].

[64] The discovery can be seen in the differences between Pollis and Schwab's 1979 essay, in which they criticize human rights using the arguments of cultural relativism, and Pollis's 2000 essay (Pollis 2000; Pollis and Schwab 1979).

we might persist with a form of cultural relativism, noting that the differences within one cultural context are different from the differences within another. Yet, it is hard to know what is gained analytically by paying attention to differences within and between cultures while ignoring similarities within and across cultures. Of course, our critical training should caution us against identifying false similarities based on unengaged or superficial observation, but we should similarly caution ourselves against identifying false differences based on similarly unengaged or superficial observation. Once we find the differences within political contexts important for our understanding of those contexts, the cultural essentialist and cultural relativist positions provide no theoretical or methodological insight. Thus, they are revealed as the tools of the powerful, able to conceal *political* oppression behind a veil, leaving us ignorant as to the ways in which inequalities and hierarchies are masked by cultural and culturally endorsed norms.

Like anti-liberal forms of anti-universalism, relativist forms of anti-universalism exhibit a form of universalism. Arguing that there is no transcendent or universally foundational basis for bridging cultural or foundational differences, they argue, essentially, there is no human essence.[65] Human essence is culturally relative.

However, such relativism exhibits its own universalizing assumption about morality. This universal account begins with a characterization that across contexts social and political values emerge out of "culture" (and traditional culture at that) rather than out of responses to changing material conditions, intercultural interaction, or major events.

Sustaining this view requires another universalizing and strong assumption about the possibility of delineating between "cultures." Though empirically suspect,[66] such delineation is required for what is suggested as a universal preference for local responses to moral questions. These assumptions work together to treat cultures as static, isolated, and internally homogeneous, though such characterization is not explicitly made. From the relativist's view, the questions raised by the politics of diversity, dissent, and epistemology are not questions to be raised within contexts, but rather only between cultures.[67]

[65] Zerilli 2002.

[66] Benhabib 2002; 2004b; Goodhart 2003; 2005; Gould 2004; Song 2005.

[67] Goodhart has a similar critique of relativism, specifically as it relates to the possibility for a universal theory of human rights (2003).

Anti-liberals and relativists turn to assertions of community and shared values. In so doing they offer a non-transcendent form of essentialist universality. All those in this community have this essential commonality; universally, cultures have uncontested common values. Exhibiting their own form of universalism, neither of these is an argument against universalism *per se* but only against the particular varieties of universalism that treat a characteristic of one as a standard by which to measure all.

The challenge is to develop the methodological tools to deploy the theoretical tools of critical reflection in the constructive project of developing a politically legitimate basis for cross-cultural and intra-cultural technique.

## What can we do?

Not all philosophical argument has to have this political problem. If an argument is attentive to the politics of knowledge, difference, and dissent, the political legitimacy of an argument can become part of the argument itself. This requires we interrogate our epistemological assumptions for their expressed or masked politics. *For political reasons*, those who respect human rights must look beyond epistemologically unchallenged norms of philosophical argument to justify that respect.

In short, cross-cultural and intra-cultural rights-based criticisms require a source of legitimacy that is external to any and every *particular* epistemological framework. Such a source of legitimacy is engaged with many particular politics, but married to none, and in fact keenly aware of the ways in which power is exploited in each. Therefore, it can be appealed to by those wishing to make criticisms of human rights violating practices either in their own context or in other contexts. Intuitively, it may seem that it is impossible to have a form of universal that at once is immanent and transcends the particulars of time, space, material conditions, and politics. I want to push our imaginations here. I want to respect and share the intuition Benhabib offers:

> in moral theory as in everyday morality, in political theory as in everyday political discourse, we are always situated within a horizon of presuppositions, assumptions, and power relations, the totality of which can never

become wholly transparent to us. This much we must have learned from all the criticisms of rationalism in the last three centuries.[68]

And yet, I want to make sure we understand its implications. We are all *multiply* situated on that horizon. Not even a powerful, raced-white, gendered-straight male, classed-wealthy, citizenship status-birthright citizen, etc. person could be singly situated on that horizon. Some of us may be more aware of our multiple situatednesses and some of us may be more dedicated to recognizing the multiplicities on the horizon. But my point is that we have *multiple* particularities and with them the potential to move between worlds and to adopt a destabilizing epistemology rather than any singular epistemology. That potential, not our sentimentality, is the basis for universal human rights.[69]

Because the politics of epistemology, diversity, and dissent always and everywhere potentially lead to exploitable hierarchies, a theory of human rights must be universal. Yet the theory cannot rely on any transcendental foundation for its political legitimacy. Even while for any individual or part of a community a transcendental source – like God or philosophical truth – may be the moral or spiritual basis for respect for human rights, individuals and communities must look elsewhere to justify human rights *politically*.

Such an approach requires distinctive methodological reflection. In this chapter we considered the ways in which scholars have thought about universality in normative theorizing, focusing when possible on what that understanding means for their understanding of human rights. Taken together, these arguments and their criticisms do not lead us to conclude that we should abandon the effort of deriving a politically legitimate theory of human rights, but they do demonstrate that the political legitimacy of such an argument would be impossible if the theory relied on intermediaries for its political legitimacy. More generally, a methodology for theorizing universally without reifying particular transcendental commitments to metaphysical or secular authorities is an essential aspect of such a theory. The foundation of a universal theory in a world of difference is a destabilizing epistemology – one that makes us treat our epistemologies (as necessary as they

[68] Benhabib 1995.

[69] The reference to sentimentality is a reference to Rorty (1993). For other ontological perspectives that can be fruitfully juxtaposed to Rorty's see White (2000) and Gould (2004).

are for life and thought) as incomplete and inconstant. The destabilizing epistemology itself fills the role that a justificatory principle fills in secular transcendental theories.[70] As White calls for, it enacts, not just announces, its contestability.[71] To strengthen a metaphor others have used, the anchor "knows" it is set in "terrain" or "sand" that is likely to shift due to myriad unknown forces and commitments.[72]

Theorists of differing normative concerns share the recognition of contestable foundations in normative theorizing without drawing the conclusion that such contestability renders philosophical reflection apolitical. In *States of Injury*, *The Subject of Liberty*, and *Political Theory and Feminist Social Criticism*, Wendy Brown, Nancy Hirschmann, and I respectively argue that normative political theory of democracy has to have a democratic character in this shared respect: while each of our arguments have normative implications, we are each open to the political appropriateness that our arguments not be taken up by all of our audience. Respecting difference means appreciating in politics the value of differing knowledges and dissent for theory. The challenge of normative political thought on this view is not to transform political thinking to one view or family of views, but rather to transform political theory so that our normative arguments are not bound by the particularities of particular theorists.[73]

Perhaps unexpectedly, criticisms of transcendental universalisms offer evidence that we should aspire to a normative theory of social justice that *does* rely on universality, but a universality that is politically constituted, derived by engagement with the politics of epistemology, diversity, and dissent. As we will see in chapters 5 and 6, women's human rights activists are a wonderful resource for considering the politics of diversity, dissent, and epistemology because they vary widely around the world and within countries, because they often disagree profoundly, and because they often have different languages and ways of knowing.[74]

[70] Cf. Cohen 2004; Sen 2004. [71] White 2000: 8.

[72] Cochran 1999: 15; White 2000: 8.

[73] Cf. Gould, who seeks a substantively foundational conception which is "true" (2004: 63).

[74] The challenge for this chapter was to answer: does a criticism of universal liberal individualism mean that there are *no* universals or only that certain strands of Western liberal individualism are not universal? Similarly, in conversation with the author, Melissa Snarr asks: "Does the criticism of liberal individualism mean

Those who draw our attentions to the *challenges* of articulating and using a universal notion of human rights for criticism offer us advice as to the importance of paying attention to the ways in which universals can be false and politically laden. However, they do not offer evidence that transcultural and intra-cultural normative theorizing cannot be done; only that it is hard. I mean to argue that we should try to rise to the challenge using all of the methodological resources familiar to theorists, developing new research tools by drawing on the empirical fields of inquiry that have been attentive to the politics of knowledge, diversity, and dissent, *and* using those methodological resources that can be known to theorists by observing the work of women's human rights activists themselves.

Together, the arguments of chapter 2 and this chapter lead us to conclude that only an account of human rights that is *both* immanent and universal can have the political legitimacy necessary to challenge interstate and intra-state rights violations.

that freedom is Western, or only that individualism is Western? Or, is there a form of liberal individualism that is particular to the West and other forms that are not?" Drucilla Cornell suggests that liberal individualism based on the autonomy of the individual is not universal, but that other forms of liberal individualism may be (1998: 63).

Many have been critical of those who have treated a non-universal as universal. However, in their criticisms and related constructive theory projects we see a tendency to conflate universalism and the theoretical contribution. For example, most notably in her criticism of liberal individualism, Gould (2004) may be read as offering a critique of universalism as well. Read in this way, she might be accused of recreating that which she criticizes in her reconstruction of democratic theory. Instead she should be read as articulating a new universal, one that does not repeat the mistakes of those she criticizes.

# 4 Immanent and universal human rights: more legitimate than reasonable

## Introduction

When I was revising the preceding chapter and this one – arguably the most theoretically demanding chapters of this book – Marie and her family were called in for their refugee interviews. I wrote everyone I knew for advice on how to support her at this stage. One wrote back with expertise and confidence, "Uganda is not accepting Rwandan refugees any longer and is sending them back to the best of my knowledge." Others encouraged me to write a supportive letter that would convey "'personal knowledge' of this family and their plight." I used my past correspondence from her to reconstruct their life story since 1992.

Here was my opportunity to ignore structural injustices and to affect one injustice, to make one family's specific injustices visible. Would it matter? I reread her life history as it had unfolded to me in letters and emails in order to make visible to me and to the Ugandan judge why Marie was not a typical Rwandan refugee. Prior to the urgency of the letter, I had thought of her life experience as revealing to me circumstances that were not unique but that were invisible to international human rights discussions. Now, I wanted to read those same life experiences as evidence of the family's *unique* fear of persecution.

The shift in my perspective revealed, yet again, the argument that I am making in these chapters, that *how* we look at a question and *how* we argue a point has political import. The implications of looking at Marie's circumstances as unique versus typical were politically important and would determine whether she was forced to return to Rwanda where some people who feared that she was a witness to post-genocidal violence had already threatened her.

This same week an advisor to a candidate for national office asked me for some "ninety-second" sound bites on human rights. "Do you have anything that would be useful? Stats, anecdotes, big picture goals, etc?" What could be a winning punch line? She knew how ridiculous the request was: "He especially needs strong 'punch lines.' I know it's a serious subject to reduce to sound bites, but it's a sad fact in a ninety-second reply."

Here I was trying to construct a careful argument, attentive to the politics of *how* we make an argument, not even considering the political perspective from the campaign trail: the demand for the ninety-second reply punctuated by the memorable punch line. If someone is willing to allow torture under some circumstances, what ninety-second reply, let alone sound bite size punch line, could convince them otherwise, or convince the viewing voter otherwise? Most of my punch lines appear in the concluding chapter of the book. Each such punch line is attentive to the power of argument, but I don't think that the need for attentiveness to the power of epistemology and argument can be laid bare to those inexperienced in being attentive to these forms of power in a ninety-second reply or a punchy sound bite.

In order for sound bites about the power of ideas *not* to fall on deaf ears, we need to reveal the power of epistemology and methodology as it is practiced even by the most thoughtful of theorists, unconstrained by the political expedience of a refugee hearing or the ninety-second reply in an election debate. In this chapter, I look closely at the power dynamics of such thoughtful arguments. If we can see them here – in the arguments of those who are attentive to certain aspects of power in human rights discourse – we might be able to see why we need to be attentive to them in each and every argument.

## An immanent moral universal and cross-cultural inquiry

Can we offer an account of universal human rights that is not defended by an ethical framework dressed up as a moral one? Given that we all live situated lives, that the historical texts that inform our engagement with the past reflect their authors' own particular contexts, and that it is particular violations of human rights that stir our inquiry into the meaning of human rights in the first place, is it possible for us to reflect on moral precepts that transcend time, place, and politics?

The answer can be "yes" if we seek a form of immanent morality. That is, a notion of universal human rights that transcends time, space, material conditions, and particular politics, without relying on a transcendent form of authority. Perhaps counter intuitively, the moral authority for universal human rights must be immanent, but not particular to time, space, material conditions, and particular politics. Assuming that, as we have seen, it is not possible to have an epistemologically neutral source of political justification or theoretical methodology, we need an approach to human rights theory that gives adequate critical attention to the political dimensions of its justificatory scheme and its theoretical methodology.

My proposal is a form of immanent theorizing about human rights which will be developed in Part II and its implications made concrete in Part III. Readers unfamiliar with the theorists whom I discuss in this chapter – Charles Taylor, Joshua Cohen, and Martha Nussbaum – may prefer to jump ahead to Part II, and then come back to this chapter to see how my epistemology and methodology differs from those discussed here even though I share with these theorists an interest in the use of immanent critique for human rights theorizing.

This is a specific theoretical application of a more general and familiar critical practice. Immanent critique, that is, criticism that draws from the resource within a context to offer social criticism of that context, is a form of relativism that offers a more muted essentialism about cultures than the relativist stance. The immanent critic notices the diversity and dissent within a context and seeks to use the political legitimacy of internal resources to justify internal critique. For example, in *The Company of Critics* and *Interpretation and Social Criticism* Michael Walzer celebrates immanent criticism as a tool for bringing about political change in contexts where there is political dissent and where the political, social, economic, and epistemological differences do not suppress political dissent (as they do in contexts of human rights violations).[1] Early Habermas develops "universal pragmatics," a tool for using language as the key to connecting the "external"(material), the "social" (relational and political), and the "inner" (subjective) worlds.[2] Carol Gould uses a form she calls "concrete universality."[3] Martin Luther King Jr. used immanent critique. Women's human rights activists are masters of immanent critique.

Immanent critique is a form of non-transcendental theorizing. Interestingly, just as a transcendental universal might function to exclude even as it posits the inclusivity of universality,[4] immanent criticism runs the same risk. By seeking to identify within a community's visible

[1] Walzer 1987; 1988. [2] Habermas 1979: 67. [3] Gould 2004: 32.
[4] Butler using Hegel cautions against this (2000).

structures and practices a means for critical evaluation of invisible structures and practices, it risks excluding some experiences within the community – excluding some basis for criticism and excluding some subjects of criticism. If adequately attentive to all parts of a community, immanent criticism within a social group should be challenged by the same questions of pluralism as criticism across social groups. The assumption that any group shares a history, values, language, and economic circumstances is naive and risks committing the sins of a false universal discussed in the preceding chapters.

Thus, an immanent theory of human rights must be attentive to the political concerns raised by critical theorists: the politics of diversity, of dissent, and of knowledge.

Not all theorists working in the burgeoning field of comparative political theory of human rights seek *immanent universal* human rights. Some comparative work supports a transcendental form of ethical universal; some the rejection of ethical universals. A third seeks to find a moral universal from within different contexts of experiences, practices, norms, values, histories, and institutions. The concerns of my argument thus far would ask us to consider *how* these approaches pay attention to those marginalized within the traditions on which they focus their inquiry. Consequently, whereas in previous chapters I surveyed the field more broadly, in this chapter I look very closely at the theoretical methods of three theorists – Charles Taylor, Joshua Cohen, and Martha Nussbaum – in order to examine closely three methodologies. Although none of these has written as extensively about human rights as some of those discussed in preceding chapters, each has a body of work through which their contributions to an immanent universal human rights theory and methodology can be read.

## Methodological considerations

To repeat myself, given that we all live situated lives, that the historical texts that inform our engagement with the past reflect their authors' own particular contexts, and that it is particular violations of human rights that stir our inquiry into the meaning of human rights in the first place, is it possible for us to reflect on moral precepts that transcend time, place, and politics? Yes, if we pay attention to our methodology.

When working cross-culturally, to whom and to what should we pay attention? Examples of women's human rights activism help us see the otherwise invisible rights violations that are experienced by women as a result of patterns of practice and institutional structures that conceal power dynamics behind norms of society, culture, and economics that vary across contexts. The theoretical discussions of the preceding chapters illustrate the need to pay attention to the marginalized – differently marginalized as they are – through inequality and exclusion based on sex, sexuality, ethnicity, class, caste, religion, country of origin, national identity, aboriginal status, immigration status, regional geography, language, cultural practices, forms of dress, beliefs, ability, health status, family history, age, and education. Many of these axes of marginalization are indivisible.[5] For example, gender oppression is experienced differently by mentally disabled men, recent immigrant women from Mexico working as domestics in southern California, Muslim women from Indonesia working as domestic workers in Japan, and able-bodied white middle-class women in the professions in developed urban settings in the global North, for example. Cross-cultural inquiry should deploy a theoretical methodology that enables the theorist to consider the meaning of these differences. The theorist's methods should be attentive *at least* to these people and *at least* to the structural causes of human rights violations. So attentive, we find that the power to define knowledge systems is a political power. For example, when rights advocates assert that a particular experience constitutes a rights violation or when asylum judges deny such claims, the terrain of discussion is epistemological.

If we take epistemological concerns seriously, an immanent theory of human rights has to take into account not only the *knowledge claims* of those most marginalized, but also the practices and politics of their

[5] "Intersectionality" has become the way that feminists reference, and encourage themselves to take seriously, the ways in which certain forms of oppression are experienced (Crenshaw 1989). This helpful concept is better *understood* using a different metaphor. Students and others still seem to understand intersectionality as indicating an additive problem, whereas the experiences of those at the "intersections" illustrate that life in the intersection is qualitatively different from life in the mainstream. Moreover, the metaphor of intersections gives the illusion that we could see "just gender" or "just sexuality" at work. While our desire to use quasi-scientific methods to capture independent effects has its own culture and purposes (and power dynamics), other research on marginalization needs to help us identify the insidiously invisible indivisibility of forms of oppression. This project is focused on this latter effort.

contexts that condition the claims they make and don't make. It must take into account the *practices* that affect those most marginalized. And it needs methodological tools for reflecting on the *politics* of the places where the marginalized live and work. What tools are available to a *political theorist* for keeping our theories attentive to the ways in which oppression is experienced, embedded in practices and structures, and inconspicuously political? What methodology can give us confidence that our theory is informed by the study of "the right" experiences, practices, and politics?

The challenge is to build theory while being attentive to the epistemological concerns of those who would criticize theory-building. While attentive to marginalization as a source and consequence of the power to define meaning and knowledge, the central theoretical and methodological challenge for immanent universal human rights is the power of epistemology. The methodological challenge is to deconstruct continually the political authority of a cultural epistemology while at the same time seeking to construct or identify a conception of immanent universal human rights. Do theorists of immanent universal human rights offer a methodology that is up to the task? The political legitimacy of universal human rights depends on it.

The key moves of this inquiry are (1) to understand questions of epistemology *as* questions of political legitimacy and (2) to put questions of legitimacy before questions of justification. Questions of epistemology – What knowledge is important? What constitutes a justification? And whose experience best positions them to offer theoretical insight? – have political dimensions. In order for universal human rights to be understood theoretically as a moral system whose precepts defy the specifics of time, place, and politics, it must be derived using a theoretical method that gives full critical attention to the political dimension of its epistemological assumptions. Is it possible to do immanent universal human rights theorizing without relying on a political epistemology? I argue no, and therefore one's theoretical methodology must be attentive to those whose membership, political inclusion, economic well-being, or social value is insecure.

## Rights as immanent in history

One form of immanent human rights theorizing bases the political legitimacy of human rights in the historical fact that defining human rights has been part of the moral discourse of human history.[6] The human rights conceptual infrastructure of individual moral autonomy and eventually the human rights language itself has been handed down to the contemporary world through historical texts and spread around the globe with the political and economic successes of its bearers.[7] On this view of history, those with enough political power to have their ideas captured in texts of their day, those political winners throughout history for whom rights have been rhetorically useful, and those with the political and economic power to spread their ideas around the world have authored a political view of human rights that has some support in the historical texts of many cultural traditions. This discourse of human rights is the discourse of the politically powerful within communities and economic and political power transnationally.[8]

As international law develops, the politically successful put these historical dictates into an internationally politically legitimate contemporary language and create the political institutions for realizing human rights. However, this approach, while conceivably dispelling claims that human rights are Western and a recent Western fiction at that, offers much historical evidence that human rights have been the tool of the colonizer, the white propertied heterosexual man, and certainly not *by this definition* a tool for liberation.[9] The historical use of "rights," "freedom," and "equality" as a collective rhetorical mask of, and indeed justification for, social, economic, and political inequality and exploitation[10] potentially discredits "human rights" as a tool for movements against oppression. As Goodhart argues, "rights" were used to justify depriving the poor and working people of England

[6] Donnelly 1989; Goodman 1998; Ishay 2004.

[7] Ishay oddly seems to base her claim that human rights have theoretical resources in all the major traditions, but have a distinctly Western history, on two views: (1) that rights and duties are the same thing; and (2) that the economic might of Europeans (successful colonial exploitation) enabled them to spread their cultural, legal, and moral values (2004; Dalacoura 1998; see also Goodhart 2003).

[8] By contrast, following Nietzsche, Wendy Brown argues that rights discourse is always the discourse of the politically less powerful deployed to give moral weight to a political critique that lacks force (1995).

[9] Ishay (2004) recognizes this common quality of the historical texts she references and yet still refers to these texts as supporting "human rights."

[10] See Ackerly forthcoming-b; Gordon 2004; Pateman 2002; 2004; cf.Pollis 2000.

of basic subsistence. In the US, the granting of "rights" was a rhetorical tool for taking land way from indigenous people in the US and displacing them.[11] Because "rights" have been used to justify oppression of some humans – within and across cultures – the fact that they have been a part of global rhetorical history does *not* give them political legitimacy as a basis for justifying social, political, and economic criticism.

Moreover, the *historical* argument does not offer a universal *moral* basis for the political responses to human rights violations by nations or citizens (who are supposed to have the power to influence their nations in democracies). Because international institutions are immature and historically, politically, and institutionally weak at preventing human rights violations or at holding those responsible accountable, the historical view of human rights does not hold much promise of developing transnational responses to human rights violations that take place within or across borders. Because the history of human rights recognition is a *political* history, the historical approach will be of limited *political* value in enhancing the moral legitimacy of those whose arguments deploy human rights as a basis for social, political, and economic criticism within and across national and cultural boundaries. The historical approach is an immanent account of human rights that has no source of legitimacy outside the power structures of the contexts in which it is deployed. If agents within the power structures are receptive, the historically grounded human rights may be a tool for criticism and change, but if these are not, rights claimants have no recourse.

The political legitimacy problem with the historical approach is even more pronounced in ahistorical immanent theorizing about human rights. While immanent criticism conceivably offers an account of criticism based on values that are shared within a context, such criticism draws on the epistemologically powerful resources of a particular context. Consequently, without a method of interrogating the ways in which these arguments support the relatively more powerful in a particular context and their prospects for exploiting that power, a local immanent account of human rights is an *ethical* understanding of human rights, situated in *particular* times and places, whose sources of legitimacy are politically problematic if uninterrogated. When rights have ethical weight, that weight enhances their political legitimacy

[11] Goodhart 2003.

within a specific ethical context. However, when their political legitimacy *depends* on internal ethical standards, their efficacy at challenging those standards is limited. This is a problem for intra-cultural and cross-cultural criticism.

## The nexus and the olive branch[12]

Charles Taylor asks what it would mean to take the question of the power of epistemology seriously in working toward an overlapping consensus on human rights transculturally. He argues that there may be an overlapping consensus on a narrow set of rights at the nexus of differing community value-schemes which can be used as a common ground justified by incompatible metaphysical views.[13] That common ground can then be used for a deepening and expanding notion of universal human rights.

His approach is not one that I think we should emulate. He chooses a methodology that privileges some sources of epistemological authority over others and therefore offers minimal prospects for a politically legitimate theory or practice of universal human rights. However, because he raises the epistemological question, because he questions the reasonableness and political legitimacy of the ambition for universal human rights, he is an important contributor to immanent universal human rights theory.

The first move toward a universalist immanent account of universal human rights has to take seriously the concerns discussed in the preceding chapter from critical perspectives including strands of Feminism, Queer Theory, Cultural Studies, Critical Race Theory, Bioethics, Post-colonial Theory, Anthropology, Critical Theory, Multiculturalism, and Comparative Political Thought. What methodological choices are necessary to mitigate the myriad ways in which politics are used to ignore some kinds of pluralism while addressing others? Charles Taylor addresses some of the epistemological questions raised by multicultural and comparative theoretical perspectives. He acknowledges processes of reform, change, reinterpretation, and reappropriation within cultures and differences between cultures. The flaw

[12] With apologies to Thomas Friedman (1999).

[13] Taylor is globalizing the Rawlsian concept of "overlapping consensus" from *Political Liberalism*, as I explain shortly (Rawls 1993; Taylor 1999).

in his thinking is twofold: (1) he doesn't recognize the political and contested character of these reforms, changes, reinterpretations, and reappropriations; and (2) he treats the transnational dialogue as between cultures, treating cultures as community wholes, rather than as subcultures within communities. Taylor is more concerned that the West treat the rest with respect than he is with thinking through what these observations about change and conflict within contexts mean for an immanent theory of universal human rights. I argue that *respect* for epistemological differences is not enough to maintain *political* neutrality.

Taylor treats respect for different ways of knowing across cultures as a principal "condition of an unforced consensus on human rights." Yet, despite giving many examples of different ways of knowing *within* contexts, Taylor does not explore the political implications of these observations for his argument that requires cross-cultural respect. Within their communities, many are politically marginalized by a cross-cultural dialogue that treats cultures as distinct and the "responsibilities [that people] owe to the whole community or to its members"[14] as apolitical.

Although Rawls coined the term "overlapping consensus" and developed its use as a tool for thinking about normative issues globally, as we saw in chapter 2, he did not use it to develop an account of universal human rights.[15] Agreement between peoples on human rights – "a special class of urgent rights, such as freedom from slavery and serfdom, liberty (but not equal liberty) of conscience, and security of ethnic groups from mass murder and genocide" – is a key component of the law of peoples.[16] However, in *The Law of Peoples*, human rights are not the result of an overlapping consensus between liberal and decent societies; rather, they are the source of the definition of a decent society. Thus, Rawls's own account of human rights does not make methodological use of the concept of an overlapping consensus in any way that we might say would yield an *immanent* account of universal human rights.

Charles Taylor, by contrast, does see theoretical and political potential in the methodological innovation of the overlapping consensus as an objective of international discourse[17]. However, Taylor sees its

[14] Taylor 1999: 130. [15] Rawls 1993; 1999b. [16] Rawls 1999b: 79.
[17] Taylor 1999.

political legitimacy as contingent on a methodological openness to epistemological differences. Though acknowledging the "overlapping consensus" as Rawls's innovation, the model of an overlapping consensus that Taylor proposes is not Rawls's as developed in *Political Liberalism*, *The Law of Peoples*, or "The Idea of Public Reason Revisited." For Taylor political legitimacy comes from mutual respect, not from the justificatory scheme. Because there are multiple justificatory schemes in the world, universal human rights must be a political agreement.

Taylor's view is reflected by one of the authors of the United Nations' Universal Declaration of Human Rights, Jacques Maritain.

> I am quite certain that my way of justifying belief in the rights of man and the ideal of liberty, equality, fraternity is the only way with a firm foundation in truth. This does not prevent me from being in agreement on these practical convictions with people who are certain that their way of justifying them, entirely different from mine or opposed to mine ... is equally the only way founded upon truth.[18]

For Maritain, the Universal Declaration is a political agreement, not a metaphysical one. Likewise for Taylor, such an agreement is a *political* agreement, not a theoretical one:

> different groups, countries, religious communities, and civilizations, although holding incompatible fundamental views on theology, metaphysics, human nature, and so on, would come to an agreement on certain norms that ought to govern human behavior. Each would have its own way of justifying this from out of its profound background conception. We would agree on norms [of conduct] while disagreeing on why they were the right norms, and we would be content to live in this consensus, undisturbed by the differences of profound underlying belief.[19]

For Taylor, such agreement may set the ground for future development of greater shared background justificatory schemes.[20]

Taylor outlines two political methodological approaches to developing such an overlapping consensus. Both begin with recognition of a subset of human rights consistent with universal condemnation of "genocide, murder, torture, and slavery, as well as of, say, 'disappearances' and the shooting of innocent demonstrators."[21]

[18] Maritain 1949: 10–11, cited in Taylor 1999: 124; cf. Ramadan 2004.
[19] Taylor 1999: 124. [20] Taylor 1999: 140. [21] Taylor 1999: 125.

A first approach is to start with this common ground and engage in mutual respect, understanding, and learning so that we may identify institutions and values in common and develop these. He argues that there is a potential variety of institutional mechanisms for preserving human rights (ones that are not so specific to a Western liberal legal culture) that have their own sources of moral authority necessary for political trust. Such an approach could also lead to greater common ground on the underlying fundamental values which support universal human rights. He suggests that the Thai monarchy has the moral authority to serve this institutional role and discusses Reform Buddhists in Thailand as sharing norms of universal human rights that are justified using seemingly very different epistemological assumptions.

Taylor's second approach starts by recognizing the lack of capacity for cross-cultural dialogue that exists between certain Western and Eastern cultures. Where this is the case he argues that Western interlocutors need more humility about their own cultural past acceptance of practices that are now considered human rights violations and more openness to the *possibility* of common ground as they engage in cross-cultural dialogue. Those Taylor calls "fundamentalists" from non-Western countries have been responding to a form of experienced cultural condemnation. On Taylor's second approach, there needs to be some defusing and focus on the possibility of mutual respect *before* the possibility of an overlapping consensus can emerge.

Taylor's view is so contingent on actual political dialogue that – though positing an overlapping consensus on universal condemnation of "genocide, murder, torture, and slavery, as well as of, say, 'disappearances' and the shooting of innocent demonstrators" and suggesting that in his criticism of Singapore there *should be* universal recognition of other rights like freedom to speak dissent and democratic participation or at least accountability to the demos[22] – his argument contains no anticipation of a broader list of rights on which a world might find consensus. His purpose is rather political: to identify the conditions under which a global overlapping consensus on universal human rights might be recognized as a legitimate basis for cross-cultural criticism. For Taylor, the legitimacy of human rights depends on an overlapping consensus's being derived through a political process in which mutual respect plays a significant role. To use Ramadan's words again: "it is in

[22] Taylor 1999: 131.

the very name of the universality of my principles that my conscience is summoned to respect diversity and the relative."[23]

To this end, Western and feminist critiques of "Western" rights are oddly missing from Taylor's account.[24] As discussed in the preceding chapters, the rights framework has been the subject of criticism from within the West for its failure to recognize structural forms of rights violations and for its focus on rights violations that take place at the hands of state action while ignoring violations that take the form of state inaction or failure to prevent rights violations of some individuals' rights by other individuals. Cultural patterns *in the West* create contexts of rights violations. And these can prove difficult to change even with significant legal reforms.[25]

Feminist critics in particular have argued that when a human rights argument focuses on individual actors and legal mechanisms at the expense of criticizing the broader structural contexts in which rights violations take place, it is not contributing to a *universal* human rights framework. A notion of human rights based on liberal individualism (and its myths of equality, freedom, agency, and consent) are the subject of feminist critiques of human rights from within and outside the West.

As we will see in chapter 8, for women's human rights activists, the universal rights framework enables immanent criticism in which activists argue that in order to sustain their societies, political, economic, and social changes need to take place so that all *members* of a society are sustained by the institutions that sustain the *society*. With an understanding of rights that puts the social dimensions of rights violations and rights recognition in full view, our rights would be more secure through a strengthening of the social fabric – not any social fabric, one that sustains rights. According to women's human rights activists, one of the most effective theoretical building blocks for using universal human rights for intra-cultural criticism is that its subject is

[23] Ramadam 2004: 6; recall the discussion of relativism in chapter 3.

[24] Taylor makes an argument that is similar to ones we criticized in chapter 1. In his criticism of individualism and the deterioration of social fabric and political trust in Western countries, he takes as axiomatic the relationship between this deterioration and individual rights. However, it is not clear from his discussion that individual *rights* rather than individualism is to blame (Taylor 1999).

[25] Jhappan 2002; Manfredi 1993; cf. Song 2005.

*an individual in a community in a state in an international system.*[26] Theoretically, every aspect of the structural contexts of human rights maintenance is the subject of universal human rights.

An immanent universal human rights theory needs a methodology that forces the *theorist*, the inquirer, to consider dimensions of pluralism which he has yet to imagine. Taylor's attention to cross-cultural epistemological differences is appropriate, but the relationship between justification and methodology should be inverted. Taylor "knows" that there are epistemological differences across cultures, so he argues that a justifiable overlapping consensus must have as its condition respect for differences between cultures. Even though he "knows" that there are other kinds of difference, he is methodologically attentive only to one. He "knows" that cross-cultural respect is important for political dialogue and he secures that through one methodological scheme. Internal political life, including the political dimensions of cultural, economic, and social life of the states or cultural groups that deliberants represent, are outside the scope of Taylor's interest in epistemology, and the political power of epistemology.

A complete account of the politics of an international overlapping consensus would need an account of (1) who deliberates, (2) who they represent, (3) how they come to represent those they represent, and (4) the cultural, social, political, and economic contexts of each of these. The politics (including the politics of epistemology, dissent, and difference) of each of these illustrate the point that the process of identifying an overlapping consensus on human rights should be ruled by the norms of dissensus not consensus. Marginalized potential deliberants, such as women's human rights activists, have argued that women have historically been inadequately included in deliberations about human rights, that those who have deliberated have not represented women's rights claims, and that they have not come to be spokespeople for their states through representative processes. Women's human rights activists have argued that the social, political, and economic contexts of both national and global deliberations have functioned so as to marginalize or exclude entirely the rights claims of women, or to give equivalent weight to the claims by women for certain rights and to the claims by cultural representatives that women should not have such rights. Despite many advances for women's human rights in many contexts,

[26] See Galtung 1994.

particularly through the last decade of the twentieth century, universal human rights are still a necessary tool for women to use to demand examination of global and national deliberative processes, including discussions about the meaning of human rights.

As we can see from women's human rights activism and as we will be able to see more clearly from the discussions in Part II of the book, respect for cultural difference is an inadequate condition for politically legitimating an overlapping consensus on universal human rights because it does not challenge questions of hierarchy within contexts. Universal human rights requires some form of legitimation that is *not* dependent on existing forms of hierarchy (be they the subject of open debate or accepted and naturalized). Clearly, a theory of universal human rights that is dependent on the politics of an overlapping consensus will not have the requisite legitimacy to be a resource for cross-cultural or intra-cultural criticism.

Taylor makes an important methodological move in paying attention to the epistemological differences around the world, but he doesn't propose a methodological approach for dealing with the political implications of disagreement *within* cultures, epistemology, and difference.[27] He offers us no methodological solution for reminding ourselves that *all* epistemological differences are potentially politically important. Certainly, epistemological reflection is an important "condition of an unforced consensus on human rights"; however, it is not enough to yield a notion of universal human rights that has political legitimacy within and across cultures (particularly within, but, because it doesn't have it within, not across either).

Given what little we know about differences and challenges to human rights around the world, it seems that in order to get a hint about what conditions are necessary for an overlapping consensus on universal human rights to be legitimate, we should try to examine all

[27] Despite an interest in the reforming movement within Buddhism and references to communitarian and liberal perspectives within the West, despite attention to changes in identities within the West (Taylor 1999: 139–140), despite discussion of "the possibilities of reinterpretation and reappropriation that the tradition itself contains" (p. 142), Taylor's theory of human rights is inattentive to the politics of these reforms, changes, reinterpretations, and reappropriations. Note, Taylor refers to cross-cultural dialogue between the West and the rest. Even if we understand the discussion as having more than these two monolithic sources of insight, as presumably Taylor does, differences, dissent, and disagreement within any culturally delimited context would need critical attention.

and at least examine many of the obstacles to a legitimate overlapping consensus process of political justification. Certainly, Taylor is right that a lack of mutual respect between some representatives of the West and some representatives of the rest is problematic.[28] However, there are so many other obstacles – economic, social, political, and cultural– to an unforced consensus, so many other contexts of failed mutual respect, and so many failures beyond the failure to respect.

Methodologically, it does not have to be wrong to defend a view of universal human rights justified through practice, as Taylor's overlapping consensus approach attempts. However, because *human rights* are in question, our methodology should also require us to *question* the ways in which power inequalities may generate a particular overlapping consensus and work to minimize the substantive scope of the overlapping consensus on rights. Attention to varieties and to competition within cultures and political contexts is an important methodological modification for redeploying the study of overlapping consensus as a resource for understanding human rights.

Taylor provides not so much an argument for the overlapping consensus approach to universal human rights as an argument for making epistemological reflection an important part of the theoretical methodology of the attempt at developing a human rights framework that is sustained by an overlapping consensus. The overlapping consensus envisioned by Taylor will be the result of sustained global engagement.[29] This engagement will involve learning and mutual transformation of ideas around what constitutes the list of human rights that should be protected, their philosophical foundations, and the legal and social institutions that best secure them.[30] For Taylor the terms of debate about an overlapping consensus on universal human rights are not epistemologically neutral. Although Taylor does not neutralize their political dimensions with cross-cultural recognition and respect, at least he sees the problem.[31]

[28] See also Yasuaki 1999.

[29] The emphasis on sustained global engagement is echoed by Etzioni (2004).

[30] Taylor 1999: 143.

[31] My methodology of immanent universal human rights requires the theorist who notices the problem of mutual respect to seek out other obstacles to an unforced consensus. While the search for these may not be complete – in fact the methodology anticipates that one should never be satisfied that she has identified all of these – the commitment to search itself renders the approach more legitimate.

## Taking "others" seriously

In this section we consider a view that is more definitive than Taylor's about the possibility of offering a reasonable cross-cultural argument for using universal human rights as a basis for social criticism. In contrast with Taylor, Joshua Cohen follows Rawls more closely in deploying the overlapping consensus and "global public reason" as tools of theorizing about universal human rights.[32] In "Minimalism About Human Rights: The Most We Can Hope For?," Cohen takes a comparative approach to arguing that global public reason can *justify* commitment to universal human rights from within illiberal intellectual traditions. Using the intellectual and theoretical resources of the cultures of the people with whom we engage in public reason, Cohen argues that there is a universal and minimalist rationale for human rights: membership. This minimalist justificatory scheme for universal human rights does not in his view mean that the content of a list of universal human rights is minimal. He argues that this approach can yield a list of universal human rights that is more expansive than Rawls's "special class of urgent rights," but the list of universal human rights is a subset of injustices that occur within states.[33] Because Cohen does not take Taylor's cue and reflect about the politics of epistemology in the Rawlsian approach, he succeeds only in broadening the subset of human rights recognized as universal human rights by the nexus approach to overlapping consensus. Cohen's methodology is not epistemologically neutral, but rather conceals a politics of discourse that relies on certain epistemological assumptions that devalue or ignore the dynamics and internal contestations of cultures, peoples, and nations.[34] The rationale of membership is not the apolitical rationale for immanent universal human rights to which he aspires.

[32] Cohen 2004.

[33] It is unclear exactly what Cohen means by this: that legal systems define injustices that are context-specific and therefore not necessarily human rights violations or that cultural systems outline norms of justice that may be more or less expansive than human rights norms.

[34] Cohen tellingly doesn't want to discuss the question of what is the unit of analysis, but suggests "nations" by preferring the term "international society" (Cohen 2004: 194). Rawls uses "Peoples." Buchanan argues that, given how Rawls defines "Peoples" and given how states function now, there is no difference between a Rawlsian People and a contemporary state (Buchanan 2000).

According to Cohen, public reasoning in search of immanent universal human rights requires cross-cultural respectful engagement. In his argument, Cohen makes use of his own thoughtful, respectful reflections on one of the key Confucian texts, *The Analects*, and on the key Islamic text, *The Qur'an*.[35] I wholeheartedly agree with Cohen's desire to justify universal human rights through intellectual resources that are immanent sources of legitimacy. If they are to be truly *universal* the justification of human rights cannot rely on any single metaphysical framework and every culture needs to have the conceptual language necessary to recognize human rights as something valuable and to argue for them. The need for a conceptual language is different from having the word for something. Although the world (including the Western world) has not always deployed the language of human rights nor had the underlying material conditions necessary to understand rights as *entitlements*, around the world, across time, and across historical material conditions, the metaphorical resource of rights as in *right of way* has been available.[36] Abdullahi An-Na'im offers an example of immanent human rights justification from a Muslim perspective on Islam.[37]

Cohen's methodology falls far short of an immanent justificatory scheme. According to Cohen, we can justifiably claim that there is a universal basis for human rights if it *could be argued for* using local intellectual resources.[38] He does not claim that he offers the best argument for his case; that could be done only from within those traditions themselves, he argues in an unusual *ad hominem* move.[39] Rather he claims only that "the terrain of argument of a global public reason that comprises a conception of human rights" seems to be "available from within Confucianism"[40] and within Islam.[41]

[35] According to Cohen it is possible to discuss the *rationale* for human rights (their justificatory scheme) separately from their *role* (as standards according to which political societies treat their members), and separately from their *content* (the list of rights) (2004: 193–194ff). I have trouble telling if he means to be offering cross-cultural content or rationale. I think he wants to be showing that in Confucianism and Islam membership bestows duties and responsibilities which can be read as proposing rights. On this reading, Cohen is offering a rationale for rights from within Confucianism and Islam that is consistent with his argument.

[36] See Lakoff 1999: particularly 305.

[37] An-Na'im 1990. [38] Cohen 2004: 192, 193ff, 202. [39] Cohen 2004: 202.

[40] Cohen 2004: 207. [41] Cohen 2004: 209; Donnelly 1982.

Cohen does not reflect on the possibility that engagement with different intellectual traditions might yield a change in his own thinking. By contrast, many engaged in cross-cultural theorizing expect it to be transformative for both "cultures."[42] Cohen's concept of a justificatory minimalism is intellectually useful, but his methodology does not make use of the tensions within intellectual traditions, nor does he *engage* within an intellectual tradition about *its* meaning but rather shows that it can be used to justify a fixed understanding consistent with Cohen's "global public reason." Cohen's justificatory minimalism is only interested in that aspect of an intellectual tradition that best supports a fixed and known "global public reason." Even though he acknowledges the diversity and disagreements within Confucianism, Islam, and Catholicism, his assumption is that these differences have nothing to *contribute* to a dynamic global public reason.[43]

There has been significant debate about the questions of human rights and Confucianism[44] and of human rights and Islam.[45] There are disagreements within those traditions themselves about whether rights can be understood within the tradition, if some transformation of the tradition is necessary to recognize them, and if so, how to transform the tradition in order to accommodate human rights.[46] The histories of these intellectual traditions offer examples of past tensions and transformations.[47] Cohen's discussion of Islam exhibits some knowledge of these. However, by focusing so narrowly on each tradition (primarily the two texts, the *Analects* and the *Qur'an*), Cohen loses the range of historical and contemporary critical debates within Confucianism and Islam. Additionally, even a more broad range of historical texts would yield only the critical perspectives of those who have been favored by history. These texts are often not written by or about women, minorities, indigenous peoples, or conquered peoples.

[42] Bell 2000; Etzioni 2004; Taylor 1999. [43] Cohen 2004: 200, 202.

[44] For example, presenting a range of views see Bauer and Bell (1999), Davis (1995), and de Bary and Weiming (1998). Chenyang Li is especially constructive for helping notice Cohen's epistemological (indeed ontological) underpinnings (1999). See also Alford 1992; Angle 2002.

[45] For examples presenting a range of views see Ali (2000), An-Na'im (1990), Baderin (2003), Dalacoura (1998), Khan (1967 [1970]), Mayer (1995b), Muzaffar (2002), and Safi (2003). See some competing views discussed in Bielefeldt (2000).

[46] For an example in Islamic studies see Ramadan (2004) and An-Na'im (1990).

[47] For an example in Jewish studies see Goodman (1998).

Feminist and post-colonial literatures reclaim women and the colonized as authors, audience, and subjects of the texts that have been written out of dominant intellectual traditions. Further, even within these written traditions there is evidence of dissent; perhaps these reflect only a subset of the dissent and disagreement within their cultural pasts. Appropriately, then, Cohen is cautious about:

> taking those traditions as fixed and given ... inasmuch as each ethical tradition has competing formulations, with often sharp contests within the tradition about which formulation is best – a point that is tirelessly reiterated by postmodernists and postcolonialists.[48]

Although he acknowledges them, these intra-cultural discussions and related intra-cultural silences are not important to Cohen's argument.

Another form of politics – the debates among secondary scholars of these traditions – is masked by Cohen's focus on his own reading of these texts. Others who have developed a more rich understanding of Confucian and Islamic reflections on human rights have made use of this richer body of material much of which is not available in English.[49]

However, the selective use of primary and secondary sources is not the most subtle politics at work in this approach to an immanent universal human rights. As discussed with reference to Rawls in chapter 2, the device of "public reason" and its dependence on a "political community" is the more insidious theoretical tool for protecting the facade of epistemological neutrality. As Taylor calls us to do, others who engage in comparative political thought begin their queries with questions of epistemology[50] and are constantly called to return to epistemological issues by the challenges of translation, interpretation, and differing emphases on revelation.[51] Comparative political thought should bring even greater attention to the structural differences in individual reasoning and cognition that affect how people assess and

48 Cohen 2004: 200.

49 Note he does cite a couple of secondary sources and these are good choices.

50 Bell 2004; Dallmayr 2004. In addition to Dallmayr's own discussion, see many of those he cites, including Derrida 1992; Gadamer 1989; Heidegger 1971; 1996; Panikkar 1988.

51 Badiou 2001; Chenyang 1999; dé Ishtar 2005; Euben 2004; Gunning 1992; Nagar 2002; Williams 1996; Ackerman 1994; Braithwaite 1999; Cornell, Rosenfeld, and Carlson 1992; Fraser 1991; Matilal 1989; Nelson and Grossberg 1988; Povey 2001; Sedgwick 1990; Spivak 1988; Stoller 1997; Walzer 1987; Warnke 1989–90; Warnke 1993; Goodman 1998; Ramadan 2004.

participate in social and political life[52] and to the political, social, cultural, and economic differences in people's ability to participate in public life that deliberative theorists and their critics have brought to our attention.[53] In sum, this scholarship confirms in cross-cultural context the theoretical concerns voiced by a broad range of critical perspectives. Attention to difference between cultures requires attention to differences and to the politics of discourse *within* cultures, including our own.

Because of the differences in how people think and how they experience political, social, cultural, and economic life, public reason itself is an inadequate tool for developing an immanent account of universal human rights. "Public reason" is not external to any and every particular cultural framework. It is a source of legitimacy familiar in some contexts, but for example, if understood as distinctly different from revelation, it is incommensurable with Islam[54] (and certain Christian beliefs).

Despite the questionable political legitimacy of his sources and the questionable political legitimacy of public reason as a theoretical guide of immanent inquiry into contested terrain, Cohen argues that the cornerstone of human rights is membership in a political community.[55] The claim is essential to his argument. People who are members of political societies that are part of international political society have human rights as recognized in the human rights principle of the law of peoples. According to Cohen, by showing that universal membership is a value within each tradition, he offers evidence that there is a universal rationale for human rights: membership.

It may be enough to refute Cohen's account of universal human rights to argue that it is inadequately informed by historical and contemporary debate and that it exercises a political power of epistemology in selecting his sources for cross-cultural theorizing as I have just done. But such critique does not take us beyond the epistemological critics of theory-building. Yet, by reading Cohen closely we can learn even more about the range of ways in which the power of knowledge can work to obfuscate questions of political legitimacy. Thinking *through* epistemological and potentially relativist concerns, a theory

52 Rosenberg 2002.
53 For a recent summary and discussion see Ackerly (2006; 2007a).
54 Ramadan 2004. 55 Cohen 2004.

of human rights is not paralyzed by epistemology, difference, and dissent, but rather enriched theoretically and politically by them.

First, I dispute the claim that membership is the preferred basis of universal human rights within Confucianism; this isn't a challenge to the universality of human rights, only to Cohen's account of membership as its universal rationale. Second, I think that Cohen is wrong about what gives immanent universal human rights legitimacy: I argue it is political legitimacy, not reasoned argument. Third, by studying intellectual and political traditions more closely, by being interested in their internal dynamics, not just in how a theorist might manipulate them, we find a more universal basis for human rights. This basis is a universal responsibility to worry about the marginalized, particularly those disempowered by the manipulation of the power over the authority of knowledge. Interestingly, this could bring us to a more firm footing on which to argue that *membership* is the universal rationale for human rights. Anticipating the argument, if we understand membership not as a state of being, but a terrain of contestation, then Cohen and I share more of a common view of universal human rights than my concerns about his methodology would suggest. The norms of public reason under conditions of inequality might lead us to understand a rights-bearer not as a member, but as a stakeholder with an obligation to support local, national, and global contexts in which social, political, and economic practices and institutions function such that all members of a society are sustained by those practices and institutions that sustain that society.[56] Even if the view of membership as a rationale derived using my justificatory scheme is that which Cohen intends (using his), because my approach is methodologically attentive to epistemological concerns with power, my argument offers *political legitimacy* as well.

Let me first illustrate the importance of attention to epistemology and methodology by describing how I evaluate Cohen's sources of insight and what further sources of insight I seek. First, beginning at the level of epistemology, I expect that by engaging in cross-cultural dialogue I may learn something about what I am looking for. Cohen is seeking a rationale for human rights (membership) which is distinct from its content (the list) or its roles (institutions). However, looking at

[56] The implications go beyond just members. I phrase this obligation in multiple ways in this chapter and flesh it out in detail in chapter 6.

the dynamics of the marginalized seeking inclusion and the role of power over epistemology in their marginalization might lead us to focus on the role of critical discourse and its rationale as interrelated during times of dissensus. In times of hardship we observe two practices: we see those who experience the hardship demanding change[57] and we see those demanding change appealing to legitimate norms to justify their demands. Even if these practices are universal (as suggested by the practice of criticism within Confucianism,[58] Islam,[59] and women's human rights activism[60]), the rationales that sustain individual criticisms may not be. Observing these ranges of views would suggest at least the need to reconsider membership as the foundational rationale *and* to reconsider whether the focus of universality should be on rationales rather than roles. If founded in an immanent universal, human rights may fill the role of the legitimating norm. One might be able to defend the view of Jacques Maritain and Rawls by arguing that political legitimacy does not rest on a universalized rationale such as membership, but might instead rest on a universal practice (such as criticism) or on a universal role, such as the obligation to support those social institutions that sustain *all* those affected by the institutions of that society.

Second, continuing at the level of epistemology, whose views should inform our understanding of the content, roles, and rationales for human rights? Many people whose special class of rights are violated don't have membership in political communities, but certainly that should not be a moral or political basis for tabling our recognition of and criticism of their rights violations or of considering what their claims may teach us about the roles (and content and rationale) for human rights. If all Cohen means by the essential role of political membership is that no one will have secure human rights without membership in a political community, then I agree with his empirical claim.[61] States do most of the human rights protecting and if your state doesn't treat you as a member of the political community, it creates the conditions of the violations of your human rights. Marie and most refugees whether externally or internally displaced tell stories that

[57] Chen 1995; Moody-Adams 1998. [58] Ackerly 2006.
[59] Ramadan 2004. [60] Ackerly 2001b.
[61] See discussion by Nussbaum and her attribution of this view to Kant (1997: 273 and footnote 275).

illustrate the centrality of membership in this fuller sense for rights recognition. The status of membership may be the practical prerequisite for political and civil rights, but it cannot be the theoretical prerequisite for human rights. Many people without political membership status claim rights violations. It may be that past rights violations created their current status as stateless humans,[62] but it cannot be that the theoretical recognition of their human rights (even of a narrow list of human rights) depends on their having a state to which they claim membership. Just because within the *Analects* and the *Qur'an* there are arguments for membership that could be used to define a rationale for human rights does not mean that this view should be privileged over other views.[63] We should have in mind here not just refugees but also indigenous people whose membership and rights were designated by the same authority that appropriated their ancestral lands and displaced them.

Of course, we cannot infer that just because someone makes a rights claim there is a theoretical basis for that rights claim as a universal human right. However, the claims of people without membership in states have been internationally recognized as human rights.[64] Further, even if they had not, wouldn't the fact of the potential violations of their "freedom from slavery and serfdom, liberty (but not equal liberty) of conscience, and security of ethnic groups from mass murder and genocide" make us question whether membership is a prerequisite for human rights either empirically or theoretically?

The focus on membership gives marginal terrain for rights-based claims of injustice to stateless people[65] and to people whose rights violations are not experienced as uniquely political.[66] Asserting membership as the *a priori* rationale for human rights moves the political debates about the indivisibility of rights and the interrelatedness of the rights of all humans to a post-consensus terrain. Given the contestability and

[62] These include many refugees, immigrant children of deported or deceased parents, and people whose citizenship is not recognized by their resident state (for example the Bihari in Bangladesh) (see Bhabha 1998).

[63] An-Na'im's political reading of Islam's use of membership could be informative here (1992b).

[64] United Nations 1989; Universal Declaration of Human Rights 1948.

[65] See Bhabha 1998.

[66] See for example the literature on women's human rights (i.e. Bell 1992; Bunch 1990; Burrows 1986; Cook 1994; Gallagher 1997; Peters and Wolper 1995).

politics surrounding the indivisibility of rights and the interrelatedness of the rights of all humans, this reasonable way of justifying universal human rights is politically illegitimate. Once we consider rights as indivisible and thus a broader list of rights as important to debate *at least*, the fact that membership does not give all people the same rights or obligations makes the focus on political societies as loci of rights justification even more problematic. However, because many rights violations take place in social, political, and economic patterns, the problem is not necessarily more visible. In short, attention to whose claims are heard in a scheme of universal human rights justified by reference to a universal rationale of membership, devalues the epistemological contributions of those marginalized. Recognizing that their knowledge offers important theoretical evidence leads us to appreciate membership as a matter of degree, not status, and to appreciate rights as secured through practices and institutions, not through membership status.

Third, moving to a level of interpretation, Cohen's comparative inquiry should lead him to question the theoretical gain and universalizability of understanding human rights as dependent on the exclusionary category of political membership *and* the justificatory device of global public reason. On one reading of Confucianism there are no boundaries of membership;[67] on one reading of Islam the boundary of political society is faith.[68] Likewise, comparative reflection might ask one to reflect on how the boundaries of political membership have been determined in the history of Western political practice and theoretical reflection. The record is *at least* that the boundaries have been the subject of much political and theoretical contestation such that the standards for membership status are *at least* a problematic basis for the recognition of human rights.

The focus on membership has implications for what Cohen interprets to be the content of universal human rights. He asserts that there is a category of practices that are unjust but not human rights violations. Cohen offers that, under certain understandings of global public reason, this is a reasonable distinction. However, he offers no evidence that this is a politically legitimate distinction. Is the distinction between

[67] According to Chenyang Li, persons are not ontologically distinct, but identity and being are "contextually situated" such that there is no basis for a political move to establish connection such as is evoked by membership (1999: 2 and chapters 1 and 4).

[68] An-Na'im 1990; 1992b.

injustice and human rights violations a matter of degree or substance? If a matter of degree, what degree of injustice is bad enough to be called an injustice, but not so bad as to be called a human rights violation, and what institutional mechanisms are in place to prevent the injustice from becoming a human rights violation? If a matter of substance, then what category of injustice does not yield a human rights violation, if not now, over time, either to an individual, a community, or descendents?

The histories of internal contestation about the extent and the meaning of membership would lead us to reflect on whether a *justification* for human rights could depend on Cohen's Rawlsian notion of political community and whether global public reason can be a source of the justification for universal human rights. We should worry with Chantal Mouffe that the turn to public reason is a way of masking a *political* decision: the decision to tolerate certain kinds of arguments (and not others) as "reasonable."[69] As Rawls invites, we must ask if the turn to global public reason is politically legitimate.

We need to question whether global public reason will reflect the understanding of human rights principles of everyone throughout the globe. As Rawls acknowledges, three kinds of conflicts are obstacles to public reason: different "comprehensive doctrines," differences in social and economic status, and "the burdens of judgment," that is, differences in interpretation of facts related to particular questions of justice at hand. Cohen's argument deals only with the first of these and not with the ways in which differences within and between political societies – differences in socioeconomic status, differences in interpretation – weaken the tool of public reason for reflection on human rights.

In sum, while I agree with Cohen that cross-cultural theorizing should be an important source of legitimizing universal human rights and while I agree that that justification will have a minimalist metaphysical basis – that is, the theoretical justification will not require adherence to universalized substantive claims about comprehensive notions of the good life, good society, or good person – I disagree with *his* minimalist justification because it is not minimal enough. It assumes too much cohesion within political societies and common ground among political societies. It is not reasonable, tolerant, liberal, or politically legitimate to treat a people or an intellectual history as homogeneous or static in either their politics or their beliefs.

[69] Mouffe 2000.

Interestingly enough, as I will argue in the second part of this book, methodological attention to the practices and institutions of marginalization, and to diverse sources of insight into universal human rights from within a range of contexts and from a range of perspectives within those contexts, leads us to a view of immanent universal human rights in which membership is important. However, its importance is not as a rationale and basis for a justificatory scheme but rather as part of a hermeneutical lens for identifying the values, practices, roles, and institutions that sustain a society. Methodological attention to those marginalized by these values, practices, roles, and institutions leads us to seek an immanent theory of universal human rights that is conducive to social values, practices, roles, and institutions that sustain all those affected by them. These may be members of a society, or globally distant economic actors connected by the exploited power of a dominant trading partner. Global justice demands our attention to the range of rights violation's contexts and sources. A notion of membership as bounded and static is not conducive to our interrogating these and methodologically puts them outside the bounds of human rights inquiry.

The discussion of Cohen illustrates that Taylor and many other comparative theorists are right to draw our attention to the political relevance of epistemology. We need a way of theorizing about human rights that attempts to stand above the politics of a particular way of reasoning (or at least be *very* attentive to it). From the discussion of Taylor we see that we need a methodology that reminds us that the sources of knowledge which were repressed in given contexts were important resources of understanding what human rights are. From the discussion of Cohen we see that we need a methodology that interrogates the politics of justification. Our reflections on the work of Martha Nussbaum in the following section will lead us to recognize the importance of methodological reflection as to what experience best positions one (or many) to offer theoretical insights about immanent universal human rights.

## A theoretical methodology

The implication of the foregoing critiques of theoretical methods that are inadequately attentive to the potential political power of epistemological difference is that a theorist needs an explicit methodology that guides one to be attentive to all potentially exploitable forms of epistemological bias. Without such a methodology, the theorist can be only naively confident in her or his attention to difference. Taylor and Cohen are insufficiently reflective about their epistemologies. Without an argument for *why* they choose the sources of knowledge (the dominant sources of cultural authority within a given context) for respect and for *why* the relevance of more marginalized views within each context are not explored, an otherwise reasonable theoretical justificatory scheme lacks *political* legitimacy because the politics of authority that informs their epistemology has not been deconstructed.

Martha Nussbaum's view of universal human rights is that they are the political tool for advocating for human capabilities, but that themselves they lack theoretical and conceptual clarity.[70] A human right involves "an especially urgent and morally justified claim that a person has, simply by virtue of being a human adult, and independently of membership in a particular nation, or class, or sex, or ethnic or religious or sexual group."[71] By understanding rights in terms of human capabilities theory we can see clearly (1) state policy goals, (2) global social justice goals, and (3) the challenges for legal and distributive justice that they pose. Moreover, because Nussbaum is explicit about her theoretical method for developing the capability basis of social justice, her theory of human rights is theoretically attentive to methodology.[72] Nussbaum offers us methodological reflection on the insights of those who suffer the injustices that a theory of social justice might seek to assess, redress, or mitigate.[73] She explicitly justifies her theoretical project using a Rawlsian model of political objectivity.[74]

In contrast with Cohen and Taylor and others in comparative political theory, Nussbaum intends to work for the marginalized and to some extent from the perspective of the marginalized. She has given some attention to questions of epistemology raised by Taylor and engaged in cross-cultural inquiry between Western and Indian contexts of the sort that Cohen engages in. Going further than Taylor, Nussbaum begins her inquiry with mutual respect but does not think

[70] Although her project did not set out as a theory of human rights, it has become one, as she argues that human rights may be the appropriate political tool for bringing about the realization of human capabilities in national and political life (Nussbaum 1997: 273–275; Nussbaum 2000b: 102, 104).

[71] Nussbaum 1997: 292.

[72] Nussbaum 1995a; 1997; 1999c; 2001; 2003b.

[73] See also Galtung 1994.

[74] Nussbaum 1999a; 2001. See also Rawls 2001.

that mutual respect is a sufficient condition for engagement. She worries about those who would engage in dialogue with only the dominant sources within a tradition. Going further than Cohen, Nussbaum relies on a more rich range of sources, including contemporary women's activists, scholars of women's activism, literature, and religion.

Importantly, Nussbaum's work is self-conscious of her theory of knowledge and its relationship to political justification.[75] Political legitimacy is based on applying "reasonable principles" on which people agree.[76] She is attentive to the fact that human minds do not all think alike,[77] that language, culture, and conceptual schemes that we might use to understand what constitute "reasonable" principles vary significantly across contexts. According to Nussbaum, attention to this kind of difference requires attention to theoretical methodology; these are political not conceptual obstacles to finding an acceptable standard of political legitimacy.[78]

There are three steps to Nussbaum's methodology for identifying universal values. First, the philosopher deploys an Aristotelian methodology of looking within human experience to identify that which is definitive of the *human* experience and which should therefore be the focus of global political, economic, and social examination. She determines that there are human functionings which are universal and that the corresponding capability to choose to exercise those functionings are the standards by which we should measure social justice within and across contexts.[79]

Second, this methodology functions like a Rawlsian choice situation[80] in which the philosopher and those seeking a universal standard of social justice compare the human capabilities approach to other available approaches.[81] This approach exhibits a holistic view of a way of life, philosophy, or world interpretation.[82] Though she

[75] Nussbaum 1999a; 2001.
[76] See also Nussbaum 1997: 297; 2001: 896; 2000b: 103.
[77] Cf. Misak 2004; Nussbaum 2001; Rosenberg 2002.
[78] Nussbaum is explicitly following Satya Mohanty and Noam Chomsky (cf. Butler, Laclau, and Žižek 2000; Harris 2000).
[79] The main arguments regarding the capability aspect of the methodology are found in Nussbaum (1995a; 2000a; 2004). In the last she is defending her account of methodology from criticism by Okin (2003).
[80] Rawls [1971]1999: 102. [81] Rawls and Kelly 2001.
[82] Nussbaum 1993: 260. Moody-Adams criticizes Nussbaum's holism but also argues that it is not necessary (1998: 265ff).

recognizes dynamism within cultures in other contexts of her work, this aspect of her methodology treats cultures as static.

And third, she tests out the view against the views of others. For this aspect of the methodology she works cross-culturally: a scholar familiar with her own cultural traditions learning about another, preferring to focus on one cultural context but inviting others to work with other contexts. For this phase of the methodology, she tests her view in explicit dialogue with activists or scholars of activism during her travels in India.[83]

From within her framework, it is hard to see what is wrong. She has a theory of justification in which she is attentive to the potential politics of justification. She has a method for developing a theory of social justice that seeks to circumvent those politics and that is explicit that its purpose is to do so. What is wrong?

Despite her carefully articulated and defended methodology, despite her explicit account of political objectivity, Nussbaum's framework is not that different from the universalists' frameworks described in chapter 2 or from Taylor and Cohen just discussed *in one important respect*. All of these theorists rely on a justificatory scheme which they assume (or argue) is neutral. Based on that neutrality they do not question the political dimension of their methodology. The possibility that the methodology is *not* neutral is not reflected in the research design.

The problem with Rawlsian political neutrality is twofold: (1) having a confidence in a justificatory scheme that is not reexamined after the initial argument for the scheme; and (2) assuming that the legitimacy of the justificatory scheme secures the methodology itself from needing to be examined as a source of political legitimacy. The general point being made here is akin to the critical theorists' argument that a theoretical argument needs to be tried out in practice. A theoretical argument developed in consideration of other theoretical arguments and certain sociological information needs to be tested out in practice. By assessing our arguments against the "truisms" of human experience, we can generate political theory that is more coherent and actionable. Why do we need to reflect on our methodology? Because maybe we have been asking the wrong question, maybe we have been asking it in the wrong way, and maybe we have been asking it of the wrong people.

[83] Nussbaum 2000b.

Confidence in the justificatory scheme secures the methodology from needing to be examined (and reexamined) as a source of political legitimacy. However, if, as the experience and insights of the marginalized argue we must, we raise epistemological questions at the level of justification, we cannot be confident that related epistemological questions need not be explored at the methodological level. Let's review Nussbaum's methodology.

First, consider the Aristotelian method of identifying human functioning. How do we know that she could see all human functioning? In the 2000 account of her list of capabilities, Nussbaum includes sexual orientation as a basis on which one could expect protection against discrimination.[84] She argues in footnote 84 that in earlier versions she excluded it because there was little consensus on the issue, but that since the movie *Fire* sparked discussions within India among liberals and feminists, now it was reasonable to assume a cross-cultural consensus on the issue. As my surveys and the huge national and state debates within the US, India, and other countries demonstrate, there is by no means a consensus, even among liberals and women activists, that sexual orientation should be universally protected.[85] Her explanation of this decision illustrates that her methodology leaves a lot up to her own judgment. That judgment needs to be interrogated. Nussbaum's change of view is sparked by awareness of a new dialogue, not attention to existing ones she may have overlooked or to a reevaluation of her own initial use of the methodology.

Second, consider the Rawlsian choice situation. Does it matter what other views are considered? When evaluating Rawls's reasoning in *A Theory of Justice* we chose between justice as fairness, Utilitarianism, and a hybrid.[86] What other options does Nussbaum offer us in her choice situation? Once we decide that a capability framework is the best, can we choose again which capability framework? Perhaps we should not be choosing between one static capability framework and another, or an alternative framework? Perhaps instead we should be working within a tested framework to further develop it.[87]

84 Nussbaum 2000b: 79. 85 Ackerly 2007a.

86 Rawls [1971]1999: §§21, 26–30.

87 One such alternative would be Sabine Alkire's approach of operationalizing Sen's general human capability framework (2002).

Third and finally, why is it that when Nussbaum engages in locally informed inquiry, everyone agrees with her? I cannot find two feminists working on women's human rights who agree with each other, let alone two women in India. Some at the Feminist Dialogues 2005 wanted to define feminism such that we could exclude some feminists from future feminist dialogues. Didn't Nussbaum meet any of these women?

Consider Nussbaum's own discussion of this problem:

> In some ways the list goes beyond what the two women are currently thinking. For example, it is possible that Jayamma does not formulate issues of nondiscrimination and fundamental liberties to herself in just the way the list does.[88]

Does this mean that there is something wrong with Jayamma – "like many women in India and the rest of the world, [she lacks] support for many of the most central human functions"[89] – as Nussbaum suggests? Or could it mean there is something wrong with the list. Perhaps the non-discrimination paradigm is problematic because it allows one to reflect on an issue (say, sexual orientation) without appreciating the indivisibility of all rights. Further:

> neither of the women seems to value education in quite the same way the list does, although Jayamma is beginning to see changes in her own family that may alter her perception.[90]

Shouldn't part of praxeological inquiry be to ask *why not*? Shouldn't the methodology require we consider that at least *possibly* the disconnect is not with a capability failure on the part of the women, as Nussbaum's reference to Jayamma's shift in thinking indicates she reads it, but rather, again, perhaps that there is something wrong with the list. It may be, as I just proposed, that the list allows one to reflect on an issue without appreciating the indivisibility of all rights. Or it may be that, as Nussbaum defines the list, the way in which these women enjoy their capabilities is not well captured. For example, a woman may value the education of her son over herself because her educated son can get a job in a city or overseas which will enable her to educate her daughters who can become doctors and marry well

[88] Nussbaum 2000b: 109. [89] Nussbaum 2000b: 110.
[90] Nussbaum 2000b: 109.

and therefore not be subject to the same kind of dowry-related violence she feels her generation faced. This would lead us to an understanding of the rights of all as interrelated.

In sum, at each step in Nussbaum's methodology, her methodology privileges her own analysis over the experiences, practices, politics, *and analysis* of the marginalized. She often refers to revisions of her capabilities list, but never to a revision of her methodology.[91] She has no methodological requirement to reevaluate her methodology.

## Conclusion

The concerns raised in this book so far would suggest that an immanent universal human rights theory needs a way of challenging both explicit political power and the power associated with defining what constitutes an acceptable argument. None of the approaches to immanent universal human rights discussed in this chapter is politically legitimate by the second measure. They each deploy rather than interrogate the power associated with their own terms of argument. Is it possible to offer an account of universal human rights that is not the result of what Tariq Ramadan calls a "dialogic monologue" between the most powerful interlocutors and the less so?

The methodological solution I offer in the next chapters addresses each of these concerns individually, and all of them together. My argument is that all three levels of inquiry – our assumptions, our justificatory scheme, and our methodological scheme or research design – rely on epistemological certainty where we should have no certainty but rather a healthy dose of actively engaged skepticism. Should this skepticism impede our search for universal human rights and their theoretical justification? No, but it cries out for our inquiry to reconsider its understanding of methodology and to begin that inquiry where many feminists begin *at the level of epistemology*.[92]

How should we ask the epistemological question about universal human rights? I argue in the next chapter that a "curb cutting" feminist epistemology leads to methodological reflection that has political legitimacy across contexts because it relies on *a priori* and ongoing epistemological reflection combined with perpetual attention to the possibilities for differences to be deployed as power inequalities. As

[91] Nussbaum 1997: 286 and footnote 266; 2000b. [92] Harding 1987.

important as it is to take seriously differences between traditions, differences within traditions, their respective cultural resources, and the political potentials of each of these, we must also look for invisible differences. Immanent inquiry cannot hope for politically legitimate conclusions if the sources of its insights are limited to the most visible, most influential, most famous, or most familiar within any particular context. Where values are seemingly broadly held, we should worry about the power of those articulating the dominant view to render inaudible, if not invisible, those who might dissent.

Consequently, the form of immanent universal human rights I propose in the second part of the book is self-consciously political, treats universal human rights as provisional, and continually interrogates them for their potential both to mask and to reveal and criticize dominant strains in existing ethical systems, be they the political practices associated with legitimating theoretical arguments or the cultural practices associated with legitimating local political arguments. As we will see in chapter 7, this doesn't mean that the notion of human rights derived from this theoretical methodology will be unstable. However, it will be informed by a broad range of views – views that do not agree with each other and views that taken together will make a beautiful sound, the cacophony of democratic engagement. As we will see in chapters 5 and 6, attention to the voices in this cacophony requires examination of the ways in which social, economic, political, and cultural practices work visibly and invisibly. This attention is an important application of the immanent human rights framework.

In order to find an immanent source of political justification that does not reenact the power dynamics of its context, we need to interrogate the epistemological neutrality of an approach to political justification generally, and to a justification for human rights more specifically. Arguing that there is *no* epistemological perspective that is apolitical, I call for a theoretical methodology for normative inquiry in the context of pluralism that does not assume away the politics of epistemology as a first step of political theory. Such a theoretical methodology enables me to make (or so I claim) a theoretical argument that is politically legitimate *and* that has the moral force of a metaphysical argument without particular metaphysics.

PART II

# *A methodology for immanent theory*

In Part I, we saw that a human rights theory is a non-ideal theory, that is, it is a theory that guides our criticisms of injustice from a context in which we have never known justice. The politics of epistemology, diversity, and disagreement require that a theory for criticism has a methodology that expects that theorists and critics continually reevaluate our commitments. As a non-ideal theory, the theory requires the tools of its own interrogation. It requires humility.

Humility is more than an attribute; it is a mindset. The political theory jargon I use to describe this mindset is that "the theory has a destabilizing epistemology." The basis of what it means to know anything, our confidence in the building blocks of our arguments, may always be shaken. This does not mean that we are always shaking them such that we never get to build a critical argument. No. It means that every time we build a critical argument, we poke at the building blocks, all the way down to the foundation of the argument, to reveal whether we have inadvertently built our argument on unjust premises. For that is the risk. When we build a critical theory in a non-ideal world, we may *without thinking* build a criticism using unjust premises. Therefore, when doing critical theory for a non-ideal world, we have to have a methodology for revealing where we were unthinking. In Part II, I set out a methodology that keeps us thinking without sidelining the practical role of human rights *to criticize*.

As will become clear from the examples discussed in chapter 5, I focus on women's human rights activists because such a perspective requires that our analysis respect a *huge range* of issues from citizenship rights of indigenous people to economic rights of laborers in the world market in the production of consumer goods, to property rights and environmental sustainability.

# 5 *Feminist curb cutting: a methodology for exposing silences and revealing differences for the immanent study of universal human rights*

## Prologue

On a 2004 trip to India for the World Social Forum[1] and to see grantees of the Global Fund for Women, Susan Okin observed two kinds of women's rights activism – one focusing on specific demands and another focusing on the consciousness of one's right to make those demands. Unfortunately, our conversation with Okin about her observation of women's rights activism and what normative implications could be drawn from it was cut short by her premature death. This chapter is about *how* theorists should go about drawing normative insights from those critically affected by the political problems on which we reflect.

## Introduction

Normative, social scientific, and experienced-based analyses are all crucial to the task of political theory that is engaged with the "struggles and wishes of the age."[2] Normative analysis turns our attention to the theoretical roots of contemporary political problems and provides a normatively defendable solution that we might actively work toward politically. Social scientific analysis elucidates the processes that constitute the historical material conditions of contemporary political puzzles. This same sociological analysis helps explain the political, social, and economic obstacles to realizing a particular normatively defendable solution. Experienced-based analysis helps us focus our

[1] The World Social Forum is a gathering of progressive activists that began in Porto Alegre, Brazil, in 2001 to offer critical assessment of neo-liberal economic globalization and has become a space for anti-globalization activists, anti-war activists, and other resistance movements.

[2] Marx [1843] 1967: 215.

normative analysis on a theoretical puzzle as it is lived by those particularly adversely affected by the problem and such analysis can suggest context-appropriate possibilities for advancing social justice and expanding human freedom. Critical theorists call this "praxeological" inquiry.

In the case of human rights theory, such activist-oriented inquiry can tell us not only to what rights people aspire, but also how they conceptualize those rights and their right to realize them. Importantly then, social scientific and experienced-based analyses should inform our normative analysis of human rights. This chapter defends a method of experience-based inquiry that can broaden the insights of normative theorizing about contemporary critical issues.

Many normative theorists have often made use of sociological inquiry.[3] More recently, in their attention to global inequality and vulnerability, contemporary political theorists have turned to first-hand experience-based inquiry to inform their normative theory.[4] Iris Marion Young calls for political theorists to do more theorizing not just *about* the most pressing political problems people face, but by drawing on the insights and experiences of those facing them.[5] In fact, since Aristotle, theorists have looked to practice for normative insights.[6] However, since Aristotle we have been doing so without a methodology that requires us to focus particularly on those hurt – and differently hurt – by existing institutions and practices.[7]

Critical theorists attempt to connect theory to practice by testing their scholarship against human experience: does the theory guide human action, coherently and consistently in a way that enables the

[3] For a fairly recent example, in *Democratic Justice* Ian Shapiro makes use of his own study of the law and institutions related to childhood, marriage, work, and the final stage of life (1999). In *Justice, Gender and the Family*, Susan Moller Okin makes extensive use of others' research on families (Okin 1989).

[4] Ackerly 2000; Nussbaum 1992; 2000b; Okin 2003.

[5] Young 2001b.

[6] Recent examples include Brettschneider (2002; see also Dean 1996; Dietz 2002; Mohanty 2003; Moody-Adams 1997; Nussbaum 2000b; Sandoval 2000).

[7] See my discussion of the Aristotelian Method in *Political Theory and Feminist Social Criticism* (2000). In addition, political theorists have borrowed from philosophy the heuristic device of the illustrative case. Both Nussbaum and Hirschmann make use of such cases. The illustrative case helps the reader see the concrete dimensions of the theoretical discussion offered by the scholar (Hirschmann 2003; Nussbaum 2000a). My intent here is to further the agenda set out in *Political Theory and Feminist Social Criticism* and that Young calls to be developed (Young 2001b).

theory itself to be revised by engagement with practice?[8] Further, feminist and post-colonial scholars have tried to invert the traditional theory–practice relationship by drawing theoretical insights from activist discourse. However, in theorizing from social activism Jodi Dean, Chela Sandoval, Chandra Talpade Mohanty, and Martha Nussbaum[9] have been vague about the ways in which their insights are derived from the actual experience of those whose conditions are evoked in the theorists' arguments, though they each have much to contribute to our understanding of oppression, resistance, social change, and human capabilities.[10] While political theorists have methods for reading texts within intellectual traditions, within geopolitical contexts we haven't yet developed our methods of practical inquiry.

This is a relatively new move in political theory, inspired by our interest in human experience but challenged by our collectively limited experience in observing it. Outside of political theory, feminists have made rich advances in collecting and analyzing insights from marginalized sources or about marginalized topics.[11] Yet, their arguments don't exhibit the tools for seeking the normative insights of their informants.

Although political theorists have not given much attention to research design for such inquiries, they have offered some insights as to what a researcher should worry about. Ayelet Shachar demonstrates

[8] Ackerly 2000; Geuss 1981.

[9] Dean 1996; Mohanty 2003; Nussbaum 2000b; Sandoval 2000.

[10] We can see glimpses of what must be required for sociological and praxeological inquiry into normative questions in some political theorists' efforts to draw on human experience for their normative analysis. Fung and Wright have assembled an edited volume on the experience of deliberative democracy in which many of the authors attempt to draw theoretical insights from empirical observation of specific deliberative practices. These authors may describe their methods of data gathering, but not the way in which their theoretical perspective guides their empirical inquiry nor the way in which it guides their analysis of the data (2003).

Critical and feminist scholars of International Relations (IR) have explored the relationship between theory and practice for IR theory. In Andrew Linklater's view, "there is more to critical theory than normative inquiry, since critical approaches seek to understand how social systems marginalize and exclude certain groups and how actual or potential logics of change might deepen the meaning of human freedom and expand its domain" (Linklater 1994: 130; cf. Cox 2001). The importance of these insights can be seen in recent feminist work (including Ackerly, Stern, and True 2006; Moon 1997; Prügl 1999; True 2003; Whitworth 2001).

[11] Naples 2003; Risman 2004; Smith 1999.

the importance of focusing on institutional design and ways in which affected group members can influence institutional design.[12] Seyla Benhabib emphasizes the importance of equal voice in the design process,[13] which suggests the importance of mitigating inequalities, creating opportunities for deliberation, and simulating deliberation in existing forums.[14] Theorists interested in theorizing from experience should respect the importance of culture to individual identity,[15] but avoid granting monopoly power for defining cultural norms to a subset of a population.[16] Theorists should respect the views of those most affected by an issue,[17] but recognize that determining group membership is itself a political act.[18] Further, if their inquiry is inclusive, theorists should expect disagreement among informants.[19] Experience-based theory needs to be attentive to the social process of identity and preference formation while respecting the agency of individuals[20] *and* the constraining liberal focus on individuals as those who exercise choice.[21] Since determining the perspective of the affected or marginalized requires making political judgments that could benefit from this epistemological attention, rather than seeking out the least well-off, we should pay attention to the processes of marginalization and the range of practices and structures through which they operate. Such research should be attentive to social and economic power[22] and to the ability of certain powerful actors to convert or extend one form of social, economic, or political power over to another.[23] Theorists observing practices and institutions must be attentive to the fact that the institutionalization of inequality may become reified such that the institutions that sustain certain inequalities become invisible and individual actions and choices of those who would seem to be disadvantaged by them appear instead to embrace them.

In this chapter and the next, I describe a general method of feminist activist-informed theoretical inquiry appropriate for when that inquiry is destined to inform normative theorizing. I give an account of the methods for gathering and interpreting insights from what activists do and say in order to give specific substance to practice-informed inquiry

[12] Shachar 2001. [13] Benhabib 2002. [14] Ackerly 2006.
[15] Kymlicka 1995; Taylor, Gutmann, and Taylor [1992] 1994.
[16] Benhabib 2002; Okin 1999; Shachar 2001. [17] Young 1990.
[18] Appiah 1994a; 1994b; Hirschmann 2003. [19] Brown 1995; Mouffe 2000.
[20] Hirschmann 2003. [21] Zerilli 2005.
[22] Fraser 1997; Okin 1989; Young 1990. [23] Walzer 1983.

generally. Further, I illustrate the method by describing the data collection and interpretation processes.

The argument proceeds in three parts which correspond to three stages of praxeological inquiry for normative theory. In order to reveal my epistemological assumptions and the ways in which they manifest themselves methodologically, I first use the example of the access ramps cut into sidewalk curbs to illustrate the value of the knowledge of those made nearly invisible by existing practices and institutions. The purpose of this epistemological discussion is to enable each reader to suspend his or her epistemological assumptions long enough to be able to judge the theoretical methodology proposed here against *its* epistemological assumptions. Second, I argue that this curb cut epistemology requires specific methods for gathering data and give examples of these from my own activist-based human rights inquiry. Third, while one might imagine that the data collection is the experience-based dimension of the method and the analysis is the normative dimension, instead I describe tools for experience-based analysis. These tools enlist the informants themselves in the analytical process. Just as the data-collection methods are designed to seek out a range of experiences, the analytical methods are designed to seek out alterative, even competing, analyses. For experience-based inquiry to be more than mere window dressing on normative theory, praxeological inquiry requires methods of analysis. Central to this argument, the analysis also illustrates the importance of a theoretical methodology that is (1) specific about its sources of data, (2) specific about its methods of analysis, and (3) particularly attentive to the prospect that assumptions can be masked by the norms of argument themselves. For expository purposes, I divide the discussion into data collection and analysis and develop these in this chapter and the next, but the dynamics between data collection and analysis will be evident throughout both.

Stephen White articulates the challenge shared by mine and similar forms of theorizing:

> One aspect of constructing such contestable foundations involves the embodiment within them of some signaling of their own limits. Felicitous weak ontologies cannot simply declare their contestability, fallibility, or partiality at the start and then proceed pretty much as before. The reason for this is that an ontology figures our most basic sense of human being, an achievement that always carries a propensity toward naturalization, reification, and unity, even if only implicitly. A weak ontology must possess resources for deflecting

this propensity at some point in the unfolding of its dimensions. Its elaboration of fundamental meanings must in some sense fold back upon itself, disrupting its own smooth constitution of a unity. In a way, its contestability will thus be enacted rather than just announced.[24]

In political theory jargon, feminist curb cutting is a destabilizing epistemological device set out to enact, not just announce, contestability. In plain English, it reminds us of our fallibility and encourages our humility. However, it does not allow us to enact contestability through self-reflection alone. It *requires* that we enact our theory in the real world, proving (in both senses of the word) its emancipatory potential.

## Feminist curb cutting – the epistemology behind the methodology[25]

In feminist theory, the sociological and practical dimensions of a normative theoretical question are interrelated. The engagement is dynamic, yet it begins with the practical experience of those who suffer under the form of oppression being studied. Sociological study of the practical impact of various oppressions may lead to insights into the ways that the oppression is institutionalized. The scope of institutionalized power may lend weight to the normative import of the question at hand. But, because so much gender hierarchy gets institutionalized in ways that render it invisible, this analysis needs to be informed by a range of experiences of marginalization.[26] Hence feminists' need for

[24] White 2000: 8.

[25] As I will illustrate, "feminist curb cutting" is a pedagogical heuristic. It is useful in the classroom and at the outset of this argument to get us thinking in a certain way, to help us to take up a critical perspective. Curb cutting functions in my exposition as the veil of ignorance does in Rawls's original position, or as the lawgiver in Rousseau's *Social Contract*. In addition, curb cut feminism functions as a method of critical assessment of our own ability to interrogate our own epistemological assumptions and to reason while imagining. Wendy Brown offers a critique of non-curb cut arguments. She holds up Marx as a theorist who is offering an example of such criticism: "Marx's characterization of rights as egoistic rests on a reading of the ways in which the historical emergence of the 'rights of man' naturalizes and thus entrenches historically specific, unavowed social powers that set us against each other, preoccupy us with property, security, and freedom of movement, and economically and socially stratify us" (1995: 113).

[26] Nussbaum draws on her observations of women in developing contexts because (1) their experiences exhibit the deficiencies of GDP-based approaches to

experience-based inquiry of many differently situated informants. They need a device that (1) teaches them to see invisible privileges (a pedagogy) and (2) fosters their reflection on that which is concealed by those privileges (an ongoing self-reflective methodology). Finally, they need (3) a shared theoretical objective of emancipatory theories that free everyone, not just the privileged or visible among the oppressed or marginalized. I am going to describe curb cut feminist epistemology as practiced through pedagogical, methodological, and emancipatory commitments. Through these commitments, the theorist cultivates habits of attentiveness to her own privileges and marginalizations and to the ways in which privileges and marginalizations in general are concealed. The research skills of being attentive to privilege and marginalizations need to be continually cultivated. In unfamiliar contexts, patterns of normalization and therefore masked privilege may be more difficult to identify. Therefore, a curb cutting, destabilizing epistemology and the skills of attentiveness it requires are best honed in familiar environments.

Post-World War II international human rights conventions and practices offer an example of invisibly institutionalized gender hierarchy. Despite sex being an illegitimate basis of discrimination in all human rights documents since the Universal Declaration of Human Rights,[27] women's human rights violations were persistently unseen or ignored by mainstream policy and human rights organizations until relatively recently.[28] Working often independently, often in tandem, women's human rights activists, scholars, and policy entrepreneurs have demonstrated that while occasionally a prudential tool for social criticism in a given moment of time, the international instruments for promoting human rights, even the international instruments for promoting women's human rights, have been inadequate for securing women's human rights.[29] Despite significant progress in integrating gender into mainstream international agreements – such as Security

development, (2) such attention may compensate for past inattention to sex inequalities, and (3) because feminist philosophy "should increasingly focus on the urgent needs and interests of women in the developing world, whose concrete material and social contexts must be well understood" (2000b: 7).

27 Universal Declaration of Human Rights 1948.

28 See Mills on the "epistemology of ignorance" (1997). In this project, I am equally concerned with the epistemological myopia of the theorist.

29 Ackerly 2001b; Askin and Koenig [1999] 2000; Bunch 1990; 1995; Jalani 1993; Mayer 1995a; 1995c; O'Hare 1999; Stamatopoulou 1995.

Council Resolution 1325[30] which requires gender analysis in the design and evaluation of UN peace-keeping missions and the Rome Statute of the International Criminal Court[31] – and in getting gender-specific international conventions, declarations, and platforms passed, the realization of women's human rights still depends on the work of grassroots activists to challenge local laws, practices, and norms. Given the political viability of local laws, practices, and norms that violate women's human rights, intra-cultural criticism and cross-cultural criticism are essential tools for realizing women's human rights. And yet, "human" rights do not help women in many local contexts because what it means to be "human" is locally determined.

In order to reveal processes that are made invisible through social institutionalization, we need to employ what I describe as "curb cut feminism." Curb cut feminist analysis follows the activist model of the Americans with Disabilities movement and *begins* by privileging the knowledge of people with disabilities in designing the solution for existing infrastructure and the design of future structures such that the full range of capabilities inform their design.[32] While designed with attention to people in wheelchairs, the curb cuts, access ramps, automatic doors, multiple access points, and clearly indicated wheelchair accessible routes enhance the mobility of others as well. People pushing strollers and delivery dollies, people carrying lots of books, and people recovering from an injury, for example, are all able to move more freely. By becoming aware of mobility privilege, we can become aware of design that enable the freedom of movement of all. Further, the ramifications of improved mobility are felt far beyond the initial focus on freedom of movement. For example, in the United States, with reliable and predictable wheelchair access, parents with children whose age or ability require them to be in strollers are able to bring their children to museums (and a range of other venues) to further their children's and their own education. Older people are afforded similar opportunities for continued learning despite declining mobility.

Particularly because I use the metaphor of curb cuts, one might misunderstand me to be privileging some forms of disability over

[30] United Nations 2000.

[31] Rome Statute of the International Criminal Court 1998.

[32] The idea came to me during a radio interview with a disability activist about the architecture of the Internet.

others. Instead, I am working within the general and familiar feminist criticism of the power of normalization. This is predominantly an epistemological power that is manifest in all sorts of values, practices, norms, and institutions. A world designed to accommodate the visible norm (to use the language of statistics) will by design ignore most of the population, and all of their unique ways of falling outside the norm. Will Kymlicka argues that by including among the oppressed "women, blacks, Native Americans, Chicanos, Puerto Ricans and other Spanish-speaking Americans, Asian Americans, gay men, lesbians, working-class people, poor people, old people, and mentally and physically disabled people"[33] Iris Young "would seem to include 80 per cent of the population" in the United States in her list of oppressed groups.[34] This may be evidence for how challenging it is to define systemic disadvantage as Kymlicka argues. The fact that *so many* people fall into the category of "oppressed group" is not itself evidence that it is hard to develop criteria for identifying privilege, but it may partly explain why it is hard to help people see their own privilege.[35]

Generally, curb cut feminists begin with gender analysis of political, social, and economic conditions and processes. These analyses reveal the ways in which political, social, and economic contexts impede, exclude, ignore, or marginalize some women, not all women, and not only women. Curb cut feminist epistemology assumes that: (1) the oppression of those "differently" oppressed than the inquirer may not be visible to the inquirer, to the theorist, or to the relatively powerful; (2) when the conditions of the "differently" oppressed are identified and analyzed, greater insights than those possible from positions of relative privilege are possible; and (3) identifying the "differently" affected is a political dimension of this methodology that is itself an important subject of critical attention.[36]

I put "differently" in scare quotes to indicate the problematic character of the term: (1) the perspective not yet imagined is more marginalized than the most marginalized one can imagine; (2) the claim to being "differently" oppressed or marginalized (like the claim to be

[33] Young 1989: 261. [34] Kymlicka 1995: 145.
[35] For other examples of this genre of pedagogy see McIntosh (1988).
[36] See the discussion of insiders, outsiders, multi-sited critics, and multiple critics in chapter 6.

"most" marginalized[37]) is a political claim; and (3) the point is not to identify *an* unprivileged perspective to privilege but to deploy a device that destabilizes the epistemology of the speaker or epistemic community. The point is not to privilege marginalization or oppression but rather to deploy epistemological processes that do not marginalize or at a minimum are self-conscious about the epistemological power exercised through marginalization. Feminist analyses generate empirical and theoretical insights for understanding the struggles and wishes of those disadvantaged by hierarchies that affect political, social, and economic processes, thus enabling all of society to understand these better.

In the search for universal human rights, curb cut feminist inquiry assumes that to answer the question "Are there universal human rights?," we need to know (among other things) *women's* experience of human rights and their violation. Women's experiences and theoretical insights are *the starting point* of our inquiry, because women's human rights violations often differ in kind and location from men's human rights violations. However, when women's previously invisible human rights violations are revealed, new theoretical and practical avenues for promoting the human rights of *all of humanity* open up.[38]

Women and others disadvantaged by exploitable hierarchies experience exclusion and human rights violations even under institutions which include many of the democratic features theorists tell us are important.[39] By drawing on women's experiences, particularly on those of women who are multiply-situated, feminist theorists and activists have drawn our attention to the range of shortcomings of human rights theory and human rights regimes in practice.[40]

Importantly, curb cut feminism must start with actual women in a place and time. We will learn different things from beginning with different actual women. For example, if we begin our analysis with African American women workers in the US, as Kimberlé Crenshaw

[37] See also Maria Stern's discussion of studying a "most" marginalized subject (2006: 178).

[38] Furthermore, attention to the rights of humans leads to reflection on anthropocentrism.

[39] Moreover, oppression may not take the form of one group oppressing another (Young 1990: 41).

[40] Among so many others see Askin and Koenig [1999] 2000; Bunch 1990; 1995; Mayer 1995a; 1995c.

does,[41] we will learn that political accommodations intended to end discrimination led to unpromising institutional changes for promoting their socioeconomic equality and economic recognition. Crenshaw reveals the ways in which social norms make it difficult for African American women to bring employment discrimination suits. Social norms influence both workplace employment patterns and judges' perspectives on who represents a class (that is, that "Blacks" are black men and "women" are white women). We might not see the problems with anti-discrimination if we study white women's employment discrimination suits.

However, anti-discrimination doesn't alleviate the patterns of injustice perpetuated by hierarchies that are sustained and mutually reinforced across private business practices, social norms, and public political practices. We might begin with Inuit women's attempts to hold someone accountable for the toxicity in their bodies and of their own breast milk, both a function of a diet of caribou, seal, and other animals that are far up the food chain and that store toxic chemicals in their fat tissues.[42]

We might juxtapose one experience with another.[43] The challenge for curb cut theorizing is to offer an analysis that has broader *explanatory, not normalizing*, power. For example, the cycle of vulnerability which Susan Okin describes as existing between gendered families and gendered workplaces is a complicated process with no beginning and no end in which individual actions and choices collectively create the limiting conditions of individual action and choice.[44] While individual action may be explained (and even understood by the actor) as one of individual choice, collectively these actions yield social patterns of vulnerability that condition such choices.[45] Okin's subjects in analyzing the cycle of vulnerability were women in or destined for heterosexual marriage. Yet the same phenomenon of a cycle of constrained

[41] Crenshaw 1989. [42] Tenenbaum 1998. [43] Lucas 2004; Narayan 1997.

[44] Okin 1989. Giddens called this "structuration" (1979). Nancy Hirschmann doesn't name it as such but discusses in thorough richness the complexities of the construction of social values, practices, norms, and institutions, and of ourselves and agents living in and constrained by these (2003). Rosenberg explores the differences in how people know (2002).

[45] Mary Rowe uses the metaphor of Saturn's rings to describe the individual character of each instance of sexism, that is its invisibility as a social phenomenon, but the impressive visibility of patterns of exclusion generated by such individual acts taken together (1990; see also Sen 1999b).

agency in which actors create, perpetuate, and render invisible institutions and social norms of oppression can be revealed to underlie most exploitable hierarchies. As we see in Crenshaw, background social and economic conditions make it difficult to see public remedies if the problem itself is in part characterized by public invisibility. The more general (but not normalizing) account of this cycle is that without evidence to the contrary we must assume that: (1) no vulnerability or hierarchy is sustained through either the public or private spheres of interaction alone; (2) no vulnerability or hierarchy is a function of sex, sexuality, ethnicity, class, caste, religion, country of origin, national identity, aboriginal status, immigration status, regional geography, language, cultural practices, forms of dress, beliefs, ability, health status, family history, age, or education alone; and (3) no vulnerability or hierarchy is a function of economics or social recognition alone.

Feminist curb cut analysis does *best* when it works with women in various intersections because their positions are often more visibly dynamic and therefore can help to reveal these interrelated processes which are often insidiously invisible.[46] Again, feminist curb cut analysis depends not on the "most" marginalized perspective but rather on understanding the variety of ways in which different kinds of power marginalize. Feminist curb cutting critical promise is pedagogical: it gives us each a tool for destabilizing our own epistemological confidence, our own confidence that our analysis is "true," and our own confidence that we are analyzing without normalizing.[47]

Returning to the disability metaphor, in designing our architectural landscape, we could rely on our own intuitions to do our best to think about the needs of people with mobility-related disabilities, or we could develop specific guidelines (like the International Building Code)[48] for making appropriate design choices. Neither approach

[46] Although Nancy Fraser recognizes this interrelation in practice, she persists in trying to discuss redistribution and recognition as analytically distinguishable (1997). Such distinctions may be necessary for the purposes of research design, as Robert Bailey notes (1999). However, such distinctions are not unproblematically useful because, as Jeffrey Weeks and Janet Holland note in their introduction to *Sexual Cultures*, "sexuality takes many forms, is patterned in a variety of different ways, and moreover, cannot be understood outside the context in which it is enacted, conceptualised and reacted to" (1996: 1; cf. Butler in Bell and Butler 1999: 168).

[47] In the language of statistics, feminist curb cut theory is theory with no one in the tails.

[48] International Code Council 2002.

would insure that our actual designs did not privilege certain forms of mobility over others.[49] Architects and city planners seek out "rules" to help guide their choices, yet the insights of users are still the most valuable for accommodating disability.[50] In one US city, the first sidewalk access ramps were too steep for a wheelchair because the designers forgot to consider that the footrest of a wheelchair extends in front of the front wheels. Further, certain access ramps seem very attractive to skateboarders who can *inhibit* the mobility of others; certain curb cuts facilitate cyclists' going on the sidewalk to avoid automobile traffic, which has the impact of making sidewalks more harrowing for pedestrians, disabled and able-bodied.[51] We need a method that enables us to *see* that the risks of bicycle travel should not be transferred *to* the disabled and others using the same mechanism that was designed to improve the mobility of the disabled. Rather than relying on our best efforts, which can be fruitless or even harmful despite our intentions, we should help develop *a method of thinking* that is always informed by the experience of the disabled. With such a

[49] Again, curb cutting is a heuristic device inspired by a politics and architectural landscape familiar, and largely successful, in the United States. Of course, the concept of curb cuts is not US-specific (accessible accommodations were supposed to be made at the World Social Forum 2004, but were often an inadequate gesture: a ramp with a huge lip or erosion at the base for example). The ability of curb cuts to be effective at de-privileging certain forms of mobility and accruing unanticipated advantages to unanticipated groups such as delivery people and parents is quite context-specific. Each place may have its own heuristic that better captures the spirit of a destabilizing epistemological standpoint that enables us to see beyond our initial concerns. I am grateful to students at the Maxwell School seminar on methodologies for raising the issue. I am also inspired by the pedagogy of Peggy McIntosh and those who have used her work creatively to stimulate student thinking about privilege (1988).

[50] To illustrate the point, I have students do basic daily activities – go to a coffee shop, get their mail, park, and ask directions at the campus information booth, etc. – in or as if they were in a wheel chair. Devoting less than thirty minutes to these activities, the students gain a range of insights about mobility and the value of a curb cut epistemology. For expository purposes I have articulated this approach in expressly anthropocentric terms; however, curb cut feminism's destabilizing epistemology does not lend itself to androcentrism, or to a privileging of the environment and animals over humanity.

[51] The word "pedestrian" is problematic, but I am using it in the sense of those who want to go where people on foot can go and to do so at approximately the same speed. I share the challenge of tripping over this word in order to illustrate a problem of curb cutting: it is based on an able-body normative assumption of what "normal" access should be.

method, we *constantly* reflect on the problem of mobility and *constantly* work to improve mobility in a respectful way and we are reminded *by the method* to do so and to do a better job of doing so.

Likewise, rather than relying on theorists to do our best in thinking about the challenges and opportunities of marginalized people which could end up reflecting the theorist's epistemological myopia (that is her unexamined view of what constitutes knowledge and of what data constitute evidence), theorists need a *method* for thinking about lived experience and about what it tells us for normative political theory.[52] As noted above, critical theory offers the theoretical foundations for such a suggestion. However, despite its intent, critical theory need not generate the critical practice of social criticism. For example, society might have a coherent explanation for the exploitation of certain groups. Exploitation or discrimination can be seen as appropriate to the social roles of both those advantaged and those disadvantaged by the norms that sustain that hierarchy.[53] Social criticism is made possible by an ability to challenge the coherence of accepted hierarchies to reveal that coherence as an institutionally sustained pattern of unjust or exploitable hierarchy.

According to Michael Walzer, some immanent critics are able to gain a critical distance that enables them to reinterpret social values in light of the experience of those harmed or disadvantaged by them.[54] However, in a world where inequalities frequently exhibit coherent patterns, normative theory must do more than require actionability, consistency, and self-reflection. It needs to offer immanent, external, and cross-cultural critics the tools to wrestle with the struggles and wishes of people in society by challenging *seemingly* coherent political, social, and economic values, practices, and norms and reveal them as mutually reinforcing potentially exploitable hierarchies.

People cannot easily disaggregate their life experiences in order to distance themselves from the bonds that oppress them.[55] Feminist social criticism helps us see this clearly. Gender hierarchy is embedded in all sorts of social relationships that women find valuable.[56] For

[52] Ackerly 2000; Sandoval 2000.

[53] See for example many of the reservations to the Convention for the Elimination of all forms of Discrimination Against Women (United Nations 1979).

[54] Walzer 1987; 1988. [55] Narayan 2003.

[56] As noted above, gender hierarchy is even embedded in movements against certain forms of hierarchy. In attempting to work within the World Social Forum process, feminist and women's groups work to help progressive movements to

example, in a particular family, a woman and a man may be better off together than either would be alone, but the relationship between them may still be hierarchical. Thus "cooperative conflict" is an apt characterization of the way in which families resolve distributional questions and conflict-prone cooperation may describe everyday life within families.[57] Because people are integrated into the social life that oppresses them, theorists need methodological resources for thinking about, critiquing, and changing that life such that the changes proposed respond not only to the struggles and wishes of the vulnerable but also *to their loves and commitments*.[58] To address women's human rights violations we need a theory of human rights that is critical of cultural norms that define "human" *such that to be "human" is to live a raced and gendered life* and that claim epistemological authority such that a raced and gendered life is beyond criticism.[59] In a particular context one's raced, gendered, classed, caste, and otherwise over-determined life may seem from the perspective of the dominant epistemological authority the result, not of inappropriate discrimination, but of *appropriate* culturally defined roles. In designing appropriate political action for securing human rights, the epistemological perspective of curb cut feminism encourages us to focus not only on holding individuals and states accountable for human rights violations, but also on transforming underlying social, cultural, political, and economic institutions and practices such that conditions for the realization of human rights are fostered by the ways in which we live.

An appropriate epistemological perspective for normative theory, curb cut feminism prompts us to ask the questions that enable society

recognize and understand their blinders to those forms of hierarchy with which they are less familiar.

57 Iversen 2003; Sen 1990a.

58 Nussbaum, Honig, and Al-Hibri express their concern along these lines in their responses to Okin (Al-Hibri 1999; Honig 1999; Nussbaum 1999b).

59 Actually, any aspect of one's identity (religion, ability, age, national heritage, immigration status, etc.) which social, political, and economic forces treat as important to the roles and opportunities of those to whom that identity is attributed needs to be the subject of such scrutiny. As Beetham notes, the move from "natural" rights to "human" rights entails the recognition that human rights are a *social*, not natural, design (1998: 60). See also the discussion of essentially contested concepts in chapter 7.

to discern and discuss the difference.[60] Curb cut feminism enables us to see human rights – in the lived experiences and the theoretical articulations of women's human rights activists. The purpose is *not* to privilege the epistemological standpoint of the most marginalized, but rather to adopt an epistemological perspective that requires the curb cut feminist theorist to inform her inquiry with a range of perspectives.[61] In order for curb cut feminism to live up to its theoretical aspirations, its arguments need to be revisited from perspectives initially not considered. If the logic of the original argument holds up under consideration of this subsequent context of marginalization, then the argument is a curb cut feminist argument. Previously unconsidered contexts of marginalization may require a range of modifications. If these are consistent with the underlying logic of the original theory, then we can describe that effort as curb cut feminist theory. The epistemological perspective of the most marginalized and the differently marginalized will be very valuable for developing curb cut feminist theory, but the epistemological practice of continually reevaluating the theorist's epistemological sources and analysis against the aspirations of curb cut feminism are definitive of curb cut feminist theory.

## The method for gathering data

Feminist curb cut analysis starts with the bottom-up analysis encouraged by many feminists.[62] This approach is necessary in order to be attentive to the possibilities identified by Kimberlé Crenshaw of "under-inclusion" and "over-inclusion" of a range of experiences into a falsely universal experience of oppression.[63] Crenshaw cautions that the standpoint approach to identifying forms of oppression risks under-inclusion of certain forms of oppression, that is, it risks not noticing the

[60] Elsewhere I proposed a model of feminist social criticism which I mean to apply here as a guide to the questions that need to be asked (Ackerly 2000).

[61] However, the influence of standpoint theory and standpoint-informed feminist fieldwork is important to this project (Acker, Barry, and Esseveld 1983; Cotterill 1992; Fonow and Cook 1991; Gorelick 1991; Harding 1987; Hartsock 1983; 1998; Kirsch 2005; Smith 1974; 1987; Wolf 1996). Such feminist research places women's experience at the center of inquiry, and rejects positivist frameworks in favor of a more critical perspective.

[62] Ackerly, Stern, and True 2006; Crenshaw 1989; 2000; Enloe 2004; Harding 1987; esp. Stern 2006.

[63] Crenshaw 2000.

problem of forced sterilization as important because it isn't experienced by all women, but only by some women of some races and in some places when in fact it is a symptom of the ways in which multiple oppressions work together to marginalize and to isolate the marginalized from one another. Likewise, she worries about the risks of over-inclusion, for example of treating the trafficking issue as a "gender" issue when, in order to understand and deal with it properly, it needs to be understood as varying by place, and raced, classed, and gendered all the way down.[64] Crenshaw summarizes these dual concerns: "in under-inclusive approaches to discrimination, it is difference that renders a set of problems invisible, while in over-inclusive approaches, it is the difference itself that is invisible."[65] As I specify it, a feminist methodology for experienced-based theoretical inquiry tries to anticipate and mitigate the problems of the epistemological myopia of the theorist and the risks of under-inclusive and over-inclusive conclusions by drawing on a range of critical perspectives and by putting those perspectives in dialogue with one another.[66]

The specific tools will vary by research question, but generally the inquiry will require tools for identifying a range of informants, for promoting deliberation among the informants, for employing provisionally fixed guidelines (such as an interview format, however open), and for promoting critical reflection at all stages of the enterprise. The

[64] Crenshaw doesn't say all this. I think she would agree, but probably because of the audience of the piece from which I cite, I expect she under-theorizes her objections.

[65] Crenshaw 2000: 6.

[66] Glover 1995; Moody-Adams 1997; O'Neill 1995. Also relevant are the principles of participatory action research (PAR) and participatory rural appraisal (PRA) in development studies (Chambers 1994; 1997; Parpart 2000). See Cooke (2001) for a critical assessment and Kesby (2005) for a transformative reinterpretation. Common to each of these traditions is the articulation of a direct connection between research and action, and a devotion of particular attention to power relations in the research process. Perhaps as important in informing my thinking are the feminist iterations and critiques of PRA and PAR which seek to capitalize on the benefits of participation while attempting to mitigate possible androcentric bias and suppression of views on the margins. Notable among these are Patricia Maguire's articulation of a framework for feminst participatory action research (1987), Allison Goebel's discussion of gendered perspectives in PRA (1998), and Guijit and Shah's edited volume devoted to primarily gender-based criticism of participatory research (1998). See also Crawley 1998; Gatenby and Humphries 2000; Harding and Norberg 2005; Hawkesworth 2006a; Kesby 2005; Lennie, Hatcher, and Morgan 2003.

tools for gathering and analyzing the data will differ but have similar qualities. In this and the following section I give examples of these for experience-based inquiry into the normative question of whether there are universal human rights. My exposition follows a nomenclature for and description of normative inquiry set out in *Political Theory and Feminist Social Criticism* (2000) although there I do not apply the methods for achieving the methodological aspirations I support.

## *Insiders, outsiders, multi-sited critics, and multiple critics*

Identifying the silent, the marginal, the unobserved, or those observed by only a few, has been part of feminist activism and scholarship. One interview subject was part of an oral history on Women of Color activists and found herself participating in the project more fully because of the questions she asked:

> I asked them, "well who else are you collecting in terms of women of color? It turns out they didn't have a clue about other women of color to collect. So I started identifying and the next thing I knew I was the one behind the camera. So now I'm on the team collecting activists that they usually don't know a whole lot about. These are women who books haven't been written about. These are not the celebrity women of color but the women of color like the woman who started the first household workers' union in New York City, or the woman who founded the first gay and lesbian center down in Texas. These are great women but they don't get the media play so only other activists know how great they are.[67]

My human rights inquiry has multiple sources of insight about feminist and women's activism: online working groups of women's activists focused on women's human rights and violence against women;[68] five workshops which I organized on networking for women's human rights among donors, activists, policy makers, and scholars; thirty-five workshops and panels at the World Social Forum (WSF) 2004 (Mumbai, India) which Lyndi Hewitt and I observed; interviews conducted at the WSF 2004 by me; interviews conducted in Australia by Bina D'Costa in 2004; interviews conducted in Porto Alegre by Sonalini Sapra and myself at WSF 2005; and the Feminist Dialogues (a feminist meeting preceding WSF 2005) and email questionnaires. During this

[67] IB13 2005. [68] Ackerly 2001b.

project, the collaboration of Bina D'Costa, Lyndi Hewitt, and Sonalini Sapra enriched the project by enabling the data to include a broader range of views, not only because there was more than one person gathering the data, but also and more importantly, because there were multiple ears listening for the silent voices.[69]

The online working groups provided postings that were part of a dialogue about women's human rights which I could observe without intervening to ask questions. The two online working groups, End-of-Violence and CEDAW-in-Action, were sponsored by the United Nations Development Fund for Women (UNIFEM) and moderated and managed by Education Development Center, Inc., Cambridge, MA (EDC).[70] Running October 1998 through January 2000 and February through September 1999 respectively, these working groups invited participants from around the world to share their program experience and their knowledge and experience working against violence against women and for the Convention on the Elimination of all forms of Discrimination Against Women (CEDAW) respectively. Membership was open to all and there was overlap between the groups. Participants were activists, scholars, and policy makers. The activists shared their knowledge of concrete experience in their own organizations or in the work of alliances or partnerships with other organizations.[71]

The workshop participants were activists, scholars, policy makers, and donors. Their proportions varied with each venue.[72] Activist

[69] Lyndi Hewitt and Sonalini Sapra provided invaluable research assistance. Bina D'Costa is a co-author on another project and this data was shared with that project (Ackerly and D'Costa 2004).

[70] CEDAW-in-Action was cosponsored by UNIFEM and International Women's Rights Action Watch. The entire texts were publicly available at http://www.globalknowledge.org/english/archives/mailarchives/endviolence/home.html (last accessed February 2006). The text of the CEDAW working group was available at http://www.sdnp.undp.org/ww/lists/cedaw/threads.html#00128 (last accessed February 2006). For reports on these working groups see www.undp.org/unifem/w@work/, www.undp.org/unifem/campaign/violence/unfpatxt.htm, www.un.org/womenwatch/forums/beijing5/ (the report on violence) (last accessed February 2006). CEDAW-in-Action continued to operate as a listserv after the end of the working group.

[71] For more on these lists and their participants see Ackerly (2001a).

[72] These were held at the University of Southern California (2001), International Studies Association Annual Meeting (2001), Association for Women's Rights and Development in Guadalajara (2002), Sustainable Feminisms Conference at Macalester College, St. Paul, MN (2002), and The World Social Forum in Mumbai, India (2004).

participation in the University of Southern California (USC) conference was funded by USC (though the participation of some scholars was made possible by a Ford Foundation grant for a conference that preceded our workshop). Activist participation was unrelated to any programmatic funding the activists may or may not have received from donors. More than half of the activists at the USC conference did not support themselves by working for their organizations, but rather worked so that they could support their organizations. At USC, the Association for Women's Rights in Development (AWID), Macalester, and WSF there were grassroots activists whose trips had been funded by outsiders or the conference. At WSF there were grassroots activists who participated without external funding, using personal or organizational funds, or by raising money by selling products from their region.

At the WSF panels or workshops, we took copious notes and recorded certain presentations and questions from the audience when the occasion allowed us to ask for permission.

Those interviewed are international and local activists and scholars from fourteen countries. Some of our interview subjects are internationally known spokeswomen for women's interests; some have national reputations; some are unknown beyond their locales. Some have garnered support from national or international sources; others have not; still others eschew any funding. We interviewed activists with a range of ages, working in a range of organizational contexts, from each human-inhabited continent, differently positioned within their local socioeconomic and political contexts, differently positioned in global politics, some able to move about freely, others confined;[73] some more theoretically oriented, some more materially oriented, some who eagerly shared their analysis of the material concerns of feminists, some from culturally accepted movements, others who challenge cultural norms or who are socially outcast. Our informants include those feminists who are visible organizers and participants in transnational feminist dialogues and those at the margins of these dialogues – some aware of them, but not invited to participate; others

[73] Nilofar Sakhi was able to come to the World Social Forum 2004 in India with the support of the Global Fund for Women, but her subsequent email correspondence has been limited by the insecure environment in which she works in Afghanistan (I14 2004).

unaware of them. I did not focus on finding those scholars or activists who were known to me before arriving in Mumbai, though we observed many of their panels and I interviewed some. We focused on identifying those whose critical perspectives we would not have been able to know had we not traveled to India – for example those of francophone African feminists who experienced WSF as language outsiders. Finally, we followed up with many who did not have time to be interviewed at WSF and interviewed them via email. In Australia, D'Costa interviewed activists in exile from Asian countries for their human rights activism and Australian women activists from indigenous and mainstream communities.

We sought multiple critics from a range of critical perspectives, yet none of our sources was interviewed as a collective voice representing others. All were asked to identify key components of women's agenda for the next decade; in their responses, while offering their own perspectives, they often supplied evidence for why their account could be taken to speak for many and not just themselves. Our sources had a range of experience with the multi-sited critical perspective. All were minimally multi-sited in that by participating in a transnational online working group, coming to a workshop, living in exile in Australia, or working in and outside indigenous communities, they had moved between worlds. WSF was a world of transnational activism which was new to most grassroots activists. No interview subject was representative in the sense of capturing an essential quality of her group.[74] Moreover, no interview subject displayed an interest in speaking for all women or for all women's human rights activists, though some occasionally spoke for all of humanity. In Mumbai, almost every interviewee shocked me with some aspect of her insight or a turn in her account that could be interpreted as exclusionary.

No matter how we count these sources – online participants or only those who posted to the online working groups; WSF panelists or those who participated from the audience or those who were in the audience; interview subjects; workshop participants; authors or the people cited by authors – they are but a small percentage of those actively interested in promoting feminist and women's issues. While this is an informative sample, it is not a representative sample.

[74] Phillips 1996.

Moreover, there are many silent informants. I documented two forms of this silence in two interviews I conducted of pairs of women. In both, one of the interlocutors hardly spoke and always deferred to the other. In one interview the silence seemed to be in deference to the other's title and in one it seemed as a result of personal style. In the audience of the panels there were those who never voiced the question or comment that was on their minds, nor an affirmation or disaffirmation of the insights being shared publicly by others. In the online working groups, there were those who never posted their own views, nor an affirmation or disaffirmation of the insights being shared publicly by others. Others were silent due to myriad conditions that meant they were *not* in the online working groups, *not* at the WSF, *not* my interview subjects, *not* at the workshops and panels I organized, *not* at the panels we observed.

I used a semi-structured interview format with different questions designed to stimulate responses from different kinds of thinkers.[75] Some questions invited explicit analysis. Others invited story-telling. The point was to offer the interview subject a range of opportunities for expressing her ideas.[76]

## *Reflective opportunity*

What all of these informants have in common is that they are stepping out from their daily lives to reflect on what they are doing. I draw my insights from them at the moment of their stepping out. The online working group participants step away from their work to reflect on their work as participants in the working group. The conference and workshop participants step away from their work and family obligations to participate in the conferences. Interviewees are most often conference participants and therefore are likewise interviewed at a moment of stepping out of their daily lives.

This is important. I am not observing them in their activism, though secondary scholarship on women's activism informs this inquiry. I am not studying their leaflets, their speeches, their organizational decision making, or the interpersonal dynamics of their daily lives. Future work could do so.

[75] Rosenberg 2002. [76] Cf. Bickford 1996; McAfee 2000; Young 2000.

Distinctively, this is participant observation of feminist and women's activists stepping out of their daily lives and work and into a reflective moment. Especially for those interviewed at the World Social Forums or at the Feminist Dialogues, the moment of our interview is set in a broader context of reflection. Reflection is not the only thing that people do at these larger gatherings when they are away from their daily routines and obligations, but reflective opportunities abound in such settings and are encouraged by them.

### *Political moment*

In addition to being reflective spaces, the World Social Forums and Feminist Dialogues were also political spaces. They are spaces where organizers articulate a political purpose to the gathering. And they are spaces that sensitize participants to political issues. Further, many of my interviews took places after a political moment. I often identified interview subjects because I had observed them to experience a political moment – a moment in which they had freshly articulated a new understanding publicly or a moment when they had been silenced by patterns of interactions or by a particular interaction. By interviewing people in a political moment, they were expected to be attuned to questions of power that under everyday circumstances may have been invisible due to the normalization of privilege.

### *Scholar as critic: promoting inquiry, deliberative opportunity, and institutional change*[77]

This project takes advantage of some opportunities for stepping out created by others: the World Social Forum, Feminist Dialogues, and the Association for Women's Rights and Development Tri-annual Meeting. I also created opportunities by hosting a workshop at the University of Southern California 2001, organizing a panel for AWID 2002, organizing panels at WSF 2004, and supporting Sonalini Sapra's panel at WSF 2005.

[77] On the roles of critics see Ackerly (2000: chapter 4). Cf. Nussbaum's mention of "women's collectives as both supporters of women's capabilities and incubators of good thought about women's problems" in her acknowledgments (Nussbaum 2000b: xx).

### *Deliberative inquiry*

Dynamic exchanges among people reflecting together and over time on a subject can yield valuable insights. There were three opportunities for deliberative inquiry in this study. First, the participants in the online working group were engaged in deliberative inquiry. They asked each other questions and responded with great variety and interchange when they were asked questions by the moderator. Second, all of the workshops enabled deliberative inquiry, both those organized by me for the purpose of this project and those we observed at WSF. Third, the workshops organized by me benefited from an ongoing dynamic quality that resulted from my using the learning of one workshop and the circulation of workshop reports to stimulate different kinds of discussions or greater depth of inquiry in the subsequent ones.

### *Guiding criteria*

Guiding criteria are the artificial boundaries created for heuristic or expository purposes that are necessarily limiting and therefore understood as guiding, not definitive. At the outset of experience-based research, the guiding criteria are the general questions of the research project and the more specific assumptions and questions which manifest themselves differently by research method (e.g. structured interviews, semi-structured interviews, content analysis, etc.). Generally, guiding criteria are a working list of issues and concerns, revealed by the experience-based inquiry as important to the struggles and wishes of the age. Some of these may have emerged historically as important and, though they are secured in most places for most people most of the time, they remain important guiding criteria either because of their historical significance or because they are always being reinterpreted in the present.

Defining the guiding criteria of a project signals the deliberative moment in which the scholarship is situated. In addition to its heuristic purpose, defining the guiding criteria of a project signals the literatures and other sources of knowledge that the research is building upon and enables researchers to reflect on the scholarship in its particular context.[78]

[78] Jacqui True and I call this the "deliberative moment" of feminist critical research (Ackerly, Stern, and True 2006).

In my project I asked by what standards do feminists and women activists guide their activism at the dawn of the twenty-first century? Do they use a human rights discourse? What issues do they think should be on the agenda of feminist and women's activists in the coming decade? At the stage of data collection, the guiding criteria are these questions. I ask these, not other, questions. These questions situate my work as being aware of *a* range of feminist and activist discourses and aware of *some* of the strategic choices activists make.

Employing the guiding criteria as a dimension of my theoretical method, during the research process I treat the notion of human rights as *immanent* and *dynamic*. I do not assume that any of my interlocutors has the same list of rights in mind when she or he reflects upon human rights. I do not even assume that they think that "human rights" or "feminism" describe their concerns. I ask them about feminists' and women's agendas in the coming decade and the past decade. I ask them about common experiences and cultural and material differences. I ask them about obstacles and opportunities. Each set of questions offers an opportunity for interlocutors to reveal their understanding of human rights – through what they actually *do* and how they *speak* about their work. A provisional characterization of what human rights are comes into being only at the analytical stage, not at the data collection stage.

## *Skeptical scrutiny*

As the preceding discussions demonstrate, skeptical scrutiny is a part of the proposed method, used in identifying sources, promoting deliberative inquiry, and defining and refining guiding questions. When identifying appropriate sources, I used skeptical scrutiny to stretch my imagination as to who would constitute "good" interview subjects and where I might find them. When identifying how to gain a broad spectrum of perspectives, I used skeptical scrutiny to suggest the range of sources I ultimately use – online working groups, workshops, and individuals – and to mitigate hierarchies or perceptions that have the potential to inhibit deliberation.

Similarly, I subject my participant observation techniques and interview methods to skeptical scrutiny. When evaluating the field research questions as the guiding criteria, I looked for ways in which the ways I ask my questions and collect my data abuse or mask power inequalities, excluding certain possible answers by not asking certain questions or by asking questions in a certain way. As curb cut analysis would suggest, it is most important to direct skeptical scrutiny toward power inequalities, misuse of power, and exclusionary processes and outcomes whether these are masked within institutions or hidden in individual actions.

Nussbaum and Cynthia Enloe assert the value of skeptical scrutiny for data collection when they endorse curiosity as a research method.[79] Nussbaum writes: "I believe that through curiosity and determination one can surmount these hurdles – especially if one listens to what people say."[80] In the next chapter, I describe some specific methods for focusing our curiosity and determination and for listening in the analytical aspects of the inquiry. These methods enable us to be attentive to the ways in which we scholars are positioned (by our race, class, nationality, etc.) within the power dynamics related to the subject under scrutiny.

## Does experienced-based inquiry stop here?

Susan Okin and I did not see each other at the World Social Forum in Mumbai. There was so much feminist activism to observe that over five days she and I were never in the same place. She had been to see grantees of the Global Fund for Women and I had spent my entire time at WSF. Over a kitchen table a few weeks later we reflected on our observations. Individually and collectively we had seen so much. She was already able to tell one story: that there were two kinds of women's activists, those fighting for their rights and those working to make women aware of their rights. For her the consciousness of one's rights was practically and theoretically important. My picture was more messy. I heard women aware of some rights, but not sure that rights related to sexuality or even that cultural rights were as important as material rights. My research assistant, Lyndi Hewitt, heard one woman discover for herself the rights discourse as a way of talking about all forms of violence against women (over ten years after this insight had a catalytic affect on transnational feminist organizing).[81] And just as soon as Lyndi Hewitt heard one woman discover the activist

[79] Enloe 2004; Nussbaum 2000b. [80] Nussbaum 2000b: 10.

[81] "Overcoming Gender-Based Violence in the Private Sphere." January 19, A11, 5–8 p.m. Organized by Bread for the World.

framework, I heard some academic women abandon the human rights framework or accuse other women of using it for professional advancement.[82]

What does this feminist noise teach us about human rights? Two potential hypotheses emerge from Okin's and my observations: (1) that awareness of rights is an important precondition for rights activism, but that lack of awareness of one's rights doesn't mean rights are not universal; and (2) that the human rights discourse is a political discourse whose effectiveness in working for women's human rights is not related to an underlying moral argument. Without a methodology for gathering and analyzing our experience-based data, the argument for either of these views relies on sociological and normative work. Of course, with good field notes, one could illustrate the argument the way that the *Voices of the Poor* series illustrates the World Bank's argument about poverty by citing the words of those who were previously only the faces of poverty.[83] But the *analysis* would remain at the normative, sociological, economic, or political level. Praxeological inquiry requires seeking from experienced informants how *they* theorize about human rights (whether or not they make use of theoretical or social science resources such as a post-colonial critique of neo-imperialist capitalism). We might learn from our empirical observation that consciousness is a definitive characteristic of a global citizen aware of her rights in an international system or that a range of social, material, sexual, and identity differences mean that there is no theoretical basis for a global citizen or her claims to universal human rights.

If we terminated our use of experience-based inquiry at the stage of data collection, it would be difficult to say which view (or some more sophisticated version of either) should hold sway. Competing views could be amply supported by quotations from interview subjects and descriptions of social action. However, the curb cut method of empirical inquiry for normative inquiry I have been describing here requires analytical engagement.

82 "Crises, Violence, and Rights: Finding Human Security in a Globalising World." January 19, 2004, C78, 5–8 p.m. Organized by the National Council for Research on Women.

83 Narayan, Chambers, Shah, and Petesch 2000a; Narayan, Patel, Schafft, Rademacher, and Kochi-Schulte 2000b; Narayan 2003.

# 6 *Listening to the silent voices, hearing dissonance: a methodology for interpretation and analysis*

## Introduction: theoretical analysis with methodology?

The purpose of applying curb cut feminist epistemology to developing the methodology for acquiring insights from activists in chapter 5 is to enable us to derive from women's human rights activists' actions and insights an immanent account of universal human rights. For those unfamiliar with women's activism, it may seem that such sources would *obviously* yield a singular view. For those familiar with women's activism, it may seem that drawing on women's human rights activists for immanent insights about universal human rights *could not possibly* lead to universal agreement because of the vast differences among such activists. In fact, despite the range of differences, a shared theory of universal human rights does emerge from immanent inquiry with women's activists. (As we will see, it is a theory according to which attentiveness to differences is necessary to know and secure human rights.)

The challenge of applying curb cut feminist epistemology to developing a methodology for analytical purposes is to be respectful and appreciative of the range of views yet not to let any particularly well-said or resonating accounts be offered as representative of the range of audible and inaudible views. Theorists can destabilize our epistemology by noticing that through our disciplinary training and practice, we are inclined to be seduced by a well-phrased and convincing argument. In this project, however, I need to take all arguments as *data* and develop analytical methods for thinking through all arguments. The methodology presented here requires theorists to be attentive to the ways that values, practices, and norms (while important subjects within our inquiry) work their magic on us too. Further, the challenge is to use insights from within the data and from outside the data to determine whether a coherent and actionable account of human rights emerges from the analysis and can withstand sustained self-reflection.

The analytical process can include seeking additional data (requiring us to cross back and forth across a boundary between data and analysis that is not crossed in positivist research designs). And it can require that we seek out or even develop additional normative resources (requiring us to loop back and forth between our theoretical framework and our analytical models, again violating the norms of positivist research designs).

Coherence in the context of such diversity means finding a theoretical account that coheres with that diversity, one that is universal not universalizing, one that is theoretically respectful of that diversity, not in search of an epistemological justification for ignoring it. The destabilizing epistemological perspective that is the basis of the methodology lends coherence to the search for an immanent universal in the face of diversity, by reminding us that such a search is always ongoing. The key to carrying out this project, then, is epistemological: we have to be able to understand the justificatory scheme and the content of a theory of human rights to be inextricably and multiply linked: the methodology of analysis is both a source of the legitimacy of the justification for the particular argument *and* a way of determining the content of the theory of human rights.

As discussed in chapter 5, in gathering data we faced two main challenges: (1) those associated with seeking out silences; and (2) those associated with seeking out differences among activists. In the analytical phase, these are likewise important. We need to be attentive to views that did not get voiced in this project, to the differences among those that did get voiced in the project, *and* to the differences between these. Thinking critically about my data collection methods and drawing on the insights about silence and marginalization offered by my informants themselves, I can be attentive to absences and silences in the data. Likewise, I give extra critical attention to the meaning of the differences, not just the similarities, among the ideas of my informants. Given the desire that experience-based inquiry be informed by such a broad range of participants, and given the ever-expanding understanding of what constitutes a marginalized source of insight, it is not surprising that my informants offer broadly differing views. Taken at face value, they do not agree about problems, solutions, strategies, or conceptual framing. What methodological tools enable us to learn from this diversity and disagreement?

The intuition of curb cut epistemology inspires us to notice and consider these dilemmas. How do we make analytical choices and evaluate analytical insights with political legitimacy of the justificatory scheme in mind? That is, what does attentiveness to epistemology, diversity, and disagreement require in this context? In short, what and how can praxeological inquiry contribute to normative inquiry?

The activists themselves help inform the answer. One informant says that by working across issues we are able to enhance our analyses.[1] Another informant argues the opposite. In one of the small meetings of the Feminist Dialogue (2005), a group leader argued that feminism is held back by too broad an inclusiveness. A third, Pramada Menon, Director of Programs for Creating Resources for Empowerment in Action, helps us see why the first view, that we must be attentive to difference, offers greater long-term analytical potential and is more inclined to strengthen the movement. She argues that working through the diversity of views, even those incompatible with one another, keeps movement activists going and challenged.[2]

Under the methodological view of experience-based theorizing presented here, the scholar–social critic is not merely a spokesperson for activists. Nor can she walk away from the theoretical disharmony of the range of feminist voices, echoing their dissonance without analytically working through the differences that cause it. In interviews and in mixed gatherings of scholars and activists, activists asked academics not to be confined to thinking in or outside of a given box, and not to waste the time resource of activists.[3] As an academic with significantly more comfort and freedom than most of my informants, my ethical obligation to my informants and to those with whom and for whom they struggle is to try to work through their differences using the time and resources that they don't have.[4] However, the luxury of time should not be combined with exuberant self-confidence in my own analytical abilities, but rather with the reflective insights of the informants themselves. Interviews (and postings to working groups) offered

[1] IS5 2005.

[2] IB2 2005. See Lakoff's argument that progressive movements need to do a better job of identifying strategic issues (2004: 29–32).

[3] IB18 2005; IS5 2005. These two interview subjects reiterate ideas that activists discussed together in the 2001 Scholar–Activist–Donor conference at USC.

[4] One of the things that time gives activists is trust (I18 2004; IS5 2005). With trust activists are able to work through their differences, so while scholarship cannot replace the relationship of trust between people, it can substitute for the dialogue that would be possible with time and trust.

only a segment of the informants' thinking on women's human rights and women's activism. After ending the interview, they may continue to reflect. Had they heard the views of one another, they might have changed their views, modified them, or been inspired to develop them. Therefore, the analytical stage of this project includes sharing with the informants the theoretical account derived from reflecting on their insights so that they could assess the view developed through my reflection on their insights.

Alternatively, theoretical reflection can lead academic theorists to abandon activists. For example, at a WSF workshop entitled "Crises, Violence, and Rights: Finding Human Security in a Globalizing World," Uma Narayan proposed a move away from women's human rights discourse. By contrast, but to similar effect, in an interview with Vikki Bell, Judith Butler shied away from answering the question "'What is to be Done?' [because] it pre-empts the whole problem of context and contingency, and ... political decisions are made in that lived moment."[5] Both are moves away from practice: Narayan abandons those who may use human rights discourse for social criticism whereas Butler merely leaves such political moves to activists. However, both leave to activists (who are very busy and not trained in theoretical analysis) the challenge of designing political action with theoretical coherence, action that reveals rather than masks institutionalized forms of exploitable hierarchy. Not that they couldn't do it, but why should we make them do it alone?

Instead, I argue that academics can (and therefore should) gain theoretical insights from what activists do and use those insights to strengthen the intellectual and material resources of their activism. The understandings can then be further challenged and developed by being put into dialogue with other normative theories such as those discussed in Part I. Furthermore, the challenge for praxeological inquiry is to gain theoretical insights *from* the activists not only by working with their *often conflicting* views and not merely bringing order to their conflict with normative coherence derived *outside* of their world of experience, but also by engaging with them about the insights that I have had by reflecting on their insights.

These experience-based insights need to be brought into dialogue with other normative theory, but the contribution of praxeological

[5] Bell and Butler 1999: 167.

inquiry derives not from a premature return to normative theorizing when the data analysis gets tough. When the theoretical data analysis gets tough, the tough should get analytically tough and work harder and better with the experienced-based data. Normative theorists interested in experience-based inquiry should not be too quick to resort to their more familiar normative resources to resolve the difficult theoretical challenges posed by the data itself.

When asked how to do political theory by a graduate student, a colleague once answered: "just pick a hard problem and take a whack at it." While that may serve as ample guidance for many, I want to try to be more transparent in this chapter about *how* I use activists' insights to theoretical ends.

To summarize the guiding methodological aspirations laid out so far: (1) attention to epistemology is essential for the political legitimacy of an immanent theory of universal human rights; and (2) curb cut feminist intuition should guide our theoretical methodology for reflecting on the empirical information that can inform our theory. The methodological challenge is to stay attentive to the prospects for power dynamics to become masked behind epistemological claims about what constitutes legitimate analysis. These methodological aspirations guide our gathering of grassroots understandings of universal human rights, as we saw in chapter 5, and they guide our analysis of that data in this chapter.

In this chapter, I offer an exposition of a methodology for theoretical analysis and interpretation. The methods of chapter 5 are designed to reveal differences, particularly some invisible differences. The theoretical methods of this chapter attempt to work within those differences and to be attentive to those yet unnoticed. These methods attempt to reveal additional silences, absences, and marginalizations that are not captured in the data. Importantly, these methods are designed not to ignore, obfuscate, homogenize, or normalize. I intend them to work against our instincts to do so. Finally, these methods are ways of using the insights of the informants themselves to reason through the differences among them. Thus, the fact that so many of my informants offer their insights to this project at moments of reflection – having stepped away from their daily routine – is very important to the way in which the analytical methodology is deployed. Further, that they are asked to assess the final argument when they are back in their contexts – short on time and patience – for lack of clarity or relevance is also just right.

One final comment on exposition: of course, I have worked through the full texts of the interviews, but I can only share part of these. When sharing their reflections, I often cite informants at length, in part so we can appreciate the development of each reflection, in part to model that I am interested in content of the ideas, not the pithiness of their articulation. In general, I don't want to privilege the cleverness of the turn of phrase an informant may use to make her argument seem more compelling over the ideas of someone who meanders through her point, never succinctly articulating the idea, but clearly having a point that needs to be given due consideration. I cite from the interviews and correspondences not to "illustrate" a point, but to invite the reader to join me in engaging with the interviewee and not to entrust to me interpretation of my interviews. I mean to engage my readers in this analysis not merely to relay it to you.

## The method for analyzing data

How are we to make sense of the range of views, characteristic of many, but representative of none, yet individually and collectively full of insights? Should all insights be taken at face value, or could we contextualize our readings of them, just as the interviewees contextualized their own arguments? Can we say that some arguments are wrong or that some activists are wrong and others right? Does employing a feminist methodology of social criticism as political theory mean that we can only repeat what our sources say or can we develop and clarify an understanding of human rights based on what we have learned from them? What does it mean to be true to the activists?

In my practice of feminist praxeological inquiry, the theorist does not merely reflect or represent the views of singular or plural others, but rather joins their efforts by offering her *theoretical* analysis of the activists' analysis, using the argument of one to develop or contest the argument of another.[6] In order to engage with the insights of these critical voices, we need to employ a method. The parts of that method are similar to those used in gathering the data. These work

[6] One way to think about the different roles of critics is to use the idea of comparative advantage. In *Political Theory and Feminist Social Criticism* I observe a range of roles of social critics. Currently some of the theoretical insights about the women's human rights framework are under consideration by many of those who contributed to the project by being interviewed.

together in a dynamic way to challenge static notions within any given interlocutor or the researcher herself. Moreover, they make the relationship between data gathering and data analysis dynamic. Curb cut feminist epistemological reflection is active in this way. And consequently, the relationship between theory-building and theoretical critique is likewise dynamic.

### *Insiders, outsiders, multi-sited critics, multiple critics, and silent or silenced critics*

The methods of acquiring information about silences and absences were described in the preceding chapter. In this chapter, I focus on the analytical methods for filling in some of the silence that will always exist in praxeological inquiry. We will not always be able to fill those silences once aware of them, so we need to develop tools for interpreting absences and silences. We may further develop analytical methods of studying silence that are informed by scholarship and our own empirical evidence.

Absences are particularly difficult to interpret. How do we know why something is not observed: because it doesn't exist, because it is unobservable, or because it is invisible? Many aspects of heterogeneity are invisible, not absent. As we have noted in chapter 2, a range of critical scholars have worked on tools for revealing and interpreting absences; activists also can contribute theoretically to this challenge. For example, women's human rights activists have tried to expose many of these: trafficking for sex work,[7] slavery in domestic work, bonded sweatshop work, death due to illegal abortion,[8] and domestic violence,[9] to name a few.[10] Health, labor, homeless, and indigenous activists similarly attempt to make the invisible visible.

How do we make meaning of silence?[11] Are the silent silenced by overt oppression, as in the case of political dissidents and those

[7] Orhant 2001. [8] Jen Ross 2005. [9] DeFrancisco 1991.

[10] For discussions of women's human rights as needing to be made visible see also Bunch (1990; 1995; 2003), Engle (1992), Fraser (1999), and Mayer (1995a, 1995c).

[11] Bianco 1991; Gal 1991; Glenn 2004; Hedges and Fishkin 1994; Hults 1991; Johannesen 1974; Kramarae and Jenkins 1987; Li 2004; Mitchell 1999; Rich 1979; Taylor, Gilligan, and Sullivan 1995. Many of the contributions to *Feminist Methodologies for International Relations* (Ackerly, Stern, and True 2006) deal with silence as a research question, a methodological challenge, and as difficult to interpret (Ackerly 2007a; also Benhabib 2002: 117).

subjected to domestic violence, silent in their invisibility, as in the case of female immigrant workers,[12] or politically silent as in the case of the Bangladeshi rape-in-war survivors who did not speak about the crimes against them because such speech would only invite other forms of oppression?[13] Are people silent because words cannot express their ideas?[14] Or does silence convey a lot of meaning?[15] Or does silence convey a *particular* meaning?[16]

Most commonly, perhaps, we think of silent voices as *silenced* voices. Those who live in insecure conditions do not feel free to speak their full thoughts or to speak them in certain venues. We might like to think that the venues described above were environments in which all felt comfortable speaking; however, many circumstances create conditions for inequality of voice. These include experience in public venues, experience at international conferences, familiarity with some or none of the audience or panelists, the presence of someone who (for whatever reason, intentional or otherwise) intimidates. Some may be silenced merely by the norms of the venue. Some may not even know about transnational networks, online working groups, or transnational meetings. Even for those who do, it may be hard to get to email regularly so that the opportunity to contribute to a thread of an online discussion is captured by those most able to participate regularly. Or, one may not have been aware of the process of becoming a panelist at WSF until the opportunity to do so passed. Or, in a workshop with donors present one might be intimidated from voicing her views for fear of foreclosing prospective funding opportunities.

Second, as Bina D'Costa argues about survivors of rape during Bangladesh's war of independence, some silent voices are *political voices*.[17] Having had their circumstances and their past words used for the political purposes of nation building often in ways that harmed them, the survivors chose to be silent about their experiences so that their experiences could not be appropriated for others' political purposes.

Third, there is the silence of habituated experience. Maria Stern describes interviewing Mayan women about their sense of security and they answer, "No, I have not received any death threats this month."[18]

[12] Bernstein 2005. [13] D'Costa 2003; Kurzon 1996.
[14] Basso 1970; Bauman 1983. [15] Braithwaite 1999; Bruneau 1973.
[16] Kostash 2004; Nthabiseng 2004. [17] D'Costa 2003. [18] Stern 2006: 180.

Likewise Patricia Foxen describes the rural Maya of Guatemala as perceiving of human rights as a threat.[19] Habits of survival, developed in particular social, political, and economic contexts, can leave insecure people unable to talk about their insecurity or their rights violations.

Fourth, there is the silence of coincidence. For whatever reason, political, economic, and social, macro-level conditions or micro-level circumstances, personal or institutional, some activists who would otherwise be valuable informants were not participants in the online working group, did not come to my attention as a potential workshop participant, came to my attention but for reasons of wanting to create certain kinds of balance in the overall workshop were not asked to participate, did not come to my attention as potential interview subjects, did not come to WSF, or went to WSF but were never at a panel that Lyndi Hewitt, Sonalini Sapra, or I observed. Addressing the analytical challenges posed by the silent voices and other limitations on sources requires making use of the other aspects of the research method.

Given activists' experience with silence and invisibility, comparative political theorists might use the insights of activists to try to see and interpret that which is otherwise invisible. Political theorists should not turn to this mode of interpretation with overconfidence. The challenges of interpreting invisibility and silence include having to guess or suspect that there is silence or invisibility when all she sees is absence. Where to look? Where to listen? Even seasoned ethnographic researcher Sonia Alvarez observes that she has been mistaken, writing about an absence of women's activism[20] when in fact that activism had moved to a different arena.[21]

Observing silence is a resource-intensive research method. Two graduate students and I went looking for women's activism and "silence" at the World Social Forum and Feminist Dialogues. We hypothesized that we would find women both visible and silent in the full range of social movements. This hypothesis was born out, strikingly, within the transnational women's movement. For example, in 2004 at a workshop on Overcoming Gender-Based Violence in the Private Sphere, Lyndi Hewitt observed an audience member propose using the human rights discourse to politicize the issue of violence

[19] Foxen 2000: 358. See also discussion in chapter 9, this volume.
[20] Alvarez 1999. [21] Personal discussion.

against women. The woman was apparently unaware that this has been a common rhetorical and political strategy in many parts of the world and in transnational feminist discourse for well over a decade.[22] By hearing her speak, we were able to observe another form of silence: that transnational feminist activism was not reaching all women activists, nor even all feminist activists. Despite the United Nations conferences of the 1990s, despite global efforts of activists and donors, many activists continue to work in isolation from global dialogue. Through participating in WSF 2004, this audience member was joining the global dialogue. By exhibiting that she had not been part of that dialogue until that panel, she also told of those who continue to be outside of global feminist dialogues.

This means that the empirical basis of an immanent universal theory will always be incomplete. The epistemological assumptions of this project anticipate as much. They anticipate that the theory will have a dynamic quality at the empirical level. However, by further reflecting on the *experience* of those marginalized through the political processes of rights activism we can see that *for the analytical process* we need methodological tools for hearing the silences of the women like the woman who spoke up at the workshop Overcoming Gender-Based Violence in the Private Sphere. We need analytical methods that can give us more confidence than a simple confidence in our mere abilities to imagine "others." Fortunately, this reflection, while demanding, is not resource intensive. The possibility of learning about silences and absences by drawing on our analytical tools privileges those with the luxury of time and a cup of tea to think. But it is not nearly as resource intensive as the transnational travel that constituted a significant aspect of the empirical methods described in the preceding chapter.

This openness is actually open-endedness: open to the experiences of absence, of those not yet included, and thus of ideas that are not yet known, perhaps not yet formulated.

Though we tried to go looking for silences, in one sense no one can. In meetings, I would often select to interview someone who had been silent during the meeting or someone who had asked a question that did not get answered. Sometimes these yielded interesting interchanges, as with Nilofar Sakhi, a women's activist from Afghanistan. For example, Hulan and I never connected for an interview after I initially

[22] See also Ackerly 2001b; World Social Forum Panel 2004.

approached her, so after WSF 2004 we corresponded and she did an email interview. She writes:

> In past 5–10 years the main achievements of women activism and feminist are that now they can widely and easily speak about their rights even in countries like Afghanistan and Iran which is totally captured by religious fundamentalist … [B]efore, talking about women rights meant something awkward not related to the world, not nationally known by the countries mentioned.
>
> Secondly by being active women have created a sense of strength-ship for the other local women and they feel strong support while taking any action against of their traditional restriction and religious fundamentalist.[23]

Analytically, I cannot take the insights of Sakhi, or others to whose breaking of silence I bear witness, as a speaking for those whose silence I did not hear break.

However, the breaking of such silences often brings new ideas into the forum. At a plenary of the 2005 Feminist Dialogues, a meeting of feminists that preceded WSF 2005, Natalia Flores, part of the coordinating group of young Chilean feminists, asked that the plenary discuss the relationship between capitalism and patriarchy. These were two themes that had been repeated throughout the Feminist Dialogues. She shared her thought in Spanish for which there was simultaneous translation, but the plenary facilitator moved on and did not discuss it. We don't know why. For whatever reason, this young person's idea was not explored in the plenary, so I asked if I could interview her and her friends.

[23] I14 2004. One of the ideas that brought me back to political theory from fieldwork in Bangladesh in 1993 was the idea of "strength-ship," as Nilofar Sakhi puts it. I witnessed women becoming aware that their seemingly isolated acts of resistance were not particular acts, but rather collective resources that they shared and could deploy. The practice of rural women living with their husband's family in isolation from their natal family or from potential friends inhibited the realization of their collective resources for social action. The most impressive of these was a "sit-in" to end domestic violence. In a provocative blurring of the lines between public and private, a group of women would stage a sit-in at the home of an abusive husband. Though the home was private and women were generally not out in public, the family space became public when filled with women. The strategy took a more public face when the women sat outside the house of the husband. But given that houses are set off in family *baris* or modest compounds, the sit-in exhibits the "strength-ship" of the women. I cite her in her own English to remind us of the complicated role of language and interpretation in work that depends on the *words* of informants.

Young women activists, such as Flores, feel challenged to talk anew of ideas that older feminists feel they have covered. As another young woman from Brazil, wishing to remain anonymous, illustrates, they struggle to be included for their analytical and experiential contributions to feminism, not just (because they are young) as the voice of "the young." For them age should not be an identity category and in their analysis older feminists are treating youth as an identity:

> My insertion in the social movement, in feminism, is not necessarily [because I am a young person], but, also I deal with these questions. With regard to being a young feminist ... I think there is always a question in mind, in relation of your thinking about the specificity of the [younger] generation. What is that that can be different? What is there that is new?[24]

Her perception was confirmed by much of what the women of the conference said in English about the role of young women: the future leaders of the movement, the energy of the movement, the note-takers, the reporters. None of these appellations exhibit an interest in the analytical insights of young women. She continues:

> to be a young feminist is not simply to be in a meeting of women or in a feminist meeting and then "ah, now we will open the floor and see what young women have to say." No. That is not how to incorporate the young in the process of this feminist movement. [Instead] we need to understand them and to listen to them as part of those who are building something and not simply on a few topics. It should be, not that we listen to what the young have to say about *some themes* ... rather, to me what interests me as a young woman is to occupy all of these spaces. I think that this is a discussion we need to have. ... for instance, here in this very meeting, suddenly all the young women were being asked to be volunteers, to translate, to take notes and I said no, and I could be doing these things, but I said no, I want to pay attention, to make questions and to listen also.[25]

This activist and her colleagues struggle against being identified as young feminists. They want to be feminists, contributing to all feminists discussions, and they feel that they are asked to contribute only in certain spaces at certain moments. In this space, young feminists are

[24] IB7 2005. [25] IB7 2005.

treated as an identity category with ideas on *certain* topics and certain *roles* to fill in the feminist movement.[26]

Even when they come to be heard as young women, as in the case of Elizabeth, an activist with REDLAC, which is a Latin American and Caribbean network of youth for sexual and reproductive rights, they find the space of deliberation delimited by what the organizers expect to hear from them:

> why did we come to this meeting? ... We came because ... well, we are part of a feminist movement and we understand that [it] will be a space for the movement to reflect and think ... where to take the movement, [which] new strategies. [In addition], we believe that the youth, we have to be in this construction of strategies, sources of debates, and we believe that we can contribute from the standpoint of the experience that we have.[27]

Elizabeth goes on to reflect on the challenges facing the movement. One that she identifies is that there are issues within feminism about which feminists themselves disagree. She gives the examples of prostitution, sexuality, reproductive rights. By not debating those "open" issues, as she calls them, feminists are not meeting their challenges:

> What are the challenges that our work faces today? ... It seems to me ... many [challenges] have [been] mentioned in the [plenary and] the discussions [of the Feminist Dialogue 2005] ... but I believe, for instance, that to the organizations that work with sexual and reproductive rights there is a challenge ... of how to reflect on these rights, what are or are not sexual and reproductive rights. And this makes me think that there is [in the] movement ... a challenge of debating open themes, like these themes of [sexual and reproductive rights] and how to include [them], of how are the power relations within the movement, if prostitution is a right or not, which is an old open theme ... Right now ... there are more themes that are not discussed, right?[28]

Though these informants do not represent the views of all young feminists, they indicate that some young women are anxious to participate in the *analytical* work of transnational feminism and are ready to take on the questions that have divided feminists. And these women are concerned that these divisive issues are not being discussed.

[26] This is not unique to feminist movements. Young activists in other movements such as environment, human rights, and peace activism may feel marginalized in the same way.

[27] IB8 2005. [28] IB8 2005.

There may be political reasons outside of the global feminist movement that prevent the breaking of silences. For example, when I wrote to Nilofar to ask her permission to cite her she belatedly responded:

> Thanks for your nice concern and yes!! You can publish my interview anywhere you want as you asked me in your last email.
>
> As you know we are living in a society where religious extremist are capturing all the social and political Sector, and my activities are very democratic so while launching some of my projects and programs for women empowerment I am receiving different threats, and I have to be careful about my life because they are very good in shooting people like us.[29]

In essence, she asked me to use her insights, whether or not I could find her. Her fear, particular to her case, is not unique to her case. Many women's human rights activists live and work in fear.[30]

The theoretical insight from reflections on these silences is that the immanent theory of human rights has to include a dynamic understanding of the political use of human rights. The silencing of the young women at the Feminist Dialogues 2005 was evidence of the ways in which age, familiarity, use of sophisticated concepts, and speaking in English create hierarchies within the transnational feminist movement. While the hierarchy itself is a problem, the loss of big ideas and willing engagement with the tough questions is equally disturbing. Both are the cost of silence; both exhibit why feminists need to be attentive to silences and debates among themselves. The meaning of human rights outlined by the theory has to make room for the debates not yet settled within feminism, let alone those not yet anticipated by feminism. However, ideally, this theory would help us resolve some that still trouble us and anticipate those not yet on our agendas.

Although we can never be confident that we have identified the marginalized perspective that will best challenge our epistemological assumptions, at some point, in order to do justice to those who have given their time toward our research, we need to analyze and share our findings which necessarily requires a form of truncating the search for unfamiliar, marginalized, or oppressed perspectives on human rights. However, even once this process has been truncated, the analytical

[29] Personal communication, February 25, 2004, from Afghanistan (I14 2004).

[30] Rothschild, Long, and Fried 2005; Special Representative of the UN Secretary General on human rights defenders 2001.

work on informant silence must continue in order for experience-based inquiry to bring to normative theory that which normative theory cannot get from sociological inquiry or text-based normative inquiry.

To summarize the theoretical implications that we have seen so far, the issues important to, and the analytical perspectives of, women's and feminist activists are broad and contested such that an immanent theory of human rights needs to include a terrain where disagreement, dissent, and epistemological differences can be the subject of collective reflection *without* consequently undermining the political legitimacy of the universal theory of human rights. The analytical methods discussed so far suggest that we need a theory of human rights that has both unequivocal political legitimacy and openness to unresolved and unimagined differences. The theory needs to be informed by a range of critical perspectives, *particularly* those of the silenced and silent. In the next three sections I describe three general dimensions of a dialogical, always ongoing methodology for analysis of experience-based data. My purpose is to mine this data for theoretical insights about whether there can be a theory of universal human rights and the content of that theory. The method would need to be significantly adopted for the purposes of making empirical claims. The three dimensions of methodological tools used here – deliberative inquiry, guiding criteria, and skeptical scrutiny – were themselves identified in experience-based inquiry about the normative theoretical methods of Third World feminist activists and researchers.[31]

## *Deliberative inquiry*

Deliberative inquiry challenges the ontological perspective of research subjects as objects of study and theorists as constructors of knowledge. While the theorist assumes the constructive role, she can also reflect on the ways in which by doing so she enacts or breaks down a power relationship with her research subject.[32] In addition, deliberative inquiry is a methodological tool for acknowledging that, because we conduct research in time and space, both the data collection and data analysis processes get truncated in a way that is theoretically arbitrary.

As a part of a theoretical method, deliberative inquiry makes it difficult for the theorist to sustain epistemological myopia.[33] Of course, it

[31] Ackerly 2000. [32] Ackerly 2003; Smith 1999. [33] Cf. Mills 1997.

is possible and skeptical scrutiny can help undermine it further, but the point is that by using deliberative inquiry, the theorist exposes herself to a range of views that in all probability will not be consistent with each other. In this way, deliberative inquiry lays bare the role of the theorist in *constructing* a theoretical argument from her observations. The observations themselves are not theory, nor can she credit the interview subjects with authoring the theory. Deliberative inquiry is a methodological way of preventing the theorist from relying on too few observations, on the particularly well-phrased insights of one or a few interlocutors, or on insights that confirm a provisional theory she may consciously or unconsciously hold.

Using tools for deliberative inquiry, I try to solicit the perspectives of those who have been silent in the online working group and in meetings. For example, with the online working group, I shared my findings in a summarized form with the End-of-Violence group, which continued after I completed my study of the group, and got feedback on my insights. I also offered to share a paper based on the group with its participants. Some accepted and some sent back brief comments.

In the case of the online working group, it was easy to contact participants, including individuals whom I wished to cite in order to enable them to approve of their words. This one-on-one correspondence also enabled authors to explain the context of their remarks as necessary.

In order to engage deliberatively with the interview subjects, when possible, respondents receive the transcript of their interview or posting, a summary of my findings that uses accessible and familiar language and concepts, a copy of the context in which I place their remarks (a draft paper or chapter), and the opportunity to comment on my work or to modify or develop their contributions to the project. For many WSF-based interviews, post-interview contact was difficult. However, where successful, these exchanges enabled interviewees to make verbal some of the non-verbal communication not captured in the transcriptions.

Other feminists have interpreted the methodological requirements of deliberative inquiry differently. For example, Maria Stern constructs a narrative text in collaboration with her interview subjects, but once leaving the field, she no longer communicates with her research subjects.[34] The methods of deliberative inquiry enable the interview

[34] Stern 2006.

subjects to be aware of the differences they have with other activists if they were not and to assess and comment on my analytical resolution of those differences on their own familiar linguistic and conceptual terrain. Seeing their thoughts in their own full interview transcript reminds them of their thinking in a moment of critical distance from their daily work. Juxtaposed with the ideas of others in the book manuscript and in the short letter that summarizes the major arguments of the book, the contributor is able to see her ideas in dialogue with others' ideas. She is invited to share her insights on both her own contributions and on the overall argument.

While I share my academic writing with my informants, I do not expect this chapter to satisfy their conceptual or practical interests. The findings and evaluation of activists' strategies that may be of practical interest to activists are in chapter 9 and have been circulated to them in a letter when I was soliciting final approval for my use of their citations.[35] Having heard so many activists say they wondered if anything ever came of the work a researcher did with them, I think that the attempt to share findings with those who granted permission to use their ideas long ago is an ethical dimension of the methodology that is as important to the credibility of research as it is to the informant. It is a way of enacting the theory.[36] In other kinds of research the sharing of findings might look much different.[37] In this project, I enact this theory by joining their effort to analyze and inviting them to join mine.

A discussion of my exchange with a participant in the online working group who had written to the group to discuss her organization's work on domestic violence and rape in Rome illustrates one role of deliberative inquiry in theoretical analysis. From this discussion, we see that immanent theorizing is neither a method of taking ideas from grassroots sources nor of imputing to grassroots sources our own preconceived theoretical insights. But rather it is a dynamic process of theoretical engagement some of which is done with sources and some of which is made possible by those sources but not narrowly reflective of any source's insight.

[35] Approval packets contain a cover letter, a summary of findings, the book manuscript with their text highlighted, the transcript of their interview, the translation of their interview if relevant, and a thank you gift.

[36] White 2000: 8. [37] Ackerly forthcoming-a; Smith 1999.

Francesca Pesce worked for an organization that did and tried to do many of the things that others who had written into the online working group had described. She shared perspectives with women from Russia, India, and Turkey. The posting of Women for Women's Human Rights (WWHR) from Turkey about their work on the civil code prompted her to write.

To follow up on her posting to the working group and to gain her permission to be cited, I contacted Francesca Pesce. In personal correspondence she revealed that in her posting to the online group she had censored her criticism of her own organization's approach, which had become more narrowly focused on support for survivors of domestic violence and rape and on some training for police and other social services who come into contact with survivors. Instead, in her posting she portrayed the organization as continuing to do work that she thought it should do even though it was no longer doing so. After posting her message to the online working group, she left the organization and was now working in an organization that in her view did a better job of dealing with domestic violence and rape because it worked to change the social context, not just to support women in dealing with gender violence in the existing social context.[38]

This exchange with Francesca Pesce illustrates that deliberative inquiry can reveal silences and contestation. Without my personal exchange with her, the view of her former organization – that support and training for survivors was more strategically appropriate than the more expansive socially oriented perspective of Pesce – might have been absent from this inquiry.

How do we analyze these two views? I cannot privilege the Pesce view that the realization of human rights requires a structural transformation of social, political, and economic practices, a view with which I have great sympathy and which I recognize in many feminist and women's activism and scholarship.[39] With both views available – the service provision view and the structural criticism view – we might be inclined to use the structural view, the one that comports well with other feminist work on violence against women. However, our first insight from this analysis is not about which view to use at all. Rather, it is an epistemological reminder that sometimes views of which

[38] See Pesce 1998 and personal correspondence, May 16, 2001.
[39] E.g. Bunch 1990; Carrillo 1990.

I am aware may have other views that conflict with them, and even when I am unaware of a specific conflicting view, I must suspect that there are some. The key theoretical insight from the Pesce story is not actually about violence against women, it is that knowledge provided by any source is always partial and contested. The immanent theory of human rights needs to take seriously that in a single context both structural and individualistic approaches can be seen as strategically appropriate.

As Pesce describes in her original message to the working group, activists and the Minister for Women's Equality had proposed:

> the introduction in the civil code of the possibility of provisional measures aiming at sending the violent man away from the family home, in order to prevent the woman from having to escape the violence and coming to our shelters, hiding away with her children and having to start her life all over again somewhere else. ... [A] bill in this sense ... has been "resting" in the Parliament drawers since.[40]

As in many of my informants' analysis of their successes and failures, Pesce places the blame for the bill's failure in culture. People see:

> this kind of provision as a menace to the unity of the family; the Catholic culture in Italy has for many years fought against (and still is trying to prevent) any kind of measure that "poked" into family issues.[41]

Given these constraints, Pesce's focus on social outreach – "a series of tailored seminars called 'Bullies and dolls' in high schools of the city and province of Rome," police and social worker training, and media outreach – seems at once necessary and of dubious promise. With this context understood, when another organization chooses to deal with gender violence with a focus on the individual survivor, we cannot be certain whether the difference between the two approaches exhibit different theoretical understandings of human rights, different experientially informed understandings of the appropriate strategic approaches for that context, different experiential and financial resources, or different temporal pressures (for example the immediate needs of current survivors versus long-term social needs for ameliorating the problem). Attentive to differences and silences, our analysis cannot lead decisively to one of these interpretations.

[40] Pesce 1998. [41] Pesce 1998.

However, taking these different views together, we can see that because activists' actions are constrained by social context, we cannot analytically determine from their strategies alone if they view human rights in a particular theoretical way.[42] Therefore, while our immanent argument for human rights may at some times be inspired by activists, this example illustrates that it can also be *shaped* by activists. Using curb cutting reflection, whatever theoretical framework we offer for universal human rights, if it is to respect difference and disagreement, then the theory cannot side with one approach or another. It must describe a path that either would take. From this example we see that an immanent theory of universal human rights has to offer a theoretical foundation for both individual-oriented activism in which survivors are the focus of attention *and* socially-oriented activism in which social, political, and economic values, practices, norms, and institutions are the subject of attention.

Taking their arguments together, as immanent theorizing through difference requires, a universal human rights theory cannot treat as separable the individual and social experiences of rights violations. Individual rights violations must be interrogated for their structural supports and the enabling structural causes of human rights violations must be interrogated in order to determine if a focus on these may make some others whose rights are violated not visible.

From this practice of deliberative inquiry we see specific implications for analysis of human rights strategies for their theoretical insights and general theoretical implications. First, in order for the analysis to be fully informed, structural *and* individual analyses need to be part of experienced-based inquiry. Second, taking these strategic insights analytically, an immanent universal *theory* of human rights needs to treat as theoretically important both structural and individual factors of rights violation. Both are necessary for creating the conditions of rights violation.

Feminist theoretical reflection on what it would mean to take such reflection seriously can be useful here. Moira Gatens argues that this dual approach to women's rights has been part of women's rights

[42] Loretta Ross discusses the need to work within social justice movements in the United States to develop the theoretical and strategic understanding of human rights as a resource (IB13 2005).

activism since the Enlightenment.[43] Consider, further, the arguments about vulnerability, capability, and freedom put forward by Okin, Sen, Nussbaum, Gould, and Hirschmann.[44] Each gives us a way of understanding the relationship between individual choices and the socially constructed constraints on those choices. Okin argues that social and economic conditions make women and men choose patterns of private and economic life that put women in a vulnerable economic position. This vulnerable economic position makes them vulnerable within families as well.[45] Further, each of these feminists, but particularly Hirschmann, helps us understand that the structural conditions that constrain our choices actually end up influencing who we are and influence our choice-making processes.[46] Of course, our choices and choice-making processes influence the context in which we make those choices. How much of something worthy of being called freedom we realize in this process might be measured by our ability to realize our capabilities (as Sen and Nussbaum argue) or to realize effectively our positive freedom (as Gould argues).

While the individually and structurally oriented strategies may seem to describe analytically distinct approaches, feminist theory can help us see the activists' analyses as complementary. This is not to impose some ideas from fairly recent feminist thought on activists' insights, but rather to make sense of differences among activists that are revealed through deliberative inquiry. It may be that these differences reveal a terrain of difference as was made visible by young women in the preceding section. Or, it may be that these differences are the result of incomplete epistemological assumptions – as in the case of Pesce's new and old organizations – which, when juxtaposed, reveal a more complete theoretical understanding.

Using a destabilizing epistemology that encourages us to look past a coherent understanding that exhibits consistency with other views,

[43] This discussion is part of an exposition in Gatens (2004). In my discussion of the legitimacy of human rights, I discuss the substantive argument of her article, which is very useful to, and consistent with, the overall theoretical argument of this book.

[44] Gould 2004; Hirschmann 2003; Nussbaum 2000b; Okin 1989; Sen 1999b.

[45] Sen also considers these issues (1990a; 1990c).

[46] The power of social norms on our views of ourselves and society (our "social imaginary") inspires the use of imagination in Cornell (1998), Ackerly (2005b), and Peterson (1990).

deliberative inquiry is a theoretical method for broadening the temporary boundaries of immanent theorizing. For the academic, familiar with contemporary feminist theories of freedom, the methodological turn described here may not seem necessary for this insight about the relationship between individual and structural sources of rights violations. However, by situating the argument in this methodology, the argument gains the epistemological and political legitimacy of being informed by the rich differences of women and feminists from around the world.

## *Guiding criteria*

Our political attention to epistemology and our curb cut intuition that each liberating insight should make opportunities for further liberation more visible are guided by and inform the guiding criteria of our critical search for a universal theory of human rights.

While my research subject is "rights," I do not let my question under-determine or over-determine the range of responses. If over-determined, the research question would be defined within epistemological boundaries that would limit the theoretical possibilities for the meaning of human rights – their content, their role in criticism, and the basis of their political legitimacy. I discussed this problem in chapter 4 with reference to Joshua Cohen. If under-determined, the research question would be defined without epistemological boundaries such that no theoretical account of human rights would be possible. Thus, the guiding criteria provide yet another way of articulating *in the analytical methodology* the role that a destabilizing epistemology plays in the resulting normative theory: it sets the boundaries, boundaries that are dynamic and porous, boundaries that we crisscross.

Although I have in this project a selection bias toward those comfortable with the rights discourse among my working group participants, interview subjects, panel presenters, and audience members, and thus would expect most to be working with "rights" as at least one of their discourses of criticism, these informants do not have the same view of rights nor are their views or the views of those with whom they work necessarily well-developed.[47] The point is illustrated by a gender and development expert from Guinea-Bissau: while "many of our

[47] For a discussion of rights discourses see Gatens (1996; 2004).

people . . . work in the field of human rights," their understanding is abstract. She adds:

> We must seek out and put into place methods that can help people to work out the concepts better, to internalize them and go out and put them into practice on a day-to-day basis.[48]

The same point is made by Poonam Arora, an academic formerly from India now in the United States:

> We would be dishonest if all we did was work it out in our minds and on paper. It would be really futile. We would have no legitimacy. On the other hand, organizing and starting a movement, if we don't have a history of what went wrong or what are the dangers, what are the vulnerabilities that we learn from theorizing? If that was not informed then that would fail, too.[49]

Taken together these informants are arguing that we need to reflect and to reflect as we practice. The theme that clarifying our understandings requires engagement in activism *and* reflection recurred in many interviews. This was not so surprising given that many of the interview subjects were activists participating in a dialogue that facilitated collective reflection – the online working groups, the conferences, the Feminist Dialogue, and the World Social Forums. So we see in two ways our epistemological assumption that a theory of human rights needs to be informed by a range of perspectives leads us to have a dynamic view of human rights. The differences among critics makes us need a terrain for debate that does not undermine the political legitimacy of human rights (as we saw in the section on critics) and the need to have boundaries on our theoretical inquiry without closing off reevaluation of those boundaries requires that our guiding criteria be informed by critics of different perspectives *and* by deliberative inquiry with and among them.

In sum, guiding criteria are dynamic, immanently determined fuzzy and porous boundaries for focusing, but not narrowing, critical inquiry. Now that we know what *kind* of guidelines guiding criteria are in the analytical process, let's look specifically at which notions of human rights became the boundaries of our inquiry. I began my inquiry with no guiding criteria about what human rights were, but with the intent

[48] I1 2004. [49] IS3 2005.

of respecting the view of those who thought that human rights were a source of political legitimacy for their activism.

The curb cutting approach leads us to start with women activists, because they are active in all social justice movements.[50] As a scholar–activist with Development Alternatives with Women for a New Era (DAWN) complains:

> Just because women push for recognition for other issues, they all become women's issues. We are picking up the baggage! It should be taken up by men as well! ... We have inherited issues by involvement.[51]

When women activists pick up the full range of social justice issues, they do not marginalize men, but rather work toward solutions that achieve the human rights of all.

Given the scope of their concerns, women are a good source of guiding criteria for human rights. Guided by their perspective, the scope and content of human rights, their sources of political legitimacy, and the role they play in social criticism are less over-determined and less under-determined than other approaches might be.

Loretta Ross, the founding executive director of a human rights education NGO in the United States, starts us off with a broad guideline by which we might define the list of human rights:

> I'm interested in doing human rights education because everybody has heard the phrase "human rights" but nobody knows the eight categories of human rights protections to which we are all entitled: civil rights, political rights, economic rights, social rights, cultural rights, environmental rights, developmental rights and sexual human rights. If you don't know those eight categories then you really don't know how to develop an appropriate strategy to advance those rights.[52]

Attentive to differences among activists, we will also need to be attentive to the differences among activists about *which* rights are indicated by each of these headings.

Further, some activists might argue that *specific* rights that might seem to fall under one of these eight categories should be singled out. Mary Robinson, United Nations High Commissioner for Human Rights 1997–2002, in a 2005 speech argued that violence against

[50] I5 2004; IB13 2005. [51] ID23 2004. [52] IB13 2005.

women needed to be a focus of international human rights efforts.[53] Her argument reasserts what women's human rights advocates have been arguing for centuries, that violence against women, while intersecting with other rights issues – civil, political, economic, social, cultural, environmental, developmental, and sexual human rights – is never adequately addressed from within any one of these. The problem of violence against women intersects with each of these categories of human rights.[54]

How can that be? Women are victims of civil rights violations by the state *and* private violence against women prevents them from exercising their civil rights in public (Universal Declaration of Human Rights 1948: article 5, the right not to be tortured). Women are victims of political rights violations *and* private violence against women prevents them from exercising their political rights (Universal Declaration of Human Rights 1948: article 20, the right to assemble and associate). Violence and fear of violence keeps women from the polls (Universal Declaration of Human Rights 1948: article 21, the right to vote). Women may be free to express their views in public in the formal sense and endure violence at home for doing so (Universal Declaration of Human Rights 1948: article 19, the right to free expression). Women are victims of economic rights violations *and* violence against women prevents them from going to work (Universal Declaration of Human Rights 1948: article 23, the right to work). Women may be formally free to work and yet subject to violence against women in their place of work. Women are victims of social and cultural rights violations by the state *and* violence against women threatens them from exercising those rights even when they are formally respected (Universal Declaration of Human Rights 1948: article 26, the right to education; article 27, the right to participate in the cultural life of the community; and article 29, the right to exercise one's rights and freedoms).

Given that, guided by our epistemological assumptions, we *begin* with women activists who see women's rights as related to men's rights, it is not surprising that a notion of the rights of all humans as interrelated emerges from our analysis of their insights: they demonstrate that, by promoting the rights of women because women and men have the same rights, we will be promoting the rights of all of humanity.

[53] Robinson 2005. [54] Bunch 1990; Carrillo 1990.

However, a more complicated understanding of the interrelation of the rights of all women emerges in the activism of women. This more complicated understanding of interrelation emerges *because* of the differences among women. This understanding of human rights emerges as a result of thinking through an admittedly incomplete perception of the differences among feminists and their critical perspectives on rights.

Women – even women who see their understandings of rights as differing from the understandings of other women – often see themselves in solidarity with one another. In my research, these solidarities often appeared fragile. Differences among women in their beliefs and in their historical relationships of trust with others in the movement often seemed to exclude or marginalize some women. A feminist activist for Asian women said when reflecting on transnational feminist spaces:

> to get into this women's movement ... [you] have to be, how do you say, patient. And then, you have to know who to work with. There's, how do you say, there are also some kinds of politics here too.[55]

Despite these politics, women are committed to working through and across differences in order to change the world. They call on each other and themselves to invest themselves in what they articulate as shared work:

> "Let's cross borders together to change the world."[56]
>
> For me, feminism means that I commit myself, with all of my force, with all of my faith, in the struggle so that women succeed in this endeavor.[57]

The first is a slogan repeated at Women's World Congress 2005 and the second is a definition articulated by an activist from Burkina Faso.

In the remainder of this section I demonstrate how I used this analytical method to think through the differences among activists. Although activists come together in these transnational spaces for a brief but intense time, I can take their insights home and reflect on them and put them in dialogue with each other. In my methodology, the guiding criteria are dynamic and provisional in their guidance. They provide a fuzzy and porous boundary. Because our destabilizing

[55] IB14 2005.

[56] Slogan announced at the end of the Women's World Congress 2005. See footnote 494* and accompanying text.

[57] I2 2004.

epistemology requires us to worry about boundaries, any boundaries created by a provisional notion of the guiding criteria inspire an effort to seek out other formerly absent voices, and to use deliberative inquiry and skeptical scrutiny (discussed in the following section) to revise and enrich our understanding of the guiding criteria.

First, observing online working groups, I identified a range of activism addressing a range of issues. I witnessed activists using the human rights discourse to define that discourse for themselves and to transform its political import. They use the discourse to rearticulate either their work or the way that they think others should think about their work. For example, Turkish women noticed that the government was using the women's rights discourse to promote stiffer penalties for domestic violence. The activists argued that the appropriate way of dealing with their human rights concerns was to secure women in their communities (not by jailing abusive husbands, but by removing them from the home nonetheless) and in their homes (by requiring that abusive husbands continue to support their families and not be in jail so that they *could*).[58]

Then in my participant observation research and interviews I asked questions that would invite responses that described *at least* those experiences and understandings which the online activists had discussed. This analysis is complicated because some activists explicitly rank their rights concerns as the "big" issues and other rights issues as affecting only a small subset of their population or only a subset of women. For some activists, economic, social, and political rights can be disaggregated and prioritized. According to these women we might work on all of these rights collectively, but only as a *quid pro quo* necessary to get support for those concerns which are their greatest priority. For others, we must understand *all* rights issues as interrelated, and to disaggregate rights conceptually for strategic purposes cannot be strategically effective. The more data we have, the more differences we observe.

The theorist needs to use the range of input, deliberative inquiry, and skeptical scrutiny in order to draw normative insights from these competing pieces of experience-based information. Conflating these views or ignoring one of them is not analytically available to the theorist using my methodology. She may be inclined to turn to normative

[58] Ackerly 2001b.

theory as a resource for thinking through this issue. For example, Iris Marion Young, Nancy Fraser, and Seyla Benhabib have normative solutions to the problems presented by conflicting activists.[59] Martha Nussbaum explicitly takes up the issue of sexual and material priorities that the activists exhibit.[60] However, if praxeological inquiry is to give us something otherwise unavailable to the normative theorist or to help us evaluate competing theoretical claims, the theorist needs to work within the insights of her informants, perhaps by bringing in new informants and interlocutors, perhaps by continually submitting her research notes to skeptical scrutiny, and perhaps through deliberative inquiry.

The curb cut epistemological perspective provides some guidance here. Does privileging one conceptual framing over another hurt anyone or could it be argued that *both* or *all* would be better off if we did not choose one conceptual framing? If there are political or strategic reasons why we would be better off with one framework, do we have to propose one of the activists' framings or is there another made known to us by reflecting upon theirs together? While the destabilizing epistemology seemingly generates cacophony, that noise may be harmonious if we can hear it all.

*The first set of insights about universal human rights.* I will illustrate the methods for using guiding criteria as an analytical tool for developing a notion of the activists' guiding criteria for the theory of human rights by discussing the implications of the informants' arguments about what are the important issues of their work. For some feminist and women's activists, the interests of lesbian, gay, bisexual, transgendered, intersexed, and queer (LGBTIQ) people are identity issues, not material issues.[61] Of course, the political, social, economic, and cultural issues that lesbian women and gay men face are different. The set of political, social, economic, and cultural issues that intersexed people face are different from those of the others. And none of these can be fully understood as an "identity" issue without interrogating the sources of the construction of identities. While LGBTIQ people all experience political marginalization refracted through the social

[59] Benhabib 2002; Fraser 1995; 1997; 2001; Young 1990; 1997b.

[60] Nussbaum 2000b: 290–297.

[61] I1 2004; I2 2004; I3 2004; I5 2004; ID16 2004. The most accepted name for the movement in Argentina is "lesbian, gay, bisexual, *transvesti*, transgender, transsexual and intersex [(LGBTTTI)]" (Sardá 2007: 43).

category and political forces of gender, they each experience a different ray of the refraction, as do straight white women from the Global South, and bi-African American women from Louisiana, et cetera. Activists who see the interests of LGBTIQ people as exclusively "identity issues" fail to see that it is gender itself that causes the refraction. The epistemological power of gender is so powerful that we can fail to see the way in which it makes the interrelated political, social, economic, and cultural processes seem disaggregated.

Many activists focus on one aspect of the refraction or another. Some activists prioritize economic concerns above sexuality concerns. For others, even gendered cultural issues are not as deserving of feminist and women's activists' attention unless "they become *the* big problem"; as Professor of Economics at J. Nehru University, Jayati Ghosh, argued, Indian activists don't have an "excessive focus on cultural issues because the material problems are so big." A Burmese women's human rights activist, working on trafficking of women and children in the Asia–Pacific Region, asserts that "gay and lesbian issues are not important in the Asia–Pacific region. Asians might encourage rights but not gay and lesbian issues."[62] A scholar–activist from Papua New Guinea frames sexuality issues as a mater of luxury: "there are other areas which are 'non-luxurious.' Most of our women are just trying to survive."[63] Likewise, an activist from Burkina Faso with the World March of Women says that feminist and activists for women in Burkina Faso need to focus on:

> things that are possible. It's the visible struggle, you see, for example, for us, in our homeland, women living today die while giving birth because of health problems. This is an objective, realistic, feasible struggle. For us, there are groups of women who travel ten to fifteen kilometers in order to go get water. It is unbelievable. And at least, for example, the government can do something to solve this problem. For us, there are women who do not have birth certificates, who do not have identification cards. This is a struggle we can win. For us, there are unclear parts of the law. The law is not equitable. Depending on the person, it changes . . . These are struggles we can win.[64]

Yet, for other interviewees from South Africa, South Asia, and India issues of sexuality are central.[65] And for others from India and the

[62] ID16 2004. [63] ID23 2004. [64] I2 2004.
[65] I12 2004; I17 2004; IB2 2005.

United States, the issues of sexuality and materiality cannot be disaggregated.[66] For others, respect for sexuality rights is definitive of feminism.[67] It is apparent in the discussions of these women that activists are not united on whether issues of sexuality – or other issues that challenge cultural norms – should be part of women's common cause.

These challenges to analytical cohesion are not merely strategic. As the following shows, they can also be moral or epistemological. Consider the further thoughts of an activist from Burkina Faso, World March of Women:

> For me, feminism means that I commit myself, with all of my force, with all of my faith, in the struggle so that women succeed in this endeavor ... Nonetheless, we've had the time to ascertain that feminism, it means that we have to agree that everything is allowed and I think that, here on earth, everything is not allowed. . . . But we realized that, in the World March, there is something called sexual orientation. And we, we are not ready to commit ourselves to fight, to ask for the authorization to have a sexual orientation other than what one normally has. I am talking about homosexuality. Whether it is right or not, for us, this is a difficult situation. It is not one of our primary concerns. Therefore, this is a difference between the North and us, which means that, from time to time, there are tensions.[68]

For her, LGBTIQ issues are issues of feminists of the global North and are not a moral imperative. While her organization supports LGBTIQ issues by participating in the World March of Women, she does not understand those issues as analytically inseparable from the issues of legal rights for women and access to water, which are the focus of her work. Moreover, despite the tremendous visibility at WSF 2004 of the South–South Dialogue – a coalition of LGBTIQ activists from the global South – and the Rainbow Planet Coalition – a union of groups who are invisible in their home countries including LGBTIQ, sex workers, people living with HIV/AIDS – she maintains that sexuality is a "Northern" issue not relevant to her context.[69]

The debate about whether rights related to sexuality are *universal* or merely contextual is alive among feminist and women's activists on the

[66] I18 2004; IB2 2005; IB3 2005. [67] Feminist Dialogues 2005b. [68] I2 2004.

[69] Her perception may be because so much of WSF 2004 was in English; feminists from francophone Africa were not able to see and hear the evidence that contradicted her assumption. Or it may be that she initially became aware of LGBTIQ issues through donors, scholars, and activists from the global North.

ground even though in venues like the Feminist Dialogues[70] and the Women's World Congress[71] the tension is obscured by a language of inclusiveness. At Women's World Congress 2005 in Korea, representatives of every country in attendance went to the stage of the closing plenary and spoke the words:

"Let's cross borders together to change the world."

Some heard that language as including them even though they would exclude sexuality-related rights and others heard that language including them even though they would exclude those who would deny sexuality-related rights.

In further evidence that the repetition of the phrase masked differences among women, after a secular Iranian woman said the phrase in Farsi, a professor from Iran said "she does not speak for me," and went to the stage to repeat the phrase. At first I thought that she did not want the secular woman to speak for her, but in correspondence the professor confirmed that she wanted her voice – representative of a view that did not endorse spreading respect for sexual rights – to speak the words of the conference. By putting her voice with the others she meant to be *limiting* the "change" to which we were committed to working together.

Certain *ways* of including a range of voices can silence debate rather than stimulate learning.[72] Unison through silencing cannot be a tool of feminism. It is logically inconsistent with the project of revealing marginalization, silences, and absences. Moreover, such unison is unsettled by a destabilizing epistemology and thus, while it is perhaps a temporarily helpful strategic endeavor for feminists to try to articulate what their shared values might be, it should be understood as an endeavor to provoke interrogation of the different guiding criteria, not ossification of shared criteria.

Disagreement about the content of the list of human rights is not the only way in which feminist and women's activists exhibit different understandings of the guiding criteria. Feminists disagree as to how tolerant of intolerance feminists should be. The "Concept Note" of the 2005 Feminist Dialogues is a very inclusive document.[73] However, at the Feminist Dialogues more than one experienced leader in the

[70] Feminist Dialogues 2005b. [71] Women's World Congress 2005.
[72] Ackerly 2006; 2007a. [73] Feminist Dialogues 2005a.

global feminist movement asserted that feminism should be inclusively understood *to the exclusion of those unwilling to be so inclusive.*[74] For these activists, feminism is strengthened by being for some things *and against* others.

As with Jayati Ghosh, for some the reasons for being against some things are strategic.[75] However, as Joanna Kerr argued in her assessment of the effect of Beijing on the international women's movement, the strategy of parsing women's issues and approaching them separately is not necessarily effective.[76] The Beijing Platform encouraged activists and donors to parse their efforts along the lines of the platform's "critical areas of concern": poverty, education, health care, violence against women, conflict, the girl child, etc. as if these issues were not interrelated.[77] Such parsing works against much grassroots women activists' work and against international women's activism of the late 1980s and early 1990s when activists around the world mobilized for the 1993 UN Conference on Human Rights by building analytical links across issue areas including health, economics, patriarchy, etc. Despite the account of the interconnectedness of economics with the twelve areas of critical concern enumerated in article 44, poverty is first, but not mentioned again in the other critical issues. Economic development is not on the critical list at all.[78]

While parsing the women's agenda may have been necessary for making use of the political tools of lobbying and caucusing, it undermined efforts to work toward an integrated agenda. At Rio (environment and development),[79] Vienna (human rights),[80] Cairo (population and development),[81] women worked on the parsed agenda set by the respective conference documents to integrate women's concerns into each issue area. At Beijing, women followed the same model, a model set by the UN process. However, the result was a reversal of integration efforts as women disaggregated themselves into issue silos. Despite

[74] Participant observation, small group meetings, Feminist Dialogues 2005.
[75] I5 2004. [76] IB1 2005. [77] United Nations 1995.
[78] References to economic aspirations, institutions, changes, challenges, trade, development, structural adjustment, recession, policies, impact on peace, exclusions can be found in United Nations 1995: articles 4, 9, 10, 13, 14, 16, 17, 18, 19, 20, 21, 23, 31, 38, 39, 40.
[79] United Nations 1992.
[80] Office of the High Commissioner for Human Rights 1993.
[81] United Nations 1994.

women's ever-improving ability to articulate the interrelatedness of their issues,[82] the movement has been splintered, Kerr argues. This silo-ing of women's issues does not facilitate women's working through their different understandings of rights to see their integration.

The search for an immanent theory of human rights reveals that, while it may be possible to offer a provisional list and it may be interesting to reflect on how various pieces of the list are mutually reinforcing, an immanent account of human rights will offer a substantive list of rights that is dynamic both in its scope and in the meaningfulness of delineating any one right from another.

So, the first set of insights about what constitute human rights using an analytical method of looking for the guiding criteria used by activists themselves are a set of insights about the content of the list which reveal that the content is not universally agreed upon *and* that the opportunities for developing an integrated analysis of rights together are limited by geographic distance *and* the silencing of the women's movement into issue areas.

*The second set of insights about human rights* gained from looking at the guiding criteria of activists is about what role or function rights play. Here there is much more consistency. The rights these women describe are capabilities, as Sen and Nussbaum have been developing them.[83] For these activists, rights are not side constraints. These activists are working to foster the kind of structural, individual, and collective freedoms aspired to by Benhabib, Brown, Hirschmann, and Zerilli in their feminist political theories of freedom.[84]

These women and men are working for ways in which health and livelihood can be enjoyed. They are working toward structural change (as Pesce described above), but even when they cannot (as Pesce's first organization could not), their aspiration is to transform social structures, not merely to remove obstacles or to meet certain thresholds of capability.[85] Rights do not operate for women as side constraints, but rather inspiration for imagining the possibilities of lives fostered, not stifled, by social, economic, and political norms.

[82] Benería 2003; Beneria and Sen 1982; Correa 1994; Petchesky 2003; Sen and Grown 1987.

[83] Nussbaum 1995b; 2000a; 2003a; 2000b; Sen 1990b; 1999b.

[84] Benhabib 2002; Brown 1995; Hirschmann 2003; Zerilli 2005.

[85] Nussbaum develops the concept of a threshold and distinguishes her approach from Sen's in this point among others (Nussbaum 2000b).

A third set of insights about universal human rights comes from being willing to ask: "is it really 'rights' to which these activists aspire?" Should we consider that *really* they aspire to capability freedom, not to rights?[86] The fact that they never use capability language should not make us answer "no" immediately. Nor should the fact that they often use the concept as I just described make us respond emphatically "yes." Rather, when we look at the language and ideas of these activists, they treat rights as a moral and political claim whose legitimacy is universal.

Consider again the claims of the activist from Burkina Faso. She knows her struggle for legal rights are specific to her context – but her right to those legal changes is based on universal political legitimacy. Whereas she respects that in other contexts the important issue may be sexuality-related rights, for her such claims are context specific – "this is a difference between the North and us" – not universal.[87]

The reason activists work for their "rights" is because rights have political legitimacy. The political legitimacy of universality is important to activists. While activists may contest certain aspects of the content of the list, they do not contest that there is a list, nor that human rights claims are universally legitimate. Further, they share a confidence in the ability of their work to transform the universal understanding of the role and political legitimacy of universal human rights.

In an early draft of my first chapter, I made no reference to the Universal Declaration of Human Rights. A feminist activist and journalist from Indonesia, Umi Lasmina, responded:

> Have you considered mentioning the history of Human Rights (HR) so it will be clear to me who (whether the state, individual, or institution) you think invented the HR concept and who makes human rights violation claims? Maybe tell the story of where and when the UN empowered by certain countries (who won World War II) introduced in 1948 the Universal Declaration of HR. Maybe tell that it has become the most referenced document used by activists. The use of the Universal Declaration of HR by activists rather contradicts your argument that human rights violations are "invisible."

Her point is clear. Given that I am interested in the use of human rights by activists, shouldn't I situate my argument *vis-à-vis* "the most

[86] Cf. Nussbaum 1997. [87] I2 2005.

referenced document used by activists"? Even though the Universal Declaration of Human Rights was written in a context in which the winners of World War II had "global power," would I not contradict my commitment to activist-based inquiry by treating the Universal Declaration as a political document, when clearly it has become part of the political theory of activists? Human rights have universal political legitimacy regardless of the power politics at the time they were recognized in international law and of the debates about their content and purpose that take place at the national level still today.

For her, as for so many others, the debates among political theorists about if rights,[88] which rights,[89] and extent of rights[90] potentially undermine the political legitimacy of their activisms. Lasmina did not want me to cede her political ground, even in the name of building a better foundation for the political legitimacy of rights.

## *Skeptical scrutiny*

While clearly the account of human rights coming from women's activism is one of universal human rights, it is a theory that is likewise suspicious of universals. The theory is equally attuned to activist skepticism toward universal claims, a skepticism cultivated through a wide range of experiences with those claiming cultural authority. Skeptical scrutiny is the methodological tool that reminds us that a destabilizing epistemology requires continuous use of those tools:

- How can we look again for the silences and absences we have missed, even when we must pause to share our findings?
- How can we create again the deliberative opportunities for conflicting ideas to come to our attention and how can we make the terrain of debate a safe space to disagree without threatening our solidarity and the aspects of our work that are collective?[91]
- How can we notice the connections between various forms of oppression in order that our analyses of these can be most complete?

[88] Ignatieff and Gutmann 2001; O'Neill 2000. [89] Perry 1998.

[90] Cohen 2004; Goodhart 2005; Rawls 1999b; Taylor 1999; Walzer 1983.

[91] Note the opposition of feminists to Beijing + 10 and Cairo + 10 because the political environment has shifted such that deliberative processes would have likely yielded rollbacks of the advances for the recognition of women's human rights achieved in the 1990s.

- How can we work through our contestations in ways that maintain respect for the political legitimacy of the critical projects in which we are engaged?

Skeptical scrutiny reminds us to seek answers to (not just to ask) these questions, to destabilize our epistemological assumptions, and to deploy our curb cutting intuitions as we go. Such constant questioning can be annoying, my colleagues remind me. It can be slowing, as the pace at which I finished this book demonstrates. Fortunately, engaged with activists, we don't have to rely on ourselves for all of that critical reflection. Our interlocutors readily provide it.

I generally mean skeptical scrutiny to refer to my own critical examination of my own thought processes. Was I adequately attentive to the range of views and to the nuances among them at all moments? It might be easy to see the dichotomies of opposing views and less easy to note the differences among similar views. Did I challenge my epistemological perspective without denying having one? I document each interview (when possible) with notes, transcription, and a brief summary written immediately following the interview. These enable me to review the interview from multiple temporal and contextual perspectives.

However, skeptical scrutiny of my analytical work is made possible with the help of current and future informants, through certain forms of deliberative inquiry, by broadening the guiding criteria. For example, a peace activist from El Salvador uses skeptical scrutiny as a political tool:

> Yes. It's just like for example it used to be that they say "join the army and visit [foreign] lands and meet exotic people," something like that. I just wrote at the end of it, "and kill them." And then that shows the larger picture. Or for example, "be all you can be, join the army" and then I just added, "and get killed." You see, that's when you have this larger understanding.[92]

Her skeptical scrutiny is directed not only at government authority, but also academic authority:

> So one of the things with the academics is that they think within the box and they try to stretch it and they try to work outside the box but it's the box. That's because the guidance is from outside and not from inside, you know. So that's why it's so important to work with people regardless of which level

[92] IB18 2005.

they are, to learn to think critically but not to be just critical. It is critical that people learn to think critically, you see, and that we do it in critical numbers. You see how I play with the words?[93]

In addition to these inspirational ways of provoking skeptical scrutiny, activists ask academics to break down the boundaries between scholars and activists that we construct with our different ways of talking.[94] Clearly, I have some way to go in this department. But in researching and writing this book I have discovered the importance of stories, evidence, and argument for breaking out of the ways in which political theorists have been approaching human rights scholarship. Scholars and activists alike need to engage our own critical impulses, to ask ourselves if our critical arguments can also be constructive.[95] The skepticism of academia, even from activists who help and befriend scholars, is pervasive. And, pervasive in a good way. These activists engage with academics and call academics to be more engaged with activists' work, ideas, and politics.

## Conclusion

If we understand a feminist curb cut epistemological perspective to require an ongoing, collective, and self-reflective methodology, at what point is it appropriate to suspend Socratic interrogation for the constructive enterprise? Methodological self-reflection is never suspended, but in order to make a worthwhile contribution to those who gave of their time in supporting the project, it is important to use their insights for theory building (and not just as a basis of criticizing those who try to do so).

As one grassroots activist from India observed:

The World Social Forum gives us hope [for the possibility of unified multi-faceted activism.] We see here affluent and non-affluent people from 130 countries; [Nobel prize-winning economist and former Chief Economist and Senior Vice-President of the World Bank, Joseph] Stiglitz [bumping into activists] in the streets ... What we need is more activism in the halls and more analysis in the streets.[96]

[93] IB18 2005.
[94] Ackerly 2007a; 2007b; dé Ishtar 2005; Nagar 2002; Staeheli and Nagar 2002.
[95] Kerr 2004. [96] I4 2004.

If this respondent is right, then one of the significant roles of theorists is going to be to learn from grassroots activists (in visible and less visible non-government organizations and social movement organizations) and to articulate and disseminate in accessible language analytical tools that can enable activists and analysts to move from bumping into each other to informing each other.

Although many informants perceive a rift in transnational feminism related to different understandings of *which* women's rights are most important, curb cut feminism suggests that we analyze any rifts first as epistemological, political, or strategic, and only secondarily as evidence of the analytical incoherence of rights activism, or worse, the irrational self-interested demands of women. Further, if praxeological inquiry is to offer us something that we cannot or have not gotten from sociological or normative inquiry, we should not too hastily resort to sociological and normative inquiry when confronted with dilemmas in praxeological inquiry.

Nor can we abandon the project because it is hard. Human rights cannot be useful for cross-cultural and intra-cultural social criticism if "human rights" has complex and nuanced meanings that *differ* across contexts such that, when we share our understandings with other activists, we have little in common but the words. If activists from a range of contexts and focused on a range of issues understand these issues as indivisibly part of the same political project *and* theoretical framework, they have a tool that they can use for intra- and cross-cultural social criticism.

More generally, the normative theorist interested in praxeological inquiry needs methods for gathering and analyzing experienced-based information in an experience-informed way. To skip the step of experience-based analysis of experience-based data is to treat our informants as texts. As political theorists, this is our training. However, if we take seriously the epistemological destabilization of curb cut feminism, we must appreciate our informants as interesting not only for their experience but also for their analysis of their experience.

The epistemology of this approach to political theory is destabilizing at the beginning, the middle, and the end of scholarship. In the beginning, we challenge our assumptions; in the middle, we interrogate our processes of inquiry; in the end, we have only a provisional theory. The theory can be used for social criticism, but we recognized that in practice the critical process will include reworking the theory itself.

I have argued elsewhere using some of the data in this book that women's human rights activists deploy a dynamic human rights theory.[97] The notion of universal human rights that is institutionalized in international law instruments is reinterpreted, expanded, and redeployed as appropriate to each context without undermining the normative legitimacy derived from its universal critical aspiration. Is the method described here respectful not only of women's human rights activists' epistemological perspective but also of their ideas and political needs? Does this method defend a view of normative legitimacy that helps their work in particular contexts in which the cultural and political legitimacy of their claims are challenged by legal, traditional, or charismatic authorities?

In this chapter, while illustrating the methodology of experience-based analysis that I deployed, I have only hinted at the account of a normative theory of universal human rights that is informed by this praxeological inquiry because the purpose here has been to illustrate a method for experience-based analysis that can inform normative theory. The appropriateness of the methods should be assessed on their own merits, and not on whether the normative argument informed by the experience-based findings is attractive.[98] For this reason I have separated the exposition of the method from the account of rights I see emerging through the use of that method.

In the next chapter I will develop the account observed here, but I conclude this chapter by highlighting insights about the role of human rights, the scope of human rights claims, and the responsibilities of all of us evoked by human rights claims. Women's human rights activists make critical use of human rights in two senses. They use human rights critically in relation to the power dynamics of their context and human rights are critical (in the sense of vital) to their work. Though gender is a politically charged, vague tool for many of them and for many their interlocutors, human rights (critically deployed to critique power in varied contexts) has a vital political legitimacy that is an important resource for their activism. The scope of human rights that emerges from considering activists' differences and even contestations about

[97] Ackerly 2001b.

[98] Compare other feminist arguments, such as Brown encouraging us to be open to the outcomes of democratic processes and Hirschmann prompting us to engage in dialogue with others with a willingness to discover our own unfreedoms (Brown 1995; Hirschmann 2003).

what rights are human rights is that they are not best conceptualized as a list (narrow or broad). Rather the scope of human rights needs to be inclusive of competing sets of commitments for any to be able to function with the political legitimacy that *all* women's human rights activists give to human rights. Most touchingly, each is engaged differently within the scope of human rights activism. Though each uses and contributes to universal human rights in her own way, all exhibit a profound commitment to the responsibilities we share in securing and promoting human rights. Here it seems important to reflect on the selection bias of my choice to look for differences among women's human rights activists. Despite these differences and disagreements, they share a commitment to human rights. This is to be expected from people who have devoted significant personal resources to go to the venues where I interviewed them or who have committed themselves professionally to women's human rights, as in those who wrote into the online working groups from their organizations where women's human rights work is being done.

In chapter 7 I develop these insights about universal human rights from women's human rights activism with further normative reflection and in dialogue with other normative work on human rights. These conceptualizations of the roles, content, and responsibilities implied by human rights offer a rich complement to existing normative reflection on human rights and an immanent grounding for the normative commitments some theorists support through other means.

While there are many challenges in processing the wide-ranging views of activists, in order to use them for normative purposes, the insights that can be gained from such inquiry promise to be stimulating and powerful for normative inquiry and therefore theorists should be attentive to their theoretical methods for experience-based inquiry. In this chapter, I had with activists a dialogue that political theorists do not generally have with each other. In conventional methods of normative political philosophy, we construct arguments based on what we understand to be shared epistemological premises. In this chapter, I put into dialogue with one another people with differing epistemologies. This is a dialogue more inclusive than the conventional theoretical debate. As I suggested in the discussion, it is a dialogue more inclusive than actual forums can be. Further, it is safer, as we converse anonymously, and more powerful, as we are not forced by time to truncate our discussion. As we heard, this kind of dialogue creates a cacophony that I would argue is the sweet sound of democracy.[99]

The claim is ironic. Democratic institutions superimposed on background conditions of exploitable and exploitive hierarchies cannot yield democratic outcomes. Human rights activisms make visible some of the exploitable and exploitive background conditions so that we might be attentive to these in our efforts to support and develop democratic norms despite flawed democratic institutions. Likewise, free and open exchange of ideas superimposed on background conditions of unequal abilities to participate in the exchange and unequal abilities to be heard cannot yield epistemologically neutral outcomes. In the realm of ideas, we need analytical and interpretive methodologies for revealing concealed and competing epistemologies. Attentiveness to these methodologies has been the focus of this chapter. The theory developed in the next chapter is provisional and will likewise need to be interrogated using feminist curb cutting destabilizing epistemology and related methodological tools.

[99] Cf. Bickford 1996; Brown 1995.

PART III

# *Immanent universal human rights: theory and practice*

In Part I, I explain why human rights theory needs the immanent account of the normative legitimacy of human rights I offer. As a non-ideal critical theory, human rights criticism cannot rely on an *a priori* authority – neither the political authority of a principal interpreter of a transcendental or traditional authority, nor (for similar reasons) the epistemological authority of a principle. In Part II, I lay out the methodological turn that excavates from human rights practice an immanent universal theory – one based on imperfect practice, not on a transcendental or epistemological authority (neither principal nor principle). In this Part III, I offer an exposition of an immanent universal theory and show how theorists and activists can use it both to guide the re-theorization of the theory itself through reflection and activism and to guide activism. With these discussions I aim to put "more activism in the halls and more analysis in the streets."[1]

[1] I4 2004.

# 7 *An immanent and universal theory of human rights*

## Preface

When I met Jean-Paul, he carried a map. He would introduce himself, "je viens d'un tout petit pays" (I come from a very small country), indicating its location on a map of the Great Lakes region of East Africa. The map included Tanzania, Burundi, Congo, Uganda, and Lake Kivu, Lake Victoria, Lake Tanganyika, and Lake Albert. In India, generally, the person he was meeting would have been better able to "locate" Rwanda in his imaginary if Jean-Paul's map had included the coast of Africa, the Indian Ocean, and India. At a transnational training session organized by a large development organization in India he was meeting people who were either Indian or had traveled to India. For most of them, the location of Rwanda was outside the bounds of their ability to picture Rwanda. Even after the genocide, most people lack the reference points needed to locate Rwanda geographically and in colonial and post-colonial geopolitics.

Jean-Paul carried a couple of family photos that also did not reveal much about what life was like for him in Rwanda, a country known until the genocide as a development success story, a success story that included increasing poverty and inequality.[1] From the pictures, one understood the social norm for being photographed was to stand very still and look somber. By contrast, in his perpetual reference to friends, other farms, and increasing milk production "sur la colline" (on the hill), I came to imagine his life. In this hilly countryside, his hill was his neighborhood. The image of communities sharing life on a hill, an image evoked not by a map or pictures, constituted my imaginary Rwanda until the news of the genocide.

[1] Uvin 1998.

## Introduction

So much of our ability to understand anything hinges on our reference points. What we know conditions what we are able to know. When we see a map or pictures, learn statistics, or hear stories, we not only fill in absences and silences, but also create the infrastructure for seeing further and understanding more. A non-ideal theory of human rights is part map, part picture, and part empirical information from lived experience (conveyed through statistics or narrative). Imperfect as it is, this theory is a guide for criticism that also helps us picture otherwise invisible rights violations, making knowledge of individual and structural rights violations accessible.

The exposition of this theory exhibits also a commitment to what is conceivably an oxymoron: a theory that defends the normative universality of human rights without relying on other normative universals.

What does a theory of human rights need to be? According to women's human rights activists, a theory of human rights needs to have the authority to justify criticism of political, economic, and cultural structures, yet because some human rights violations have been invisible even to those supporting human rights, the theory needs a way to reveal and examine *its own* exercise of power *and* the ways in which it may even inadvertently contribute to the masking of exploitable power. Human rights criticism can exercise different kinds of power – the power of information when a critic makes violations visible, the power of symbolism when a critic names a visible practice a "human rights violation," the power of accountability when a critic uses human rights to call specific actors to be accountable for rights violations, and the power of leverage when a critic uses the normative authority of human rights against the political authority wielded by those in a position to do something about human rights violations.[2] A non-ideal human rights theory must be explicit about where and how power is exercised within the theory. A non-ideal human rights theory needs to be a form of, and to encourage, critical self-scrutiny.

In fact, feminist and women's human rights activists have shown us a seemingly impossible path to a theory of universal human rights. They

[2] Compare these to the four kinds of politics described by Keck and Sikkink (1998: 16–25).

have crafted through practice a theory that can guide criticism of political, economic, and cultural structures *and* of itself as a guide for criticism. In this chapter I set out the justificatory scheme of this theory, the roles of human rights for social criticism, the scope of human rights, and the responsibilities we bear for promoting human rights. These roles, scope and content, and responsibilities are an elaboration of the core theory of human rights with which we ended the last chapter. But first, let us clarify what problem women's human rights theorists think we need to be solving.

## What's the problem?

Women's human rights activists need a theory of human rights that can deal with individual rights violations *and* patterns of rights violations. They need a theory attentive to violations related both to insecurity (which on some readings might justify only a minimal list) *and* capabilities (which on some readings might justify an endlessly long and particularized list). They need a theory that recognizes rights not as entitlements, but as rights of way with no geopolitical, geographic, economic, or moral boundaries and no limits on responsibility. They need a theory that makes all of us see differently so that we become aware of our responsibilities though rights violations may be remote, concealed as a byproduct of individual choice, or masked by social, political, and economic habits and conventions. Not knowing about human rights violations is not an excuse for inaction in a feminist theory of universal human rights, even though it is often the assumed explanation for inaction.[3]

What activists know is that rights cannot be realized or even conceptualized as divisible, though often political expedience requires them to discuss political rights as distinct from civil rights, as distinct from social rights, as distinct from economic rights, as distinct from cultural rights. They know that the rights of each are related to the rights of all. And they know that human rights can be violated by individual acts and through social, political, and economic structures. They know that to change values, practices, and norms, social, political, and economic institutions also need to change, but that changing these challengingly requires changing values, practices, and norms as well.

[3] Power 2002.

While they may never articulate a theory of human rights, in their daily practice (and in their reflections about their work) these activists exhibit a non-ideal theory of human rights, one that guides their critical activities while at the same time is itself the subject of individual and collective reflection.

What theory of human rights is embedded in activist knowledge, action, and reflection? What theory of human rights can guide criticism of political, economic, and cultural structures *and* of itself as a guide for criticism?

## Justificatory scheme and responsibilities

### *Other approaches*

For some political theorists the rights that are human rights are a set of rights that can be enumerated and delineated. For them, the central challenge of a theory of human rights is to identify a justificatory scheme that can defend the legitimacy of a particular list of human rights.[4] For others, a founding principle establishes the relationship among rights claimants; for example, "membership" for Cohen or "reciprocity" for Benhabib.[5] Other political theorists of human rights work through the problems of delineation and delimitation of human rights using a principle that calls not for a finite list, but rather for an expansive list: positive freedom[6] or emancipation,[7] for example.

These principles can guide our thinking about the indivisible content of human rights, but do not provide an immanent justification for that content. Let's use the positive freedom principle – the most conceivably immanent of these approaches – to illustrate the point. According to Carol Gould:

> the common foundation that normatively grounds the conceptions of both justice and democracy is freedom, understood as the critical or distinguishing feature of human action. *Freedom* has a complex sense here: It is, on the one hand, a bare capacity for choice among alternatives; on the other, it is the

[4] Beitz 2001; Cohen 2004; Ignatieff and Gutmann 2001; Lukes 1993; Rawls 1999b; Talbott 2005; Taylor 1999.
[5] Cohen 2004; Benhabib 2004b: 130.
[6] Gould 2004; Nussbaum 1997; cf. "capability," Sen 2004.
[7] Goodhart 2005.

exercise of this capacity – individually or together with others – in the realization of long-term projects and the development of abilities. In this sense, freedom is an activity of self-development or self-transformation as a process over time, and I interpret this as the characteristic mode of human agency or life activity.[8] [*Emphasis in original.*]

Gould goes on to describe the notion of human rights that this theory of freedom gives rise to:

The particular theory of positive freedom and justice delineated here gives rise to a conception of certain rights that need to be recognized as *human rights* – that is, as rights that people possess simply by virtue of being human and, therefore, equally and universally.[9] [*Emphasis in original.*]

This positive freedom-based theory of human rights does some of what the women's human rights activists say a theory ought to do. It makes us regard human rights as unable to be enumerated. How could we distinguish between economic rights that enable us to develop our abilities and political rights that enable us to develop those abilities? Guided by this principle, what is the normative basis for distinguishing among reasons why someone cannot participate in politics? As we saw in chapter 6, how secure is any one of the rights not to be tortured, to assemble and associate, to vote, of expression, and to work, for people who do not have all of these rights?

However, this designation does not give adequate recognition to the historically recurring political phenomenon of humans making distinctions about the humanity of different humans. In different cultural and political contexts, certain groups, not all humans, are treated as deserving of equal treatment. Convicted criminals, suspected terrorists, people with severe disabilities, and survivors of sexual violence, for example, receive treatment that constitutes evidence that not all humans are treated as if they have the same humanity.

While I share Gould's normative commitment to universal humanity, that commitment is not universal. Activists may share it, but their interlocutors do not. A theory of human rights cannot offer support for setting aside the rights of a certain class of people. If the rights of any class of people can be set aside, for whatever reason – the public interest in economic development or political security have both been used – then no rights of any class of people is secure. The universality of

[8] Gould 2004: 33. [9] Gould 2004: 37.

human rights depends not only on the imbrication of rights-enabling political, social, and economic structures, which Gould's theory defends with a freedom-based approach to rights, but also on the ability of the theory of human rights to respond critically to the human impulse to classify, which Gould's freedom-based approach cannot require. For political, social, economic, physiological, and particular reasons convicted criminals, suspected terrorists, people with severe disabilities, and survivors of sexual violence do not have the same agency as other humans. A theory of human rights should respect their rights of people without freedom too.

Arguments based on a foundational principle either (1) argue that it should be shared and offer an argument for why their chosen principle is *the* universal shared principle[10] or (2) ask if it *were* shared, what would universal human rights look like.[11] Is it possible to theorize about universal human rights without relying on an *a priori* assumption of a shared foundational principle – membership, freedom, or other?

### *Immanent approach*

As with all political theory, the immanent theory of universal human rights rests on the justificatory scheme of the theory. In Part I of this book, I argue that a theory of human rights needs to be a non-ideal theory. It cannot assume away injustice or power inequalities, but rather must assume that they exist; in fact, we need a human rights theory because they exist. We cannot aspire to a human rights ideal without appreciating that it will never be maintained if achieved and probably will not be achieved. Even if it were achieved and maintained, its achievement and maintenance would be through struggle. In order to be able to be attentive to all the ways in which power can be used to exploit, no form of power, no structure, no process, nor foundational principle can be treated as an authority beyond the reach of criticism and therefore no such authority can be the basis for criticism. Any principle, even inclusion, can be exclusive.[12] The defining required to apply a principle establishes boundaries and meanings that are an exercise of power. A non-ideal theory of human rights needs an

[10] Cohen 2004. [11] Gould 2004.
[12] Connolly 2004; 2005; Mouffe 2000; Volf 1996.

immanent source of justification that can be applied within and across cultures, one that is not a principle, not itself an exercise of potentially exploitable power.

Constructing an immanent universal theory does not mean replacing a privileged *external* position with a privileged *internal* position. This would be a particularistic justification, whose basis for universality would rest in the initial claim that a certain position should be privileged. The range of views exhibited in Part II of this book demonstrates why such a foundation would be as problematic as relying on a foundational principle. Nor do I mean to build the argument on commitments that "we" or at least some of "us" already share (such as a commitment to freedom and equality, autonomy, membership, etc.). Again, this would be a particularistic argument that would require political commitment to prior shared values, and as we saw, it would require ignoring differences and disagreement. Such an approach would put the exercise of power – however democratic – prior to the construction of the theory.[13]

Rather, I ground this non-ideal, immanent theory of universal human rights in a critical methodological *practice*, one that is practiced by a wide range of activists who have a broad range of experiential perspectives, a broad range of commitments, and share profound disagreements with one another.[14] Using curb cut feminism at every step of theoretical reflection – from "What is a theory of human rights?" to "How does one research human rights practice?" to "How does one make visible invisible practices?" to "What is the best form of exposition of a theory of human rights?" – I lay bare the potential exercise of power, stay attentive to diversity, and am aware of disagreement in every step in the theoretical argument. And, following the self-reflective methodology of curb cut feminism, I recognize that I do ask and attend to these questions imperfectly.

The methodology is but one level of my justificatory scheme for the immanent universal theory of human rights. The second level is within the theory itself, as the justification for any *immanent* theory must be. The theory itself contains a political space where exercises of power are

[13] Special thanks to Michael Goodhart for offering a good example of this kind of theory and for pushing me to clarify how and why my approached differs from it (see Goodhart 2005).

[14] Cf. Habermas 1984.

made visible and mitigated, disagreements are acknowledged, and differences are worked through – likely not to the satisfaction of all, but – publicly. By making the terrain of difficulty public, the theory asks theorists and activists to take responsibility for working through political disputes about the meaning of human rights, recognizing diversity, looking out for disagreement masked as consent, and asks us to be attentive to the many ways in which epistemological power can be legitimated and abused.

The theory I describe shares many of the commitments of many human rights theorists. The difference is in the justificatory scheme. The justificatory scheme for immanent universal human rights does not rely on everyone communicating (because epistemological power, diversity, and disagreement characterize communication).[15] Nor does it rely on everyone being a member (because membership is determined through social, political, and economic values and institutions that are terrains of epistemological power, diversity, and disagreement).[16] Nor (ironically for a philosopher) does it rely on its effectiveness as an argument.

Though different from familiar forms of theorizing about universal human rights, my approach is not unprecedented. The universal justification for human rights in Amartya Sen's "Elements of a Theory of Human Rights" comes closest to the justificatory process in the terrain of difficulty I describe:

> The universality of human rights relates to the idea of survivability in unobstructed discussion – open to participation by persons across national boundaries. Partisanship is avoided not so much by taking either a *conjunction*, or an *intersection*, of the views respectively held by dominant voices in different societies across the world (including very repressive ones), but through an *interactive* process, in particular by examining what would survive in public discussion, given a reasonably free flow of information and uncurbed opportunity to discuss differing points of view. Adam Smith's insistence that ethical scrutiny requires examining moral beliefs from, inter alia, "a certain distance" has a direct bearing on the connection of human rights to global public reasoning.[17] [*Emphasis in original.*]

15 Consider by contrast Benhabib's discourse ethics of human rights (2004b).

16 Cohen 2004. Benhabib sees this point, arguing that membership is a human right, certainly not the basis of rights claims (2004b).

17 Sen 2004: 320; Habermas 1990: chapter 3; 1994: chapter 2; see also Habermas 1998: chapter 2.

A non-ideal theory of human rights needs what Sen calls a "domain of continued dispute."[18] In my view, these spaces are both imaginary (one can go there alone as a Rawlsian representative man going behind the veil of ignorance)[19] and actual (they get created when people with different views talk). Making use of the latter for empirical inquiry, anthropologist and ethnographer Anna Lownhaupt Tsing focuses her study of global connections on "zones of awkward engagement, where words mean something different across a divide even as people agree to speak. These zones of cultural friction are transient; they arise out of encounters and interactions."[20] Such terrains of difficulty can be institutionalized through international institutions like the UN conferences and corresponding NGO fora were (for women activists particularly in the decade from 1985 to 1995), or they can be assembled through transnational networking as the World Social Forums have been in the first part of the twenty-first century. It can be a large space with numerous participants (like the NGO fora or the WSFs), or an invitation-only small space (like the workshop at USC), or a virtual space (like the online working groups). Further, what gets disputed in these spaces will change over time, place, medium, size, and agenda setting. Attention to these terrains – and attentiveness to power dynamics in defining them and working within them – is a fundamental feature of the theory itself, not just of the practice of human rights. It is an element of the theory that is observed in practice.

The ideas that survive must be critically examined for the means by which they survive and the role that they may play in rendering other ideas invisible. The unobstructed discussion is scrutinized for the ways in which agenda setting and other consensus building tools create unanimity without including diverse and divergent views. Participation cannot just be open, but must be solicitous of the full range of divergent views. Partisanship is not avoided but engaged. Dominant voices within different societies are obscured by the cacophony of the range of views and their disagreements.

The process of learning from this cacophony is an iterative process, as Sen argues, but his focus on the free flow of information, the opportunity to discuss a range of views, the ethical scrutiny of moral

[18] Sen refers to this space as a "domain of continued dispute" (2004: 323); compare this to Cohen's "terrain of deliberation" (2004: 195).

[19] Rawls [1971]1999.

[20] Tsing 2005: xi.

beliefs, and the aspiration to global public reason are only half of the picture of this global iterative process.

The other half is listening. Globally, women's human rights activists practice what Susan Bickford theorized for national democratic process and citizenship: listening. According to Bickford:

> political interaction *between* subjects in a *common* world . . . does not necessarily take its meaning from, or its purpose to be, consensus. I suggest instead a different normative goal that can better guide political action in an inegalitarian pluralistic social order.[21] [*Emphasis in original.*]

For Bickford the different normative goal is listening. She knits together Anzaldúa, Arendt, Merleau-Ponty, Aristotle, and Socrates to show us the normative function of listening in and for political action. Listening draws us together by creating paths between participants through which they share what each "knows." Such listening does not take consensus as its necessary objective and requires commitment and a willingness to face one's fears:[22]

> Fear may, in fact, be what allows us to question our convictions. Fear of being "wrong" (of having an opinion that is incomplete or mistaken in some way) can contribute to our ability to listen … Someone who never feels the possibility of incompleteness will have difficulty genuinely hearing someone else, but someone who is overly frightened by it will be silent when she should speak. … Courageous listening in the face of fear means avoiding two extremes: one in which I simply, defensively, do not hear, and one in which I simply exchange my opinion for yours.[23]

Courageous listening is essential for any terrain of difficulty to be a space of transformation and learning.[24]

The universality of the immanent human rights theory I describe rests on the universality of exploitable power, the ubiquitous ability of power to render its exercise invisible, and the ubiquitousness of people willing to face their fear of that power in order to build bridges

21 Bickford 1996: 141.

22 Bickford 1996: esp. chapter 1, where she differentiates her view from Barber and Habermas.

23 Bickford 1996: 151, 153.

24 On the role of learning in global deliberative democracy see Ackerly (2006; 2007a). Consider, however, the challenges to learning in post-modern contexts (Rosenberg 2002). Compare to Aung San Suu Kyi's argument that freedom from fear is the basis of democracy (Suu Kyi 1991).

(to follow Gloria Anzaldúa) and to create pathways (to follow Maurice Merleau-Ponty) for communication. The key tool of this global public is not "reason," but rather "listening." Argument without "attention" does not have the transformative potential that listening has on the pathways of communication and therefore on the pathways for learning. Our obligation is not to *simulate* imagined inclusive argument; it is to try to *bring it about*.

A terrain of continued dispute is the theoretical and practical space in which we acknowledge the ways in which the power of epistemology, diversity, and disagreement can become part of the use of human rights. By acknowledging terrains of continued dispute as a part of the theory, we give theoretical importance to the activist practice of using human rights as a critical tool even though much of what is important to many activists – the inclusion of sexuality and reproductive rights, the critique of certain religious practices or authority – is in a terrain of continued dispute.

A terrain of continued dispute is integral to the theory in another way as well. As we will see, the theory also understands human rights as interrelated, indivisible, and sustained through social, economic, and political structures. Once we accept that the social and economic dimensions of rights are necessary for the realization of any rights, we have to acknowledge that the understanding of what it means to have, to violate, or to support human rights will have a wide range of forms. They will be sustained and violated by values and institutions that vary by context. In a terrain of continued dispute, we work through these differences in a manner attentive to wide-ranging views *and* to the human rights at stake in any resolution or failure to resolve issues in a terrain of continued dispute.

In a non-ideal theory, power cannot be assumed away in the justificatory scheme of a universal theory of human rights. The justificatory scheme has to be explicit about where and when power will be exercised and mitigated and why we are obligated to foster a global public whose fundamental building blocks include, but do not privilege, reasoned argument, but rather privilege attentiveness. Our understandings must be admittedly incomplete; our theory provisional. The justificatory scheme of this provisional non-ideal theory relies on the methodology of developing the theory (as presented in Part II of this argument) and on the ways in which the immanent theory itself is attentive to power.

## Roles and responsibilities

In chapters 5 and 6 (and in chapter 9) we see activists doing two things with human rights: using them to guide social, political, and economic criticism *and* using them to rethink what human rights are. Correspondingly, our immanent universal theory of human rights has two purposes for human rights: (1) guiding social, political, and economic criticism and calls to action; and (2) directing criticism toward identifying and adjudicating epistemologically grounded ethical differences around which rights should be recognized, whose rights should be recognized, and which social, political, and economic structures should be interrogated for their potential to violate human rights.

In order to do these two things well, as part of an immanent universal theory, human rights needs to guide our critical thinking about the many micro processes that create human rights violations in the aggregate. Human rights can be used as guiding criteria to encourage us to participate in dialogues where there are profound disagreements, to expose differences where they may be masked, and to create new opportunities for working through differences and disagreements.[25] And they guide our critical attention to possible individual and structural human rights violations.

Other theorists have understood that a complete theory of human rights requires an account of the roles or functions of human rights. For Cohen, human rights are "a set of important standards that all political societies are to be held accountable in their treatment of their members."[26] In Cohen's conception, human rights are limits on sovereignty. They are also, in Cohen's view (which is similar to Sen's in this sense), "a partial statement of the content of an ideal of global public reason."[27] If we ever achieved an ideal global society, this ideal of global public reason might be used as a guide to get us back to it were particular members to slip and not respect the human rights of other members. But this role for human rights is quite limited.

We need a human rights theory to criticize institutions and values where we are and to help us figure out what an ideal might be, to reveal invisibilities, to help us be attentive to disagreement, and to guide our

[25] See my discussion of deliberative opportunity (Ackerly 2000).
[26] Cohen 2004: 195. [27] Cohen 2004: 195.

learning from differences. These differences are known in Cohen's ideal theory of human rights:

> Disagreement is of course the normal situation when it comes to issues of justice: disagreement comes with the territory, and should not be taken as a sign of deficiency. We can assume that the disagreement is genuine – not simply a matter of people talking past each other ... Thus global public reason – and the ideal of human rights in particular – provides a terrain of deliberation and argument about appropriate norms ... not a determinate and settled doctrine awaiting acceptance or rejection.[28]

I agree, but would add that in a non-ideal human rights theory there is a role for human rights in building connections between people by fostering listening.[29] In a non-ideal theory, we cannot assume that all people have membership in some state. The Universal Declaration and the Child's Rights convention both include the right to membership and by so doing indicate that membership cannot be assumed in a non-ideal world.[30]

Amartya Sen makes a move toward non-ideal theory by arguing that "human rights generate reasons for action for agents who are in a position to help in the promoting or safeguarding of the underlying freedoms."[31] According to Sen, human rights may be used as a guide for legislation and activism.[32] In Sen's view, human rights violations are not confined to acts of commission or omission by states. Rather, the web of social, economic, and political life that are the context of humans' freedom are the subject of legislation and activism guided by human rights.

The immanent universal theory of human rights outlined here makes more explicit the roles of human rights and the obligations of all of us – not just those positioned to help – in promoting them. In the immanent universal theory of human rights, before and after criticism and call to action, the essential role of the human rights concept is to enable us to notice invisibility, diversity, and disagreement and help us to work through them. Path-building listening is essential to this project. Path-building listening also helps us see the connections between our actions and the environments in which we and the rest of the world live and

[28] Cohen 2004: 195.
[29] Connolly develops the ethical commitment to this kind of listening (2004; 2005).
[30] United Nations 1989; Universal Declaration of Human Rights 1948.
[31] Sen 2004: 319; cf. Shue [1980] 1996. [32] Sen 2004: 319–320.

work. It helps us see that we are all "agents in a position to help" in one sense or another.

Both activists and theorists use human rights in these ways and both can contribute to a better understanding and use of human rights by doing so. Their success in changing social, economic, and political structures through such critical engagement depends in part on the political legitimacy attributed to human rights and on the scope (or content) of human rights.

## Content, scope, and responsibilities

Any theory of human rights needs to identify the content of human rights. The challenge is how to define a concept that is inherently dynamic such that it can be useful for the critical function just discussed without compromising its legitimacy. As Jeremy Waldron argues, attention to the meaning of human rights is an indication of their legitimacy. Dispute, deliberation, and disagreement about human rights "is a sign – the best possible sign in modern circumstances – that people *take rights seriously*."[33] The question remains, what are they? Do they include cultural, social, and economic rights? Do they include sexuality rights? Reproductive rights? Are they best articulated by a long specific list that requires certain institutions that are the result of particular histories often associated with colonization, imperialism, and specific beliefs and debates about religion and culture?[34] Or can they be described by a short, vague list?[35] Or should the list be specific and short?[36]

According to the immanent theory of universal human rights emergent in women's human rights activism's attentiveness to silence and marginality, the content of human rights is not best articulated in the form of a list. Human rights violations are sometimes observable at the individual level and sometimes observable with society-level analysis; they are sometimes visible in formal legal, social, and economic institutions and sometimes concealed in practices and values that we enact at

[33] Waldron 1999: 311, emphasis in original.

[34] An-Na'im 1992a; Maritain 1949; Universal Declaration of Human Rights 1948.

[35] When Sen describes rights as capabilities, he is giving us a short vague list that includes social, political, and economic rights (2004).

[36] Cranston 1967; 1983; 1973; Ignatieff and Gutmann 2001; Perry 1998; Rawls 1999b; Taylor 1999.

the individual level, generally unconscious of the rights violations that happen or could happen as a result of our aggregated patterns of behavior; human rights are differently prioritized, but inextricably linked; and they are universalizable for intra-cultural and cross-cultural criticism, but not in the same ways by all people. Enumeration of such rights is not best done with a list.

If human rights are not a list of rights, then what is the content of human rights? What are they? To anticipate, the content of human rights is better understood as their scope. Three insights from activists analyzed using the theoretical methodology described in the preceding chapter determine the scope of the content of universal human rights.

(1) The rights of all humans are interrelated; no human's rights are secure if all humans' rights are not secure. No specification of the content of human rights can exclude some people from realizing those rights that are *not* in a terrain of difficulty.
(2) Rights are integrated, that is, rights are "indivisible," each right is secure only if the others are secure; a list of human rights is a gesture at describing what it would mean to be able to exercise one's human rights, but the delineations between rights is heuristic not conceptual.
(3) Human rights are secured through a fabric of social, political, and economic life; no narrow set of institutional changes will change that fabric.[37]

To develop this account, I argue that the rights violations of women reveal the importance of paying attention to the ways in which rights violations can be obscured by disaggregating rights claims, by over-inclusion and under-inclusion,[38] and by the functioning of the basic structure.[39] Through many social practices which women value (marriage and family) or in which women engage because they value affiliated practices, women contribute to the construction of social structures that oppress themselves, other women, or women more

[37] In the next chapter, I argue that this understanding of universal human rights, shared by many human rights advocates of all stripes, has implications for the strategies of human rights activism, from its grassroots work to its global coalitions.
[38] Crenshaw 2000. [39] Cf. Young 2006.

generally.[40] I argue that it is not necessarily the general practices themselves, but rather the specific forms they take that create the opportunities for rights violations. Consequently, the implications of this theory of human rights for social change must be context-informed, whether the accusation of human rights violations comes from an intra-cultural or cross-cultural source.[41] Moreover, no rights claim – right to health, to information, to food, etc. – is illegitimate by definition as the minimalist approaches might allow.[42] At most such claims belong in a terrain of difficulty for consideration. Further, as we will see, the shared understandings of human rights as indivisible, integrated, and structurally sustained enable us to think through many of the issues that activists relegate to a terrain of difficulty, despite a lack of agreement as to the moral foundations of human rights or as to how we might specify a list of human rights.[43] These three – interrelation, indivisibility, and structure – are inextricably linked in practice, and consequently each will be mentioned in the exposition of the other. The important thing is not the distinctions among these three aspects but rather the connections among them.

An immanent theory of human rights needs to recognize that at any given moment in history and over time, interpretations of the content of human rights and specific understandings of what rights are and are not will vary. Even the subjects of differences and disagreement are not universally shared *even among those using human rights to guide their activism.*

## *Rights extended to all: the interrelatedness of people*

In the immanent universal human rights theory, the extension of rights to all humans is based on the curb cutting epistemological and political

[40] Cf. Hirschmann 2003; Okin 1989. For an analysis of the ways in which even Black Feminist women can be implicated in the structures of silence and representation see Wallace (1990: especially chapter 2).

[41] One of the important contributions of feminist theory on rights and cultures has been to deconstruct the notion of culture as internally homogeneous and inter-culturally differentiated (Benhabib 2002; Okin 1998; 1999; Song 2005).

[42] Cf. Cohen 2004; Lukes 1993; Taylor 1999.

[43] On foundations, see Gould (2004); Talbott (2005). In the end, I return to the challenges of diversity and to the arguments of my informants to explore why this view of universal human rights is only widely, not universally, shared among women's human rights advocates.

commitment to listening for and noticing exclusions. Feminist and women's activists, devoted to revealing the rights violations of those made politically invisible by social values, practices, and institutions, practice an embracing form of human rights theory based on the commitment to attentiveness to other human beings, particularly to vulnerable or marginalized human beings.[44] This attentiveness to marginalization leads to expanding paths of learning among humanity.[45] And from this experience, women's human rights activists show us that the rights of any depend on recognizing the rights of all. In the immanent universal theory of human rights, the theoretical understanding that social roles or social differences are not a basis for discriminating in the extension of human rights to humanity is based on the practical observation of the interrelatedness of all of humanity.

How could human rights have legitimacy in bringing our attention to the marginalization of anyone anywhere, if it does not have such legitimacy for everyone, everywhere, and always? How could it be used for social criticism anywhere, if it could not be used for social criticism by anyone, anywhere, and always? An immanent theory of human rights requires the recognition of all of humanity. Of course, not all of humanity agrees. How should we deal with the argument that certain people should not have certain rights recognized?

Let's consider addressing the lack of recognition of the human rights of all of humanity by arguing that human rights require reciprocity as proposed by Gould.[46] While we can see evidence of a universality of a principle of reciprocity, it takes different forms, not all of which are conducive to recognizing the human rights of all of humanity. The Aristotelian notion of reciprocity does not help us think critically about the social bases of reciprocity. In Aristotle's *Ethics*, reciprocity means

[44] Carol Gould argues that care feminism offers three insights for democratic community: reciprocity of respect, cooperative reciprocity necessary for social, economic, and political institutions, and concern for the vulnerable. She characterizes this last concern as a "benign form of non-reciprocity" (1993: 409).

[45] In this aspect this theory is speciesist, because humans share with other humans the need to build obligations to one another for survival. Humans need human community. As Sen argues, the human desire to exercise freedom is also an appropriate concern for human rights and a useful tool for thinking about the content of human rights (2004: 328).

[46] Gould 2004; cf. Benhabib 2002; 2004b. Singer notes that reciprocity is one of the "common themes of primate ethics" (1994: 57ff). Reflecting on disability, Benhabib considers that reciprocity is not universalizable (2002: 190–192 note 7).

giving each person his due in proportion to his merit. Because merit is contextually relative, Aristotelian merit does not require egalitarian reciprocity. Judith Steihm has argued that this is a problem in US legal practice and Catharine MacKinnon that it is a problem in international human rights practice.[47] As MacKinnon argues, discrimination and human rights violations occur when the natural differences between people are treated as an appropriate basis for different treatment for different people. Such difference is not precluded by the Aristotelian application of reciprocity. Historically, the perceived natural differences between people have rendered invisible the unjust, inhumane treatment of some people.[48]

The invisibility of this inhumane treatment is a byproduct of the logic of Aristotelian reciprocity. Inhumane treatment must be seen for what Frederick Douglass calls us to see it as, an unwillingness to extend to others the rights and freedoms that those in power take for themselves.[49] If we take as the solution to this dilemma that we must make the argument that "these people" are just like "our people" and therefore are worthy of rights, which the reciprocity principle and anti-discrimination paradigm call us to do, we are committing ourselves to making the argument another day in the same way. *This is unacceptable from a curb cutting perspective*. When we argue for an extension of human rights to some group made visible, we are accepting for today those exclusions that we have not noticed in the past.[50] The political legitimacy of human rights and their role in guiding social, political, and economic criticisms cannot be sustained if every

[47] MacKinnon 1993; Stiehm 1983.

[48] Consider the historical treatment of African American women in the US (Cannon 1988; Cole and Guy-Sheftall 2003; Guy-Sheftall 1990; Kapsalis 1997; Wallace-Sanders 2002). When judges and the media compare discrimination against gays to racial discrimination, they are using Aristotelian reciprocity. Sometimes the comparison leads to a challenge of discrimination against gays and sometimes it does not. This ambiguity is evidence of the problem with Aristotelian reciprocity.

[49] See discussion in chapter 2, this volume.

[50] Cf. the theological use of embrace rather than inclusion in Volf (1996). As the comparison of gay discrimination with racial discrimination illustrates, anti-discrimination also invites us to ask, "How bad is the treatment?," "How inappropriate is the treatment?" These are not curb cutting questions, as the respect for human rights depends on whether we *see* the treatment as bad or inappropriate. The test of human rights cannot be how well the treatment sits with our traditional (past) understandings but rather how resilient they are in challenging long-held, but oppressive, practices and values.

argument requires a prior argument about the relative merit of people or classes of people. Regardless of our success in proving the equal merit of these people in this context, we will have undermined human rights more generally by giving legitimacy – in the form of any consideration at all – to the view that reciprocity or the reciprocal recognition of others is a basis for recognition of human rights.

Instead, the curb cut epistemology of the immanent universal theory of human rights assumes that there is inhumane treatment of some humans occurring now, somewhere, out of sight or beyond the reach of the political will to end such treatment. Commitment to human rights means a responsibility to seek out and mitigate those violations, not just those of the people we can see today and not just those violations we are in a position to mitigate today.[51] It is a commitment to listening, to building the communicative pathways necessary to be able to hear those voices to which we were previously deaf. From this perspective, no characteristic, visible or invisible, known or unknown, can justify understanding some humans as having some human rights and others not having those rights. The security of universal human rights depends on *not* having to negotiate local particulars prior to asserting or defending human rights.

With this commitment, there is (at first) no difficulty in determining whose rights are protected. Everybody's. And there is no challenge in identifying who is responsible for protecting these. Everyone.

But the curb cut epistemology prompts us to ask, just who do we think everybody is? For many, this is a subject for a terrain of continued dispute. Should human rights apply to all of fully functioning humanity?[52] To LGBTIQ people? To children?[53] To those with disabilities?[54] To convicted criminals?[55] To terrorism suspects? To the unborn – both particular (conceived) and general (the un-conceived of future generations)?[56] To animals?[57] In the next chapter, I show how we might use the immanent universal theory to think through some of these questions, but in order to do that we need a more complete picture of the content and scope of human rights.

[51] Cf. Sen 2004: 319. [52] Nussbaum 1997; Talbott 2005.
[53] Nussbaum 1997: 292. [54] Corker and French 1999.
[55] Schaffer and Smith 2004: chapter 6. [56] Rawls [1971]1999.
[57] Singer 1993; 1994.

## *Indivisibility and structures: useful obstacles to delimiting the content of human rights*

The understanding of the rights of all people as interrelated is not alone sufficient for working through these questions. In order to work through these challenges, we need an account of *how* the rights of all are integrated and indivisible.[58] This will require thinking about the relationships not only among humans but also among their human rights claims. How is health related to poverty?[59] How is present violence related to past conditions?[60] How are present economic conditions related to future environmental conditions?[61]

Some of these connections can be illustrated by social science. For example, holding other things constant, in those developing countries or regions of developing countries where women are employed outside of household production, the ratio of women to men is relatively higher than in places where women do not have the economic autonomy that comes with non-domestic employment.[62] Such use of social science can be an attempt to shift a political agenda by getting us to *see differently* and to be better able to listen. For example, Richard Cizik, Vice President of Governmental Affairs for the National Association of Evangelicals, an organization long politically and theologically committed to anti-abortion, guides his thinking about *how* to end abortion in part with the social science that a 10 percent decrease in the poverty rate would decrease the number of abortions by 30 percent.[63]

Social science can help illuminate the empirical relationships at stake, by making the invisible visible and revealing the structural dimensions of the things we are used to seeing. In an immanent universal human rights theory, the content and scope of human rights commits human rights critics to analyzing of the indivisibility of, and of the structural relationships among, rights claims that are seemingly able to be disaggregated.

[58] Ackerly 2001b; Basu and McGrory 1995; Bunch 1990; Charlesworth 1994; Mayer 1995c.
[59] Petchesky 2003; Sen and Grown 1987.
[60] Bullard 2005; Christian Aid 2006; Gray and Kevane 2001; 1999; Silliman and King 1999; Uvin 1998.
[61] Gray and Kevane 2001; 1999; Kevane and Gray 1999.
[62] Sen 1990c. [63] Cizik 2006.

Amartya Sen links these theoretically by thinking of rights as the context that provides the opportunities to realize one's capabilities.[64] In the immanent universal human rights theory, the indivisibility of all rights is based on the curb cutting epistemological and political commitment to noticing silence and invisibility. Guided by attention to over-inclusion and under-inclusion and by skeptical scrutiny more generally, feminist scholars and women activists make visible the connections among an ever-broadening range of issues. In an article read around the world, "Women's Rights as Human Rights," Charlotte Bunch connects abuse in the family, war crimes, mutilation of bodies, socioeconomics, political persecution and discrimination, and trafficking.[65] In *Public Privates*, Terri Kapsalis connects the unjust control of women's reproduction to the birth of the field of gynecology in slavery, particularly to the effort of one physician to restore slave women to "productivity" after a birth or rape results in a fistula. Her historical analysis reveals the epistemological roots of contemporary gynecology and medical research, making visible the shared logic of the control of slave women and of the fertility control of poor and minority women.[66]

The ability to see and reveal these connections is not unique to feminists and women's human rights activists. From Mahmood Mamdani we learn the connections between colonialism, medical research on humans, and the European Holocaust of the middle of the twentieth century.[67] Christian Aid links poverty and conflict to climate change.[68]

Although these connections are sometimes difficult for some to see, feminists and women's human rights activists have a lot of experience identifying and making explicit such connections.[69] Women's activism makes indivisibility visible. For example, Loretta Ross's activism in the US and that of the 1400 organizations which were part of the March for Women's Lives exhibit this understanding.[70] Other examples from around the world include the Rainbow Planet Coalition in India, the Right to Food campaign in India, the Right to Information campaigns in Kenya[71] and India,[72] and the

[64] Sen 2004. [65] Bunch 1990; see for example Soares *et al.* 1995.
[66] Kapsalis 1997: particularly 31–59.
[67] Mamdani 2001; see also Madley 2005. [68] Christian Aid 2006.
[69] Bunch 2003; IS5 2005; cf. MacKinnon 1993. [70] IB13 2005.
[71] IB17 2005. [72] I4 2004.

*dalit*[73] movement since that movement's preparation for the World Conference Against Racism (Durban, South Africa, 2001). The sociological and economic logic of their work – the logic that sees social and economic particulars as analytically inseparable – is sustained by social science.[74]

The view of human rights as indivisible is captured in the Universal Declaration of Human Rights,[75] reiterated by many transnational feminists, and affirmed in activists' accounts of their work. Here an activist with an Indian women's organization gives an account of the evolution of the view of issues of patriarchy, capitalism, neo-imperialism, political religious fundamentalism, and war as indivisible:

> Earlier on, when the feminist groups started in India, we had lots of differences with them because they didn't want to see anything except patriarchy in a context that was divorced from everything else. I am putting it very bluntly and I'm being a bit unfair also. Because many of them did, you know, stick up for the issues also, but the whole thing was this . . . woman against man, and they . . . would say they were very anti- any kind of Marxist or socialist interpretations. . . . But now, of course, there are socialist feminists and there are radical feminists and there are different kinds of feminists, and I think all feminists now are realizing that globalization is really taking over everything that they have fought for and that common religious fundamentalism is just the biggest, the biggest enemy of women's movements. And also, that war has brought home the real nature of globalization as imperialism actually.[76]

This activist has heard women disaggregate their issues. She shares the concern of Joanna Kerr about the splintering of the women's issues.[77]

[73] According to Anupama Rao, "Dalit means 'ground down,' or 'broken to pieces' in both the Marathi and Hindi language. First used by B. R. Ambedkar around 1928 in his newspaper *Bahishkrit Bharat*, the term gained new visibility in Maharashtra during the 1970s in the context of the literary and cultural efflorescence that saw the birth of Marathi Dalit *sahitya*. Today, the widespread currency of the term is also a belated recognition of Dalit militant claims upon a history of humiliation and suffering" (Rao 2006).

[74] Benería 2003; Petchesky 2003.

[75] This document was the result of political contestation and while the document outlines a consensus going forward on the indivisibility of human rights, at the time there were struggles over whether social, economic, and cultural rights should be included. The political compromise was that the Declaration would be all-inclusive and in the subsequent Conventions political and civil rights would be outlined in one document and social and economic rights in another (cf. Donnelly 1989; Humphrey 1984; Waltz 2001).

[76] I10 2004. [77] IB1 2005. See discussion in the preceding chapter.

Others see transnational dialogue as increasing the possibilities for treating rights as indivisible.[78]

Both those who worry about splintering and those who see increased possibilities for integration demonstrate that they share the theoretical insight that feminist issues and the rights claims that are articulated through feminist activism are indivisible. Peace and security are analytically and practically unable to be isolated from sexual violence as a weapon of war and as an expression of patriarchy.[79] Ending poverty, improving health, stemming the spread of AIDS, and improving education are all inextricably linked issues.[80] While we sometimes observe and hear women disaggregating these issues, by using the methods of analysis discussed in the preceding chapter, we can understand their issues as indivisible, such that none of women's rights claims would be secure if all such claims were not secure.

Recognizing the connections among rights issues, when we recognize that some rights claims are disputed, we at once acknowledge the dispute *and* commit to working through that disagreement. Acknowledgement of difference does not signal recourse to toleration of difference in order to avoid engaged listening. Nor does recognition of difference lead us to defer difficult listening. Often it does require more research or new analysis.

The range of feminist and women's issues requires analytical tools that enable us to conceptualize and analyze social justice issues as *indivisible* and the experiences of humanity *interrelated* through the *structures* of power.[81] Although some activists do not see *all* rights as indivisible (for example, the assertion by the professor from Iran mentioned in the preceding chapter reminds us that sexuality-related rights are not indisputably part of feminists' collective agenda[82]), all activists see some bundle of rights as indivisible. For example, inheritance rights, voting rights, divorce rights, and parental rights are related legal rights with social, cultural, economic, and political dimensions. Advocates in Burkina Faso and other parts of Africa are working on these as a bundle. The Rainbow Planet Coalition is a second example of an organization viewing social, cultural, economic, and political rights

[78] IB2 2005; IS5 2005. [79] Confortini 2006. [80] Benería 2003.

[81] By contrast, Fraser argues that we can analyze recognition and redistribution issues distinctly even while we understand them as integrated in practice (1997; cf. Francisco 2003).

[82] See the discussion in chapter 6.

as indivisible; health, economic, civil, and political rights are interdependent for large numbers of women, sex workers, and people with HIV/AIDS. Without civil and social rights and protections, people conceal their HIV status with detrimental effect – on their own lives and on the economy overall.

The advantage of the immanent universal approach over the principle-based justification is that it is informed by curb cut epistemology and does not rely on a transcendental claim in order to justify the critical capacity of indivisible human rights here, there, now, and in the future. In the practice-informed immanent universal human rights theory, the view that rights can be disaggregated in order to be enumerated is subjected to scrutiny. Though activists may try to distinguish between rights as they list them out in order to clarify which claims are being made, such efforts at listing universal human rights and setting priorities among them elaborate not delineate the scope of human rights.[83] The human rights violations of those made invisible by social, economic, and political structures are not made more visible by enumerating rights in the form of a list.

Activists are not alone in understanding the way that social, political, economic, and cultural structures render rights indivisible. Many political theorists argue that social structures can conceal rights violations behind social processes and institutions, particularly in the form of social roles.[84] The view that structures are important comes both from theorists who view the content of human rights as including a narrow list of rights that can be delineated[85] and from those who view human rights as providing a context that cannot be secured by a narrow list of rights.[86] So, even Steven Lukes argues:

> To defend human rights is to protect individuals from utilitarian sacrifices, communitarian impositions, and from injury, degradation, and arbitrariness, but doing so cannot be viewed independently of economic, legal, political and cultural conditions and may well involve the protection and even fostering of collective goods, such as the Kurdish language and culture. For to defend human rights is not merely to protect individuals. It is also to protect the activist and relations that make their lives more valuable, activities and relations that cannot be conceived reductively as merely individual goods[87]

[83] United Nations 1979; 1989; Universal Declaration of Human Rights 1948.
[84] Ali 2000; An-Na'im 1990; Benhabib 2002; Okin 1999.
[85] Lukes 1993: 30, 38. [86] Goodhart 2005; Gould 2004: 37, 63.
[87] Lukes 1993: 30.

Lukes goes on to enumerate the rights, but note that he insists, despite the argument just quoted, that:

> the list of human rights should be kept both reasonably short and reasonably abstract. It should include the basic civil and political rights, the rule of law, freedom of expression and association, equality of opportunity, and the right to some basic level of material well-being, but probably no more.[88]

Why? Why would attention to the ways in which "economic, legal, political and cultural conditions" can foster "injury, degradation, and arbitrariness" lead to "no more" rights? He answers:

> For only these have a prospect of securing agreement across the broad spectrum of contemporary political life.[89]

As the women's human rights activists show us, Lukes draws the wrong conclusion from observing contemporary political life. He recognizes that structures are important and powerful in constraining the recognition of human rights, but then gives those same constraints normative force by arguing that they are the reason that we cannot recognize more rights than these.

The activist-informed immanent universal theory of human rights is not constrained in its scope of normative legitimacy by existing practices that oppress human rights. Such a constraint would undermine the meaning of the concept.

Rather, it is strengthened throughout the scope of its application by the recognition of the power of structure in fostering or oppressing human rights.[90] This means understanding the rights-enabling conditions of local, national, and international legal contexts – the institutions from local police to the UN human rights treaty bodies – that provide legal resources.[91] But it also means understanding the ways in which social and economic practices and norms enable one to use those institutions to promote human rights. It means understanding the institutions of national economic policy and international trade.[92] But it also means understanding the ways in which local social norms and practice, including patterns of migration and patterns of paid and unpaid labor, condition the impact of these on life and livelihood.

[88] Lukes 1993: 38. [89] Lukes 1993: 38.

[90] In the next chapter we will see examples of activists' strategies for transforming the rights recognizing structures in which they operate.

[91] For a fabulous study of these see Rahmani (2005).

[92] Benería 2003; Ghosh 2005; Sen and Grown 1987.

For example, social, political, and economic issues are structurally integrated for the immigrant prostitute sending money regularly to her mother in her home country in order that the mother may care for her son who has HIV/AIDS and to whom ownership of the family property fell when her husband/his father died. There is no practical or analytical advantage to disaggregating the many vulnerabilities this woman and her family experience. There is an important analytical reason not to disaggregate. By not disaggregating we see that formal and informal economic systems, legal and social inheritance practices, and the identity and material vulnerabilities they create are interrelated. Changing inheritance practices will help the family keep the farm when the son dies, but economic pressures toward large-scale agriculture and the need to compete with Western farmers who receive large subsidies from their governments mean that the family land is decreasingly able to support the family. Illegal but well-established paths, such as that of Nigerian women working in prostitution in Italy and repatriating funds to their families, create conditions of vulnerability in which women choose to engage because of the economic landscape. Again, to analyze in isolation any one of the rights violations these women experience in Italy would be distractingly inaccurate and render an incomplete picture of the violations and of the opportunity and obligation to address these violations.[93]

The immanent universal human rights theory of women activists requires attention to all of the ways in which the background institutions, practices, and norms of society establish a human rights respecting culture. We see them targeting this structure in their activism.[94] Looking at this activism, we can also see the challenges in transforming the basic structure.

First, we need to have tools for identifying the visible and invisible ways in which women's human rights are violated. Women may be visibly exploited through paid labor in insecure working conditions, but their exploitation could be more subtle as being the vehicle through which a family gains access to microcredit. Whether working conditions and credit program designs are mechanisms for exploiting women

93 Achebe 2004; Aghatise 2002; 2004; Angel-Ajani 2003; Bamgbose 2002; Fitzgibbon 2003.

94 Ackerly 2001b; Ain o Salish Kendra 2000; I4 2004; I10 2004; I12 2004; I17 2004; IB2 2005; IB12 2005; IB13 2005; IB18 2005; IB19 2005; ID13 2004; IS5 2005; see also the discussion in the following chapter.

depends on the specifics of the institutions and their normative contexts.[95] Where gender hierarchy is used as an economic resource, that is, a substitute for collateral by the institutions employing or loaning money to women, women's rights violations may be less visible.

Second, such hierarchies may become part of our second nature and through social processes in fact attributed to nature. The social processes of naturalization take place in different ways in different contexts, making them difficult to identify. In chapter 1, I introduced Joyce King's concept of dysconsciousness to help us be attentive to our obliviousness to these processes even as we enact them.

Third, and most challenging, the cultural institutions, norms, and practices in which women's rights may easily be violated may be perpetuated by women themselves. Women experience human rights violations in their families, their religious communities, their social communities, their economic communities, and their political communities. These are the same contexts which provide their personal, spiritual, economic, and political support, however unstable that support may be. Although plausibly attributed to false consciousness or to dysconsciousness, women also experience this as cognitive dissonance, irony, and even ironic humor when the circumstances allow it.[96] What does a theory of universal human rights look like for those attentive to the politics of epistemology, difference, and disagreement?

## Non-ideal theory at work: responsibilities without boundaries

As we saw in chapter 2, an ideal theory sets out the just conditions to which we strive to return should injustice occur. In non-ideal theory, we need theoretical resources for guiding our construction of a just world, resources that do not include a blueprint, or even an outline sketch of what the just conditions might be. In my view, this means that responsibility is the building block of a non-ideal theory of justice. If we are committed to building a just world, we must be committed to more than a God, a leader, or a principle, we have to be committed to a process.

[95] Ackerly 1995; 1997; Bender and Greenwald 2003; see also Freeman, Hersch, and Mishel 2005; Goetz and Gupta 1996.

[96] Narayan 1997; White 1992.

The immanent non-ideal theory of universal human rights sets out the responsibilities of those who are committed to human rights, sure that they are interrelated, indivisible, and structurally sustained, but also sure that they are in dispute and sometimes invisible. These responsibilities include commitment to participating in an immanent and critical justificatory process at both the meta-theoretical level and the level of a terrain of continued dispute. These require a willingness to listen attentively, thus building bridges unconstrained by geographic or geopolitical boundaries. They include commitment to looking for the invisible, and a willingness to think differently. They include a commitment to reflect continually on the ways in which seemingly separable injustices are in fact interrelated, indivisible, and sustained through visible and invisible values and institutions.

These are the responsibilities of those committed to an immanent non-ideal theory of universal human rights. But they do not describe the sum total of human rights activists' work. These are merely the responsibilities dictated by the theory.

### *Transcendental universalisms (God or principles) in a non-ideal world?*

Does it matter whether those committed to universal human rights use a theological justification or a principled foundation for human rights' role, content, and ultimately normative legitimacy instead of an immanent theoretical justification? Does the immanent universal theory's expectation of non-decisive, curb cut path-building and listening among all people as the foundation for thinking through disputes about which rights are universal human rights exclude those whose reasoning relies on theological or philosophical commitments? It matters if in order for human rights claims to be legitimate, we all must connect all rights violations to a single faith commitment or principle. Immanent universal human rights requires us to connect some rights violations to each other in some places. Does it matter if some people connect certain human rights arguments to faith or to a principle first?

Yes. It matters. Even if all three arguments (faith-based, principle-based, and immanent) conceivably justify the same rights claims, the immanent approach facilitates the building of a human rights sustaining community as it encourages all to learn more about the structural connections among experiences of rights violations.

Turning to faith or a principle may come first in one's experience, one's life journey, one's sense of commitment, or one's belief system. Respect for the faith-based commitment means respecting it as a basis for understanding what is true. A destabilizing epistemology with regard to human rights does not require questioning the foundations of faith (or even faith in public reason), but it does require a willingness to suspend belief that the basis for human rights is theological (or reasoning) and only theological (or reasoning).[97]

As a peace activist from El Salvador said, universal human rights guide all of us to become more aware of our responsibilities for the human rights conditions of our own lives and those of others.[98] Sharing in responsibility for the human rights of all does not require prior religious commitment or commitment to a principle of reciprocity or positive freedom. It doesn't *require* prior reflection on one's commitments to see if those commitments are consistent with a shared religious commitment or commitment to an authoritative principle. It requires recognizing the individual role in collective responsibility for the realization of human rights for all, but it does not require a particular route to that realization.

This is *not* to say that activists *cannot* reflect religiously, abstractly, or theoretically using principles. As Iris Marion Young describes, principles of justice serve an important pragmatic function:

> to the extent that people require justification from one another for their claims and proposals, they must often appeal to principles and values of justice. To the extent that some people doubt or disagree with the principles that others appeal to, reasonable political discussion also calls for justifying principles, theorizing their coherence with one another, or arguing that some take precedence over others. Appeals to principles of justice have a more pragmatic function in political interaction than many theories of justice attribute to them. Where practical judgements are the result at which discussants aim, appeals to principles of justice are steps in arguments about what should be done.[99]

Young describes the use of reason *and* listening. She describes discussion that builds paths and bridges among people. Those who respect

[97] For the view that human rights is a religious idea and not a secular idea see Perry (1998).

[98] IB18 2005; cf. Suu Kyi 1991. [99] Young 2000: 29.

human rights have a responsibility to participate in the building of such bridges.

Recognizing the pragmatic politics of principles, the immanent universal theory rejects not the use of principles in discussion but their *theoretical authority*. The immanent theory of universal human rights should not require activists to use transcendent principles or any other guiding authority in order for their rights-based activism or criticism to be normatively legitimate. The legitimacy of an immanent theory of universal human rights for guiding criticism of values, institutions, and individual actions comes from the methodology that developed the theory *and* from the role of terrains of continued dispute within the theory.

Let me illustrate the difference between principle-based criticism and immanent theory-based criticism by drawing on the insights of Loretta Ross, founder of the National Center for Human Rights Education in Atlanta, Georgia. For Ross, the indivisibility of rights is both a strategic tool and a conceptual tool, but it is not a delimiting principle. It does not tell her who to include and who not to include, rather it guides with whom she builds bridges and how she builds those bridges. For example, her organization works with a range of social justice activists. How does she identify those partners?

> We really focus on social justice activists, people coming from the women's rights movement, the anti-poverty movement, the anti-racism movement, the anti-fascist movement, the immigrant rights movement, the gay and lesbian movement. We go after people already in struggle because we feel that those are the people most likely to quickly use the human rights framework.[100]

Her organization uses the understanding of rights as indivisible to identify and develop partners and to mobilize and work in coalition.

Further, her organization seeks to develop and spread the use of the human rights framework. How do they develop the use of the human rights?

> Sister Song, Women of Color for Reproductive Health which is a collective of seventy women of color organizations which use the human rights framework to talk about reproductive health issues.[101]

Now and into the future, Sister Song works on health issues, recognizing that women's health is part of human rights.

[100] IB13 2005. [101] IB13 2005.

Further, from this platform, they have sought to spread the conceptualization of health as indivisible from other rights. This effort was visible in the discussions that led to their participation in the March for Women's Lives.[102] The March for Women's Lives (a march on Washington, DC, in April 2004) was originally a march for women's "choice" and anticipated to be much smaller than its April 2004 turnout estimates.[103] By understanding reproductive choice in its broader context of women's health, access to contraception, sex education, and global family planning, the movement spoke not only for women who were afraid of the loss of health privacy and reproductive choice, but also for women who already lacked these due to economic circumstance or local legal and social restrictions. A right, such as reproductive choice, might be separately enumerated so that we can see clearly what is being claimed and why it is being claimed. But to secure that right, economic, social, and political circumstances need to secure men's and women's health, including but not limited to their access to contraception (not just to abortion), sex education, and family planning.[104]

Loretta Ross and the organizations with which she works exhibit commitments to building the bridges and paths necessary for making visible human rights violations, analyzing their causes, and developing strategies for mitigating these.

If we don't need the political theorist's principle, maybe we don't need political theory at all.[105] Perhaps we do not need a normative argument for indivisibility that reconciles activists' competing attitudes on specific rights. Perhaps it is enough to rely on the political legitimacy of the Universal Declaration.[106] The Universal Declaration outlines an

[102] Loretta Ross 2005. [103] IB13 2005.

[104] As we will see shortly, Loretta Ross understood the purpose of the March even more broadly to include the war in Iraq, the environment, and the debt crisis. Ross's reflections on the impact of hurricane Katrina on African American women offer another illustration of *her* thinking about interrelatedness, indivisibility, and structures as essential to articulating and defending human rights claims. However, in the text I constrain myself to the organizational example (Loretta Ross 2005).

[105] Donnelly 1989: 44, fn 17.

[106] Talbott calls this the "Overlapping consensus interpretation of human rights," attributes it to Charles Taylor, and considers that this methodology justifies a much more narrow view of human rights than the Universal Declaration (Talbott 2005: 8–9).

understanding of rights as integrated based on what René Cassin, a drafter of the document, calls the four pillars of human rights: human dignity,[107] civil and political rights,[108] social and economic rights,[109] and cultural rights.[110]

Given the commitments that all states have already made *to* all the rights in the Universal Declaration, why do we need a normative argument *for* all of them? Does a normative argument *for* them undermine the universal commitment *to* them?

No; as John Stuart Mill would argue, to hold our commitments to human rights dogmatically, is not to hold these commitments in any meaningful way.[111] If we want to use human rights to guide activism and policy, our commitment to human rights must be moral and political not merely prudential and legal.[112] Thus, a commitment to human rights is a responsibility to think through the ways in which rights are indivisible and to think through what conditions need to change for rights to be understood as mutually reinforcing rather than conflicting.

## *Immanent responsibility in a non-ideal world*

One peace activist who survived the authoritarian regime of her Latin American country did not have much confidence that the conceptual resources of industrialized nations enable their citizens to see these structural conditions and the role of individual and collective action in sustaining them:

> I really look at the US people and people in industrialized nations with a lot of love . . . because I don't know how you can all live like that, without meaning and talking so wrong. And living in the illusion, and talking about poverty

107 Universal Declaration of Human Rights 1948: articles 1–2.
108 Universal Declaration of Human Rights 1948: articles 3–19 and 26–27.
109 Universal Declaration of Human Rights 1948: articles 20–27.
110 Universal Declaration of Human Rights 1948: articles 26–28. Note, I read article 26 on education and article 27 on scientific knowledge as having implications for political, social, economic, and cultural rights. Further overlaps could be offered. The point of the indivisibility argument of feminists is that beyond the obvious connections between education and culture, between scientific knowledge and economics, the meanings (not just the realization) of all rights are indivisible (cf. Ishay 2004: Introduction).
111 Mill [1859] 1989.
112 Kellenberger 2003: 115; cf. Donnelly 1989: 44; see Gatens 2004: 280ff.

and poor people and not knowing that poverty and poor people are created by human beings, and that these so called developed nations are not developed. They are industrialized nations. I don't know how people can tell me, "oh, I am so glad that I wasn't born in your country. I am so fortunate to be born in this country" when your country is the other side of having created my country. And then for example, even peace organizations and charitable organizations. How can we have charity about things that we are supposed to be responsible for? How can we have the March of Dimes to take care of people who are born like that whom we are responsible for and it shouldn't be that we walk so many miles to be taking care of them, that this is something that our state, but our state, I'm not talking about government. I'm talking about society being responsible. I don't understand that part. ... I understand it in a sense, you know. That's how people are because they are in the illusion and a lot of things are like that. Then they'll be calling us undeveloped nations or nations in development, or talking about our debt. How can these industrialized nations that call themselves developed talk about the debt of our countries when we were made slaves and when all our resources were taken? I don't understand how academic people don't understand that. Or the churches. That I try, you know? The only thing I know is that the reason I can see with love is because I see that they don't see it. And it's sad not to see. But I know that one day everybody's going to see.[113]

A former nun, she is not confident that we can reason our way to understanding structural interrelatedness and the responsibilities that these entail. Her concern is not that we cannot find an argument, but rather that we cannot find an argument that moves people to *think differently*. In the meantime she extends patient love and compassion. From her epistemological perspective, love and compassion enable sustained engagement across profound conceptual differences and the epistemological failings of (among others) the academics of industrialized nations.

Just as we need, but cannot rely on, philosophical argument to reveal our human rights commitments, so too many will need religion to make visible our human rights responsibilities. Immanent universal human rights theory requires that we see our connections. However, religious commitments are also social commitments. As this survivor of political violence attests, even broadly shared religious commitments may not be sufficient to challenge human rights violations. If argument cannot

[113] IB18 2005.

challenge the "illusion" that we are separable and not responsible for one anothor's fate, perhaps "love," perhaps bridge-building listening, can.

## Conclusion

The challenge to listen and to think differently as we engage with difference, diversity, and the power of epistemology is an elemental part of the practice of human rights activism. Doing so while engaging in the terrain of continued dispute is essential to sustaining the legitimacy of human rights-based criticisms. The terrain of continued dispute is the space where we acknowledge that working through questions that draw out our differences is necessary for maintaining the legitimacy and critical worth of universal human rights. In the next chapter, I illustrate how *one* theorist uses the immanent universal theory to think through some of the hard questions in the terrain of continued dispute.

Throughout this chapter, I have signaled which questions are likely to be important to work through in the terrain of continued dispute. What are the critical boundaries of rights? Can they be used to criticize family, religion, and community in addition to local, national, and international legal authorities? Whose human rights are respected by an immanent universal theory: fully functioning adults, people with disabilities, children, the unborn, the unconceived? Do these rights include sexuality rights and reproductive rights? Some issues in the terrain of continued dispute are a continual question in my own mind; others are decided in my own mind, but remain politically recognizably in dispute.

The essential pieces of the immanent universal theory of human rights set out in this chapter and which guide the reflection in the next are the justificatory scheme, the roles, and the content of human rights. This theory is a non-ideal, provisional theory that guides both criticism and, through attentiveness to power and to others, the building of communicative pathways that are the building blocks of human community. In the next chapter I illustrate how the theory guides *my* theoretical reflection on these hard questions. In the subsequent chapter, I show how the theory guides transnational feminists in building communicative pathways while advocating for the recognition of women's universal human rights. (To anticipate, it is no wonder that the transnational network is the social movement organization of women's human rights activism.[114])

In both the theoretical and the activist discussions we will see that global public reason alone is an inadequate tool for adjudicating difficult issues. In practice, attempted adjudication needs to take place in ways that build trust, pathways and bridges that acknowledge and are open to continued dispute – no matter how frustrating that is. By building a global listening infrastructure as we theorize and engage in activism for human rights, we are expressing a belief in the power of humanity to live up to its human rights obligations: that is, to think differently, and then act differently. And here, as I move on to show how *I* reason guided by this theory, I lay bare my own epistemology and transcendental commitment – a belief that exercises of power are the obstacles to our mutual learning. The better our spaces for continued dispute are at mitigating power inequalities in those spaces, the better we will be at building listening pathways as we think through and learn to think differently. To be attentive to the vulnerable or invisible, we need to listen attentively, which means being open not only to changing what we think, but also to changing *how we think*. We need to be open to treating global public reason as an essentially contested concept, rather than a guide. Ironically, global public cacophony sounds better.

[114] Moghadam 2005.

# 8 *Terrain(s) of difficulty: obligation, problem-solving, and trust*

## Preface

What is in a name? In my discussion of Jean-Paul, Marie, and their family, I have changed their names and some facts for their privacy and safety. Despite this care, until their third country resettlement status was approved by UNHCR, I worried that by telling bits of their story I would introduce a full range of insecurities into their situation. The more I learn about Rwanda, the more it seems that their unbelievable story is, while perhaps unique in its particulars, not unique in the details that I have shared with you. Less than a month after this status was finalized, many registered Rwandan refugees in Uganda were repatriated to Rwanda.

Funny, but when I use these aliases and these altered details, I have trouble picturing them. When I call him "Jean-Paul" I cannot picture him coming to life when introduced to other francophone expatriates in India. When I call her "Marie" I cannot picture her newly married and thin from rural farm work or making a traditional dress from the cloth Jean-Paul brought her from India.

My memories of Jean-Paul are more vivid, not when I reread my own distorted account of their lives, but when I serve green beans for a crowd in the casserole dish he gave me as a "thank you" for hosting him and translating for him during his stay in Bangladesh. With a cook as his guide and no common language but cooking and hospitality between them, he had gone all over a certain district of Ahmedabad looking for a serving dish appropriate for hosting a crowd. He said such a casserole dish was a traditional Rwandan housewarming present.

Focusing on his false name, I forget his spirit of welcoming and the spirit he wished to perpetuate in my dinners with family and friends long after he was reunited with his.

## Introduction

Naming can distract us from what is really important. For Jean-Paul, being a good host and guest was important. For feminists trying to hear each other in the global public cacophony, it is less important what we name the spaces where we gather to notice and attend to our differences and disagreements and more important that we listen, notice, attend to our differences and disagreements, and appreciate our obligations to do so.[1]

Does it matter what we call the political spaces where disagreement and diversity characterize the background conditions of our engagements? Both Joshua Cohen and Amartya Sen identify a political space for global public reason. Cohen calls it "a terrain of deliberation."[2] I like the sound of that, except for the ideal characterization of the practice of global public reason that "deliberation" evokes in contemporary political theory. For Cohen, the terrain of deliberation is "broadly shared," not a place of epistemological and other differences.[3] Deliberation ought to require listening as Bickford theorizes it for democratic politics.[4] Deliberation ought to require attentive learning, a commitment to engagement even if a commitment to consensus is not shared, and a willingness to risk being wrong. But in contemporary deliberative democratic theory, so often it does not.[5] As we saw in Part I, theory that models the deliberative practice on Rawlsian ideal theory and the use of reasonable pluralism and public reason to define the boundaries of the political and political discourse seems inappropriate for the global cacophony we anticipate in these terrains.

What is in a name? In the preceding chapter I followed Amartya Sen's nomenclature and developed a concept of a "terrain of continued dispute." This name is open to differences beyond the limits of reasonable pluralism, differences that may include epistemological differences. In fact, as Sen describes the terrain, he seems committed to

[1] Hawkesworth gives us some understanding of why this may be hard to do (2006b: chapter 4). Sen clairifies the perfect and imperfect obligations human rights demand (2004: 321ff).

[2] Cohen 2004: 195. [3] Cohen 2004: 194.

[4] Ackerly 2007a; Bickford 1996: esp. chapter 1 and 5; McAfee 2004.

[5] See critical attention to this question by Ackerly (2000), Benhabib (2004a), Stokes (1998), and Young (2001a).

facing the differences that may surface in cross-cultural discussions and discussions between activists and scholars:

The point here is not so much whether we are *permitted* to make cross-boundary scrutiny, but that the discipline of critical assessment of moral sentiments, no matter how locally established they are, *demands* that such scrutiny be undertaken.[6]

Such scrutiny, Sen argues, is best done under the rubric of Rawlsian public reason:

I should, however, emphasize that the understanding and viability of human rights are, in this perspective, intimately linked with the reach of public discussion, between persons and across boarders. The viability and universality of human rights are dependent on their ability to survive open critical scrutiny in public reasoning. The methodology of public scrutiny draws on Rawlsian understanding of "objectivity" in ethics, but the impartiality that is needed cannot be confined within the borders of a nation.[7]

In fact, Sen argues, it cannot be confined within the boundaries of theoretical reflection:

But it is also important to note that the conceptual understanding of human rights, in turn, can benefit substantially from considering the reasoning that moves the activists and the range and effectiveness of practical actions they undertake, including recognition, monitoring and agitation, in addition to legislation. Not only is conceptual clarity important for practice, the richness of practice, I have argued, is also critically relevant for understanding the concept and reach of human rights.[8]

I argue in Part II that "considering the reasoning that moves the activists" requires a methodology to guide our attentiveness. And I argue in the preceding chapter that when we consider the "reasoning" of activists, we see that *listening* is a complementary and essential critical practice.

With a shared responsibility to listen attentively, to risk being wrong, and to work through the issues in dispute, we might resolve some of them – or at a minimum reveal that the dispute over some of them is political, not normative. Our discussions may reveal that *interests*, not normative commitments, make some people want to continue to treat

[6] Sen 2004: 355. [7] Sen 2004: 356. [8] Sen 2004: 356.

some issues as disputed when the normative commitment to oppose those issues is inconsistent with other normative commitments those people hold.

Wanting to distinguish between the terrain of political dispute and the terrain of conceptual difficulty and normative ambiguity, I am inclined to name this political space in which normative disputes are deliberated the terrain of "difficulty," even the terrain of "intractable differences." However, I do not wish the nomenclature to prejudge whether differences are irreconcilable or merely difficult, so I am going to go with "difficulty" as some difficult questions are never resolved and some might be. By calling such political and normative spaces a "terrain of difficulty," I mean to recognize not only that the issues are hard, but also that it is hard to be committed to attentive listening when the issues and views on the issues are so politically and normatively different *and* important to those who hold them.

We may *call* these spaces different things. The important thing is how we *understand* them. Do we understand this terrain as singular or plural, open or closed? Are we invited to such spaces or trapped by their boundaries? In the immanent theory of universal human rights I am articulating, the terrain is a space where those committed to human rights take on the responsibility of ongoing, attentive listing, of shared learning, and of thinking differently through epistemological and normative differences, thereby building bridges to one another over differences, with the ultimate goal of resolving them, and facing new ones together. This commitment means revealing when some political differences are being masked as normative differences.

So when one might be inclined to refer to "a broadly shared terrain of deliberation," a destabilizing epistemology makes me ask if such a characterization isn't imposing *a priori* limiting boundaries on what can be disputed. Such boundaries exercise a form of authority or privilege. By contrast, when I or another is inclined to refer to one of many terrains of continued dispute, I like to self-destabilize and ask if such a characterization will enable some people to treat an issue as cut off from or distinguishable from other issues. Such parsing of human rights, as we have seen, is itself a way of delegitimating certain rights claims. I understand this space as dynamic and unbounded, neither singular nor plural, both singular and plural. Of course the English language doesn't give me that flexibility and so I use "terrain," "terrain(s)," and "terrains" in destabilizing ways.

In the preceding chapter, in the exposition of the key features of an immanent universal theory of human rights, I compare the elements of the immanent universal theory of human rights to arguments made by other human rights theorists who have used principles to guide their thinking through the political legitimacy of certain human rights claims and to enumerate the content of legitimate human rights claims. In the examples I gave, these theorists rest the political legitimacy of human rights for criticism and political change on a transcendental argument meant to be immanent: that the human experience needs effective positive freedom (whatever else it needs); that fair treatment of others begins with reciprocity (whatever else it requires). These theorists base these principles on immanent argument: what it means to be a human being in society with others requires recognition of this principle. (This is not the same thing as basing the universality of human rights on biological membership in the human species. Their notion is distinctly social, not biological.) However, the theorists use these conceivably immanent principles transcendentally, that is, they bypass the problems in the terrain(s) of difficulty with a categorical principle rather than with adjudication. In the application of the immanent universal theory of human rights, I use the commitment to immanent universal human rights (*the responsibility itself*) to guide our thinking through the terrain(s) of difficulty.

I begin this chapter with a brief exposition of this commitment, that is, the obligation to support human rights by working through the terrains of difficulty. I discuss three such debates – how to adjudicate competing rights, whether sexuality-related rights are human rights, and whether and how to prioritize one rights issue over others. The theoretical dimensions of these questions are examples of the terrain of difficulty of immanent universal human rights. These are theoretical debates that are manifested either explicitly or implicitly in women's human rights activism.

In the following chapter, I work through another obligation of the theorist, that is, to think through the strategies of activists to evaluate the ways in which they work within (or against), while developing (or potentially undermining) the theory of human rights. That chapter (9) is meant to model the way that a deconstructing theorist, a critical abstract thinker, might be able to offer concrete, practical suggestions to activists. Such an attempt to apply theory to practice is a necessary part of the curb cut feminist methodology, though I have no delusions that buried at the end of a political theory text is the best place to share these reflections with activists. Hence, this is not the only form with which I have shared this information with activists; most of these ideas have been circulated on listservs and in gatherings of activists in 1998, 1999, 2001, 2004, and 2005. However, sharing these with theorists is likewise important for facilitating discussion about how we can and should make theoretical reflection useful to activists. In the discussions in the next chapter I suggest ways in which human rights work might become increasingly oriented toward realizing human rights as immanent universal human rights. In this way I mean to show how the activists' practice can be brought in line with the activists' theory. What obligates me as a theorist to do so?

## Working through the hard questions: obligation and tools

Of course, fieldwork with time- and resource-challenged, generous people generates a professional ethical obligation to reflect on ways to give back to research subjects from the products of the research (and in more immediate material ways).[9] Beyond these obligations of the researcher, the theory itself generates a notion of obligation.

Obligation in this immanent universal theory is the obligation to respect the legitimate use of human rights for social criticism while being committed to working through issues in the terrain(s) of difficulty. It is an obligation to listen attentively in order to build bridges across differences. In keeping with the dynamic characterization of the theory, the obligation includes guiding that work and listening with an immanent universal theory of human rights. Such reasoning and listening exhibit an epistemological commitment to seek out that which is absent, marginal, invisible, or otherwise not being given adequate consideration and to support through a broad range of actions the uncontested indivisible human rights of interrelated people, realized both structurally and through individual behavior.

The political and the theoretical intermingle in the terrain(s) of difficulty. When we use the immanent theory of universal human rights, we try to disentangle these, realizing that there may be political interests in masking political problems as theoretical ones.[10]

[9] Ackerly 2007b; Nagar 2002; Smith 1999.
[10] Englehart 2000; Langlois 2001; Weatherley 1999.

What are the hard questions we face together in the terrain(s) of difficulty? Well, political theorists don't agree. In chapter 1 I listed off four challenges that have led some political theorists to a constrained view of human rights.

(1) Human rights cannot be a legitimate basis of claims because they rely on pre-legal principles.
(2) Even if we were convinced that pre-legal ethical principles could be the basis of political demands, there can be no universal pre-legal or pre-political principles because there are no culturally universal foundations.
(3) Even if we could agree that there were universal human rights despite lacking universal moral foundations, we could not agree on what they were because we cannot agree on what their foundations are.
(4) Even if we could agree on what rights were, in order to realize them, we need to be able to assign correlative duties and obliged agents to each right.

These are not hard questions for activists. And immanent universal human rights theory dispatches with these challenges fairly quickly, but not without argument, because immanent universal theorists are committed to social change and social change cannot happen without confronting those who are not convinced. First I show how immanent universal rights theory dispatches with these four so-called challenges, and then turn to the questions that immanent universal human rights theorists see as the hard questions of the day.

First, whether codified in legal principles or just in political practice, the legitimacy of human rights cannot depend on pre-political principles, as none exist.[11] Second, universality need not depend on cultural (or religious) foundations; universality can be exhibited in universalizable practices – such as the practice of self-reflection. Third, rights need not come from foundations, but can be derived from critical practice. In fact, the meaning of human rights should be fundamentally tied to their function which is critical.[12] So, we should expect their content to

[11] In this sense, immanent universal human rights agrees with Bentham. Rights are nonsense if they are based on a hypothetical political agreement to any politically relevant principle (Bentham 1823; see also Ackerly forthcoming-b).

[12] See Kate Nash, who shows that commitment to universal human rights is consistent with the normative commitments of poststructural feminisms (2002).

be derived from their contestation and not from agreement about them. Were there universal agreement about their content, they would be rendered redundant. Fourth, as we have seen in practice, human rights violations are often invisible, thus at least *some* aspect of our obligations to promote human rights must be related to making their violation visible. This obligation cannot be directly correlated with any particular right. Rather, for human rights to mean something, the obligation has to be to use them to guide criticism and to open up possibilities for others to use them. (We will also see that because of what human rights are and do we have an obligation to participate in working through the terrain of difficulty, but that obligation is not a direct refutation of the traditional rights-require-corresponding-obligations-and-duty-bearers construction, so I will discuss it next.)

For the immanent universal human rights theorists, it is clear that there are human rights, that we need to use them for criticism and to be ever more attentive to human rights violations beyond our view, that we need to create opportunities for learning about human rights violations beyond our view, and that we need to confront our lack of political will by revealing that our lack of ability to address individual and structural rights violations is a political shortcoming, not a theoretical shortcoming. Human rights violations may be hard to see, but it is not hard to know that we should ask about that which we cannot see. It may be hard to know what to do, but it is not hard to know that the moral imperative rests with the obligation implicit in recognizing the normative legitimacy of human rights for criticism. We have the obligation to expose, mitigate, and prevent the opportunities for human rights violations. That obligation is immanent in the concept itself. Moves to limit the scope of that obligation are understood in an immanent universal theory as prudential, not theoretical. Sometimes, prudence cannot be helped. We may not know better or be able to imagine better. But in immanent universal theory, we don't delineate the boundaries of political theory with our political failures.[13]

Some hard questions may come to our attention because we are informed by (or care about)[14] those close to us, younger generations, or those whose human rights violations are unknown to us, but who are

[13] Cf. my discussion of Lukes in the preceding chapter.

[14] In this book I have not developed the connections between this theory of human rights and the feminist literature on care (see Gould 2004).

connected to us, perhaps because we consume the products of their labor, perhaps because our governments are directly or indirectly implicated in their human rights violations. What obligations do I have to Marie and her children? What is our obligation to stop global warming?[15] Is abortion a human right?[16] What can and should we do about human trafficking? The list of hard questions goes on and on. It is always a politically charged list that makes us confront not only our understanding of human rights, but also our political will to do anything and our problem-solving imaginations to bring us to solutions that would have a curb cutting quality. Though sometimes we cannot come up with curb cutting solutions, we must be vigilant in looking for them before we set precedents through action that may make other human rights violations less visible, or that may close off some future solutions.[17]

Other hard questions are brought to our attention by our research subjects themselves. In this study, women's human rights activists ask: How are we to be active in support of human rights for women in their communities? Are sexuality-related rights universal or of the same relative importance as economic rights? For strategic reasons, shouldn't we focus on the big issues?[18] In the next section, I lead us

[15] I will not answer this question here, but rather just suggest that in order to answer it, we need to know more about the structural connections between climate change and social injustice (Christian Aid 2006).

[16] Again, I cannot make the argument here, but as the Colombian government has been arguing, access to abortion may be inextricably linked with health and economic rights. These arguments are compatible with arguments that transnational feminists have been making and are not focused on a right to privacy basis for access to abortion (see *New York Times* 2006; Hitt 2006; Muse 2006; Petchesky 2003).

[17] See my earlier discussion on the use of the anti-discrimination paradigm. Relying on a shared notion of what constitutes appropriate and inappropriate differential treatment, the anti-discrimination paradigm makes each successive rights claimant articulate why her concerns are the "same as" other concerns that have previously been recognized. In other words, the approach requires each claimant to assert that human dignity is variable across different humans. It is an approach to human rights that relies on prior political recognition and therefore that undermines its own effectiveness as a critical device.

[18] Other human rights activists and theorists would recognize that these are important hard questions as well. Instead of on human rights and community, some might choose to focus on the relationship between human rights and religion (Afkhami 1995; An-Na'im 1990; Dalacoura 1998; Goodman 1998; Hertzke 2004; Howland 1999; Khan 1967 [1970]; Muzaffar 2002; Runzo,

through the terrain(s) of difficulty in reflecting on the tensions around competing rights, sexuality-related rights claims, and claims about the priority of rights even within women's human rights communities in order to illustrate the use of the immanent universal human rights theory. While the theory argues that rights cannot be itemized and disaggregated, often the terrain of difficulty of human rights is over which "rights" are universal rights.

I choose these hard questions, not because of their familiarity (though they are common challenges posed to human rights advocates), nor because of their political necessity (though they are the subject of pressing human rights demands in the world today), but rather because each exhibits a form of dilemma that is important to work through. If we are able to work through these dilemmas, we will have expanded our tools, tools that can be used to take up other questions in the terrains of difficulty.

Not surprisingly, these hard questions intersect, because (as the theory says) rights are indivisible. Many issues are framed by some political actors as problems related to *competing rights*;[19] I focus on community rights versus individual rights. Many issues are characterized by some political actors as *"new" rights* not part of universal human rights protections;[20] I focus on sexuality-related rights. Many issues are framed by some political actors as being about *priorities*; I focus on material-rights versus identity-rights priorities. These discussions reveal the politics in the characterization of rights as "competing," "new," or "more important." Aware of the ways in which politics are used to derail or prevent normative discussions, I might have set out how to answer other questions characterized as *the* hard questions.

Immanent universal human rights theory helps show us which aspects of a question are settled, where the difficulties lie, and whether those difficulties are political or theoretical. The challenge is to show which rights are uncontested and which are in a terrain of difficulty. To engage these arguments, the theorist has to work with one foot in the

Martin, and Sharma 2003; Spickard 2002; Yu 2000) or human rights and culture (Benhabib 2002; Clements and Young 1999; Crossette 2000; Ibhawoh 2000; Lentin 2004; Manderson 2004; Spivak 2005). For some, political rights are human rights and economic rights are questionably so (Cranston 1967). In my view the argument for including sexuality-related rights in the list of human rights is more difficult than the argument for including economic rights.

19 Messer 1993.

20 Discussion about "new" rights was renewed during Beijing + 10 (Omang 2005).

theory and one foot outside it – using the view that all universal human rights are indivisible to determine if the right or basket of rights in question are indivisible from those other rights indisputably recognized as universal human rights. The theory itself offers us some tools to think through issues in a terrain of difficulty.

First, commitment. The basics of a destabilizing epistemology and attentiveness to that which we cannot see condition our perspective on the problems of the terrain of difficulty. We need to look for the possibility that the use or abuse of power is rendering a problem more intractable than the underlying theoretical problem might suggest. The immanent universal theory of human rights invites us to reveal the political interests behind one framing or another. Further, it asks us to sustain our commitment to working through the problem despite its seeming intractability. The theory asks us to be committed to the use of human rights for social criticism and not to table human rights as a guide for criticism when a theoretical adjudication of a hard question is not immediately forthcoming.

Second, epistemological attentiveness. The immanent universal theory asks us to be attentive to how epistemology constrains our conception of a problem. Working through the terrain of difficulty reveals that epistemology can act as a structure constraining our imaginations. Epistemology conditions what we see as "the" problem. For example, we might see the tension between individual rights and collective rights as *itself* a problem.[21] Immanent universal human rights theory asks if the structure of the problem isn't itself an exercise of power that constrains our ability to think through an issue. To follow the example, universal human rights theory invites us to approach a rights-in-tension problem by asking the question that Walzer asked: what else are we but humans in community?[22] And to ask it with Uma Narayan's twist: how could a solution to my human rights violations require my giving up the community that sustains me?[23] A theory of human rights cannot *require* anyone to live with experiential and cognitive dissonance (though it might recognize that there is a lot going around). The immanent universal theory of human rights does however ask us to

[21] Many authors characterize these in tension (Al-Hibri 1999; Benhabib 2002; Honig 1999; Kymlicka 1995; Nussbaum 1999b; Okin 1999; Okin, Cohen, Howard, and Nussbaum 1999; Shachar 2001; Skocpol and Fiorina 1999).
[22] Walzer 1984. [23] Narayan 1997.

think through the structural forces that make some rights seem divisible, that make some people's rights violations invisible, and that make thought processes themselves partially socially constructed.

Third, indivisible rights. In the immanent universal human rights theory we use uncontested rights to work through rights claims in the terrain(s) of difficulty. We might show that recognition of an uncontested right is not possible without recognition of the contested right. In this case, resolution of the problem in the terrain of difficulty is not to identify a "new" right, but rather to use existing rights to challenge existing political, social, and economic structures that prevent its realization. We might notice when the rights of some people are not able to be realized because they are indivisibly dependent on other rights that are insecure. Whether invisible or visible, the indivisibility of rights leads us to look for the ways that values, practices, and institutions can enable the realization or violation of certain rights.

Fourth, structure. The theory asks us to consider the ways in which values, practices, and institutions, including political, social, and economic structures, prevent the recognition and realization of a basket of contested rights *for all* even though they may be recognized and realized for some. For these arguments, Sen's understanding of rights as the opportunity for, and the context of, autonomous choice is useful in guiding our listening and reasoning.[24] Do some people have fewer opportunities if this basket of rights is not legitimate? At first we may think we have found a "new" right until careful analysis of "old" structures reveals in fact this universal human right has been necessary for those with power to have the "opportunity to achieve combinations of functionings (including, *inter alia*, the opportunity to be well-nourished or in good health)."[25] Immanent universal human rights theory reveals that the right is uncontested, essential to the opportunity to achieve combinations of functionings, but that some people are deprived of that opportunity. This deprivation can be either due to a failure to realize the interrelatedness of all humans or due to social norms that make the different treatment of some people invisible. The solution cannot be to recognize the rights of these "new" people; that would undermine the universality of human rights by requiring recognition prior to realization of rights. Instead the immanent theory

[24] Sen 2004; Gould 2004.

[25] Sen 2004: 334. See also the discussion of Frederick Douglass in chapter 2.

requires us to analyze *all* structures such that no human (visible or invisible) experiences human rights violations.

Feminist activists and academics are continually cultivating new methods for assessing the practices of the daily lives that we live and love but that contribute indirectly to the context of rights violations (or maintenance). These practices are different for each of us but we all have them. Because they sustain us in certain ways, they are the source of aspects of our epistemology that are least able to be destabilized.[26] A curb cut feminist epistemology requires us to look for analytical solutions that address not only the rights violations of the women with whom we launched our inquiry, but also of others. Consequently, a curb cut approach encourages us to look for overlaps that might lead us to notice forms of marginalization that are not linked explicitly to gender. While noticing the distinctiveness of each individual experience, the curb cut epistemology does not highlight differences that would lead us to treat certain forms of marginalization as unique. Instead, while dealing with one experience of marginalization we look for other related forms made visible to us because we were attentive to the first. Although we have a history of describing oppression as discrimination on axes[27] – of race, sex, gender, sexuality, age, etc. – women's experiences, often documented through feminist research, illustrate that oppression is not experienced on axes, but rather through processes. Cynthia Enloe and Katharine Moon theorize about the experiences of local women near US military bases as subjects and objects in international relations.[28] Because they reference processes of militarization and Cold War politics, their inquiries invite us to consider the linkages between the international agreements that are predicated on the economic and political marginalization of women that serve US military bases, international trade agreements that are predicated on the economic and political marginalization of women in developing economies who are drawn into low wage labor, and international efforts to stem the trafficking of people, drugs, arms, and money. While seeing all of these linkages may make it difficult to design social science research that can study these integrated global processes, ignoring them limits our ability to promote a human rights respecting culture.

[26] Cf. Narayan 1997; Rosenberg 2002. [27] Crenshaw 1989.
[28] Enloe 1989; Moon 1997.

Fifth and finally, collaboration. The focus on visibility and invisibility leads us to notice that perspective matters. "We" cannot refer only to those whom "we" see. Therefore, we need to work through the terrain of difficulty collaboratively, building communication bridges between people so that perspectives become shared and more of "us" are visible. Through collaboration we become increasingly attentive to the invisible among us (Crenshaw's over-inclusion) and the invisible outside of "us" (Crenshaw's under-inclusion). We also can see the linkages (between micro-level analysis and macro-level analysis for example). Feminists generally talk about "feminisms" in the plural today, recognizing the reality of this diversity. Immanent universal human rights theory is built on the epistemological value of this diversity. As I work through the following issues, I work collaboratively, in dialogue with the activists whose views help articulate what is *hard* about competing rights, new rights, and setting the priority of rights.

In the next three sections I use these tools to think through three areas that many human rights theorists and activists, including feminist and women's activists, continue to treat as in a terrain of difficulty. These are areas of "continued dispute" and I am offering *my* way of using the immanent universal theory to resolve the dispute. My epistemological bias in this query is that which I laid out in chapter 5. That in order to work through difficult questions we need to be open to our own blind spots. These include being open to the possibility that our way of asking the question itself is mistaken and that our own practices (particularly consumption patterns), institutions (including markets), and epistemological blinders make our own blind spots out of sight.

So in this chapter I am doing two theoretical things while discussing particularly hard problems for human rights theorists and activists. I am showing how I, one theorist in collaborative reflection with my interviewees, use this theory to think through a problem, and I am showing that the process of thinking through a hard problem itself generates new tools that may be useful in working through other hard problems. The implication is not that it would then be *easy* to deal with other problems, but the problems may seem less intractable.

Having worked through some hard problems, the skill of attentive listening is more practiced. The evidence of shared responsibility is exposed in the bridges among people used in the process. One may not agree with how I use the theory to reason through these hard questions or with my choice of hard questions. However, using the tools of the immanent universal theory, the process of reasoning through these differences – of building bridges across differences – *itself* will reduce invisibility and silence.

## Working through hard questions: illustration

Amy Gutmann and Dennis Thompson's *Democracy and Disagreement* is really two books and I like them each for different reasons. In one book they explain the practices and principles that we ought to use in our democratic deliberations (reciprocity, publicity, accountability, basic liberty, basic opportunity, and fair opportunity). I agree that I ought to exhibit these practices and principles *with attentive listening*, encourage them when I am engaged in deliberative contexts, and that institutions that do the same promote deliberative democracy. In the other book, they explain how a deliberative democrat should decide certain illustrative issues, admittedly relying on scholarly not political deliberation.[29] I agree with many of their conclusions. However, I do not think that the argument of the first book supports the conclusions of the second because they use scholarly deliberation not political deliberation to address the issues. Uncomfortably, because I have heard lots of arguments I don't think are morally right, uncomfortably, because I live with lots of political decisions that I don't think can be sustained by normative argument, uncomfortably, because I am very comfortable with my own moral compass, the theory that I defend leaves some positions that I would defend up for continued discussion. My illustrations are illustrations.

In this section, I illustrate how this theory (which functions like an ethics) can guide our thinking through these hard questions. I will offer my conclusions based on the way in which the theory guides my thinking. But I am not arguing that the *theory* enables us to derive decisive answers to these questions. The theory *does* enable us to say that to use another human rights theory to argue decisively that certain human rights claims are illegitimate claims in all times in all places for all time is to use an epistemological authority for a political purpose. Such uses of epistemological authority (I argued in the early

[29] Gutmann and Thompson 1996: 3.

part of this book) need to be interrogated for the exercises of power that they mask. In this section I use the theory to think through specific issues. Others will use the theory differently and may come to different conclusions in thinking through these issues. However, neither the ambiguities and incommensurabilities of these arguments (mine and the imagined other) and of life experiences, nor the dynamics of crossings and translations, nor the existence and continued emergence of hard questions, are themselves *evidence* that there are no human rights.

The import of this argument is that where such differences exist, because all humans are interrelated and human rights indivisible, we must develop and strengthen our commitments to attentive listening in the terrains of difficulty. In the colloquial sense of "ideal," commitment to listening to people with whom I have profound differences over epistemological and moral issues may indeed feel like an *ideal* theory. Such attentive listening is too tall an order for an Aristotelian man of leisure, let alone for a working parent in an industrial democracy, or for a refugee seeking safety from regionalized conflict.

Recognizing epistemological differences and the profound disagreements that they generate within and across human communities, such listening is hard. It poses daunting logistical and political challenges, but it is not idealistic. Ideal theory would assume that such communication would be easy or unnecessary.

So, in this chapter I engage. I show how one might work through the difficult questions guided by the theory. The theory being provisional, and myself being individual (quite broadly informed, but imperfectly informed), my illustration is an *illustration* of the use of the theory and not *the* conclusions of the theory. I think these are the right arguments, but there are others. I willingly privilege these arguments or others that use the immanent theory of universal human rights over others that do not use the immanent universal theory of human rights. I privilege these over arguments that rely on an authoritative interpretation of tradition or a transcendental authority. I privilege these arguments over those that would use a principle or set of principles to adjudicate epistemological differences.

My arguments, then, are provisional, but they can guide theoretical reflection *and the activism of women's human rights activists.* In the following chapter, I show how activists have and can further use this theory (their own theory) of human rights to guide their activism.

## *Competing rights*

One aspect of the terrain of difficulty over the content of human rights is the question of whether *all* human rights claims should be understood as *human* rights claims. This often takes the form of a dispute as to which rights are more foundational or fundamental and is characterized by the need to adjudicate between rights claims or the debate over whether all of the "pillars" of human rights are foundational.[30] If we understand rights as a list, it is very difficult to work through these difficulties.

On adjudicating between rights, consider what it means to keep our commitments to articles 29 and 30 of the Universal Declaration:

Article 29.

(1) Everyone has duties to the community in which alone the free and full development of his personality is possible.
(2) In the exercise of his rights and freedoms, everyone shall be subject only to such limitations as are determined by law solely for the purpose of securing due recognition and respect for the rights and freedoms of others and of meeting the just requirements of morality, public order and the general welfare in a democratic society.
(3) These rights and freedoms may in no case be exercised contrary to the purposes and principles of the United Nations.

Article 30. Nothing in this Declaration may be interpreted as implying for any State, group or person any right to engage in any activity or to perform any act aimed at the destruction of any of the rights and freedoms set forth herein.

Although states have agreed to the Universal Declaration, the Declaration itself contains ambiguities such as the tension between the obligations to community that membership requires and the exercise of rights enumerated elsewhere in the Universal Declaration. Even though the Universal Declaration is universal in its scope and political legitimacy, it does not contain within it the tools for reconciling its own tensions such as the tensions between individual rights and responsibilities to communities. Nor does the document contain the methodological tools for identifying when the activities of a state or group related to maintaining itself might justifiably require the suppression of the individual rights of its members.

[30] See reference to pillars in chapter 7.

The terrain of difficulty will always include rights claims that seem to conflict. But the content of the immanent theory, based on indivisibility, interrelatedness, and structure does give us the tools to think through these difficulties. If we understand rights as indivisible, there may sometimes arise strategic or prudential reasons for why we might have to prioritize *certain* individual rights over *certain* community claims. Cases that involve the cultural defense for a crime, the headscarf affair in France, the education of Amish children, and community membership rights of indigenous women (for example) are political questions over rights, not theoretical questions about rights.[31] Theoretically, a minority culture ought to be able to thrive in a national context without courts needing to draw a legal boundary between a citizen and herself – between her citizenship and her membership in community. When such conflicts emerge politically, they are not best adjudicated by a theoretical principle that lets individual rights be trump.[32] Theoretically, it is more sound (and more consistent with the reasons that feminists put cultural issues on the table from within their cultural traditions) to argue that the political loss one rights-bearer is asked to endure is recognized for what it is, a politically expedient loss, not a theoretically justified rejection. The conditions that prevent some aboriginal women and their children from being members of their communities are political, not theoretical.[33] The conditions that make it politically problematic for girls to wear headscarves to school in France are political, not theoretical. The historical conditions that make family law decisions separate from other civil and criminal law decisions in India are political, not theoretical. The post-colonial and post-genocidal domestic and international politics that prevent Marie and her family from living in a safe place where they can provide for themselves are political, not theoretical. Keeping the commitments to articles 29 and 30 requires changing the political structures that make the less powerful within minorities confront a Hobson's choice. More generally, the theory of human rights needs a normative argument not only for what it means to keep commitments to articles 29 and 30, but also for why the committed should understand all four pillars of the human rights system as necessary moral

[31] Benhabib 2002; Green 2001; Song 2005.
[32] Benhabib 2002; Kymlicka 1995; Okin 1999.
[33] Benhabib 2002; Shachar 2001; Song 2005; Walzer 1990.

commitments with political legitimacy, as so many human rights activists do.[34]

However, to understand these as the four pillars is arbitrary. Loretta Ross argues that there are:

> eight categories of human rights protections to which we are all entitled: civil rights, political rights, economic rights, social rights, cultural rights, environmental rights, developmental rights and sexual human rights. If you don't know those eight categories then you really don't know how to develop an appropriate strategy to advance those rights.[35]

Her view is not universally held among feminists either, as we will see in the following discussion.[36]

The challenge in articulating a normative argument for thinking through conflicting views about the content of rights using the insights of activists is that activists – especially my sources who often disagreed with or were only newly connected with transnational feminist networks – do not agree on the extent of indivisibility. They all agree that some rights are indivisible, but they do not all agree as to which rights are indivisible. The challenge is to work through the terrain of difficulty using the undisputed aspects of the immanent universal theory. The theory itself guides the committed to identify structural impediments to recognizing all rights, structural impediments to recognizing the rights of some people, and structural impediments to imagining new ways of thinking. In my research, activists justified not prioritizing sexuality-related rights claims because they were not "normal" or because they were not the "big" issue. In the next section, I address the first argument, and in the following, I address the other.

[34] Cf. Habermas (2001a), in which he seems to treat human rights as theoretically linked to the rule of law because their Western liberal form is historically linked with the rule of law. On Habermas's reading, human rights are contingent on a polity. I have been arguing that their political legitimacy is *not* dependent on a polity. That to make human rights contingent on a polity would undermine human rights as a political resource for the oppressed within a society. The struggle for human rights is in a sense a contestation about the boundaries of the polity and about the rule of law within a polity and thus its political legitimacy and moral legitimacy cannot rely on the norms of the polity as bounded.

[35] IB13 2005.

[36] Focus on the "big" issues echoes the problem of identifying as "universal" only those rights on which there is an overlapping consensus discussed in chapter 3.

## *Sexuality*

Discrimination based on sexuality is a violation of most international human rights law, but the model of immanent universal human rights I have been describing extends far beyond the bounds of legal structures to create obligations for identifying and mitigating human rights violations in social, political, and economic structures. Do these include violations of sexuality-related rights?

To a certain extent we need to look beyond what people say sexuality rights are to know what they are. We need to look to their actions to see what rights they claim. But as a starting place, consider that feminists in the international sphere have described them as:

> the right of each human being to experience her/his sexuality freely, fully, and consensually, and an understanding of sexuality as a realm of experience encompassing sexual orientation, gender identity, sexual and gender expression, desire, pleasure and sexual practices.[37]

In the United States in the late 1970s feminists defined sexuality-rights in the context of women's health:

> the availability to all people of good public childcare centers and schools; decent housing, adequate welfare, and wages high enough to support a family; and of quality medical, pre- and post-natal and maternal care. It also must mean freedom of sexual choice, which implies an end to the cultural norms that define women in terms of having children and living with a man; an affirmation of people's right to raise children outside of conventional families; and ... a transformation of childcare arrangements so that they are shared among women and men.[38]

In both contexts sexuality rights are understood as dimensions of Ross's eight categories: "civil rights, political rights, economic rights, social rights, cultural rights, environmental rights, developmental rights and sexual human rights."

However, while we want to capture all of these dimensions of rights that reflect on sexuality demands, activists also caution us to notice that using "rights" in the rights-as-entitlements way (a familiar view which immanent universal human rights displaces) depends on a state

[37] Rothschild, Long, and Fried 2005: 3–4.

[38] CARASA, *Women Under Attack: Abortion, Sterilization Abuse, and Reproductive Freedom* (1979: 11), cited by Petchesky (2006).

in a way that itself is problematic for sexuality rights. As some South and Southeast Asian activists caution:

> When people use the term "sexual rights," it encompasses many aspects: the right to information, choice, well-being, pleasure, access, treatment, and services with regards to sexuality. But when we break it down and talk about the part of sexual rights that includes pleasure, it becomes even more difficult for us to discuss and define how to go about providing for its freedom/regulation. So, should we at all consider sexual pleasure as a "right" given that in doing so, it will fall under the purview of the state?[39]

These activists' definitions of (and concerns about) sexuality rights exhibit a concern for inclusiveness and attention to ways in which the rights of some people may be denied. In my interviews and participant observation, many exhibited these definitions and concerns. Much documentation of transnational feminist activism is consistent with this range of concerns.[40]

In my discussion of sexuality, I want to focus instead on a tension between those who see sexuality rights as human rights and those who do not. This tension emerged in my interviews and participant observations. Feminist theorists have brought theoretical attention to the issues raised by these activists and have offered us principles or guidelines for adjudicating between them.[41] Each balances the claims using theoretical and institutional mechanisms.[42] Further, they have discussed them in ways that reify a *dichotomous tension*[43] which serves to weaken arguments for both social recognition and material redistribution.[44] Immanent universal human rights theorizing approaches the tension in a way that strengthens the affirmative rights claims of activists on *all* sides of the tensions. Activists may see sexuality rights as in competition with material concerns (such as health, poverty, and land rights) or cultural concerns (such as *dalit* or minority issues).

[39] The South and Southeast Asia Resource Centre on Sexuality 2006.
[40] Bunch 1990; 1995; Laurent 2005; Nash 2005; Petchesky 2006; 2003; Ratna 2000; Rothschild, Long, and Fried 2005; Wilson 1996.
[41] Nussbaum 2000b: 290ff. [42] Benhabib 2002; Fraser 1997; Shachar 2001.
[43] See, more generally, Connolly 1993; 2004.
[44] In personal conversation, Joshua Cohen noted that the title of Susan Okin's "Is Multiculturalism Bad for Women?," which provocatively pits women's interest claims against cultural-based interest claims, was an editorial proposal intended to be provocative. The piece and responses brought much attention to the seemingly irreconcilable trade-off between individual and cultural rights (Okin *et al.* 1999).

Although some activism reifies this dichotomy, not all does. The shift by lesbian activists in their discourse to women's human rights from development and economic concerns did not correspond to a shift away from the material concerns that had been central to their agenda nor to a shift toward identity-based politics.[45] Rather, it seems that the discussion of "sexual orientation" and "sexual rights" was used by non-feminists opposed to both, to focus on the identity dimension of lesbian activism and thus to undermine the activists' own integrated analysis. This reframing came not from women's arguments, but rather from those opposing women's organizing.

As is illustrated by Rothschild in a book put out by the International Gay and Lesbian Human Rights Commission and the Center for Women's Global Leadership, anti-women forces have been able to draw public attention away from material issues by using a politics of distraction in which lesbian-baiting and sexuality play key roles.[46] A strategic response of focusing narrowly on the identity issue is a way of affirming the anti-women strategy of lesbian-baiting.

The activism of some women in India, for example, offers an alternative strategy that puts the issues women think are important squarely at the center of the public debate. Through their activism around the movie *Fire*, women forged an integrated analysis of gendered power that formed a platform for future activism and alliance on other issues.[47]

Of course, identity issues are important and the often successful strategy of lesbian-baiting is an illustration of why. However, when feminists and women activists focus on lesbian identity issues over

45 Wilson 1996. 46 Rothschild, Long, and Fried 2005.

47 See Rothschild, Long, and Fried 2005: 132ff. Also, Nussbaum mentions this activism as a case of political contestation precipitating context-specific reevaluation of capabilities (2000b: 292–293). She uses the example to illustrate the relationship between employment and economic autonomy-related capabilities and sexuality-related capabilities. Women's economic independence puts them in a better position to express their sexuality, but cultural stereotypes of women as having a sexuality that needs to be controlled inhibits their ability to find employment and gain economic autonomy. The movie *Fire* and its discussion within India figure prominently in her confidence that sexuality is no longer a contestable rights claim, at least within India. Rothchild *et al.* discusses women's activism in India related to *Fire* as well. While it is important to be aware of this activism, the movie and the activism around the movie invite trans-cultural and intra-national discussions as well in part because of the diasporic origins and audience of the movie (see Desai 2002).

other lesbian and women's issues, we let lesbian-baiters choreograph our politics.[48] Such performative politics is distracting and can reinforce and be reinforced by instincts to prioritize other subsets of women's issues. If we think substantively about women's issues, however, they are not easily disaggregated.

Like the lesbian activists in India that Rothschild discusses, many working in health, poverty, and the *dalit* movement have resisted divide and conquer strategies. Ross argues that because the present US administration's strategy has been to threaten women's rights from so many fronts, disaggregation is no longer a viable strategy for women and feminist activists:

> Well, the opportunities are that we all are facing an innovative, collective foe in this US Administration. Even though we may not want to, Bush and his cronies are connecting the dots for us because their attacks on our human rights are so universal. They're attacking women's rights with the partial birth abortion ban and at the same time they won't allow emergency contraception to be made available. You know they won't force insurance companies to provide birth control coverage but they will pay for Viagra.
>
> I mean we're dealing with all of that in the women's rights movement but you also have attacks on the gay and lesbian movement with the so-called Defense of Marriage Act and they're trying to change the Constitution; the attack on the environment with the withdrawal from the Kyoto Accords. So instead of being the divided and the conquered we're actually recognizing that we need to come together. I think that's why the March for Women's Lives was such a success because when we were only calling it the "March for Freedom of Choice," it was a very narrow march. But once we broadened it and called it the "March for Women's Lives" and we connected opposition to the war in Iraq with the attack on women's rights, with the attack on the environment, with the debt crisis, all of a sudden that march took off and over 1400 organizations endorsed it.[49]

In Ross's analysis, divisibility is the anti-rights strategy and indivisibility is the strategy of those committed to immanent universal human rights. Divisibility is a theoretical device anti-rights forces can use to create complicity with the use of political, economic, and social structures to constrain rights recognition.

48 Appiah cautions against letting others determine which aspect of our identity has political import to us (1994b).

49 IB13 2005.

Gigi Francisco, activist and scholar with Development Alternatives with Women for a New Era (DAWN), makes this point in a succinct way:

> Our struggle is embedded in power compacts found in institutions and social relations. For DAWN, the women's movement is not about women per se. Its analysis and advocacy is about freeing women as constructed, disciplined and objectified beings, and nurturing our agency in both private and public spaces. Moreover, gender inequity in power relations cannot be separated from other power inequalities. It is deeply entangled. Thus, it is futile to address gender issues singly, exclusively and in isolation from other struggles against unjust and undemocratic power systems.[50]

Attempts to do so are designed to fail.

Through their activism and in their reflections on their activism, women's human rights activists disaggregate theoretical and political concerns. Strategically, they may respond to lesbian-baiting by asserting a right to marry or to adopt in the United States for example, but such a claim does not mean that this disaggregation is theoretically sustained by immanent universal human rights.

However, the historical record is as much one of *not* extending rights to women as it is one of extending rights to some people. This history should make the committed keenly aware of the power of such approaches to ignore some human rights or the human rights of some people using structures and therefore shielding any particular individual from facing her human rights obligations.

As those committed to immanent universal human rights work through the problems in the terrain of difficulty, they reveal that some disputes don't belong there at all. They reveal no immanent theoretical basis for treating an issue as contested, that the contestation is wholly political. Even those who would dispute certain claims on ethical grounds can understand that the dispute over whether sexuality-related rights are "rights" is only about *some* rights. LGBTIQ people have undisputed politically legitimate claims to those human rights that are *not* in the terrain of difficulty. So whether lesbians should be allowed to adopt children might be in the terrain of difficulty, but whether lesbians are equal persons before the law (article 6 and 7) is not. One might dispute whether gays should have the right to serve in

[50] Francisco 2003: 24.

the military, but not whether they should be subjected to arbitrary arrest, detention, or exile (article 9). All humans are entitled to the indivisible rights that are not in the terrain of difficulty. The questions are: are certain other rights also indivisible? Do the structures that prevent LGBTIQ people from enjoying these other rights prevent them or others from enjoying those rights that are not in dispute?

For example, the right to have children, biologically, through *in vitro* fertilization, or through adoption is disputed.[51] If there were such a right, reproductively challenged people would be entitled to a share of medical care that might compete for resources with (for example) those claiming a right to a healthy environment or to prevent the spread of HIV/AIDS. However, the right to found a family is part of the Universal Declaration of Human Rights.[52] So how do we unpack the theoretical and political questions in order to think through the rights claim to successful procreation? There are uncontested rights to health and to found a family. Clearly, reproduction is a constitutive aspect of each of these. Politically and socially created environmental conditions and social structures may have an impact on one's ability to have reproductive health or to found a family through adoption. If we show that reproductive challenge is a result of environmentally or socially caused human rights violations, then we should bring about structural change to realize that right; the inability to successfully procreate is an indicator of other rights violations, but not a rights violation itself.

Likewise, then, the focus on ability to found a family aspect of sexuality-related rights should be on the social, political, and economic local and global structures necessary to realize that right. The right to procreate should be secured for all of society through a healthy environment, universal access to health care, universal education, political participation, and economic opportunities. Since these are rights that are not in the terrain of difficulty, they should be secured for all and all people should enjoy them, and the ability to found a family they enable. So, whereas one might argue that there is no right to found a family, therefore LGBTIQ people do not have such a right (or at least such a right is contestable), in fact, since the ability to found a family depends on rights that are uncontested, all people including LGBTIQ people should have the healthy environment, universal access to health care,

[51] Cf. Center for Reproductive Rights 2004.
[52] Universal Declaration of Human Rights 1948.

universal education, political participation, and economic opportunities necessary to found a family and no one has the explicit right to successful procreation.

Likewise, there is no uncontested right to serve in the military. However, it has been argued that in contemporary political structures, serving in the military is an important avenue to full citizenship and equality before the law. Such a notion of citizenship excludes many people from full citizenship.[53] Therefore, immanent universal human rights theory would argue that the practices of citizenship and equality need to change such that neither depends on the willingness or ability to die for one's nation-state. The strategy for allowing gays in the military to be out *because* of the citizenship-value of military service leads to an increasingly militarized notion of citizenship. Such a notion of citizenship is exclusionary. The women's rights as human rights movement of the 1990s was about exposing the politics of such arguments and revealing the theoretical incoherence of marginalizing views.[54] According to this reading of immanent universal human rights, the focus on this aspect of sexuality-related rights should likewise be on the political and social structures of citizenship, augmenting the social and political recognition for work that strengthens the citizenry, not just work that strengthens the state.

It may be that strategically, in order to change social structures society needs more visibility of gay families and more visibility of gays in the military, but the immanent universal human rights theory does not recommend strategies of advocating for rights to procreation or to serve in the military. Its curb cut epistemology cautions against strategies that close off some human rights claims or the human rights claims of some people. It does so but it also supports rights to a healthy environment, universal access to health care, universal education, political participation, economic opportunities, and full citizenship for all.

One might argue for sexuality-related rights using anti-discrimination framework. Since sexual minorities cannot have secure property and other economic rights when they are discriminated against based on sexuality, they need to have rights that prevent that discrimination. No right (the right not to be discriminated against based on sexuality)

[53] Stern 2005; Tickner 1992.
[54] Bunch 1990; 2004; Charlesworth 1994; Friedman 1995.

can be relegated to the terrain of difficulty because only some (LGBTIQ) people confront it. Because the immanent universal human rights theory recognizes that the rights of all people are interrelated, we know that no economic rights are secure for anyone if they are not secure for all. If there is a politically legitimate justification for depriving some people of their economic rights, then there is no security for economic rights. This approach yields a similar conclusion: while activists may have different strategic priorities based on their context, they need to work in a way that recognizes the conceptual indivisibility of rights and the interrelatedness of rights-bearers.

However, immanent universal human rights is more ambitious than anti-discrimination. Rather than playing into the anti-discrimination model which encourages dichotomization (in order to treat likes alike and unlikes differently), immanent universal human rights theory justifies a commitment to thinking through the structures that determine what constitutes "alike" and different.[55] Immanent universal human rights activists and theorists work toward social, political, and economic structures that reveal and sustain the indivisible rights of all of humanity.

In a given location at a given point in time, advocacy for sexuality-related rights will be strategically partial or non-existent, but the immanent universal human rights theory does not support choosing rights strategies that support structures that impede future recognition of or advocacy for sexuality-related rights.

While activists will continue to work in issue silos, in locally appropriate ways, the implications of this theoretical account of indivisibility and interrelatedness is that their activism needs to proceed in a curb cutting way. It cannot close off future or neighboring rights claims or rights claimants. The immanent universal theorist must be self-conscious of the risks of fragmentation.

This move in the theoretical argument is beyond what the activist from Burkina Faso and I ever talked about in our interview.[56] It may be that it remains beyond what she would agree to, or it may be that this is what she meant and I misunderstood her because of her reference to "*normal* sexuality." She argued that it was appropriate for women sharing a movement to support each other on their respective issues.

[55] See discussion of equality, Steihm, and MacKinnon in the preceding chapter.
[56] I2 2004.

Perhaps she did not mean this as a *quid pro quo* agreement to disagree. Perhaps she meant that *because* women's issues are interrelated, we need to support each other across issues, even while we work independently in our issue and geographic silos.

Besides being theoretically attractive, analytical coherence is the right strategic response to the divide-and-conquer strategy of anti-women, anti-gay, anti-minority, anti-labor, and anti-family forces. It is not enough for activists to agree to support one another on "their" issues. While potentially strategically useful in the short-term, *quid pro quo* strategies are not theoretically sustained and in the long-term inhibit structural analysis and contribute to fragmentable and fragmented efforts at social change.

Human rights cannot be useful for cross-cultural and intra-cultural social criticism if "human rights" has complex and nuanced meanings that *differ* across contexts such that when we share our understandings with other activists, we have little in common but the words. When activists from a range of contexts and focused on a range of issues understand these issues as indivisibly part of the same political project *and* theoretical framework, the discovery itself is a tool that enables us to work (with contestation among us) for intra- and cross-cultural social criticism. That shared theoretical project is the use of human rights to delegitimate attempts to oppress some people.

## *The big issue*

Even though indivisibility is part of the immanent universal theory of human rights, for some feminist and women's activists who are not working with LGBTIQ-informed perspectives, the variety among LGBTIQ perspectives, the differences between lesbian and intersexed identity issues, the differences between gay and transgendered health and medical issues, are unnoticed, invisible. Instead, for some activists, the interests of LGBTIQ people are understood as identity issues, not material issues, and are less important strategically for feminist and women's rights activism.[57] For them, we should focus on the "big" issues. One of the activists from Burkina Faso thought women activists should focus on the "visible" issues. The irony of committing feminists

[57] I1 2004; I2 2004; I3 2004; I5 2004; ID6 2004; ID16 2004; ID23 2004.

to working only on the issues we see should not be lost on feminists who are associated with a movement for making women's human rights violations visible.

Often tensions over which issues are the "big" issues take the form of priority. Should indigenous rights have the same priority as women's rights? Should cultural minority rights have the same priority as women's rights? Should the rights violations of LGBTIQ people have the same priority as women's other rights-based concerns? For others, even gendered and cultural issues are not as deserving of feminist and women's activists' attention unless "they become *the* big problem," as Jayati Ghosh argued; Indian activists don't have an "excessive focus on cultural issues because the material problems are so big."[58]

The juxtaposition of "big" and "identity" issues reifies an unconstructive dichotomy. Continued divisiveness on issues of sexuality and culture within feminist movements demonstrates that there is much more analytical work to be done among and with activists' insights.[59] Social and political recognition are often necessary for the political and economic security concerns of members of minority or marginalized groups.

The reason that the distinction between "big" and "small" is not *analytically* important is because, if it were, it would offer a justification for focusing on the rights of some people rather than the rights of others. Even strategically, but certainly theoretically, women's human rights activists cannot be concerned with the human rights violations that affect only a certain portion – the most visible, most numerous, most articulate – of the population. Because feminists don't want to offer analytical or strategic support to a view that argues that it is acceptable to de-emphasize human rights advocacy for the least visible, least numerous, or least articulate, feminist and women's activists need

[58] Anyone with even a passing knowledge of India's material and cultural history might guess that this activist, a well-known economist, was speaking ironically. The cross-cultural issues raised to national and even international attention, sometimes turning violent, include the Shah Bano case (a divorse and family maintenance case), the mandir–masjid controversy (conflict over a shared location of a temple for Lord Ram and a mosque), the uniform civil code, and ethnic violence in Gujurat.

[59] Remember the discussion in chapter 6 of the professor from Iran and the differences laid bare by the desire to speak words of solidarity: "Let's cross borders together to change the world."

to work to deploy theoretical tools that support the strategic priorities that power-challenged activists need to make.[60]

One could rearticulate identity issues as material issues by focusing on the material aspects of identity issues. However, while being inclusive, an analytical approach that disaggregates material and identity issues and then reaggregates them by rearticulating identity issues *as* material issues obfuscates the important *identity dimension* of most material concerns which is quite evident in my informants' work and in their accounts of their work.[61] In an ironically tautological way, people who lobby for material concerns risk being identified politically by others as having an identity of "one lacking." Without the critique of the identity dimension of material rights, those with HIV/AIDS who are lobbying for their health are heard on their material issue, but in their activism their stigma as an outcast group is reified.[62]

Some political claims are commonly conceived of as material, yet the work for recognition of these material claims starts with analytical attention to structures *and* the right to interrogate these. These include the right to information and accountability, to legal documentation of identity and citizenship, to property and inheritance, to access to impartial and transparent justice, to personal security for women generally, and to personal security for sexual minorities or other social outcasts, ultimately with the goal of changing the social structures that generate outcasts.[63]

Another set of rights claims, again, can be talked about as materially based, but only with a distortion of the meaning of material or with an under-comprehension of the extent of the demand being made. These demands include demands for peace, for recovering the hidden truths of past human rights violations in order to create a path toward reconciliation and reparations, for environmental preservation or sustainability, for economic reform generally, for agricultural reform, and

[60] In the same essay in which she argues that feminist and women's social movements need not disaggregate their activism, Francisco acknowledges that one of the paradoxes of an integrated analysis of oppression is that it too creates fragmentation as feminists spread themselves thin to be in all places all the time (2003).

[61] I read Fraser as doing this in a careful and thoughtful way (1997; 2001).

[62] The Rainbow Planet Coalition is one example of strategizing that seeks to challenge that reification through cross-issue and cross-identity-group collaboration.

[63] Bunch (2003) spoke of rights and security.

for water for livelihood. Other issues that affect the visible material conditions of women's lives are migration issues, including those related to refugees, internally displaced people, trafficking, illegal immigration, and sex work.[64] Finally and perhaps most obviously, marginalized within their own communities and as members of groups marginalized within their societies, women are concerned with the injustice of socially normalized exploitable hierarchy.

Many of these rights claims involve making claims that are *seemingly* substantively unrelated. Additionally, these rights claims have seemingly different metaphorical forms – rights as entitlements, rights as the political standing to make a claim, rights as enabling conditions. Some of these rights have conceivable individual or institutional duty-bearers (like the police or the government), but many do not.

When we analyze the rights claims of each, one at a time, considering the context of the rights claim and the conceivable parties who might bear some responsibility for securing the right, we see also that, because of the institutionalization of the rights violations in patterns of social, economic, and political behavior that are caused by many agents acting individually, none of these rights can be secured without changes in social, economic, and political institutions *and* social, economic, and political *behavior* of many, including the behavior of those whose rights are violated. None of these rights claims could be met without dealing with the multiple dimensions of social context and the individual choices and actions not only of duty-bearers, but also of the rights-bearers themselves. In the same way that patterns of rights violations become invisible through patterns of social interaction, the ways in which those patterns of social interaction sustain conceivably unrelated rights violations may also be invisible even to some of the actors engaged in challenging those rights violations. This analysis reveals that the rights-as-entitlements metaphor is theoretically and strategically constraining.

For example, though many are well aware of it, the relationship between material- and identity-based rights claims are invisible to some activists and yet in order to address *either* sort of claim the social patterns that sustain *both* need to be made visible and to be challenged.

[64] As a Burmese women's human rights activist said, "For Burmese women, migration issues, refugee issues, human rights, all are linked. Especially, in terms of trafficking . . . When you work as an illegal immigrant you are not protected by the employer. So employers also exploit them" (ID16 2004). Similar insights were shared by other interviewees (I1 2004; I2 2004; I3 2004; I5 2004).

When we are attentive to the ways in which material- and identity-based rights violations are institutionalized in any context, we discover that their very institutionalization is invisible. Furthermore, feminist curb cut epistemology and experience-based inquiry are essential to revealing these processes of institutionalization and to focusing our attention on solutions that conceive of these processes as not analytically distinct but rather as integrated conceptually as they are practically.[65]

Combating social stigma while lobbying for material claims (to health care, legal rights, and education) is the strategy of the Rainbow Planet Coalition. Sexuality is clearly a human rights issue, not unlike the way that domestic violence is. Discrimination based on sexual orientation creates a range of circumstances of vulnerability. The Rainbow Planet Coalition, a coalition of a range of activists – LGBTIQ, sex workers, people living with HIV/AIDS, groups who are invisible in their home countries – made themselves visible at WSF 2004. An anonymous South Asian queer rights activist expressed how wonderful it was to be in a place where she could be out about her sexuality. At WSF we have "found a larger space than we usually get, and no harassment." For this queer activist and so many LGBTIQ people, indigenous people, sex workers, and people living with HIV/AIDS, their material lives are affected either by their own affiliation with an identity group or by the social stigma associated with their perceived membership in a group.[66]

The *quid pro quo* approach to integrating the materially based and identity-based issues imposes a coherence at the cost of losing some of the theoretical complexity demanded by material and identity issues alike – a concern that the Rainbow Planet Coalition demonstrated through their *collective action.* Rainbow Planet Coalition make themselves visible through multiple parades, colorful and widely circulated posters, buttons, visors, and flags. Threats to individual and social identity impact not only the material conditions of people's lives, but also the material reality of what it means to have that identity. The issue is not only that people with HIV/AIDS are not healthy, but also

[65] For alternative interpretations of the possibility for analytical disaggregation of various forms of oppression see Fraser (1995; 1997; 2001), Fraser and Honneth (2003), and Young (1997a).

[66] I12 2004.

that without proper treatment, we cannot identify ourselves as healthy people. The issue is not only that LGBTIQ people cannot move safely in public in many communities, but also that we cannot identify ourselves as safe and free-moving people. The issue is not just that indigenous people are losing access to our own land, but also that we cannot identify ourselves as the people on that land. (Though we could still be people of that land, the land is changed, in no small part because we are no longer on it.) It is not that identity claims have an impact on material claims, but rather that material claims are integral to identity. When we understand material claims as constitutive of identity, we see that the reciprocal must hold as well: identity claims cannot require alienating one's own material claims.

Of course, some people claim that they have the right to treatment or that they are entitled to some material claim. These claims put the identity claim – *the right to make a claim* – first *strategically*.[67] However, both kinds of claims are better understood analytically as *enabling rights* rather than as ends in and of themselves; they are rights claims that reflect integrated material and identity concerns, not rights claims that put identity first in an analytical way. Activists need not only that which they are demanding but also the recognition that they have the right to make that demand. Thus, even the most material claims are integrally tied up with a claim for recognition.[68]

This may seem like an unnecessary nuance or a nuance that serves only a "small" problem and is not necessary for the "big" problems of feminists and women's activists. Though the distinction between "big" and "small" is sometimes politically important, the distinction between "big" and "small" is *analytically* problematic because it offers a justification for marginalizing some people based on the "importance" of their rights concerns relative to the numbers of others who share a different rights concern and thus ignores the structural interrelatedness of the rights of all humans.

[67] Rights may *also* be ends in and of themselves. Clarifying this point requires normative theorizing and provides an opportunity to put the normative insights gained from praxeological inquiry into dialogue with insights from normative theory.

[68] Though it would take us off the thread of the discussion to note in the text, I should note here that on this reading a non-ideal immanent and universal theory of human rights is a form of capability theory as developed by Sen and Nussbaum (Nussbaum 1997; 2003a; Sen 1990b; 1999a; 2004).

In boundary crossing movements – from the living wage movement in Atlanta, to Sojourners's attempt to unite Christian social conservatives on economic and race issues in the United States, to the World Council of Churches' work on the environment – people have been able to come to difference-spanning agreements on race, caste, global economic inequality, and environmental degradation. It seems common that these agreements are reached by tabling women's issues, or marginalizing them into a narrow category of concerns. Specifically, sexuality and reproduction are bracketed in order to develop other issue-based alliances. Feminists are not alone in their struggle to deal with the ethical differences across a range of other differences. Nor are they alone in finding sexuality and reproductive issues the hardest to work through. However, putting these in the terrain of difficulty is not a way of bracketing them as other movements have done, but for feminist and human rights activists it is a way of committing ourselves to working through them. Nor is it a way of saying they are not the "big" issues, as some activists have done. Issues in the terrain of difficulty are not of lesser importance than rights claims that are uncontested.[69] Nor are they more important. However, the work each requires is different. For the uncontested rights, the committed need to reveal the structural obstacles to their realization. For the contested rights, they need to reveal the ways in which social, political, and economic structures are being masked by being characterized as theoretical, not political, obstacles to the respect for universal human rights.

As they do the work of unmasking such structures, those committed to immanent universal rights may strengthen our ability to be aware of the ways in which rights are indivisible and of the structures that render some rights violations invisible. These ways can be studied with the tools of social science and they can be explored through our shared conceptual reflections. Both our social science observations and our conceptual reflection will lead us to appreciate that we cannot resolve issues in the terrain of difficulty without a conceptualization of rights as secured through social, political, and economic structures. Once we understand social structures as both social processes and institutions in

[69] Compare this approach to theorists who treat those on which there is agreement as having greater priority (including Lukes 1993; Rawls 1999b; Taylor 1999). In Part I (particularly chapter 2) I argued that such a methodological approach conceals an exercise of epistemological and political power.

which social epistemologies are reified (or deconstructed, depending on the institution), analysis of these processes and institutions becomes a powerful tool for revealing invisible sites of marginalization and rights violations. On this model, no right is a "big" or "small" issue. Any visible rights violation is conceivably a warning about other as yet invisible rights violations.

## Trust and thinking through the terrain of difficulty

The obligations of duty-bearers in the transcendental models of universal human rights are defined within a more narrow theoretical space than the obligations of those committed to an immanent universal theory of human rights.

Through the discussion of the use of the immanent universal theory of human rights for criticism, and the need to be committed to revealing the invisible, including the invisible exercise of power, trust emerges as an important resource for human rights activists. In one of the earliest interviews of this project, one of the principal leaders of the women's human rights campaign leading up to the United Nations Conferences on Human Rights and a contemporary transnational feminist leader and scholar explained that the transnational and well networked feminists of the generation, who were so successful at influencing the United Nations conferences' processes and other international areas of human rights, had developed through this work long-standing relationships of trust.[70] While for younger feminists or those who were not part of this process, the bonds among this generation of activists may feel and in fact be exclusionary.[71] Given the expectation that working through the terrain of difficulty will require destabilizing each participant's epistemology, those committed to immanent universal human rights need to work to foster trust among those engaged in the terrain(s) of difficulty.

Thinking through the structural basis for the indivisible rights of interrelated people requires attentiveness to the necessity of a destabilizing epistemology and yet cautions that such destabilization should take place in a terrain that is not just difficult, but that is safe, where

[70] I18 2004.

[71] IB5 2005; IB6 2005; IB7 2005; IB8 2005; IB9 2005; IB10 2005; IB11 2005; IS5 2005.

deliberants can trust one another. But it also cautions that even well-intentioned human rights activists, committed to making the invisible visible, may themselves make some people, some rights violations, and the rights-violating potential of some structures invisible.[72]

This is one reason why feminist activists pay such attention to agenda setting. Because of the need for trust in working through the terrain of difficulty, unreflective comments can cause disunity. When one woman assumes that young women will do the note-taking of the movement (Feminist Dialogues 2005) or a scheduled celebratory plenary is interrupted with anti-war poetry that depicts Iraqi women as lesbian (Women's World Congress 2005), trust is violated. Both speech acts violated the trust of all of the participants in one another's understanding of why each is participating. Participants who are engaged in working through the terrain of difficulty need to confront the otherwise unspoken biases that made them take offense and to confront their own biases *in an environment of trust.*

Trust does not figure prominently in Wendy Brown's encouraging us "to engage in struggle rather than recrimination."[73] Nor does trust play an important role in Seyla Benhabib's deliberative model.[74] Mistrust does play a brief role in Kate Nash's argument for why we should not consider feminist post-structuralist and pro-human rights arguments as opposed.[75] In the world of women working together to think through the issues in the terrain of difficulty, trust, and bonds that are sustained by relations *other than* the structures of power they come together to critique, are imperative.[76]

As noted throughout this book, there are resources in feminist political theory for helping us think through the problems of indivisibility, interrelatedness, and structural sources of rights violations. Feminist researchers of women's activism offer us explications of the context-based challenges to doing so. And, women's human rights activists offer us examples of how to live with such irony or cognitive dissonance.

At the Feminist Dialogues in 2005, when asked what she ever learned from academics, an activist from Goa answered, "this phrase,

[72] Ackerly 2007a; I18 2004; Peterson 1990. [73] Brown 1995: 48.
[74] Benhabib 2002: chapter 5. [75] Nash 2002: 418.
[76] Dean 1996; Mohanty 2003; Sandoval 2000. For other dimensions of building global civil society using deliberative tools see Ackerly (2006; 2007a).

'cognitive dissonance.'" The phrase was academic jargon for something she confronted regularly in her work but for which she had no name, only frustration. In addition to giving activists the jargon to describe their challenges, political theorists can also offer activists ways of thinking through their dilemmas. In this case, the theory of human rights that I have been arguing is immanent in activists' work gives her the political legitimacy to change her world despite her likely lack of political authority.

In order to communicate across conceptual boundaries, some epistemological destabilization is necessary, yet in order to come to agreement across such boundaries, the boundaries themselves should be fuzzy. The terrain(s) of difficulty must have fuzzy boundaries in order to enable us to reason together, challenging some assumptions while affirming others. This challenge is directed not only at the academics of industrialized nations that concern the peace activist from El Salvador, but also at all of us who are faced with the challenge of communicating around conceptually complex problems. Trust is a tool for working through that conceptual complexity; an immanent universal conceptualization of rights can provide background for strengthening that trust.

Curb cut feminism requires vigilant attention to the possibilities for identifying new forms of marginalization. The connections between forms of marginalization are the "windows between worlds."[77] The differences between them are what make the face of feminist and women's human rights activism distinctive in each context. The complexity of addressing problems embedded in the social, economic, and political fabric of societies means that within a given context there may be multiple distinctive approaches to activism. Yet, within and across a range of contexts, women's human rights activists exhibit an attention to the ways in which social practices are part of the social structures of society that condition women's rights violations and their ability to redress them.

Given the range of differences among activists, it is remarkable that the terrain of difficulty is as small as it is. In sum, the immanent theory of universal human rights emergent from women's and feminist activism is that human rights are politically legitimate resources for local,

[77] This is the name of the organization that inspires the discussion in the last chapter and that is supported by the cover art of this book.

national, and transnational criticism of social, economic, and political rights violations, and that the human rights of all people are indivisible, interrelated, and sustained and threatened through structural as well as individual causes. While there are aspects of the content of the list of human rights that may be relegated to a terrain of difficulty for collective consideration, these constitute challenges to a human rights practice not obstacles to a universal human rights theory. Many of these challenges can be revealed to be political not theoretical challenges.

## Conclusion

Despite all of these differences and obstacles to a universal view of human rights based on immanent not transcendent sources, there is remarkable cohesion around the view that universal human rights are indivisible, interrelated, and sustained or violated through practices, norms, and institutions and therefore that they are a politically legitimate concept for social criticism within and across contexts. *Moreover*, there is significant agreement that differences can be adjudicated, revealed to be politically motivated, not manifestations of essential uncrossable human differences. In addition to its being compelling, this view of human rights enables us to address many kinds of human rights violations and in fact, as I have shown, leaves no rights claims definitionally illegitimate.

While it does leave some room for local interpretation and strategic variation, such diversity is constrained by the account of immanent universal human rights and its curb cut epistemology. In the next chapter, I discuss the strategic implications of the immanent universal view of human rights, and in the concluding chapter outline the kinds of questions that immanent universal human rights puts on the table for theorists and practitioners.

What we have seen in our examination of ideas that are revealed through the work and reflections of activists is that there is not a single completely theorized idea of universal human rights. Yet, there is an incompletely theorized coherent account emerging through human rights practice and immanent reflection. In addition, there is a range of other views that treat some rights claims as having priority over others; some rights claims as not rights at all; some rights claims as in tension. These views may be immanent, but not universal; or they may be universal but have a transcendental, not immanent basis for political legitimacy. Human rights theorists and activists use the immanent universal account of human rights to work through these (mostly political) threats to the political legitimacy and critical purpose of human rights. In this chapter I have modeled a theorist's working though these issues. In the next chapter I will demonstrate the activists' working though these issues.

Feminists and women's activists (not just feminist political theorists) need a theoretical and analytical framework that requires them to submit to skeptical scrutiny the vulnerabilities created by the internal hierarchies of communities and yet enables women to see the sustainability of communities vulnerable to external threat as an issue indivisible from their own. In the next chapter, I will argue that the indivisible-interrelated-structural account of human rights is better supported by certain activist strategies than others. Further, I argue that strategies consistent with the non-curb cutting views inadvertently or intentionally create barriers to future feminist activism, to theoretical integration of human rights issues with other issues, and to strategic networking among issue advocates.

# 9 Feminist strategies

## Introduction

In the preceding chapters we notice that there are strategic reasons to focus on a specific priority but these strategic reasons do not undermine the normative view, observed in activist practice taken together, that all rights are indivisible and that all rights-bearers are interrelated through multiple and integrated relations of power. Yet, experience-based inquiry cautions activists and theorists alike against attempts to disaggregate rights claims in both our analysis and our activism. So while such disaggregation may be necessary for certain strategic action or for certain sociological research,[1] it is not supportable in praxeological inquiry and is normatively indefensible. To do so whether for the exigencies of activism or research is problematic. In this chapter, I will show that some women's human rights praxis is inconsistent with an immanent universal theory of human rights.

Curb cutting human rights activism is a way of doing women's and feminist activism that, even though fragmented for strategic or logistical reasons, works within an understanding of immanent and universal human rights as individual, interrelated, and structurally sustained. In this chapter we will listen to what activists say about their work for human rights and observe that sometimes they practice a curb cut feminist form of analysis and sometimes they don't. Sometimes they practice their work in ways that clear a path for themselves or others to advocate for other issues and other people, and sometimes they conduct their work in ways that close off avenues for future change. Though all activists have to make strategic choices about what to do and how to do it, our choices can be guided by a curb cut intentionality – an intention with our activism to address our priority concern in ways that do not close off opportunities for future

[1] Bailey 1999; Risman 2004; Weeks and Holland 1996.

change and other forms of potentially allied activism. Ideally, it would close off forms of exploitable hierarchies, or at least undermine their theoretical, financial, or human resources, but we may need to rely on the political legitimacy of human rights to do that.

We saw in chapters 7 and 8 that curb cut feminist methodology reveals not only a curb cut feminist practice of human rights activism, but also activist arguments which are inconsistent with curb cut feminism. That is, some women's arguments for women's human rights create barriers to other forms of women's human rights activism.

Non-curb cutting arguments get put into practice through strategies that enable some activists to work for the rights of some at the neglect or expense of the rights of others. In addition to being unlikely to succeed because they create or mimic political divisions among potential allies,[2] these strategies do not clear the way for other forms of activism – even other forms of feminist activism.[3] Non-curb cutting feminists have argued that activism for other rights will come second, that other rights claims are not feasible now in their particular context, or that other rights are not a priority.

While such views can be defended as strategically appropriate to the short term, they pose theoretical and strategic challenges for feminist activism in the long term. Successful activism sets precedents. Some precedents are codified in law;[4] others are codified in social norms and economic practices. Of course, laws, norms, and practices can be changed – many hopes of women's human rights activists are based on memories of success at bringing about such changes – but by creating and reenacting laws, norms, and practices inconsistent with curb cut feminism, non-curb cut activism splinters feminist activism politically and also generates norms that work against the indivisible-interrelated-structural analysis of curb cut feminists.

[2] See accounts of why we lost the ERA (Mansbridge 1986). See Lakoff's account of the contemporary failure of progressive activisms (2004).

[3] In future work, I expect to argue that some environmental activism has a curb cut effect and others do not. The same argument can be made about poverty reduction schemes, identity-based activism, strategies for promoting peace and mitigating conflict, etc. While developed reflecting on feminist practice and theory, curb cut feminism is a methodology appropriate for thinking about a range of issues.

[4] Vandenbergh 2001; 2005.

Curb cut feminism and the immanent and universal theory of human rights are not nearsighted. Nearsighted approaches foreclose opportunities to recognize other rights, the rights of other people, and the structural processes that presently conceal our recognition of these people and their rights. Further, non-curb cutting approaches limit our ability to identify allies and partners.[5] Further, they limit our exposure to unfamiliar arguments. Consequently, we should be wary of strategies for human rights activism that are inconsistent with curb cut feminism. The immanent and universal theory of human rights is empowering for activists' engagement with the rest of the world because it enables us to relegate challenges to our human rights claims to the realm of the terrain of difficulty rather than treating them as challenges to the theory as a whole. While our understanding of the immanent and universal theory of human rights may be destabilized by such engagement, the very legitimacy of the theory and its role in critical discourse is shorn up by such engagement.

In this chapter I review feminist activist work and strategies of the present and recent past. While each of these strategies has been developed and deployed in a specific context or set of contexts and challenges, and while each may be deployed for curb cut or non-curb cut ends, attentiveness to the theoretical meanings created by strategic choices and actions may help feminists individually and collectively to make their strategic choices with awareness of the future challenges or allies created by various choices.

Of course, some activists are aware of the effects that their choices of the past have had on the contexts in which they presently work. And likewise, some reflect on the ways in which their present choices may constrain or open up future opportunities. As we saw in chapter 7, an immanent and universal theory of human rights emergent in women's and feminist activism is based on an understanding of rights as indivisible, of the rights of all humans as interrelated, and of the structural challenges to sustaining a human rights culture. Still, activists have to face the world immediately. Fallible feminists may make mistakes by pursuing strategies that are inconsistent, but not because they have abandoned their understandings of human rights. Moreover, as we noted in chapter 5, the activists' understandings of human rights on which the theory just presented is based were articulated in moments of

5 Francisco 2003.

reflection; yet, daily activism does not often create space for moments of reflection.

With the luxury of time to reflect on the strategic choices of women's organizations and transnational feminist organizing, I assess these choices and use them to offer guiding questions for activists to ask themselves as they analyze the contexts of their work, set their objectives, plan their strategies, and, when faced with actual circumstances, respond in the moment. As I critically evaluate the strategies of activists and the movement, I will discuss as well the implications for researchers as allies of activists in helping to anticipate the impact on the future work environment of present choices.

## Are immanent human rights universal?

Before illustrating how to use the activists' immanent and universal theory of human rights for critical assessment of women's activism, let me first consider what it means to be using a guide that is universalizable but not universal. *How could an account of* universal *human rights emerge from our inquiry and yet* not *be universally observable*? There are methodological, substantive, and analytical answers to this question.

Methodologically, an immanent and universal theory of human rights with a recognizable terrain of difficulty was expected. In seeking out diverse sources, I created ample opportunity for differences and disagreements among my sources. One methodological and theoretical implication of our destabilizing epistemology is that, even as we work through those items in the terrain of difficulty, we should also always be looking to enlarge the terrain of difficulty by finding excluded issues, people, and structures that need to be considered. We should be skeptical of our methods if they did not reveal differences.

Consequently, the substantive insights of feminist and women activists are expected to vary and to reflect their differences. People work in different contexts, under different time pressures, with different social, economic, and political constraints and opportunities. Reasoning through the terrain of difficulty, we may work through many of the differences that emerge for methodological and substantive reasons. Our understanding of human rights – its political legitimacy as a concept, its function as a critical tool, and its content – are all further enriched through this process.

The analytical answer is most challenging. First, recall from chapter 2 that human rights theory is a non-ideal theory. The purpose of a non-ideal theory is to propose normatively guided reflection on problems of injustice that have occurred and will occur in forms that we recognize *and* in forms that we cannot now anticipate. Human rights is an essentially contested concept because its applications for criticism, the challenges to its political legitimacy, and the calls to adapt its content cannot be fully anticipated.

Because human rights are realized through the ways in which legal, social, economic, and political institutions function, practices are important. From those associated with local norms to those that have become the norms of transnationally networking feminists, practices condition the development of a human rights culture – a culture of values, practices, norms, and structures that treat human rights as politically legitimate and are conducive to their recognition and realization.

Sometimes vaguely sometimes explicitly, practices embody values. There are a number of reasons why the values we practice are not coherent with immanent and universal human rights. The more vaguely they do so, the more likely our practices exhibit cognitive dissonance. It may be that we are aware of competing values within us. Additionally, it may be difficult to determine what immanent universal human rights should lead us to do. Further, in some places one question may be "easy" and in others "hard."

Consequently and finally, immanent universal human rights could be manifested differently not just because of differences across contexts but also because of differences in the reasoning processes of people. By definition, immanent universal human rights offers no tool for transcending these. But it does offer tools for working through them, as I illustrated in the preceding chapter in my discussions of rights claims associated with having children and military service.

Most transnational feminists and most international human rights treaty bodies articulate a view of human rights as indivisible, interrelated, and structurally sustained (although they often do so in a way that disaggregates rights so as to enumerate and specify legitimate rights claims). However, in how transnational feminists work together and in how the UN human rights treaty bodies get used, this view of universal human rights is not universally sustained. In a thoroughly researched dissertation, Ladan Rahmani offers institutional reasons why the UN human rights treaty bodies, even the Convention on the Elimination of all forms of Discrimination Against Women, have trouble recognizing gender discrimination: they lack practices that facilitate an integrated understanding of gender.[6] Given the central importance of indivisibility in the content of human rights for criticism, her finding does not bode well for the near future of women's human rights and makes clear the challenge for global human rights.

Even within the transnational feminist activist community, practices can be habituated such that they create barriers to an integrated analysis of women's human rights violations, and certainly to an integrated strategic approach. Why would a leader in the transnational feminist movement, interested in inspiring young feminists to join the movement, call on them to be rapporteurs rather than the discussion leaders at a dialogue among transnational feminists? Habit. Her colleagues (and in a moment of reflection she too) recognized that her call for young women to play a supportive role was problematic. Another feminist leader at the Feminist Dialogues 2005 used her time to thank young women for their role in the movement, not just as worker bees, but as energetic thinkers. All is forgiven. However, in the closing plenary of the same two-day meeting, a young feminist asks in Portuguese (which is not the language of the moderator of the plenary, but which is translated with simultaneous translation) "how feminists can work together in a critique of capitalism and patriarchy?" Her question is ignored, perhaps because the panelists on the dais are tired, perhaps because the translation provided via headset is poor, and perhaps because after years of working in the feminist movement the call to integrate these is not new. Why is it ignored? Habit. Many in the room felt that that was an old question, one answered satisfactorily by the work of DAWN economists who integrated a gendered critique of economic and social power, one always already on the strategic agenda of feminists.[7]

But what if we had discussed the question as if it had never been asked before? What might we have learned about the marginalization of young women if we had explored the young woman's question with her and her friends? Following the plenary I did interview the young woman, Natalie, and her colleagues and learned that their frustration was less in being ignored by, and more in not having learned anything

[6] Rahmani 2005. [7] Benería 2003; Sen and Grown 1987.

new from, the older feminists from the movement and that they had not been invited into the circles of trust and friendship of the meetings' organizers.[8] Under conditions of struggle, what is wrong with relying on bonds of trust and friendship? Nothing in one sense. Nothing at all; such trust has enabled the movement and will be the basis of our working through the terrains of difficulty. But something is lost if feminists are in the habit of turning to each other, such that they foreclose, by force of habit, learning opportunities.[9]

I start with these two discussions – of institutions and of transnational feminist activists – to illustrate a point: the failure to practice a shared vision of universal human rights as interrelated, indivisible, and structurally sustained is not fruitfully discussed as a result of false consciousness. Instead, we can be aware of a range of reasons why this view of universal human rights, immanent in women's human rights activism, is not universally visible even to women's human rights activists.

If it is not universally visible or practiced even by the institutions and actors that articulate this account, in what sense is it universal? To answer this question, we need to return to the epistemological framework of the inquiry. Curb cut feminism is a destabilizing epistemology that invites us to know *provisionally*. We know that these three are features of a universal human rights theory that activists work toward and that international rights institutions are inadequately designed to support. However, we also know that in practice they are fully recognized nowhere: in no society, in no institutions, and in no activist practice.

This is not a moral or cultural relativist finding that there are no universal human rights. Rather, it is an empirical finding: human rights are not visible universally in social, international, and activists' practices. However, an immanent and universal theory of human rights enables criticism. Activists use the political legitimacy of human rights to argue for social change. The human rights of *all* within a society need to be sustained by the political, economic, and social institutions that sustain those *societies*, regardless of the politics of membership status. Therefore, locally, regionally, and globally women and feminist

8 IB5 2005; IB6 2005; IB7 2005; IB8 2005; IB9 2005; IB10 2005; IB11 2005.

9 This point was made explicitly by Poonam Arora (IS3 2005) and the activist for Southeast Asian women and refugees (IS5 2005).

activists work in ways that help make human rights recognition independent of community and national, social and economic boundaries. In this work, imperfect as it is, we see the practice of activism that is guided by and that contributes to our understanding of immanent universal human rights.

## Strategies of local activism: working within in order to transform

Despite working in a broad range of contexts, there are remarkable similarities in the ways in which women's human rights activists conduct their work.[10] Activists seek to:

(1) make legal changes such that domestic or international laws better conform with the CEDAW and other international agreements which recognize women's human rights (*legal change*);
(2) reinvent local legal practices (for example by training judges and police officers, establishing ombudswomen for survivors of violence, or establishing women's police stations) (*training*);
(3) support survivors of violence (*support*);
(4) educate society broadly (for example in schools, through the media, and through gender training programs) (*education*);
(5) network and promote alliances among organizations working to end violence against women; share methods, resources, and information with other organizations; promote activism (such as letter writing campaigns, marches, and boycotts), or offer funding for any of the above activities (*networking*); and
(6) integrate women's human rights efforts with other initiatives for social, economic, and political change (including but not limited to economic development, health, and environmental initiatives) (*integration*).[11]

[10] For a developed discussion of each of these forms of activism see Ackerly (2001b).
[11] This is my categorization based on working group contributions and the categories are somewhat fluid, as I discuss in the text. Other ways of categorizing women's human rights activism might emphasize the educative dimension of all aspects of activism (a point raised to me by Nelly Stromquist) or the essential role of being able to move between worlds (Ackerly 2000). Many activists move between the worlds of legal theory and human experience, between the legal system and survivors' lives, between the worlds of individual survival and public education, between local and national dialogues and action, between human

Some of these similarities are the result of a similarity of analysis: that women's human rights issues need to be addressed through multiple avenues in order to challenge and change legal institutions, political and economic practices, and social, cultural, and religious norms. Some have developed as a result of transnational networking. The first is the result of separate analyses yielding common insights and similar approaches to work.[12] The second is the result of global feminist strategies. The question is, does all women's activism exhibit curb cut feminist analysis or does some activism restrict future possibilities for women's activism and for alliances? How can we tell the difference?

While descriptively we may generalize and say that these activists all work in these six ways or some subset of these, they do not do so in the same ways. For example, some can advocate for legal change, as in the efforts of Burkina Faso women to secure property, inheritance, and land rights, in a way that ignores questions of sexuality and in fact further codifies practices around heterosexual families.[13] But activists in Burkina Faso do focus on domestic violence and property rights, indicating that they view criticizing social norms while asserting economic rights as strategically necessary. Socially enforced heteronormativity is arguably a tool for controlling women by limiting their social roles. As has been illustrated throughout Africa, it is difficult to secure women's political and economic rights with legal change alone. Securing the rights of women – married women, single women, divorced women, widowed women, girl children – requires social reexamination of the roles of women. Without rethinking women's roles and the heterosexual family, the practices of the traditional

rights and economic institutions, and between informal and formal institutions. Rather than a way of acting (educating or moving between worlds), I chose to focus on the forms of action and their intended audiences. By categorizing their actions for the purposes of discussion I do not mean to limit anyone's ability to imagine other forms of activism. After the end of the CEDAW-in-Action working group, as part of fulfilling my perceived obligation to the groups incurred by learning from them, and in order to practice networking and integration, I shared these categories with the End-of-Violence working group and received some commentary which led to my specifying some forms of integration. I shared the entire paper with those interested. Two wrote me to tell me they were incorporating the categories in their training materials. For more on the bases for a constructive working relationship between scholars and activists see Ackerly (2001a; 2007b).

12 Bina D'Costa and I discuss the strategies of women's human rights activism (Ackerly and D'Costa 2005).

13 I2 2004; I3 2004.

heterosexual family are stronger than legal changes such that constitutional and other legal changes are slow to make it into social and economic practice, or even judicial practice.[14]

By contrast others understand social, economic, and political rights violations as integrated such that they design legal solutions with the need to transform the social context as well – sometimes transforming the economic context as well (by allowing women to own property), or sometimes taking the economic context as a constraint. For example, Women for Women's Human Rights (WWHR), an NGO in Turkey, works toward legal change in a way that takes the economic context in which men are the primary financial support for families and women's work opportunities are limited as given, but seeks to use legal change to transform the political, social, and economic context that previously left survivors of domestic violence economically destitute and socially ostracized. They explain their work to an online working group:

> In the case of domestic violence, an amendment of the criminal code to increase the punishment for the perpetrator of violence did not provide women with the most effective legal mechanism. While the relevant clauses of the existing criminal code allow women exposed to domestic violence to take their partners to court, they entail criminal cases, which require relatively long procedures. During the course of this process, women encounter many obstacles: They are often faced with policemen who refuse to file their complaint or tell them to go home and make up with their partners; or with doctors, who either do not, or choose not to, recognize that a woman has been subjected to domestic violence, which prevents women from obtaining the medical report (from a government doctor) needed to file a criminal charge. Women are also very often reluctant to file criminal charges due to various reasons, for example: They are afraid that the incarceration of their partner will result in a loss of social status for the family; they do not wish to place their children in a situation where they will have to see their father in jail; they are frightened that their partner will become more violent before or after his imprisonment; they fear that the husband's family and their own community will apply pressure to them for having caused the imprisonment of the father; and they are very often worried that when their partner is in jail, they will be left without a source of income, especially if their family has only a single-earner.

[14] Bonnin 1998; Center for Reproductive Rights 2003; Fox 2003; Human Rights Watch 2003; Khadiagala 2002; Marais 2001; Mwenda, Mumba, and Mvula-Mwenda 2005; Quisumbing, Payongayong, Aidoo, and Otsuka 2001; Tripp 2004; US Department of State 2006.

We argued that a much better strategy would be not to increase the punishment but rather to introduce other laws, such as the protection order, which would provide women with other means of ending the violence to which they are subjected. The protection order, which would be under the civil code, would involve less complicated and much quicker legal proceedings resulting in the enforced separation of the perpetrator of violence from the family home for a certain period of time. In other words, it would facilitate what women who are subjected to domestic violence need the most: a cessation of the violence without them having to leave home. A protection order also allows for the enforcement of the spouse to continue to provide for his family during the time he is separated from the family home.[15]

The approach of WWHR sets a precedent and establishes new practices that, while having a positive impact on women survivors of violence, create practices that perpetuate new social norms about family obligation and family reputation within community.

Svati Shah is an activist for lesbian/gay/bisexual/transgender-rights organizations in the queer/people of color community in New York and in India. She has done activism in India, research in India for scholarship in the US, and activism in the US while also being a scholar. She compares her activism in the US with her activism in India:

one thing I really liked about the feminist organizing I did in India, was that there were queer women and straight women working together and, kind of, building a very strong analysis around sexuality. That it was just space to question a lot and challenge a lot. Which is something I kind of missed in my work in the US.[16]

[15] www.globalknowledge.org/english/archives/mailarchives/endviolence/endviolence-nov98/0021.html (last accessed February 2006), WWHR, Istanbul, Turkey, End-of-Violence Working Group posting, November 10, 1998. This message and a solicitation by the moderators spawned a discussion about legal reform and other measures. The November 17, 1998, response from Francesca Pesce describes the work of Associazione Differenza Donna in Rome, Italy. While explicitly interested in similar legal reforms, she also discusses the many other ways in which Associazione Differenza Donna has worked, including training, support, education, networking, and integration. See www.globalknowledge.org/english/archives/mailarchives/endviolence/endviolence-nov98/0039.html (last accessed February 2006). In recent years Differenza Donna has focused on support and some training. In October 1999 some former members of Differenza Donna breathed life into an existing organization, The Associazione Non Una di Meno, and began renewed efforts to promote legal change, education, networking, and integration (personal correspondence, May 16, 2001).

[16] IB3 2005.

Later on in the interview she elaborates:

in my own political analysis, I see connections with everything, I mean, I have an intersectional analysis, so I see connections with all progressive struggles, with the anti-war movement, any kind of sexuality-related rights movement whether its LGBT, sexuality, or whether it's sex work, or anything that's using a sexual rights framework. I think definitely there are connections with feminism, but also with struggles around class, around land rights. Unfortunately, I don't think that the LGBT movement in the US, where it is now, is making those connections. I think, I feel like it's become very narrow and it's a very difficult place to actually do organizing at this point in time. It's much easier to do social things, you know, have parties, go to bars and have a social life that's mostly populated by other LGBTQ people, but the political organizations, the ones that are really asking questions about power and structures, are few and far between. So, that's why I'm saying, I have that analysis, and I know that there are other people have that analysis, but I think organizationally, that those of us who have this analysis ... are feeling a little bit like that we are not representative of the trend.[17]

And again, reflecting on her activism in India:

[T]he LGBT movement in India is very intersectional, and they have to be, I mean they have to make those alliances, and in some cases they're making very successful alliances, like in Bangalore, there's an organization [that has] really worked hard to make connections with the Left, so there are a couple of, kind of, very well known Leftist organizations that are taking stands on things like the anti-sodomy law that people are trying to get repealed, and that, getting the anti-sodomy law repealed is starting to be on a lot of people's agendas. The movement in India is, I think, doing amazing work at trying to make an analysis around the anti-sodomy statute within the Indian penal code, ... making that a part of a public discourse, a broad public discourse, so that it's feeling less and less like a LGBTQ issue, but more an issue about State accountability, and the State's responsibility vis à vis citizens.[18]

The work of the LGBTIQ movement in India that Shah describes exhibits the kind of integrated analysis that enables the movement to move forward on a range of issues, closing off none with its activism.

Discrimination based on sexual orientation creates a range of legal and economic circumstances of vulnerability. The Rainbow Planet Coalition, mentioned in the preceding chapter, recognizes and educates about these interrelating structures and how they affect LGBTIQ

[17] IB3 2005; see also Rothschild, Long, and Fried 2005. [18] IB3 2005.

people, sex workers, people living with HIV/AIDS, groups who are invisible in their home countries. At WSF 2004 Rainbow Planet Coalition activists carried and shared signs in English and Hindi that denounced their marginalizations.

Some activists in many organizations have an integrated analysis of queer oppression. Some go further to work in ways that integrate queer activism with other critiques of gendered, classed, and racialized power. This latter approach is a form of activism that exhibits the understanding of human rights as interrelated, indivisible, and structurally sustained. Scholars of activism have argued for, and documented the success of and the challenges of, this kind of activism within a range of issue areas.[19]

From this brief discussion, it is clear that the kind of work activists do in the generic sense does not help us understand the underlying theory of human rights that gets enacted in practice through their work. To get this latter insight, we must look closely at each political action in its context and see if it offers us an understanding of human rights as indivisible-interrelated-and structurally sustained. Clearly, then, it is not what we do, but how we do it that exhibits theoretical information both to normative theorists who are interested in experience-based inquiry and to society responding to and living with the social change advocated by activists.

## Strategies of transnational women's human rights feminism[20]

In the following section, I discuss some transnational feminist strategies of the past decade. Problems associated with transnational feminist human rights activism include exclusions, dichotomization in analysis,

[19] Possibly the most influential of these is Bunch (1990). Rosalind Petchesky credits much of the success of the global women's health movement to its integrated and structural analysis (2003). Rothschild *et al.*, in a book reviewing women's activism around the world and the ways in which sexuality is used to marginalize women's activism, attests "to how issues central to discussing women's sexuality – questions, among others, of bodily integrity and health, of the freedom to define oneself outside traditional social structures, and of basic rights to expression and association – cannot and must not simply be called 'lesbian issues.' They are relevant to all women. Their impact, though multifarious, cuts across classes, localities, and culture" (2005: 133).

[20] The following discussion parallels work co-authored with Bina D'Costa and brings out the theoretical import of that work (Ackerly and D'Costa 2005).

oversimplification, crowding out of local activism that is unversed in the transnational lingo of global feminism and of other non-rights based approaches, drawing away of financial and human resources from grassroots activism, and provoking a cultural backlash against some feminist activism. These problems are not specific to any particular strategy. As we will see in the ten I discuss, certain of these recur. Immanent universal human rights and feminist curb cutting suggest a set of guiding questions to help activists be attentive to these and related potential problems within women's human rights activism. I will discuss guiding questions after reviewing the familiar strategies of women's human rights activism.

Though not all women and feminist activists deploy human rights as a political tool, through the 1980s to the present human rights has become a discourse that many women have used to describe their activism.[21] Working politically and analytically within the human rights discourse while challenging certain boundaries of its conceptualization and practice, transnational feminists have united feminists and women's activists, who are situated in diverse locations, in a global commitment toward achieving women's rights.

Transnational feminists have used "human rights" as a political tool not only to incorporate women's voices, but also to legitimate their influence in policy making. Some of the most important strategies adopted by the transnational feminist movement that made many successes possible include: (1) framing a myriad of concerns as "rights" issues; (2) bringing local and particular issues and those affected by them to the global stage; (3) using global discourse to raise the visibility of women's human rights at the local level; (4) channeling resources; (5) bringing those working on similar issues in different places into dialogue with one another; (6) rewriting international universal human rights such that violations of women's human rights are as visible as violations of men's; (7) strategically using women's rights to bring attention to the human rights violations of all; (8) contextualizing human rights; (9) fostering and following the movement leadership in the global South; and (10) bringing those working on separate issues into dialogue with one another. Does a curb cutting feminist

[21] Basu and McGrory 1995; Friedman 1995; Joachim 2003; Keck and Sikkink 1998; Petchesky 2003; Peters and Wolper 1995.

epistemology and our immanent universal theory of human rights make us rethink any of these strategies, and if so, how?

## *Framing a myriad of concerns as "rights" issues*

Since contemporary global networking around the human rights discourse began, activists have been employing the women's human rights discourse to oppose abuse in the family, war crimes against women, violations of women's bodily integrity, socioeconomic injustice, and gender-based political persecution and discrimination. By claiming the right to assert these problems as rights issues, activists challenge the global human rights community to support their claims. The discourse proved unifying for the critical agendas of those concerned about conceivably disparate issues such as inadequate safe water,[22] sexual and reproductive health,[23] sweatshop labor,[24] and human trafficking.[25]

Story after story from the activists' work – from education in Afghanistan, to women's health in Costa Rica, to constitutional reform in South Africa – illustrates the challenge of working for women's rights while transforming local thinking about women and human rights. Many of the feminists' ways of working are particularly conducive to a transformative approach to human rights through framing the full range of women's issues as rights issues. In particular, work which educates people through classrooms, media, and street theater can transform social norms. In Bangladesh, Ain o Salish Kendra, a human rights and legal aid organization, has a particular interesting twist on street theater which uses social hierarchies to provoke rethinking of gender and other social hierarchies. In their work, they invite the most respected leaders of the community to be the performers of the street theater. They give them the character assignments and plot line and have them role play and work out the solution. In this way, they

[22] The Gender and Water Alliance is a network of 133 organizations and individuals from around the world and links water rights with gender; www.genderandwater.org/.

[23] The International Planned Parenthood Federation (IPPF), which is a coalition of voluntary associations of 180 countries in the world, uses women's rights based advocacy training programs, social awareness, and mobilization strategies; www.ippf.org.

[24] Pearson 1998.

[25] For example, the Coalition against Trafficking in Women (CATW) advocates for effective legal reform against trafficking and the sexual exploitation of women.

give those higher up in the social hierarchy the opportunity to put themselves performatively in the shoes of those otherwise located.

However, the strategy of framing issues as human rights issues has not been uniformly successful and even in areas where there has been much success, such as sexual and reproductive health, there is still so much work to be done.[26] The challenge is for any activist to articulate her concerns as universal human rights claims and to link her concerns not just to a narrow understanding of universal human rights as say only civil rights. This is challenging because in some contexts in which activists work, the social, political, and economic environment is such that only civil and political rights are understood as human rights. Even more worrisome is when the political history of the use of "human rights" makes the human rights discourse itself a source of fear or suspicion. Patricia Foxen gives an interesting example based on her fieldwork with Mayan communities in Guatemala nearly two decades after its thirty-six-year civil war.

Discussing the UN-mandated Truth Commission (CEH) and the Catholic Church's Historical Memory project (Interdiocesan Project of Recuperation of Historical Memory – RHEMI), she argues:

> The CEH report states that "a large number of people continue to remain silent about their past and present suffering, while the internalization of traumas prevents the healing of their wounds." The report's authors acknowledge that, despite the collection of 8000 direct testimonies of human rights violations, a majority of Mayans did not come forward, presumably out of fear because the perpetrators of violence continue to live with impunity throughout the highlands. However, based on the author's own field work in a municipality where most people had lived through brutal violence but most did not participate in either the CEH or the RHEMI projects, reasons for withholding their testimonials went beyond the fear of their persecutors.
>
> Based on past experiences, many believed that "los Derechos Humanos" ("The Human Rights," a personification of the abstract concept of human rights), must not be trusted.[27]

In a footnote Foxen makes the political memory and legacy more explicit:

> Many people in this area, particularly from the outlying hamlets, perceive "los Derechos Humanos" – broadly characterized as the UN Human Rights

[26] Petchesky 2003. [27] Foxen 2000: 358.

Mission (MINUGUA), the CEH and any other organization utilizing the language of human rights – as an extension of the guerrillas. There are several reasons for this: first, the guerrillas themselves had utilized the language of rights – the right to land, education and health – to rally people in villages to support their cause; second, during the period of armed struggle, the URNG (National Guatemalan Revolutionary Unity) also participated in popular human rights organizations as part of their social strategy; and third, the army, in implementing its counterinsurgency and fear tactics, had used a discourse which demonized those who spoke of "derechos humanos." This negative discourse on human rights continues to reach every level of society; in September 1998, President Arzu told a group of graduating military cadets that human rights activists are "nearly traitors to the fatherland."[28]

Clearly, given the context of the Maya of Guatemala, framing all issues as human rights issues is not a curb cut strategy.

Does this mean that no feminists should use human rights to talk about their issues? No. Immanent universal human rights theory recognizes the contextually specific reasons for not turning to human rights language while also recognizing the political legitimacy of those who do. The challenge is not to ignore the rights of those whose contexts inhibit their asserting them. Internationally networked women themselves lobbied for recognition of the importance of recognizing the human rights of indigenous women.[29]

The point instead is that feminists can use human rights to talk about their issues in a way that gets the interests of the Guatemalan Maya on a political agenda. We should use Foxen's insights to be particularly attentive as to *how* we talk about rights and silences, so that women's silences do not become an excuse for women's political exclusion, or unquestioningly to be evidence of their fear. We may decide that in certain contexts we should not use human rights discourse (though we are still committed to human rights). However, from acknowledging that the *discourse* will differ by context does not follow the view that human rights are relative. Certainly, where human rights is the dominant discourse and a successful discourse for women, including indigenous women, we should use it to lobby for the human rights of indigenous women, even of the specific Guatemalan Maya who anthropomorphized human rights.

28 Foxen (2000: footnote 4) cites Goldman (1999).

29 Their comment on Beijing + 10 was included in actions by the Committee on the Status of Women at their March 11 meeting (United Nations E/CN.6/2005/L.10) (United Nations 2005).

As successful as the human rights framing has been, as transformative as it has been for so many contexts of activism, it is not an unproblematic strategy. Curb cut feminism requires that we be sensitive to the exclusionary potential of our strategic choices. In addition, it requires us to be attentive to the silences potentially perpetuated by limited reflection on our strategies and to use this attentiveness to hurdle or break down the boundaries created by silences. If past political exclusions make some women unable to use the women's human rights discourse, we should not allow their present silence on human rights issues or present avoidance of human rights discourse to justify inattention to the violation of their human rights.[30] Curb cut feminism cannot respect the language choices of some people at the expense of their political interests. Curb cut feminism ought to be able to distinguish between the politics of discourse and the politics of substance, recognize the substantive dimensions of discourse and the discursive dimensions of substance, without letting all of that awareness preclude them from recognizing women's interests as they articulate them.

By understanding human rights as interrelated, indivisible, and structural, activists have greater flexibility in articulating rights claims and greater resources with which to explain why and how certain norms, practices, and institutions have become rights violating. While the strategy of framing issues as rights issues may be problematic, if activists use their curb cut epistemology to anticipate the ways in which this might be so, framing issues as rights issues can continue to be a curb cutting strategy of global feminist activism.

### *Bringing local and particular issues to the global stage*

In the past two decades and particularly during the 1990s, the international women's movement became closely linked with UN conferences: four global women's conferences in Mexico (1975), Copenhagen (1980), Nairobi (1985), and Beijing (1995), Environment and Development (1992), Human Rights (1993), Population and Development (1994), and Human Settlement (a.k.a. Habitat II,

[30] See work on women's international war crimes tribunals (e.g. Cockburn and Hubic 2002: 103–121; Kempadoo and Doezema 1998; Puja 2001: 611–620).

1996).[31] The Third World Conference on Women in Nairobi has been heralded as "the birth of global feminism."[32] An inclusion of local NGOs and social movement organizations (SMOs) in these global dialogues brought certain local issues such as women's reproductive health, domestic violence, and local inheritance, property, and divorce laws to the global stage. With women's human rights visible at the global level, activists in other, less visible issues were able to articulate their concerns using the increasingly accepted language of women's human rights. Thus, these activists brought international attention to issues including war rape, comfort women, female cutting, sex work, and trafficking.[33]

Not all women's local issues have made it to the global stage. Above I discuss the role of the discursive exclusions that may come about as a result of the use of human rights language. The approach potentially leaves out those who don't or can't frame their issues as rights issues. Transnational feminists have been alert to this problem and have devised strategies to bring local activists to the attention of global audiences.[34] However, the concern is that un-networked women, particularly women from the global South, become the face of women's human rights violations rather than the voice of criticism. This is problematic for the post-colonial, race, and class dynamics of transnational feminist activism and may impede the visibility of intersectional experiences.[35]

It is substantively problematic as well. Activists who have not thought to frame their issues as "rights" issues are cut off from the transnational resources that have been mobilized for women's human rights and because they are cut off from transnational networks, they have limited access to the ideas of transnational feminists (including the women's human rights discourse). As a gender and development expert

[31] United Nations 1980; 1985; 1992; 1993; 1996; United Nations First Conference on Women 1975; United Nations 1995; 1994.

[32] "The Four Global Women's Conferences 1975–1995: Historical Perspective"; www.un.org/womenwatch/daw/followup/session/presskit/hist.htm (accessed April 28, 2004).

[33] Joachim 2003: 247–274; Keck and Sikkink 1998.

[34] Particularly at the Vienna Human Rights Conference (United Nations 1993), even more so at the Beijing Conference on Women (United Nations 1995), and most recently at the UNIFEM Video Conference: "A World Free of Violence Against Women" (UNIFEM 1999).

[35] Crenshaw 2000.

from Guinea-Bissau described in an interview at the end of the 2004 World Social Forum, while "many of our people . . . work in the field of human rights," their understanding is abstract. "We must seek out and put into place methods that can help people to work out the concepts better, to internalize them and go out and put them into practice on a day-to-day basis."[36]

Finally, international rights discourse, such as that provided by CEDAW, give legitimacy to local struggles if the participants can articulate their arguments in CEDAW's global legal language. However, CEDAW's monitoring processes demonstrate that nation-states and cultural norms have the resources to circumvent that language by undermining its local legitimacy, thus challenging the women who employ a rights discourse in their local strategies as traitors to their country or culture.[37]

Further, as D'Costa and I argue in our work for the United Nations Research Institute for Social Development (UNRISD), the use of a general universalizing discourse risks treating the local activists as the illustration (that is as the voice or the face of women's human rights violations), but denying their important analytical contribution to human rights.[38] Further, even when scholars from the global South make theoretical arguments about women's human rights locally, their arguments are not given the same critical attention (and thus respect) that the arguments of their colleagues from the global North receive.[39] Such lack of critical respect reenacts a colonial relationship in the realm of ideas.

Again, these criticisms are specific, not general. Exclusions, crowding out of some activism, and drawing away of financial and human resources from some grassroots activism are good reasons to be concerned about this strategy of activism. However, if activists use their curb cut epistemology (that is, a heavy dose of self-reflection) and the immanent universal theory of human rights (that is, attentiveness to the potential to exclude, crowd out, or detract from particular local activism) in their efforts to bring local issues to the global stage, this strategy can strengthen not just their own activism but also the activism

[36] I1 2004.

[37] Cook 2001: 109–123; Farha 1999: 483–532; Gallagher 1997: 283–333; Kapur 1999: 143–153; Otto 2001: 52–67.

[38] Ackerly and D'Costa 2004; 2005.

[39] Personal discussions with D'Costa.

of others. It can serve not only to identify, but also to mitigate, the ways in which particular practices could create these problems.

### *Rewriting international universal human rights such that violations of women's human rights are as visible as violations of men's*

In addition to using human rights to strengthen women's activism locally and globally, transnational feminist activists also use human rights to re-theorize the international human rights framework itself. One might argue that actually, women's human rights activists were able to reveal the ways in which international, national, and local practices as they impacted women were inconsistent with the world's existing commitments to the human rights of all of humanity. On this view, human rights were not re-visioned theoretically, but practically.Though we may debate the impact of this re-theorization on women's lives, in the UN rights institutions, regional human rights conventions, ad hoc war crimes tribunals, international human rights groups, refugee work, and even UN Security Council peace-keeping missions, women's human rights have become a principal concern.[40]

Having a substantive impact on these institutions has been very difficult.[41] Even a person who was for a time in charge of writing the resource package for gender mainstreaming within UN peacekeeping missions said in an interview with Carol Cohn that she did not know what gender mainstreaming meant when she started the job.[42] On the other hand one indicted Rwandan war criminal was re-indicted so that the indictment included specific mention of his gendered war crimes.[43]

Triangulating multiple research methods, in her dissertation, "The Politics of Gender in the United Nations Human Rights Treaty Bodies," Ladan Rahmani documents the narrow range of ways in which women's rights get discussed let alone redressed by the UN treaty bodies. Institutional design and the limited presence of women in

[40] Ali 2000; Amnesty International 2004; Anker 2002; Barsky 2000; Bunch 2003: 6–11; Campanaro 2001: 2557–2592; Cook 1994; Cooper 2002: 9–25; United Nations 2000; West 1997.

[41] Rahmani 2005. [42] Cohn 2005.

[43] The Prosecutor versus Jean-Paul Akayesu (ICTR-96-4-T), www.un.org/ictr/english/casehist/akayesu.html (accessed February 20, 2004).

positions of influence and authority function as structural barriers to mainstreaming gender analysis into the organizations.

Perhaps the reason that women have made such strides in rewriting international universal human rights is that the political opposition to women's human rights has focused its attention on objecting to the application of gendered interpretation of human rights. Consider the contestation at the 61st session of the Commission on Human Rights between March 16 and April 22, 2005. Sweden proposed adding to paragraph 5 text that urges:

> all States to integrate [into] their national strategies on HIV/AIDS interventions with sexual and reproductive health and the promotion of reproductive rights as well as the right to have control and decide freely and responsibly on matters related to their sexuality, free of coercion, discrimination and violence.

Those contesting such changes – China, Costa Rica, the Dominican Republic, Egypt, Ecuador, Guatemala, Iran, Sudan, Pakistan, the USA, and the Vatican – did so using the rhetoric of "no new rights."[44] In so doing opponents to the immanent and universal understanding of human rights illustrate that they accept some of its premises. First, they recognize that there is a significant terrain of human rights in which the content, role, and legitimacy of human rights are not contested. "No *new* rights" implies that some rights are not contested. Second, they recognize that the recognition of rights changes over time. In the past there have been "new" rights that became accepted as universal. The "no new rights" strategy admits that human rights is an essentially contested concept and the product of social processes which are contested. While wishing to keep gendered issues in the terrain of difficulty, no-new-rights strategists acknowledge that the use of human rights for social criticism is legitimate and that much of the content of what we understand to be human rights is not contested.[45] Women's human rights activists have been able to frame human rights as immanent and universal and opponents have had to follow suit, perhaps without realizing the implications of their strategy.[46]

44 Astra Network Online 2005.

45 Allison Brysk argues that the introduction of "new human rights norms" offers an illustration of how "new" claims about justice become international norms about human rights (2005: 29 and 3).

46 On the politics of being the first to frame an issue see Lakoff (2004).

Through their activism, transnational feminist activists have transformed non-feminist thinking about human rights. Even anti-feminists recognize that the terrain of disagreement around gender issues is political. The "no new rights" argument can be sustained only if we respect the *political* interests of those pushing the view. Even those with conservative political interests recognize that the epistemological ground of human rights is shifting, theoretically inclined toward the recognition of "new" rights and the rights of "new" people, deterred by political will, not theoretical argument. In making their argument, opponents of human rights for women did not draw on minimalist theoretical accounts. Instead, they recognize that the practice of human rights recognition is politically constrained. In this political context women's human activism may generate a backlash. However, this form of backlash affirms the universality of the immanent theory of human rights by revealing the politics of moral disagreement and, in limiting the scope of the disagreement, it affirms the political legitimacy of that which is not in dispute.

## *Channeling resources*

The women's human rights discourse enabled local NGOs and SMOs to gain access to international donor dollars by educating global donors about women's human rights and convincing them to think of their issues as women's human rights issues and by educating local actors on how to articulate their issues as women's human rights issues in order to secure such support.

Two political trends created the opportunity for such education. First, with increased democratization in Latin America, Asia, and Africa, international donors were interested in strengthening civil society. Organizations using the human rights language were able to secure funding for grassroots political participation and collective action.[47] Second, with the desire for grassroots participation in the UN Conference process (at least as the face if not the voice and analysis of women's human rights violations), donors supported local NGO participation in the preparatory processes and ultimately in the NGO forums of the UN Conferences of the 1990s. Women with access to global feminist networks advocated for funding and training resources

[47] Alvarez 1999: 181–209.

for local organizations and in addition facilitated dialogues among local counterparts in an effort to foster collaboration that could sustain these groups' local activism after the UN Conference process.

Scholar–activist individuals and networks became key to the processes of channeling global money into the hands of local activists. To donors, scholar–activists of women's human rights offer a way of leveraging donor money. When combined with others working for women's human rights, donor investment toward social change (however that is understood in each donor's mandate) has the potential for a much greater impact. Likewise, scholar–activists write reports and assist NGO and SMO activists in grant writing by describing the work of grassroots activists in the increasingly accepted language of women's human rights as understood by donor communities. Principally through networks such as DAWN, IRWIG (Institute for Research on Women and Gender), IWHC (International Women's Health Coalition), and WGNRR (Women's Global Network for Reproductive Rights), and supported by UNIFEM, UNDP, and UNRISD, the transnational women's rights movement successfully mobilized scholar–activists to channel global funding to local sources.

As Erica Lewis, National Policy and Research Officer for the YWCA of Australia argues, scholar–activists are the 'intellectual capital' of transnational feminism. Scholar–activist efforts are reflected in the funding policies of various donor agencies such as the Global Fund, Ford Foundation, EU, Cafod, Oxfam, Care, and government funding agencies such as NORAD (Norwegian Agency for Development Cooperation) and CIDA (Canadian International Development Agency). Further, the power of this intellectual activism is such that organizations with religious affiliations are no longer able to ignore women's issues. For example, over the last decade the Christian Children's Fund, Caritas, and World Vision have increasingly emphasized women's issues although their funding strategies still reflect a Women in Development (WID) perspective, that is not focused on changing gender roles as we have seen is generally necessary in order to increase recognition of women's human rights. Even though the religious attitudes of some donor agencies (for example toward homosexuality or certain reproductive health services) may conflict with certain women's human rights concerns such as security and reproductive health, these donors have contributed to promoting women's rights in other areas.

In the field of women's human rights, scholar–activists have been able to facilitate the channeling of resources by offering well-articulated explanations of the substance and meaning of human rights by making visible the often invisible violations of women's human rights.[48] While gender analysis has been essential to this endeavor, the success of the movement does not depend on activists or the people they try to persuade to have or even to develop a nuanced understanding of gender. By contrast, Margaret Snyder argues that the "gender and development" initiative, which was more theoretically nuanced than its predecessor, got the Women In Development initiative off track[49] because it did not consider the institutional, organizational, and individual limitations of those institutions, organizations, and people it sought to transform. The comparison between women's human rights work and development work is interesting. Unless people within organizations understand gender – a difficult and essentially contested concept – at the level of being able to reflect about what makes gender a difficult and essentially contested concept, they will not be able to institutionalize "gender mainstreaming,"[50] or "gender and development," or "gender in development," or "women, culture, and development."[51] Women's human rights work respects the theoretical boundary pushing that makes us wonder about the universality of universals and yet works within the language and conceptual constraints of its audience. This means at times pushing theoretical boundaries with practice and at times pushing practices in order that new conceptual thinking can be made possible in a given context.

This is not to say that the ability of a compelling framework to help channel resources is unproblematic. During her interview, an activist from Turkey whose organization works locally and transnationally within the Middle East and North Africa region reflected on the competition and accountability issues associated with the impact that the human rights discourse has had on channeling resources:

> If you were to introduce this training and research, there might be a need for broader funding, and then there is the question, who is getting this fund? Who is accountable for this fund? And then this might become a problem because our experiences are in Turkey, we work very well together on a not paid basis, a lot of organizations. The moment funds comes in it creates

48 Bunch 1990; Charlesworth 1994; Friedman 1995. 49 Snyder 2006.
50 True 2001. 51 Chua, Bhavnani, and Foran 2000.

problems. So to find funds that are flexible. For example, you have a fund that's saying look I will sign the contract but it might be I give a portion of this money to this organization who will never fund. But this would be perfect. Maybe in ten years we can formulate an institution in the Middle East where everyone takes a part of. But in the moment we are not at that stage. We need also independence. We need also trust-building situation. It would not be possible. I think it would create competition and stress and so we observe other networks. For example there's a huge woman-African network we heard about – I forgot the name. There was a conference in 2003 in South Africa, … I think this is the only example right now where I know the network with a head office is functioning. … But the other experience what I have is typical.[52]

Likewise, activists are skeptical of agenda setting by donors. She continues:

some donors come and say you should interlink with those and those countries. For example they tried it for a long time in Turkey to connect to the Eastern European states, former Soviet state, Ukraine, whatever, Turkmenistan and somehow it doesn't work. In some parts it's working but in some parts it's not working.[53]

However, not all donors are worried about their agenda-setting power. Many donors are confident that they are well positioned to see a large range of activisms and the possibilities of coordinated activism.[54] This activist from Turkey has evidence from her own experience that supports this role of donors:

We had in the past a very good funder who was also working in the Middle East. It was really the best funder I ever met. We were in a mutual understanding. They gave us addresses of people they thought they might be of interest to us … So we had the same aim.[55]

And yet she has reason to be concerned that donors distract activists from their core competencies:

I think we have some very good funding agencies in Turkey also. But in the past they gave us good ideas, they pushed a little bit but sometimes it's really dangerous because I think if people are not, or if movements are not at that

[52] IB12 2005. [53] IB12 2005.
[54] Personal correspondence with representatives of Ford, MacArthur, and Soros foundations.
[55] IB12 2005.

> stage to act like that ... Like after the earthquake it was clear after a while that there were a lot of funds available to be spent in relief effort. ... And then they left their work what they were actually doing and then after a while the fund was ending and they couldn't go back. This is something which is dangerous and I think ...[56]

The activist experience illustrates that channeling resources can be both a way of getting resources into the hands of those previously marginalized and a way of preventing resources from getting into the hands of those who are marginalized by a lack of access to human rights discourses. Again, the curb cutting perspective and the immanent and universal human rights theory guide us to think not about whether to use the human rights discourse but about *how* we use it.

## *Contextualized human rights*

The method of theorizing and re-theorizing human rights employed by women's human rights scholar–activists has led to a reform in legal thinking regarding rights. Whereas the norm of impartiality has been assumed to require neutrality, the increasing discussion of gender in rights and law has demonstrated that uninformed neutrality cannot yield impartiality. For example, gender expertise has been used to write guidelines for immigration judges determining asylum.[57] In another example mentioned above, gender expertise on the Rwanda War Crimes Tribunal led to one defendant being re-indicted so that his indictment included gender-based war crimes.[58]

When activism results in increased visibility of the violations of some people's rights, increased acceptance of the indivisibility of rights, and increased awareness of the enabling structural conditions of human rights violations, then it contributes to the immanent and universal theory of human rights.

## *Transfer of leadership to the global South*

The previous discussion shows some macro-level strategies that transnational feminists used to transform thinking about human rights. One

[56] IB12 2005. [57] Anker 2002.

[58] The Prosecutor versus Jean-Paul Akayesu (ICTR-96-4-T); www.un.org/ictr/english/casehist/akayesu.html (accessed February 20, 2004).

of the exciting things about women's human rights activism of the past decade is that the leadership of transnational feminist activism has been (at least partially) transferred from the global North to the global South.

For example, Rosalind Petchesky describes the transfer of leadership and transformation of the health rights agenda:

> Northern-based women's health and human rights NGOs that played convening roles in Cairo and Beijing and the Plus Five conferences could only do so by forming networks of allied organizations from Africa, Asia-Pacific, Latin America and the Caribbean as well as Eastern-Central Europe. This was necessary in order to sustain their legitimacy and viability in the globalizing world ... But the interesting thing is the ways in which the partner networks develop a life of their own, with their own outlooks and agendas and an independent, vocal leadership from the Global South.[59]

In one sense, the shared global leadership of the transnational feminist movement is evident in international meetings of feminists. In transnational networks such as DAWN, IRWIG, IWHC, and WGNRR, in international organizations such as UNIFEM, UNDP, and UNRISD, and at transnational meetings such as the World Social Forum (2004 and 2005) and the Feminist Dialogues (2005), agenda setters are generally not from the global North. However, as we saw in chapters 6 and 7 there are differences among activists from different geographies, different networks, with different experiences.

While leadership is not held in the global North, it does not have democratic accountability to the women of the world. Activists of the global feminist movements may practice curb cut feminism and develop the immanent and universal theory of human rights through their activism, but the institutions of the global feminist movement do not make this happen. The accountability of global feminist and women's activists is not institutionalized, thus making our shared immanent and universal theory of human rights an important tool for our own self-criticism.

### *Bringing those working on similar issues in different places into dialogue with one another*

The women's human rights framework has also enabled locally oriented activists, who are dealing with particular human rights

[59] Petchesky 2003: 67.

violations as they manifest themselves in a particular locale, to transnationalize their work. An activist from Turkey (cited above) describes her work:

So there are NGOs working on similar issues like we. Not only women's organizations. We have also some men, more individual men, we have some gay organizations from Indonesia, because they are there dealing with the movement ... also in the Muslim community. So it's a totally different discussion there. And it can help for other countries.[60]

What are their strategies?

We initiate meetings to come together, [discuss our] most concerns, where are we working, how can we together strategize, how can we learn from each other, and then we almost take care that there is a further plan, action plan, what can we do together? One example of what we are trying to do now is that because of the campaign that we led in Turkey of the penal code reform, I tell later of that, is to initiate also our network in other countries, to support law initiatives there or initiate, so civil law compares, so penal law, from a gender perspective under the aspect of sexuality and bodily rights.[61]

Her Turkish organization is one of many in which transnational feminists bring together activists working on similar issues. Some of these are regional (as in the Turkish example) and others are global. For example, at the 14th World AIDS Conference at Barcelona, Spain (2002), a coalition brought together more than 400 activists who work on HIV issues around the world to address the gendered dimension in HIV/AIDS advocacy work.[62] The Women at Barcelona coalition was founded through a joint initiative of Health & Development Networks (HDN), the United Nations Development Fund for Women (UNIFEM), and the IAS (International AIDS Society) Women's Caucus.[63]

60 IB12 2005.

61 IB12 2005; for more information see Anil, Arin, Macimirzaoglu, Bingollu, Ilkkaracan, and Amado (2005).

62 SAATHII (Solidarity and Action Against the HIV Infection in India), www.saathii.org/about_saathii/saathii_collaborators.html (accessed February 25, 2004).

63 "Women and HIV/AIDS: The Barcelona Bill of Rights"; www.actupny.org/reports/bcn/BCNwomenrights.html (accessed February 25, 2004). (Barcelona Bill of Rights 2002.) Based on Bina D'Costa's research.

The International Conference on Women, Peace Building, and Constitution Making held in Colombo, Sri Lanka, in May 2002 is another example of peace and transnational dialogue. Organized by the International Center for Ethnic Studies, the conference brought together women activists from conflict areas such as Rwanda, Sierra Leone, Bosnia, Afghanistan, the Middle East, East Timor, Colombia, Guatemala, Northern Ireland, and the South Asian countries.[64] Academics and specialists who researched the theme of women and peace made this conference a platform for sharing experiences and strategies among women across borders.

Despite their possibilities for building networks, such gatherings are expensive and require a lot of coordination and therefore as they include, they also exclude. Some activisms crowd out local activism by drawing human and financial resources away from local activities, and potentially provoke local and nationalistic backlashes.

### *Bringing those working on separate issues into dialogue with one another*

Further, with a common discourse, feminists working on seemingly separable issues such as domestic violence, health, education, safe water, peace, land rights, etc. have been brought together in virtual and physical ways through online working groups, edited volumes, and international meetings for small- and large-scale dialogue.[65]

In addition, women have sought to build bridges across movements. One reason these links have been able to be made is because, as Jayati Ghosh argues, and as much activism at the 2004 World Social Forum demonstrates, women have become the most dynamic contributors to other social movements including the *dalit*, trade unions, right to information, and right to food campaigns.[66] However, women are aware of the risk that their energy will be co-opted in such partnerships, that

[64] The International Conference on Women, Peace Building and Constitution Making, "Introduction"; www.icescolombo.org/wpc2002/intro.htm (accessed February 25, 2004). (International Conference on Women 2002: Introduction.) Based on Bina D'Costa's research.

[65] Two medium-size opportunities for such international feminist dialogue include the Feminist Dialogues (2005) and the 5th international meeting of the World March of Women (2004).

[66] I5 2004.

their gendered perspective on the broader issues will be de-emphasized when raised within the context of a larger movement, or as Angela Mandie-Filer cautions, the larger issue will be de-emphasized when it becomes politically identified as a "women's" issue. Mandie-Filer of DAWN-PNG complains:

> because women push for recognition for other issues *they* ... become women's issues. We are picking up the baggage! [These issues] should be taken up by men as well! Things like a non-violent household – that is not women's issues. We have inherited issues by involvement.[67]

Furthermore, even while such coalition-building can exhaust the women involved, like the preceding strategies of bringing those working on the same issues together, such network-building risks being exclusive, reinforcing a hegemony of knowledge within certain social movements, even critical social movements.

## Conclusion: guiding questions for activists' work

In chapters 5 and 6, I described curb cut epistemology as challenging me as a feminist researcher to be self-conscious of my epistemological perspectives, to choose research tools that would reveal certain kinds of data that were otherwise not visible in human rights theory, and to analyze that data in a dialogical fashion. Just as curb cut epistemology challenged my research agenda, methods, and analysis, so to it can be a helpful tool for feminist activists to think about the contexts in which they work, the objectives and priorities they set for themselves, and the strategies that they use to pursue these. Though it is right to distinguish between my theoretical argument and the work of activists, I now shift to using the first person plural (we) to underscore the importance of *collective* reflection and the critical *insignificance* of a distinction between academic and activists in the need for self-reflective questioning. These reflections are inspired by and contribute to contemporary discussions among transnational and global feminist activists about contemporary women's activism.[68]

[67] ID23 2004.

[68] Other reflections on the contemporary movement include Clark *et al.*(2006) and the workshops and meetings of the Feminist Dialogues and World March for Women.

In this chapter I have utilized this curb cutting perspective and the immanent and universal theory of human rights articulated in the preceding chapter to evaluate the strategies of women's human rights organizations and of the transnational feminist and women's human rights movement taken as a whole. I am concluding this chapter with a set of guiding questions that those for whom immanent and universal human rights depict our normative commitments, and the commitments that we would like to see embodied in our practices, might find useful.

### *Context assessment*

In each context, we need to ask ourselves: What are our issues? What are the social, political, and economic factors defining our issues? What are the other progressive movements in our context? Do any of those movements share our analysis of the social, political, and economic context? What are their objectives? Do any of these objectives work against our objectives?

For example, Pramada Menon understands that conceivably feminists and environmentalists have a lot in common and could conceivably pursue objectives in common. However, environmentalists have won "victories" in the form of national parks established in India. These national parks are established by displacing the people who lived in the newly designated area. This strategy works against development, women, and, upon further analysis, most likely the environment itself as the relocation of people puts a strain on the environmental resources of their new communities.[69]

This sort of analysis reveals that a partnership with environmental organizations may be difficult to develop without first establishing a shared understanding of the indivisibility of rights and the interrelatedness of people. By contrast, women's environmental organizations may be more attentive to environment and social justice. Such organizations include international networks such as the Women's Environment and Development Organization (WEDO), national movements such as the Greenbelt movement in Kenya, and local activist organizations such as Navdanya in India.

[69] IB2 2005.

## *Objectives and priorities*

Sometimes activists can choose our objectives and priorities, sometimes, as in the India activism that rose up in response to Shiv Seva's criticism of the movie *Fire*, an issue chooses us. As Maya Sharma wrote to the International Gay and Lesbian Human Rights Commission (IGLHRC) in an email message eventually included in the book *Written Out*:

> Shiv Sena's attacks on the film *Fire* led to the formation of CALERI [Campaign for Lesbain Rights]. Strange are the ways in which people come together. This attack, in fact, became our source of strength. We came together because of it. Not that one is saying it's good, but the need for the vulnerable to come together hits hardest when one is under attack. It creates a fissure in the placid, dead routine. Like stitches getting undone and the tear in the garment widens. All that is covered and hidden "comes to" and so we awakened and came together. We came together in spite of our differences.[70]

Whether activists are choosing our objectives and priorities or are seemingly having them chosen for us by the need to respond to attacks, we need to understand these priorities as dynamic and not set. Of course, it may be that the fact that we have to respond to an attack dictates how we respond to that attack. However, activists cannot let the fact that we are forced to respond to an issue dictate the way we *think* about an issue. We must remain the authors of our conceptualizations. As authors, we can respond to future circumstances and attacks with our objectives and priorities that are chosen so as to open up future possibilities for activism and alliances and close off avenues of exploitation of hierarchy.

Questions we might ask are: How is the political problem being framed and how would we like to frame it? What response to an attack will enable others to share our concern? How can we best approach our issue without foreclosing options for addressing other issues – our own, those of potential allies, those that we have yet to imagine?

## *Dialogue*

Both theorists and activists assert the need for, and demonstrate the value of, dialogue. However, not all deliberative opportunities are the

[70] Rothschild, Long, and Fried 2005: 135.

same.[71] An activist from Turkey reflects on her organization's experience with promoting dialogue:

> We are very open in our principles and in our aims. We are open communicating them, we don't have hidden agendas. One thing, people know if we have a meeting, from which source it is funded. Transparency. We invite sometimes also donor agencies to connect also with the people we invite to the meeting. This is also very important. Not all the time, but sometimes. And then, we don't say we are the leaders of the network, and we follow very, one of our principles is that we stay very good in contact with people, have a good follow-up. It's a working principle that we have in our organization and now, for example like, in this tsunami, we immediately wrote we need any help, we told about our experiences working in the earthquake relieving Turkey, so it was an immediate exchange. But the other side, as we finish the penal code reform, we got so many emails from the network congratulating, and saying, asking questions, so see, there was already a basis of interacting together, and celebrating with each other but also keeping in touch and caring for each other. So, not only on the work issue a follow-up, but also on the other occasions, and this is very important. We can support each other in various situations, and this is very important. And another thing, is that we very clear respect the work people are doing in their country. This is very important, and we don't want to influence this. We are not setting the agenda. This is very important. We are just trying to say, ok if you work mainly on domestic violence, we are working mainly, we name it sexual and bodily rights, where can we interconnect, do you see any chances? And a lot of people give their feedback that for the first time they go a step back and say yes, actually, yes I'm working on violence against women but yes it really has something to do with sexuality. And on the other hand, we are learning also of some examples of the strategies that some countries employ to get through, and it's challenging them, and this is really fantastic. And having all this knowledge, and you don't refer all the time only to Turkey. You can say something from Algeria, you can name an example from Pakistan. So the government cannot take the national interest and saying we are like that, and in other countries it's much worse. We can say also good examples from other countries and say we have to compete.[72]

How can we promote dialogues that enhance our own awareness of terrain(s) of the difficulty? How can we make ourselves aware of marginalized people and issues? How can we work through the terrain of difficulty together? How can we create opportunities for each of these?

[71] Ackerly 2000; 2007a. [72] IB12 2005.

### *Dialogue partners*

How can we dialogue with those with whom we disagree?[73] The activist from Turkey whose organization has significant experience developing and working with local, regional, and global networks underscores the challenges of dialogue:

> I think identifying other NGOs or people to work with, it took a while in the beginning. It was a long, long process. And it wasn't easy in the beginning and I can give you an example of that. But now it is easy, because we are known and we have also very simple principles. So although we are initiating and monitoring this network we are not leading it. And this is very important. And this message we give you. This work can only be successful if people are interested in, and they have the same goals, vision, and they do something.[74]

Following the activist from Turkey, we need to ask, does this partner share the immanent and universal theory of human rights? Does this partner recognize terrain(s) of difficulty, rather than treating difference as a basis for challenging the universality of human rights?

Sometimes our dialogue partners choose us as in Menon's dialogue with a *dalit* activist about whether sexuality was an important political issue because only a small percentage of the population was affected.[75] When such moments happen, they are deliberative opportunities, opportunities for us to learn, to revise, and to strengthen our commitments.

When differences become apparent, how can we treat them as part of the terrain of difficulty and not as a basis for foreclosing dialogue or as evidence that there is no basis for dialogue? One of the most exciting things about the immanent and universal theory of human rights that I have described is that it demonstrates that there is huge ground of theoretical agreement. Consequently, any claims that some or all human rights are not universal can be seen as part of the terrain of difficulty but not a challenge to the overall theory. Moreover, the theory has its own analytical methodology for working through the terrain of difficulty.

How can we dialogue with those with whom we disagree? How can we not and continue to develop our immanent and universal theory of human rights? According to our immanent and universal theory of

[73] Ackerly 2007a. [74] IB12 2005. [75] IB2 2005.

human rights, human rights are an essentially contested and always dynamic concept for dealing with existing and as yet unknown injustices. Activists with frontline exposure to emergent concerns and academics with the resources for reflection can work in partnership to guide evaluation of and responses to these emergent sources of injustice.

# 10 *"If I can make a circle"*

Far away from Rwanda, a young art teacher drives from the Berkshires of Massachusetts to the ocean of Venice, California, staying in battered women's shelters for a few days to a week at each shelter. In each shelter she does art with the residents. She teaches them art techniques, simple ways of using various media. Each uses the opportunity to create something beautiful. Sometimes the teacher paints portraits of the survivors of domestic violence. Sometimes she records their words. Their words become part of the portraits.

The cover of this book is such a portrait. The words inspired the founder of what became A Window Between Worlds, an organization that develops art curricula for shelters of survivors of domestic violence and that fosters survivors' circles, which bring women together to do art. The title of this chapter (and of the cover art) come from three women's reflections on surviving, power, building trust, fostering community, and listening. The text that appears in italics is text from their reflections and is incorporated into the portrait.

*IF I CAN MAKE A CIRCLE – TRIO*

(Acrylic on Paper 32" × 37")

I

The relationship that I've been in with myself is a type of freedom that I never believed that I could feel: I can express that it's not okay to be beat, it's not okay to molest children, it's not okay to hurt another person. I feel happy and sad. I feel sad because there's still women and children out there getting beat and hurt and perpetrated. But I feel happy that I can tell the world that it's not okay.

I hang on to my spirituality, my Native American spirituality, because it's a belief, it's a simple belief that everything that breathes needs to be respected.

*If I can make a circle, a grand circle of people saying that it's not okay to be hurt, then I've done my part.*

II

I don't ever want to be on the streets again. *If you go through that, you're lucky if you come out halfway OK.*

Nobody, unless I told them, would know that I did that. They think I look innocent, or kind of young and naive. I felt like I was dirty and worthless. It takes a long time to get over it, and I'm not over it.

I think I need to concentrate on myself, instead of relationships with guys. I think it'd be better to just be alone for a while, and concentrate on my daughter too. She's most important to me.

III

I don't want to be here. I really don't. It's hard, knowing I have a house, I have a place to go, I have furniture, I have clothes. It's hard knowing that I can't get to these things. It's hard knowing that he's out there and I'm leery of going out.

In a relationship, I want to feel safe. I want to feel like there is this big out stretched hand or arms wrapped around me to keep me safe. I want this not just for me, but for everybody. *I would like to be that person who's looking down with my hands surrounding the whole world*, just protecting it from all evil, all wrong doings, everything. *I wish I had that kind of power.*

Individually, most of us don't feel that we have "that kind of power." However, the immanent universal theory of human rights says that we do have that power collectively if we exercise it.

A graduate student in California, I was driving toward Palm Drive down El Camino Royale on my way to be a teaching assistant for Peace Studies when I learned of the Rwandan genocide in 1994. In the course, we were studying conflict after conflict (Vietnam, Somalia, Croatia, Bosnia) and the students joked that the course title constituted false advertising. After my lecture on "societal security" in which we reviewed non-militarized forms of insecurity from domestic violence, to economic insecurity, to environmental insecurities, the first question from a student was: "What should I do?"

Indeed, assuming I have an obligation to do something, what should I do? For this student and for most of the students self-selecting into an optional course called "Peace Studies," the question was not about whether one had an obligation, but about how to fulfill that obligation. In the immanent theory of human rights, the primary obligation is to participate in the "grand circle" by promoting human rights and by engaging in the terrain(s) of difficulty. Thus, immanent universal human rights theory is both an ethic and a political theory. It can be used to inspire individual behavior. In addition, institutionally, it expects us to foster multiple, differentiated and overlapping, institutional and informal settings for informing our understandings, making transparent the linkages between actions (and in actions) and human rights violations, and promoting accountability.

I had met Jean-Paul about six months prior to the genocide and last saw him when he was going home to Rwanda, to his cows that produce four times as many liters per day as the cows we saw together in India. Hearing of the genocide on the radio, I pulled over to the side of El Camino Royale and cried. All I knew was that Jean-Paul and his family, caught in the cross-fire during the Burundi violence, would likely be caught in this violence too. I wrote the Jesuits he worked for and heard nothing. Then in 1998 or 1999 I received a brief cryptic letter from Marie and began my long (incomplete) education about the history of the region, its colonial past, its post-colonial history, its hills, and its politics. As a theorist I am skeptical of texts and the interests they served, yet from the United States I relied on texts to help me understand the threat she was experiencing. During this time there was no US media coverage of violence or human rights violations in Rwanda (and only scant mention of the violence in Uganda after the 2006 elections). Scholarship with thorough histories exposed multiple aspects of the far and recent past histories.[1] However, each revealed different views of what could stabilize the politics of the region going forward.[2]

Marie is not an activist like those I interviewed and observed in writing this book. She is a woman surviving brutal attacks on her person, only to have to be retested for HIV/AIDS in six months; a mother, protecting her children with half-baked plans and her own body; a friend, generously taking in the child of murdered friends.

1 Adelman and Suhrke 1999; African Rights (Organization) 1995; Eltringham 2004; Khan 2000; Mamdani 2001; Reyntjiens 2004; Scherrer 2002; Semujanga 2003; Twagilimana 2003; Uvin 1998.

2 One argued that even in an academic setting, you could close your eyes and guess someone's "ethnicity" by the position they advocated for Rwandan rule.

Writing a theoretical book while Marie and children moved from Rwanda, to Uganda, finally approved for refugee status and resettlement in Australia as the book went to press, meant living an irony. While I was writing an academic book about human rights, I went from compassionate friend, to unbelieving bystander, to useless confidante, and to her only hope. The question, "What should I do?" was often on my mind.

I had no doubt I had an obligation to do something for her and her family, but I had no idea how to direct my political will. What should I do? Having written a book on human rights, I have no better answer for myself than I did for my student in Peace Studies in 1994. No single person created the geopolitics we live with now and no single actor can undo them. We can, however, become increasingly aware of the multiple actors and structures that perpetuate our circumstances today and draw on our own strengths to address them. My obligation is not limited because Marie and her family are not proximate. It is not limited because I have limited ability to aid her. My obligation is not limited because I don't know what to do.

My answer for myself is, "If I can make a circle ..."

This is the same answer that Samantha Power gives in *A Problem from Hell*.[3] None of us alone will end a genocide, but we can be attuned to the political forces that structure what we are able to learn about human rights violations around the world and we can challenge these. We can become more aware of the ways in which the governments that are accountable to us are complicit in human rights violations around the world.[4] And, we can become more aware of the ways in which our own actions make us complicit in human rights violations around the world. And here is the socially awkward part: we can build a circle by listening and talking about human rights with people we know and with people we don't know.

Perhaps it is exhausting to be attuned to the politics of the places where our clothes and sneakers are made, to the child labor conditions under which our bananas are grown, to the economic risks to those who grow broccoli for a global market, to the health of those who live downstream from the strip mining that delivers the coal that powers our light bulbs, to the people who are displaced by hydropower dams, and to the lives of the people who for morally arbitrary reasons (and

[3] Power 2002. [4] E.g. Klinghoffer 1998.

political reasons beyond their influence) live in places where conflicts over resources are life-threatening.[5] Perhaps the insecurity of people in conflict zones, in violent families, in hunger is outside of our circle of influence. Perhaps we cannot live up to moral obligations toward those whom we cannot hear or see. Perhaps we cannot live up to moral obligations when our imaginations cannot generate viable political solutions, let alone a credible picture of the people and places in question. I keep coming back to this feeling of *incredibility*. Though I correspond with her with increasing frequency, sometimes I cannot believe that Marie's life is a real life that someone is living.

Actually, it is here, where our failure of imagination meets our moral theory, that we have been falling down. Just because we cannot come up with a good political solution for ending human rights violations does not mean we are not morally obligated to try. Certainly, in immanent universal human rights we have a theory of human rights that sees us as normatively committed to trying, and always uncertain that our efforts are adequate. If human rights are to mean anything, those who say they are for them need to mean that they are willing to work on political solutions. It is not hard to find a theoretical reason for setting aside political challenges. Most of the theories of human rights we have been considering could keep a theorist busy on a theoretical puzzle that must be resolved prior to facing the political puzzle of any instance of human rights violations.

But activists and survivors don't need answers to theoretical puzzles prior to action. They need a stronger circle. They participate in the global cacophony of "human rights." For them, human rights are a legitimate basis for social, political, and economic criticism; the challenge is in coming up with political strategies that enable everyone to realize those rights. Human rights are often a legitimate goal, but an ineffective political tool. Being an ineffective political tool makes them no less a legitimate goal. Using human rights in this way may mean being active for property inheritance rights in Burkina Faso, for freedom of movement and association for LBTIQ women in India, for citizenship rights in countries whose governments protect each member including indigenous women and their children, and for refugee status in countries for those whose governments will not.

[5] http://hrw.org/english/docs/2002/04/25/ecuado3876.htm

From the perspective of immanent universal human rights theory, attempts to formulate transcendental human right theories undermine human rights practices. Such transcendental (or tradition-based) theories take what activists consider are given – that claims for social justice may be rhetorically framed as political claims based on the normative legitimacy of human rights – and reframe them as contested. They move the content of the human rights debate back from the front lines. They move the discussion from the terrain(s) of difficulty to a terrain of principles where power rests with those able to make a better argument.

Of course, in one sense activists (particularly, scholar–activists) would *love* to have the success of a political claim rest on the ability to make a better argument, but in fact human rights claims are about claims of power. When theory undermines the normative legitimacy of a rights claimant, it attempts to remove from activists the one thing they count on, the normative legitimacy of universal human rights.

Activists have been challenged by such arguments: the primacy-of-sovereignty argument of anti-human rights voices during the drafting of the Universal Declaration of Human Rights,[6] the priority of sovereignty over human rights in the founding of the Organization of African States,[7] and Asian Values political arguments of the 1990s.[8] Each was an attempt to delegitimate claims to human rights.

But activists are undeterred by these political arguments. Of course, activists too have tried to expand our understanding of human rights and the political viability of human rights arguments. However, in contrast with the theoretical critiques of the anti-rights advocates, these human rights critics strengthen the immanent universal theory of human rights as they reflect upon it. Each of their criticisms affirms the normative legitimacy of human rights.

These activists do warn us of woefully inadequate analysis and information in our humanitarian action.[9] They caution us against mistakes made because some people or some rights violations are invisible. But, each such criticism again strengthens the normative legitimacy of human rights theory – imperfect as its recognition may

[6] Glendon 2001; Humphrey 1984; Ishay 2004. [7] Ibhawoh 2000.

[8] Chan 1997; Dalai Lama 1999; Dallmayr 2002; de Bary 1998; Donnelly 1999; Englehart 2000; Trowbridge 2000; Xiaorong 1998; Yu 2000.

[9] Uvin and Kennedy give us a similar warning (Kennedy 2004; Uvin 1998; 2004).

be in practice. Further, it guides us to create institutions and institutional mechanisms that can inform, make our actions and the impact of our actions transparent, and hold us (individually and in our institutions) accountable for them.

Human rights theory is a non-ideal theory in three senses. It is non-ideal because human rights are not currently universally secure. Human rights theory needs to provide a normative account of injustice and to offer a normative account of the moves necessary to promote human rights where they are lacking, not just to know that they are lacking. Human rights theory is non-ideal in another sense: because of the structural causes of human rights violations and the ways in which those causes are constructed through social, political, and economic practices, the normative theory of human rights needs to incorporate methodological attentiveness to the emergent possibilities for human rights violations. Finally, human rights is a non-ideal theory because we cannot now imagine what social, economic, political, geographic (etc.) conditions may change so as to precipitate conditions for human rights violations.

Non-ideal theory is concerned with the politics of knowledge, diversity, and dissent that prevent shared idealized theoretical justifications. Because of the political dimensions of non-ideal theory, the methodologies appropriate to ideal theory – that might rely on shared agreement about norms of argument or shared respect for the authority of certain arguments – cannot be appropriate for non-ideal theory. Therefore, we needed to develop a methodology for doing non-ideal theory. This methodology is attentive to the politics of knowledge by using a destabilizing epistemology. It is attentive to the politics of diversity by interrogating structures and seeking out invisibilities and silences for their political import. This methodology is also attentive to the politics of dissent by deploying methods for making dissent voiced and working toward political legitimacy, not consensus.

We may have growing international consensus on the ideas that some have called basic or core human rights, particularly on what philosophers call our "perfect" obligations. Further, we have come to demand more from national governments and international institutions. Not all of these battles are about law. Some of these rights are better achieved through changing basic social institutions. Thus, the political work inspired by Rawls's egalitarianism may not be best handled by parties at the national level or international organizations globally. Rather, this kind of egalitarianism requires grassroots social movements. Perhaps, such movements are lacking in the United States.[10] Or perhaps they exist in the US and in many places but are less visible to observers of traditional politics because they defy traditional norms.[11]

However, such grassroots movements can be seen globally and among women activists in the United States. Without United Nations sponsorship, since 2000, the World Social Forum process has brought grassroots activists together in global, regional, and national forums. Around the world activists and advocates have challenged a range of forms of human rights violations within their states or of some people within their state.

Institutions are important to our realizing our universal human rights. The immanent theory of universal human rights relies on and fosters multiple, differentiated and overlapping, institutional and informal settings for informing our understandings of human rights violations, for making transparent the linkages between individual and instititutional actions and inactions and human rights violations, and for holding institutions and each other accountable for our actions and inactions.

For the foreseeable future, human rights – perfect and imperfect obligations – will be political struggles. What are human rights? Who is responsible for sustaining them? Who must act and how when rights violations are observed? How do we know when they are being violated? We cannot answer these questions for any "we" without political struggle. That struggle will take place between states and peoples, between sovereign states in the international system, and, as this book has argued, within the power relations of the institutions, structures, values, practices, and norms of our collective lives. These political struggles will take place in constitutional conventions, legislatures, and courts, in public administration, in schools and police departments, in the halls of conferences and higher education, and in the streets. These political struggles will take place in families, among friends, at security checkpoints and immigration counters, and in the myriad places where our lived experiences of violence and hunger intersect with the social, political, and economic institutions of our

[10] Eliasoph 1998; Putnam 2001; 2002; Skocpol 2003; Skocpol and Fiorina 1999.
[11] Bullard 2005; Williams 1993.

local and globalized world. An immanent and universal theory of human rights emerges through those political struggles.

Women's and feminist activists for human rights use that theory to end their human rights violations and to transform the theory itself. Terrains that are difficult to navigate remain. Our collective awareness of the terrains of difficulty is a testimony to our commitment to an emancipatory epistemology, our commitment to seek and to reveal power relations and their potential abuses. While we do not deny the terrains of difficulty, we are empowered to work through those difficulties by our mutual trust and by our appreciation for how much of the terrain of human rights is uncontested in our immanent and universal theory of human rights. With each such effort, we do our part to make the "grand circle."

# Bibliography


Abeysekara, Ananda. 2002. *Colors of the Robe: Religion, Identity, and Difference*. Columbia: University of South Carolina Press.

Achebe, Nwando. 2004. "The Road to Italy: Nigerian Sex Workers at Home and Abroad." *Journal of Women's History* 15, 4: 178–185.

Acker, Joan, Kate Barry, and Johanna Esseveld. 1983. "Objectivity and Truth: Problems in Doing Feminist Research." *Women's Studies International Forum* 6: 423–435.

Ackerly, Brooke A. 1995. "Testing the Tools of Development: Credit Programs, Loan Involvement, and Women's Empowerment." *IDS Bulletin* 26, 3: 56–68.

1997. "What's in a Design? The Effects of NGO Choices on Women's Empowerment and on Family and Social Institutions in Bangladesh." In *Getting Institutions Right for Women in Development*, ed. Anne Marie Goetz. New York: Zed Books, 140–158.

2000. *Political Theory and Feminist Social Criticism*. Cambridge: Cambridge University Press.

2001a. "Learnings from Scholar–Activists' Dialogues." Paper presented at Annual Meeting of the International Studies Association, Chicago, February 21–25.

2001b. "Women's Human Rights Activists as Cross-Cultural Theorists." *International Feminist Journal of Politics* 3, 3 Autumn: 311–346.

2003. "Ethics in Networking: Learnings from Scholar–Activist–Donor Dialogues." Paper presented at Sustainable Feminisms Conference, Macalester College, Minneapolis.

2005a. "Is Liberalism the Only Way toward Democracy? Confucianism and Democracy." *Political Theory* 33, 4: 547–576.

2005b. "Transnational Feminist Human Rights Activism: Local and Global." Paper presented at Annual Meeting of International Studies Association, Honolulu, March 2–6.

2006. "Deliberative Democracy Theory for Building Global Civil Society: Designing a Virtual Community of Activists." *Contemporary Political Theory* 5, 2: 113–141.

2007a. "'How Does Change Happen?' Deliberation and Difficulty." *Hypatia* 22, 4: 46–63.

2007b. "Sustainable Networking: Collaboration for Women's Human Rights Activists, Scholars, and Donors." In *Sustainable Feminisms: Enacting Theories, Envisioning Action*, ed. Sonita Sarker. UK: JAI Press, 143–158.

forthcoming-a. "Feminism and Methodological Reflection, ed. Audie Klotz.

forthcoming-b. "Human Rights and the Epistemology of Social Contract Theory." In *The Illusion of Consent*, eds. Dan O'Neill, Mary Shanley, and Iris Marion Young. University Park, PA: Pennsylvania State Press.

Ackerly, Brooke A., and Bina D'Costa. 2004. "Transnational Feminism and the Human Rights Framework." United Nations Research Institute for Social Development.

2005. "Transnational Feminism: Political Strategies and Theoretical Resources." The Australian National University, Department of International Relations, Working Paper 2005/1.

Ackerly, Brooke A., Maria Stern, and Jacqui True, eds. 2006. *Feminist Methodologies for International Relations*. Cambridge: Cambridge University Press.

Ackerman, Bruce. 1994. "Rooted Cosmopolitanism." *Ethics* 104, 3: 516–535.

Adams, Scott, and David Neumark. 2005. "The Effects of Living Wage Laws: Evidence from Failed and Derailed Living Wage Campaigns." *Journal of Urban Economics* 58, 2: 177–202.

Adelman, Howard, and Astri Suhrke. 1999. *The Path of a Genocide: The Rwanda Crisis from Uganda to Zaire*. New Brunswick: Transaction Publishers.

Afkhami, Mahnaz, ed. 1995. *Faith and Freedom: Women's Human Rights in the Muslim World*. Syracuse: Syracuse University Press.

African Rights (Organization). 1995. *Rwanda: Death, Despair, and Defiance*. London: African Rights.

Aghatise, Esohe. 2002. "Trafficking for Prostitution in Italy: Concept Paper." Turin: Associazione Iroko Onlus.

2004. "Trafficking for Prostitution in Italy: Possible Effects of Government Proposals for Legalization of Brothels." *Violence Against Women* 10, 10: 1126–1155.

Agnew, Vijay. 1998. *In Search of a Safe Place: Abused Women and Culturally Sensitive Services*. Toronto: University of Toronto Press.

Ain o Salish Kendra. 1997. *Human Rights in Bangladesh: A Report by Ain o Salish Kendra, Bangladesh Legal Aid o and Services Trust, and Odhikar*. Dhaka: University Press Ltd.

1999. *Human Rights in Bangladesh*. Dhaka: University Press Ltd.

2000. *Human Rights in Bangladesh*. Dhaka: University Press Ltd.

Al-Hibri, Azizah Y. 1999. "Is Western Patriarchal Feminism Good for Third World/Minority Women?" In *Is Multiculturalism Bad for Women?*, eds.

Susan Moller Okin, Joshua Cohen, Matthew Howard, and Martha Craven Nussbaum. Princeton: Princeton University Press, 41–46.

Alexander, M. Jacqui. 2005. *Pedagogies of Crossing: Meditations on Feminism, Sexual Politics, Memory, and the Sacred.* Durham: Duke University Press.

Alford, William P. 1992. "Making a Goddess of Democracy from Loose Sand: Thoughts on Human Rights in the People's Republic of China." In *Human Rights in Cross-Cultural Perspectives: A Quest for Consensus*, ed. Abdullahi Ahmed an-Na'im. Philadelphia: University of Pennsylvania Press, 65–80.

Ali, Shaheen Sardar. 2000. *Gender and Human Rights in Islam and International Law: Equal before Allah, Unequal before Man?* The Hague: Kluwer Law International.

Alkire, Sabina. 2002. *Valuing Freedoms: Sen's Capability Approach and Poverty Reduction.* Oxford: Oxford University Press.

Alvarez, Sonia. 1999. "Advocating Feminism: The Latin American Feminist NGO 'Boom'." *International Feminist Journal of Politics* 1, 2: 181–209.

Amnesty International. 2004. *It's in Our Hands: Stop Violence against Women.* London: Amnesty International.

2005. "Amnesty International Report 2005." London: Amnesty International.

An-Na'im, Abdullahi Ahmed. 1990. *Toward an Islamic Reformation: Civil Liberties, Human Rights, and International Law.* Syracuse: Syracuse University Press.

ed. 1992a. *Human Rights in Cross-Cultural Perspectives: A Quest for Consensus.* Philadelphia: University of Pennsylvania Press.

1992b. "Toward a Cross-Cultural Approach." In *Human Rights in Cross-Cultural Perspectives: A Quest for Consensus*, ed. Abdullahi Ahmed An-Na'im. Philadelphia: University of Pennsylvania Press, 19–43.

Angel-Ajani, Asale. 2003. "A Question of Dangerous Races?" *Punishment Society* 5, 4: 433–448.

Angle, Stephen C. 2002. *Human Rights and Chinese Thought: A Cross-Cultural Inquiry.* Cambridge: Cambridge University Press.

Anil, Ela, Canan Arin, Ayse Berhtay Hacimirzaoglu, Mehves Bingollu, Pinar Ilkkaracan, and Liz Evcevik Amado. 2005. "Turkish Civil and Penal Code Reforms: The Success of Two Nationwide Campaigns." Report published by Women for Women's Human Rights (WWHR) – New Ways, Turkey.

Anker, Deborah E. 2002. "Refugee Law, Gender, and the Human Rights Paradigm." *Harvard Human Rights Journal* 15, Spring: 133–154.

Antony, Louise M. 2000. "Natures and Norms." *Ethics* 111, 1: 8–36.

Appiah, Kwame Anthony. 1994a. "Identity against Culture: Understandings of Multiculturalism." Paper presented at University of Berkeley, September 14.

2001. "Human Rights as Politics and Idolatry." In *Human Rights as Politics and Idolatry*, ed. Amy Gutmann. Princeton: Princeton University Press, 101–116.

1994b. "Identity, Authenticity, Survival: Multicultural Societies and Social Reproduction." In *Multiculturalism: Examining the Politics of Recognition*, ed. Amy Gutmann. Princeton: Princeton University Press, 149–163.

Aristotle. 1996. "The Politics." In *The Politics, and the Constitution of Athens*, ed. Stephen Everson. Cambridge: Cambridge University Press, 11–207.

Askin, Kelly Dawn, and Dorean M. Koenig, eds. [1999] 2000. *Women and International Human Rights Law*. Ardsley: Transnational.

Association for Women's Rights in Development. 2005. "Interview with Mineke Schipper – Friday September 9, 2005" (Friday File Issue 243). Retrieved December 13, 2005, from www.awid.org/.

Astell, Mary. [1694] [1697] 2002. *A Serious Proposal to the Ladies. Parts I and II*. Orchard Park: Broadview Press.

Astra Network Online. 2005. "Burning Issue – Human Rights Commission." In *CEE Bulletin on Sexual and Reproductive Rights*.

Baderin, Mashood A. 2003. *International Human Rights and Islamic Law*. Oxford: Oxford University Press.

Badiou, Alain. 2001. *Ethics: An Essay on the Understanding of Evil*, trans. Peter Hallward. London: Verso.

Bailey, Robert W. 1999. *Gay Politics, Urban Politics: Identity and Economics in the Urban Setting*. New York: Columbia University Press.

Bamgbose, Oluyemisi. 2002. "Teenage Prostitution and the Future of the Female Adolescent in Nigeria." *International Journal of Offender Therapy and Comparative Criminology* 46, 5: 569–585.

Barber, Benjamin R. 1995. *Jihad vs. Mcworld*. New York: Times Books.

Barber, Elizabeth J. Waylan. 1994. *Women's Work: The First 20,000 Years: Women, Cloth, and Society in Early Times*. New York: Norton.

Barcelona Bill of Rights. 2002. "Declaration from the 14th International Aids Conference," Barcelona, July.

Barsa, Pavel. 2005. "Waging War in the Name of Human Rights? Fourteen Theses About Humanitarian Intervention." *Perspectives* 24: 5–20.

Barsky, Robert F. 2000. *Arguing and Justifying: Assessing the Convention Refugees' Choice of Moment, Motive, and Host Country*. Aldershot: Ashgate.

Bartik, Timothy J. 2004. "Thinking About Local Living Wage Requirements." *Urban Affairs Review* 40, 2: 269–299.

Basso, Keith H. 1970. "To Give up on Words: Silence in Western Apache Culture." *Southwestern Journal of Anthropology* 26: 213–230.

Basu, Amrita, and C. Elizabeth Mcgrory, eds. 1995. *The Challenge of Local Feminisms: Women's Movements in Global Perspective*. Boulder: Westview Press.

Bauer, Joanne R., and Daniel A. Bell, eds. 1999. *The East Asian Challenge for Human Rights*. Cambridge: Cambridge University Press.

Bauman, Richard. 1983. *Let Your Words Be Few: Symbolism of Speaking and Silence among Seventeenth-Century Quakers*. Cambridge: Cambridge University Press.

Beetham, David. 1991. *The Legitimation of Power*. Atlantic Heights: Humanities Press International.

1993. "In Defense of Legitimacy." *Political Studies* 41, 3: 488–491.

1998. "Human Rights as a Model for Cosmopolitan Democracy." In *Re-Imagining Political Community: Studies in Cosmopolitan Democracy*, ed. Daniele Archibugi, David Held, and Martin Köhler. Cambridge: Polity Press, 58–71.

Beitz, Charles R. 2001. "Human Rights as a Common Concern." *American Political Science Review* 95, 2: 269–282.

Bell, Daniel. 2000. *East Meets West: Human Rights and Democracy in East Asia*. Princeton: Princeton University Press.

2004. "Human Rights and Social Criticism in Contemporary Chinese Political Theory." *Political Theory* 32, 3: 396–408.

Bell, Diane. 1992. "Considering Gender: Are Human Rights for Women, Too? An Australian Case." In *Human Rights in Cross-Cultural Perspectives: A Quest for Consensus*, ed. Abdullahi Ahmed An-Na'im. Philadelphia: University of Pennsylvania Press, 339–362.

Bell, Vikki, and Judith Butler. 1999. "On Speech, Race and Melancholia: An Interview with Judith Butler." *Theory, Culture and Society* 16, 2: 163–174.

Bellah, Robert Neelly. 1992. *The Good Society*. New York: Vintage Books.

Bender, Daniel E., and Richard A. Greenwald, eds. 2003. *Sweatshop USA: The American Sweatshop in Historical and Global Perspective*. New York: Routledge.

Benería, Lourdes. 2003. *Gender, Development, and Globalization: Economics as If All People Mattered*. New York: Routledge.

Benería, Lourdes, and Gita Sen. 1982. "Class and Gender Inequalities and Women's Role in Economic Development: Theoretical and Practical Implications." *Feminist Studies* 8, 1: 157–176.

Benhabib, Seyla. 1986. "The Generalized and the Concrete Other: The Kohlberg-Gilligan Controversy and Feminist Theory." *Praxis International* 5, 4: 402–424.

1995. *Feminist Contentions: A Philosophical Exchange (Thinking Gender)*. New York: Routledge.

1996. "Toward a Deliberative Model of Democratic Legitimacy." In *Democracy and Difference: Contesting the Boundaries of the Political*, ed. Seyla Benhabib. Princeton: Princeton University Press, 67–94.

2002. *The Claims of Culture: Equality and Diversity in the Global Era*. Princeton: Princeton University Press.

2004a. "On Culture, Public Reason, and Deliberation: Response to Pensky and Peritz." *Constellations* 11, 2: 291–299.

2004b. *The Rights of Others: Aliens, Residents and Citizens*. Cambridge: Cambridge University Press.

Benhabib, Seyla, and Drucilla Cornell. 1987. *Feminism as Critique: On the Politics of Gender*. Minneapolis: University of Minnesota Press.

Benson, Koni, and Richa Nagar. 2006. "Collaboration as Resistance? Reconsidering the Processes, Products, and Possibilities of Feminist Oral History and Ethnography." *Gender, Place and Culture* 13, 5: 581–592.

Bentham, Jeremy. 1823. "Anarchical Fallacies." In *The Works of Jeremy Bentham*, ed. John Bowring. Edinburgh: W. Tait; London: Simpkin, Marshall, & Co.

Berman, Antoine. 1984. *L'épreuve De L'étranger: Culture Et Traduction Dans L'allemagne Romantique*. Gallimard.

Bernstein, Nina. 2005. Invisible to Most, Women Line up for Day Labor. *The New York Times*, August 15, A.1.

Bhabha, Jacqueline. 1998. "'Get Back to Where You Once Belonged': Identity, Citizenship, and Exclusion in Europe." *Human Rights Quarterly* 20, 3: 592–627.

Bianco, Frank. 1991. *Voices of Silence: Lives of the Trappists Today*. New York: Paragon House.

Bickford, Susan. 1996. *The Dissonance of Democracy: Listening, Conflict, and Citizenship*. Ithaca: Cornell University Press.

Bielefeldt, Heiner. 2000. "'Western' Versus 'Islamic' Human Rights Conceptions? A Critique of Cultural Essentialism in the Discussion of Human Rights." *Political Theory* 28, 1: 90–121.

Bohman, James. 2004. "Toward a Critical Theory of Globalization: Democratic Practice and Multiperspectival Inquiry." *Concepts and Transformation* 9, 2: 121–146.

Bonnin, Debby. 1998. "Identity and the Changing Politics of Gender in South Africa." In *South Africa in Transition: New Theoretical Perspectives*, ed. David R. Howarth and Aletta J. Norval. New York: St. Martin's Press.

Booth, William James. 2006. *Communities of Memory: On Witness, Identity, and Justice*. Ithaca: Cornell University Press.

Bradstock, Andrew, ed. 2000. *Winstanley and the Diggers, 1649–1999*. Portland: Frank Cass.

Braithwaite, Charles A. 1999. "Culture Uses and Interpretations of Silence." In *The Nonverbal Communication Reader: Classic and Contemporary Readings*, ed. Laura K. Guerrero, Joseph A. Devito, and Michael L. Hecht. Prospect Heights, IL: Waveland Press, 163–172.

Brettschneider, Marla. 2002. *Democratic Theorizing from the Margins*. Philadelphia: Temple University Press.

Brooks, Ethel. 2003. "The Ideal Sweatshop? Gender and Transnational Protest." In *Sweatshop USA: The American Sweatshop in Historical and Global Perspective*, ed. Daniel E. Bender and Richard A. Greenwald. New York: Routledge, 265–286.

*Brown v. Board of Education*. 347 U.S. 483 (1954).

Brown, Donald E. 1991. *Human Universals*. Philadelphia: Temple University Press.

Brown, Wendy. 1995. *States of Injury: Power and Freedom in Late Modernity*. Princeton: Princeton University Press.

Bruneau, Thomas J. 1973. "Communicative Silences: Forms and Functions." *Journal of Communications* 23: 17–46.

Bruton, Henry J. 1997. *On the Search for Well-Being*. Ann Arbor: University of Michigan Press.

Brysk, Alison. 2005. *Human Rights and Private Wrongs: Constructing Global Civil Society*. New York: Routledge.

Buchanan, Allen. 2000. "Rawls's Law of Peoples: Rules for a Vanished Westphalian World." *Ethics* 110, 4: 697–721.

Bullard, Robert D. 2005. *The Quest for Environmental Justice: Human Rights and the Politics of Pollution*. San Francisco: Sierra Club Books.

Bunch, Charlotte. 1990. "Women's Rights as Human Rights: Toward a Re-Vision of Human Rights." *Human Rights Quarterly* 12, November: 486–498.

1995. "Transforming Human Rights from a Feminist Perspective." In *Women's Rights, Human Rights: International Feminist Perspectives*, ed. Julie Peters and Andrea Wolper. London: Routledge, 11–17.

2003. "Feminism, Peace, Human Rights and Human Security." *Canadian Woman Studies* 22, 2: 6–11.

2004. "A Feminist Human Rights Lens." *Peace Review* 16, 1: 29.

Burrows, Noreen. 1986. "International Law and Human Rights: The Case of Women's Rights." In *Human Rights: From Rhetoric to Reality*, ed. Tom Campbell, David Goldberg, Sheila Mclean, and Tom Mullen. New York: Basil Blackwell, 80–98.

Butler, Judith. 1993. *Bodies That Matter: On the Discursive Limits Of "Sex."* New York: Routledge.

1995. "Contingent Foundations: Feminism and the Question of Postmodernism." In *Feminist Contentions: A Philosophical Exchange*, ed. Judith Butler, Seyla Benhabib, Nancy Fraser, and Drucilla Cornell. New York: Routledge, 35–57.

1999. "On Speech, Race and Melancholia: An Interview with Judith Butler." *Theory, Culture and Society* 16, 2: 163–174.

[1990] 1999. *Gender Trouble: Feminism and the Subversion of Identity.* New York: Routledge.

2000. "Competing Universalities." In *Contingency, Hegemony, Universality: Contemporary Dialogues on the Left*, ed. Judith Butler, Ernesto Laclau, and Slavoj Žižek. London: Verso.

Butler, Judith, Ernesto Laclau, and Slavoj Žižek. 2000. *Contingency, Hegemony, Universality: Contemporary Dialogues on the Left.* London: Verso.

Bybee, Keith J. 1997. "Essentially Contested Membership: Racial Minorities and the Politics of Inclusion." *Legal Studies Forum* 21, 4: 469–483.

Campanaro, Jocelyn. 2001. "Women, War, and International Law: The Historical Treatment of Gender-Based War Crimes." *Georgetown Law Journal* 89, 8: 2557–2592.

Cannon, Katie G. 1988. *Black Womanist Ethics.* Atlanta: Scholars Press.

Carrillo, Roxanna. 1990. "Violence against Women: An Obstacle to Development." In *Gender Violence: A Development and Human Rights Issue*, ed. Center for Women's Global Leadership. Highland Park, NY: Plowshares Press.

Center for Reproductive Rights. 2003. "Burkina Faso." New York: The Center for Reproductive Rights.

2004. "Center Joins Couples' Legal Battle against Costa Rica's IVF Ban. Case before Inter-American Commission Could Have Repercussions in US," December 10, 2004. Retrieved May 25, 2006, from www.reproductiverights.org/tools/print_page.jsp.

Chambers, Robert. 1994. "Participatory Rural Appraisal (PRA): Challenges, Potentials and Paradigm." *World Development* 22, 10: 1437–1454.

1997. *Whose Reality Counts? Putting the First Last.* London: Intermediate Technology Development Group.

Chan, Joseph. 1997. "An Alternative View." *Journal of Democracy* 8, 2: 35–48.

Charlesworth, Hilary. 1994. "What Are 'Women's International Human Rights'?" In *Human Rights of Women: National and International Perspectives*, ed. Rebecca J. Cook. Philadelphia: University of Pennsylvania Press, 58–84.

Chen, Martha Alter. 1995. "Engendering World Conferences: The International Women's Movement and the United Nations." *Third World Quarterly* 16, 3: 477–494.

Chenyang, Li. 1999. *The Tao Encounters the West: Explorations in Comparative Philosophy.* Albany: State University of New York.

Chin, Christine B.N. 1998. *In Service and Servitude: Foreign Female Domestic Workers and the Malaysian "Modernity" Project*. New York: Columbia University Press.

Chodorow, Nancy. 1978. *The Reproduction of Mothering: Psychoanalysis and the Sociology of Gender*. Berkeley: University of California Press.

Christian Aid. 2006. "The Climate of Poverty: Facts, Fears and Hope." Christian Aid. Retrieved March 30, 2007, from www.christianaid.org/indepth/605caweek/caw06_full_embargo.pdf.

Chua, Peter, Kum-Kum Bhavnani, and John Foran. 2000. "Women, Culture, Development: A New Paradigm for Development Studies." *Ethnic and Racial Studies* 23, 5: 820–841.

Cingranelli, David L., and David L. Richards. 1999. "Measuring the Level, Pattern, and Sequence of Government Respect for Physical Integrity Rights." *International Studies Quarterly* 43, 2: 407–417.

Cizik, Richard. 2006. "The Evolution of American Evangelicalism." A transcript of radio program on file with the author, interviewed by Krista Tippett.

Clark, Cindy, Ellen Sprenger, Lisa Vaneklasen, and Lydia Alpízar Durán. 2006. *Where Is the Money for Women's Rights?* Washington: Just Associates.

Clements, Luke, and James Young. 1999. "Human Rights: Changing the Culture." *Journal of Law and Society* 26, 1: 1–5.

Cochran, Molly. 1999. *Normative Theory in International Relations: A Pragmatic Approach*. Cambridge: Cambridge University Press.

Cockburn, Cynthia, and Meliha Hubic. 2002. "Gender and the Peacekeeping Military: A View from Bosnian Women's Organizations." In *The Postwar Moment: Militaries, Masculinities, and International Peacekeeping*, ed. Cynthia Cockburn and Dubravka Zakrov. London: Lawrence and Wishart, 103–121.

Cohen, Joshua. 1989. "Deliberation and Democratic Legitimacy." In *The Good Polity*, ed. Alan Hamlin and Philip Pettit. Oxford: Blackwell, 17–34.

1996. "Procedure and Substance in Deliberative Democracy." In *Democracy and Difference: Contesting the Boundaries of the Political*, ed. Seyla Benhabib. Princeton: Princeton University Press, 95–119.

2004. "Minimalism About Human Rights: The Most We Can Hope For?" *The Journal of Political Philosophy* 12, 2: 190–213.

Cohen, Susan A. 1993. "The Road from Rio to Cairo: Toward a Common Agenda." *International Family Planning Perspectives* 19, 2: 61–66.

Cohn, Carol. 2005. "The Rhetorical Construction of the United Nation's Women, Peace and Security Agenda: From Crafting Documents to Changing Practices." Paper presented at Annual Meeting of International Studies Association, Honolulu, March 5.

Cole, Johnnetta B., and Beverly Guy-Sheftall, eds. 2003. *Gender Talk: The Struggle for Women's Equality in African American Communities*. New York: One World.

Collins, Patricia Hill. [1990] 1991. *Black Feminist Thought: Knowledge, Consciousness, and the Politics of Empowerment*. Boston: Unwin Hyman.

Collins, Sara R., Karen Davis, Michelle M. Doty, and Alice Ho. 2004. *Wages, Health Benefits, and Workers' Health*. New York: The Commonwealth Fund.

Confortini, Catia. 2006. "Galtung, Violence, and Gender: The Case for a Peace Studies/Feminism Alliance." *Peace and Change* 31, 4: 333–367.

Connolly, William E. 1993. *The Terms of Political Discourse*. Princeton: Princeton University Press.

2004. "Response: Realizing Agonistic Respect." *Journal of the American Academy of Religion* 72, 2: 507–511.

2005. *Pluralism*. Durham: Duke University Press.

Convention on the Rights of the Child–Adopted November 20, 1989, G.A. Res. 44/25, U.N. GAOR, 44th Sess., Supp. No. 49 (1989) (Entered into force, September 2, 1990).

Cook, Rebecca J., ed. 1994. *Human Rights of Women: National and International Perspectives*. Philadelphia: University of Pennsylvania Press.

2001. "Advancing Safe Motherhood through Human Rights." In *Giving Meaning to Economic, Social, and Cultural Rights*, ed. Isfahan Merali and Valerie Oosterveld. Philadelphia: University of Pennsylvania Press, 109–123.

Cooke, Bill, and Uma Kothari. 2001. *Participation: The New Tyranny?* New York: Zed Books.

Coomaraswamy, Radhika. 2002. "Integration of the Human Rights of Women and Gender Perspective." United Nations Economic and Social Council. Retrieved August 23, 2005, from www.unhchr.ch/huridocda/huridoca.nsf/AllSymbols/42E7191FAE543562C1256BA7004E963C/$File/G0210428.pdf?OpenElement.

Cooper, Sandi E. 2002. "Peace as a Human Right: The Invasion of Women into the World of High International Politics." *Journal of Women's History* 14, 2: 9–25.

Corker, Mairian, and Sally French. 1999. *Disability Discourse*. Philadelphia: Open University Press.

Cornell, Drucilla. 1998. *At the Heart of Freedom: Feminism, Sex, and Equality*. Princeton: Princeton University Press.

Cornell, Drucilla, Michel Rosenfeld, and David Carlson, eds. 1992. *Deconstruction and the Possibility of Justice*. New York: Routledge.

Correa, Sonia. 1994. *Population and Reproductive Rights: Feminist Perspectives from the South*. London: Zed Books.

Cotterill, Pamela. 1992. "Interviewing Women: Issues of Friendship, Vulnerability, and Power." *Women's Studies International Forum* 15: 593–606.

Council of Europe Convention on Action against Trafficking in Human Beings. 2005. "Recommendation 1695 – Adopted January 25 2005 by the Parliamentary Assembly."

Cox, George O. 1974. *Education for the Black Race*. New York: African Heritage Studies Publishers.

Cox, Robert W. 2001. "The Way Ahead: Toward a New Ontology of World Order." In *Critical Theory and World Politics*, ed. Richard Wyn Jones. Boulder: Lynne Rienner Publishers, 45–59.

Cranston, Maurice William. 1967. "Human Rights, Real and Supposed." In *Political Theory and the Rights of Man*, ed. David Daiches Raphael. Bloomington: Indiana University Press, 43–53.

1973. *What Are Human Rights?* London: Bodley Head.

1983. "Are There Any Human Rights." *Daedalus* 112, 4: 1–17.

Crawley, Heaven. 1998. "Living up to the Empowerment Claim? The Potential of PRA." In *The Myth of Community: Gender Issues in Participatory Development*, ed. Irene Gujit and Meera Kaul Shah. New Delhi: Vistaar Publications, 24–34.

Crenshaw, Kimberlé. 1989. "Demarginalizing the Intersection of Race and Sex." *The University of Chicago Legal Forum*: 139–167.

2000. "Gender-Related Aspects of Race Discrimination." Paper presented at Expert Meeting on Gender-Related Aspects of Race Discrimination, Zagreb, Croatia, November 21–24.

Crossette, Barbara. 2000. "Culture, Gender, and Human Rights." In *Cultural Matters: How Values Shape Human Progress*, ed. Lawrence Harrison and Samuel Huntington. New York: Basic Books, 178–188.

D'Costa, Bina. 2003. "The Gendered Construction of Nationalism: From Partition to Creation." Ph.D. Dissertation. Canberra, The Australian National University.

Dahl, Robert. 1997. "On Deliberative Democracy: Citizen Panels and Medicare Reform." *Dissent*, Summer: 54–58.

Dalacoura, Katerina. 1998. *Islam, Liberalism and Human Rights: Implications for International Relations*. London: I.B. Tauris.

Dalai Lama. 1999. "Buddhism, Asian Values, and Democracy." *Journal of Democracy* 10, 1: 3–7.

Dallmayr, Fred R. 1998. *Alternative Visions: Paths in the Global Village*. Lanham: Rowman & Littlefield.

ed. 1999. *Border Crossings: Toward a Comparative Political Theory*. Lanham: Lexington Books.

2001. *Achieving Our World: Toward a Global and Plural Democracy*. Lanham: Rowman & Littlefield.

2002. "'Asian Values' and Global Human Rights." *Philosophy East and West* 52, 2: 173–189.

2004. "Beyond Monologue: For a Comparative Political Theory." *Perspectives on Politics* 2, 2: 249–257.

Daly, Mary. [1978] 1990. *Gyn/Ecology: The Metaethics of Radical Feminism*. Boston: Beacon Press.

Danner, Mark. 1994. *The Massacre at El Mozote: A Parable of the Cold War*. New York: Vintage Books.

2005. "What Are You Going to Do with That?" *The New York Review of Books* 52, 11: 52–56.

Davis, Michael C., ed. 1995. *Human Rights and Chinese Values*. Hong Kong: Oxford University Press.

De Bary, William Theodore. 1998. *Asian Values and Human Rights: A Confucian Communitarian Perspective*. Cambridge, MA: Harvard University Press.

De Bary, William Theodore, and Tu Weiming, eds. 1998. *Confucianism and Human Rights*. New York: Columbia University Press.

Dé Ishtar, Zohl. 2005. "Striving for a Common Language: A White Feminist Parallel to Indigenous Ways of Knowing and Researching." *Women's Studies International Forum* 28, 5: 357–368.

Dean, Jodi. 1996. *Solidarity of Strangers: Feminism after Identity Politics*. Berkeley: University of California Press.

Defrancisco, Victoria L. 1991. "The Sounds of Silence: How Men Silence Women in Marital Relations." *Discourse and Society* 3: 413–423.

DeNavas-Walt, Carmen, Bernadette D. Proctor, and Robert J. Mills. 2004. "Income, Poverty, and Health Insurance Coverage in the United States: 2003." In *Current Population Reports, P60–226*. Washington, DC: U.S. Census Bureau.

Derrida, Jacques. 1992. *The Other Heading: Reflections on Today's Europe*, trans. Pascale-Anne Brault and Michael B. Nass. Bloomington: Indiana University Press.

Derriennic, Jean-Pierre. 1972. "Theory and Ideologies of Violence." *Journal of Peace Research* 9, 4: 361–374.

Desai, Jigna. 2002. "Homo in the Range: Mobile and Global Sexualities." *Social Text* 20, 4 (73): 65–89.

Dewey, John. [1927] 1954. *The Public and Its Problems*. Chicago: Swallow Press.

[1932] 1990. "The Making of Citizens: A Comparative Study of Methods of Civic Training, by Charles Edward Merriam: University of Chicago Press, 1931." In *John Dewey: The Later Works, 1925–1953*, ed. Jo Ann Boydston. Carbondale: Southern Illinois University Press, 112–114.

[1942] 1989. "Religion and Morality in a Free Society." In *John Dewey: The Later Works, 1925–1953*, ed. Jo Ann Boydston. Carbondale: Southern Illinois University Press, 170–183.

Di Leonardo, Micaela, ed. 1991. *Gender at the Crossroads of Knowledge: Feminist Anthropology in the Postmodern Era*. Berkeley: University of California Press.

Diamond, Jared M. [1997] 2003. *Guns, Germs, and Steel*. New York: Spark Publications.

Dietz, Mary G. 2002. *Turning Operations: Feminism, Arendt, and Politics*. New York: Routledge.

Donchin, Anne. 2003. "Converging Concerns: Feminist Bioethics, Development Theory, and Human Rights." *Signs* 29, 2: 299–324.

Donnelly, Jack. 1982. "Human Rights and Human Dignity: An Analytical Critique of Non-Western Conceptions of Human Rights." *American Political Science Review* 76: 303–316.

1989. *Universal Human Rights in Theory and Practice*. Ithaca: Cornell University Press.

1999. "Human Rights and Asian Values: A Defense of 'Western' Universalism." In *The East Asian Challenge for Human Rights*, ed. Joanne R. Bauer and Daniel A. Bell. Cambridge: Cambridge University Press, 60–87.

Douglass, Frederick. *What to the Slave Is the Fourth of July*? Archives of American Public Address, June 14, 2002 [1852] [cited]. Available from http://douglassarchives.org/.

Dryzek, John S. 2000. *Deliberative Democracy and Beyond: Liberals, Critics, Contestations*. Oxford: Oxford University Press.

Dunne, Timothy, and Nicholas J. Wheeler. 1999. "Introduction: Human Rights and the Fifty Years' Crisis." In *Human Rights in Global Politics*, ed. Timothy Dunne and Nicholas J. Wheeler. Cambridge: Cambridge University Press, 1–28.

Dworkin, Ronald. 1977. *Taking Rights Seriously*. Cambridge, MA: Harvard University Press.

1990. "Foundations of Liberal Equality." In *The Tanner Lectures of Human Values*. Salt Lake City: University of Utah Press.

Economic Research Service. 2004. "Rural Income, Poverty and Welfare: Rural Poverty." Retrieved August 3, 2005, from www.ers.usda.gov/Briefing/IncomePovertyWelfare/ruralpoverty/.

Ehrenreich, Barbara. 2001. *Nickel and Dimed: On (Not) Getting by in America*. New York: Metropolitan Books.

Eliasoph, Nina. 1998. *Avoiding Politics: How Americans Produce Apathy in Everyday Life*. Cambridge: Cambridge University Press.

Ellacuría, Ignacio. 1990. "Historiziación de los Derechos Humanos Desde Los Pueblos Oprimidos y Las Mayorías Populares." *ECA* 502: 590.

Elson, Diane, and Ruth Pearson. 1997. "The Subordination of Women and the Internationalization of Factory Production." In *The Women, Gender, and Development Reader*, ed. Nalini Visvanathan. Atlantic Highlands: Zed Books, 191–202.

Elster, Jon. 1998. *Deliberative Democracy*. Cambridge: Cambridge University Press.

Eltringham, Nigel. 2004. *Accounting for Horror: Post-Genocide Debates in Rwanda*. London: Pluto Press.

Engle, Karen. 1992. "International Human Rights and Feminism: When Discourses Meet." *Michigan Journal of International Law* 13, Spring: 517–610.

Englehart, Neil A. 2000. "Rights and Culture in the Asian Values Argument: The Rise and Fall of Confucian Ethics in Singapore." *Human Rights Quarterly* 22, 2: 548–568.

Enloe, Cynthia H. [1989] 1990. *Bananas, Beaches and Bases: Making Feminist Sense of International Politics*. Berkeley, CA: University of California Press.

2004. *The Curious Feminist: Searching for Women in a New Age of Empire*. Berkeley: University of California Press.

Estlund, David. 1998a. "Debate: Liberalism, Equality, and Fraternity in Cohen's Critique of Rawls." *The Journal of Political Philosophy* 6, 1: 99–112.

1998b. "The Insularity of the Reasonable: Why Political Liberalism Must Admit the Truth." *Ethics* 108, 2: 252–275.

Etzioni, Amitai. 1996. *The New Golden Rule*. New York: Basic Books.

2004. "The Emerging Global Normative Synthesis." *The Journal of Political Philosophy* 12, 2: 214–244.

Euben, Roxanne L. 1999. *Enemy in the Mirror: Islamic Fundamentalism and the Limits of Modern Rationalism*. Princeton: Princeton University Press.

2004. "Traveling Theorists and Translating Practices." In *What Is Political Theory?*, ed. Stephen K. White and J. Donald Moon. Thousand Oaks: Sage Publications, 145–173.

Falk, Richard A. 2000. *Human Rights Horizons: The Pursuit of Justice in a Globalizing World*. New York: Routledge.

Farha, Leilani. 1999. "Women and Housing in Law." In *Women and International Human Rights Law*, ed. Kelly Dawn Askin and Dorean M. Koenig. Ardsley: Transnational, 483–532.

Feminist Dialogues. 2005a. "Concept Note for the Feminist Dialogues," on file with the author. Feminist Dialogues, Porto Alegre, January 23–25.

2005b. "Feminist Dialogues." World Social Forum, Porto Alegre, January 23–24.

Fishkin, James S. 1991. *Democracy and Deliberation: New Directions for Democratic Reform*. New Haven: Yale University Press.

1995. *The Voice of the People: Public Opinion and Democracy*. New Haven: Yale University Press.

Fitzgibbon, Kathleen. 2003. "Modern-Day Slavery? The Scope of Trafficking in Persons in Africa." *African Security Review* 12, 1: 81–89.

Flax, Jane, and Susan Moller Okin. 1995. "Race/Gender and the Ethics of Difference: A Reply to Okin's 'Gender Inequality and Cultural Differences' – Comment/Reply." *Political Theory* 23, 3: 500–510.

Fonow, Mary Margaret, and Judith A. Cook. 1991. *Beyond Methodology: Feminist Scholarship as Lived Research*. Bloomington: Indiana University Press.

2005. "Feminist Methodology: New Applications in the Academy and Public Policy." *Signs* 30, 4: 2211–2236.

Foucault, Michel. 1978. *The History of Sexuality*. New York: Pantheon Books.

[1978] 1995. *Discipline and Punish: The Birth of the Prison*. New York: Vintage Books.

Fox, Diana J. 2003. "Women's Human Rights in Africa: Beyond the Debate over the Universality or Relativity of Human Rights." *African Studies Quarterly* 2, 3. Online journal available from http://web.africa.ufl.edu/asq/v2/v2i3a2.htm.

Foxen, Patricia. 2000. "Cacophony of Voices: A K'iche' Mayan Narrative of Remembrance and Forgetting." *Transcultural Psychiatry* 37, 3: 355–381.

Francisco, Josefa S. 2003. "Paradoxes for Gender in Social Movements." *Development* 46, 2: 24–26.

Fraser, Arvonne S. 1999. "Becoming Human: The Origins and Development of Women's Human Rights." *Human Rights Quarterly* 21, 4: 853–906.

Fraser, Nancy. 1991. "What Is Critical About Critical Theory?" In *Feminist Interpretations and Political Theory*, ed. Mary Lyndon Shanley and Carole Pateman. Cambridge: Polity Press, in association with Basil Blackwell, UK.

1995. "From Redistribution to Recognition? Dilemmas of Justice in a 'Postsocialist' Age." *New Left Review* 212: 68–93.

1997. *Justice Interruptus: Critical Reflections on The "Postsocialist" Condition*. New York: Routledge.

2001. "Recognition without Ethics?" *Theory, Culture and Society* 18, 2–3: 21–42.

Fraser, Nancy, and Axel Honneth. 2003. *Redistribution or Recognition?: A Political-Philosophical Exchange*. London: Verso.

Freeman, Richard B., Joni Hersch, and Lawrence R. Mishel, eds. 2005. *Emerging Labor Market Institutions for the Twenty-First Century*. Chicago: University of Chicago Press.

Friedman, Elisabeth. 1995. "Women's Human Rights: The Emergence of a Movement." In *Women's Rights, Human Rights: International Feminist Perspectives*, ed. Julie Peters and Andrea Wolper. London: Routledge, 18–35.

Friedman, Thomas L. 1999. *The Lexus and the Olive Tree*. New York: Farrar, Straus, Giroux.

Fukuyama, Francis. 1992. *The End of History and the Last Man*. New York: Free Press.

Fung, Archong, and Erik Olin Wright, eds. 2003. *Deepening Democracy: Institutional Innovations in Empowered Participatory Governance*. London: Verso.

Gadamer, Hans Georg. 1989. *Truth and Method*. New York: Crossroad.

Gal, Susan. 1991. "Between Speech and Silence: The Problematics of Research on Language and Gender." In *Gender at the Crossroads of Knowledge: Feminist Anthropology in the Postmodern Era*, ed. Micaela Di Leonardo. Berkeley: University of California Press, 175–203.

Gallagher, Anne. 1997. "Ending the Marginalization: Strategies for Incorporating Women into the United Nations Human Rights System." *Human Rights Quarterly* 19, 2: 283–333.

Gallie, W. B. 1962. "Essentially Contested Concepts." In *The Importance of Language*, ed. Max Black. Englewood Cliffs: Prentice-Hall.

Galtung, Johan. 1969. "Violence, Peace, and Peace Research." *Journal of Peace Research* 6, 3: 167–191.

1985. "Twenty-Five Years of Peace Research: Ten Challenges and Some Responses." *Journal of Peace Research* 22, 2: 141–158.

1990. "Cultural Violence." *Journal of Peace Research* 27, 3: 291–305.

1994. *Human Rights in Another Key*. Cambridge: Polity Press.

Gandhi, Leela. 1998. *Postcolonial Theory: A Critical Introduction*. New York: Columbia University Press.

Gatenby, Bev, and Maria Humphries. 2000. "Feminist Participatory Action Research: Methodological and Ethical Issues." *Women's Studies International Forum* 23, 1: 89–105.

Gatens, Moira. 1996. *Imaginary Bodies: Ethics, Power, and Corporeality*. London: Routledge.

2004. "Can Human Rights Accommodate Women's Rights? Towards an Embodied Account of Social Norms, Social Meaning, and Cultural Change." *Contemporary Political Theory* 3, 3: 275–299.

Gaus, Gerald F. 1990. *Value and Justification: The Foundations of Liberal Theory*. Cambridge: Cambridge University Press.

1996. *Justificatory Liberalism: An Essay on Epistemology and Political Theory*. Oxford: Oxford University Press.

1999. "Reasonable Pluralism and the Domain of the Political: How the Weaknesses of John Rawls's Political Liberalism Can Be Overcome by a Justificatory Liberalism." *Inquiry* 42, 2: 259–284.

2003. *Contemporary Theories of Liberalism: Public Reason as a Post-Enlightenment Project*. London: Sage.

Geertz, Clifford. 2000. *Available Light: Anthropological Reflections on Philosophical Topics*. Princeton: Princeton University Press.

Geuss, Raymond. 1981. *The Idea of a Critical Theory: Habermas and the Frankfurt School*. Cambridge: Cambridge University Press.

Ghosh, Jayati. 2005. "Integration of Gender Perspectives in Macroeconomics." In *United Nations Commission on the Status of Women – 49th Session*. New York, March.

Giddens, Anthony. 1979. *Central Problems in Social Theory: Action, Structure, and Contradiction in Social Analysis*. Berkeley: University of California Press.

Glendon, Mary Ann. 2001. *A World Made New: Eleanor Roosevelt and the Universal Declaration of Human Rights*. New York: Random House.

Glenn, Cheryl. 2004. *Unspoken: A Rhetoric of Silence*. Carbondale: Southern Illinois University Press.

Glover, Jonathan. 1995. "The Research Programme of Development Ethics." In *Women, Culture, and Development: A Study of Human Capabilities*, ed. Martha Craven Nussbaum, Jonathan Glover, and World Institute for Development Economics Research. Oxford: Oxford University Press, 116–139.

Goddard, Cliff, and Anna Wierzbicka, eds. 2002a. *Meaning and Universal Grammar*. Amsterdam: John Benjamins Publishing Company.

eds. 2002b. *Meaning and Universal Grammar: Theory and Empirical Findings*. Amsterdam: John Benjamins Publishing Company.

Goebel, Allison. 1998. "Process, Perception and Power: Notes from 'Participatory' Research in a Zimbabwean Resettlement Area." *Development and Change* 29, 2: 277–305.

Goetz, Anne Marie, and Rina Sen Gupta. 1996. "Who Takes the Credit? Gender, Power, and Control over Loan Use in Rural Credit Programs in Bangladesh." *World Development* 24, 1: 45–63.

Goldman, Francisco. 1999. "Murder Comes for the Bishop." *The New Yorker*: 60–77, March 15.

Goodhart, Michael. 2003. "Origins and Universality in the Human Rights Debates: Cultural Essentailism and the Challenge of Globalization." *Human Rights Quarterly* 25: 935–964.

2005. *Democracy as Human Rights: Freedom and Equality in the Age of Globalization*. New York: Routledge.

Goodin, Robert E. 1985. *Protecting the Vulnerable: A Reanalysis of Our Social Responsibilities*. Chicago: University of Chicago Press.

Goodman, Lenn Evan. 1998. *Judaism, Human Rights, and Human Values*. New York: Oxford University Press.

Gordon, Neve, ed. 2004. *From the Margins of Globalization: Critical Perspectives on Human Rights*. Lanham: Lexington Books.

Gorelick, Sherry. 1991. "Contradictions of Feminist Methodology." *Gender & Society* 5: 459–477.

Gould, Carol C. 1988. *Rethinking Democracy: Freedom and Social Cooperation in Politics, Economy, and Society*. Cambridge: Cambridge University Press.

1993. "Feminism and Democratic Community Revisited." In *Democratic Community*, ed. John William Chapman and Ian Shapiro. New York: New York University Press, 396–413.

2004. *Globalizing Democracy and Human Rights*. Cambridge: Cambridge University Press.

Government of Bangladesh, Bureau of Democracy, Human Rights and Labour, 2001. "Country Report on Human Rights Practices: Bangladesh." Bureau of Democracy, Human Rights and Labour, February 23, 2001. Retrieved August 15, 2005, from www.state.gov/g/drl/rls/hrrpt/2000/sa/692.htm.

Gramsci, Antonio, Quintin Hoare, and Geoffrey Nowell-Smith. 1971. *Selections from the Prison Notebooks of Antonio Gramsci*. London: Lawrence & Wishart.

Gray, Leslie, and Michael Kevane. 1999. "Diminished Access, Diverted Exclusion: Women and Land Tenure in Sub-Saharan Africa." *African Studies Review* 42, 2: 15–39.

2001. "Evolving Tenure Rights and Agricultural Intensification in Southwestern Burkina Faso." *World Development* 29, 4: 573–587.

Green, Joyce. 2001. "Canaries in the Mines of Citizenship: Indian Women in Canada." *Canadian Journal of Political Science/Revue canadienne de science politique* 34, 04: 715–738.

Guijt, Irene, and Meera Kaul Shah, eds. 1998. *The Myth of Community: Gender Issues in Participatory Development*. London: Intermediate Technology Publications.

Gunning, Isabelle. 1992. "Arrogant Perception, World Traveling and Multicultural Feminism: The Case of Female Genital Surgeries." *Columbia Human Rights Law Review* 23: 189–248.

Gutmann, Amy, and Dennis F. Thompson. 1996. *Democracy and Disagreement*. Cambridge, MA: Belknap Press of Harvard University Press.

Guy-Sheftall, Beverly. 1990. *Daughters of Sorrow: Attitudes toward Black Women, 1880–1920*. Brooklyn: Carlson Publishing Inc.

Habermas, Jürgen. 1979. *Communication and the Evolution of Society*. Boston: Beacon Press.

1984. *The Theory of Communicative Action*. Boston: Beacon Press.

1990. *Moral Consciousness and Communicative Action*. Cambridge, MA: MIT Press.

1994. *Justification and Application: Remarks on Discourse Ethics*. Cambridge, MA: MIT Press.

1996a. *Between Facts and Norms: Contributions to a Discourse Theory of Law and Democracy*. Cambridge, MA: MIT Press.

1996b. "Three Normative Models of Democracy." In *Democracy and Difference: Contesting the Boundaries of the Political*, ed. Seyla Benhabib. Princeton: Princeton University Press, 21–30.

1998. *The Inclusion of the Other: Studies in Political Theory*. Cambridge, MA: MIT Press.

2001a. "Constitutional Democracy: A Paradoxical Union of Contradictory Principles?" *Political Theory* 29, 6: 766–781.

2001b. *On the Pragmatics of Social Interaction: Preliminary Studies in the Theory of Communicative Action*. Cambridge, MA: MIT Press.

Hampton, Jean. 1989. "Should Political Philosophy Be Done without Metaphysics?" *Ethics* 99, 4: 791–814.

Harding, Sandra G. 1987. *Feminism and Methodology: Social Science Issues*. Bloomington: Indiana University Press.

Harding, Sandra G., and Kathryn Norberg. 2005. "New Feminist Approaches to Social Science Methodologies: An Introduction. (Editorial)." *Signs* 30, 4: 2009–2015.

Harding, Susan Friend. 2000. *The Book of Jerry Falwell: Fundamentalist Language and Politics*. Princeton: Princeton University Press.

Harris, Angela P. 2000. "Equality Trouble: Sameness and Difference in Twentieth-Century Race Law." *California Law Review* 88, 6: 1923–2015.

Harris, Dean A., ed. 1995. *Multiculturalism from the Margins: Non-Dominant Voices on Difference and Diversity*. Westport: Bergin & Garvey.

Hartsock, Nancy. 1983. "The Feminist Standpoint: Developing the Ground for a Specifically Feminist Historical Materialism." In *Discovering Reality: Feminist Perspectives on Epistemology, Metaphysics, Methodology, and Philosophy of Science*, ed. Sandra G. Harding and Merrill B. Hintikka. Boston Hingham: Kluwer Boston, 285–311.

1998. *The Feminist Standpoint Revisited and Other Essays*. Boulder: Westview Press.

Hauerwas, Stanley. [1988] 2001. "Why the 'Sectarian Temptation' is a Misrepresentation: A Response to James Gustafson." In *The Hauerwas*

*Reader*, ed. John Berkman and Michael G. Cartwright. Durham: Duke University Press, 90–110.

Hawkesworth, Mary E. 2006a. *Feminist Inquiry: From Political Conviction to Methodological Innovation*. New Brunswick: Rutgers University Press.

2006b. *Globalization and Feminist Activism*. Lanham: Rowman & Littlefield.

Heaney, Tom. 1984. "Action, Freedom, and Liberatory Education." In *Selected Writings on Philosophy and Adult Education*, ed. Sharan B. Merriam. Malabar, FL: R. E. Krieger, 113–122.

Hedges, Elaine, and Shelley Fisher Fishkin. 1994. *Listening to Silences: New Essays in Feminist Criticism*. New York: Oxford University Press.

Heidegger, Martin. 1969. *The Essence of Reasons*. Evanston: Northwestern University Press.

1971. *On the Way to Language*, trans. William Kluback and Jean T. Wilde. New York: Harper and Row.

1996. *Being and Time: A Translation of Sein Und Zeit*, trans. Joan Stambaugh. Albany: SUNY Press.

Held, David. 1995. *Democracy and the Global Order: From the Modern State to Cosmopolitan Governance*. Stanford: Stanford University Press.

2003. "From Executive to Cosmopolitan Multilateralism." In *Taming Globalization: Frontiers of Governance*, ed. David Held and Mathias Koenig-Archibugi. Cambridge: Polity Press, 160–186.

Held, Virginia. 1987. "Non-Contractual Society." In *Science, Morality and Feminsit Theory*, ed. Marsha Hanen and Kai Nielsen. Calgary: The University of Calgary Press, 111–137.

Hertzke, Allen D. 2004. *Freeing God's Children: The Unlikely Alliance for Global Human Rights*. Lanham: Rowman & Littlefield.

Hirschmann, Nancy J. 1992. *Rethinking Obligation: A Feminist Method for Political Theory*. Ithaca: Cornell University Press.

2003. *The Subject of Liberty: Toward a Feminist Theory of Freedom*. Princeton: Princeton University Press.

Hitt, Jack. 2006. "Pro-Life Nation." *The New York Times Magazine*: Section 6: 40–47, April 9.

Hobbs, Frank, and Nicole Stoops. 2002. "Demographic Trends in the 20th Century." Census 2000 Special Reports. CENSR-4. Retrieved August 21, 2005, from www.census.gov/population/www/cen2000/briefs.html#sr.

Honig, Bonnie. 1999. "My Culture Made Me Do It." In *Is Multiculturalism Bad for Women?*, ed. Susan Moller Okin, Joshua Cohen, Matthew Howard, and Martha Craven Nussbaum. Princeton: Princeton University Press, 35–40.

Howland, Courtney W., ed. 1999. *Religious Fundamentalism and the Human Rights of Women*. New York: St. Martin's Press.

Hults, Linda C. 1991. "Durer's Lucretia – Speaking the Silence of Women." *Signs* 16, 2: 205–233.

Human Rights Watch. 2002. "World Report on Women's Human Rights." Retrieved August 11, 2005, from www.hrw.org/wr2k2/women.html#labor%20rights.

2003. "Double Standards: Women's Property Rights Violations in Kenya." Retrieved August 15, 2004, from http://hrw.org/reports/2003/kenya0303/kenya0303.pdf.

Humphrey, John P. 1984. *Human Rights and the United Nations: A Great Adventure*. Dobbs Ferry: Transnational Publishers.

Huntington, Samuel P. 1996. *The Clash of Civilizations and the Remaking of World Order*. New York: Simon & Schuster.

Ibhawoh, Bonny. 2000. "Between Culture and Constitution: Evaluating the Cultural Legitimacy of Human Rights in the African State." *Human Rights Quarterly* 22, 3: 838–860.

Ignatieff, Michael. 2001. "Human Rights as Politics and Idolatry." In *Human Rights as Politics and Idolatry*, ed. Amy Gutmann. Princeton: Princeton University Press, 1–98.

Ignatieff, Michael, and Amy Gutmann. 2001. *Human Rights as Politics and Idolatry*. Princeton: Princeton University Press.

International Code Council. 2002. *International Building Code 2003*. Country Club Hills, IL: International Code Council.

International Conference on Women, Peace Building and Constitution Making, Colombo, Sri Lanka, May 2–5, 2002.

Ishay, Micheline. 2004. *The History of Human Rights: From Ancient Times to the Globalization Era*. Berkeley: University of California Press.

Iversen, Vegard. 2003. "Intra-Household Inequality: A Challenge for the Capability Approach." *Feminist Economics* 9, 2–3: 93–115.

Jaggar, Alison M. 1992. "Feminist Ethics." In *Encyclopedia of Ethics*, ed. Lawrence C. Becker and Charlotte B. Becker. New York: Garland Publishing, 361–370.

1994. *Living with Contradictions: Controversies in Feminist Social Ethics*. Boulder: Westview Press.

Jalani, Hina. 1993. "Diversity in Character and Role of Human Rights NGOs." In *Claiming Our Place: Working the Human Rights System to Women's Advantage*, ed. Margaret Schuler. Washington: Institute for Women, Law and Development, 107–114.

Jhappan, Radha. 2002. *Women's Legal Strategies in Canada*. Toronto: University of Toronto Press.

Jieun, Leehan. 2005. "Queer Girls Negotiating Identities." Paper presented at Women's Worlds Conference, Seoul, Korea, July 19–24.

Joachim, Jutta. 2003. "Framing Issues and Seizing Opportunities: The UN, NGOs, and Women's Rights." *International Studies Quarterly* 47, 2: 247–274.

Johannesen, Richard L. 1974. "The Functions of Silence: A Plea for Communication Research." *Western Speech* 38: 25–35.

Jones, Richard Wyn, ed. 2001. *Critical Theory and World Politics*. Boulder: Lynne Rienner Publishers.

Kant, Immanuel. 1997. *Lectures on Ethics*, ed. Peter Heath and J.B. Schneewind, trans. Peter Heath. New York: Cambridge University Press:

[1887] 2002. *The Philosophy of Law: An Exposition of the Fundamental Principles of Jurisprudence as the Science of Right*. Union, NJ: Lawbook Exchange.

Kapsalis, Terri. 1997. *Public Privates: Performing Gynecology from Both Ends of the Speculum*. Durham: Duke University Press.

Kapur, Ratna. 1999. "The Two Faces of Secularism and Women's Rights in India." In *Religious Fundamentalism and the Human Rights of Women*, ed. Courtney W. Howland. New York: St. Martin's Press, 143–153.

Keck, Margaret E., and Kathryn Sikkink. 1998. *Activists Beyond Borders: Advocacy Networks in International Politics*. Ithaca: Cornell University Press.

Keith, Linda Camp, and Steven C. Poe. 2004. "Are Constitutional State of Emergency Clauses Effective? An Empirical Exploration." *Human Rights Quarterly* 26, 4: 1071–1097.

Kellenberger, James. 2003. "Human Rights, Environmental Rights, and Religion." In *Human Rights and Responsibilities in the World Religions*, ed. Joseph Runzo, Nancy M. Martin, and Arvind Sharma. Oxford: Oneworld Publications, 115–128.

Kelley, Steve. 2002. "Title IX Saved Dunn; She's Ready to Return the Favor." *Seattle Times*: D1.

Kelly, Erin. 2001. "Editor's Forward." In *Justice as Fairness: A Restatement*, ed. Erin Kelly. Cambridge, MA: Harvard University Press, xi-xiii.

Kempadoo, Kamala, and Jo Doezema. 1998. *Global Sex Workers: Rights, Resistance, and Redefinition*. New York: Routledge.

Kennedy, David. 2004. *The Dark Sides of Virtue: Reassessing International Humanitarianism*. Princeton: Princeton University Press.

Kerr, Joanna. 2004. "From 'Opposing' to 'Proposing': Finding Proactive Global Strategies for Feminist Futures." In *The Future of Women's Rights: Global Visions and Strategies*, eds. Joanna Kerr, Ellen Sprengers, and Alison Symington. London: Zed Books,

Kesby, Mike. 2005. "Retheorizing Empowerment-through-Participation as a Performance in Space: Beyond Tyranny to Transformation." *Signs* 30, 4: 2037–2065.

Kevane, Michael, and Leslie C. Gray. 1999. "A Woman's Field Is Made at Night: Gendered Land Rights and Norms in Burkina Faso." *Feminist Economics* 5, 3: 1–26.

Khadiagala, Lynn. 2002. "Justice and Power in the Adjudication of Women's Property Rights in Uganda." *Africa Today* 49, 2: 101–121.

Khan, Muhammad Zafrulla. 1967 [1970]. *Islam and Human Rights*. Zürich: Oriental Publications.

Khan, Shaharyar M. 2000. *The Shallow Graves of Rwanda*. London: Tauris.

King, Joyce. 1991. "Dysconscious Racism: Ideology, Identity, and the Miseducation of Teachers." *The Journal of Negro Education* 60, 2: 133–146.

King, Martin Luther. 1963 [2007]. "I Have a Dream." Retrieved February 17, 2007, from www.savethemall.org/moments/mlk_02.html.

Kinoti, Kathambi. 2006. "Fighting for The 'Right Not to Be a Prostitute'." *Association for Women's Rights in Development*. Retrieved November 20, 2006, from www.awid.org/go.php?stid=1639.

Kirsch, Gesa E. 2005. "Friendship, Friendliness, and Feminist Fieldwork." *Signs* 30, 4: 2163–2172.

Klinghoffer, Arthur Jay. 1998. *The International Dimension of Genocide in Rwanda*. New York: New York University Press.

Kostash, Myrna. 2004. "Visible Silence: Women in Black in Edmonton." *Signs* 29, 2: 591–594.

Kramarae, Cheris, and Mercilee M. Jenkins. 1987. "Women Take Back the Talk." In *Women and Language in Transition*, ed. Joyce Penfield. Albany: State University of New York Press, 137–156.

Krause, Keith, and Michael C. Williams. 1996. "Broadening the Agenda of Security Studies: Politics and Methods." *Mershon Internatonal Studies Review* 40, 2: 229–254.

Kurzon, Dennis. 1996. "To Speak or Not to Speak." *International Journal for the Semiotics of Law* 25: 3–16.

Kymlicka, Will. 1995. *Multicultural Citizenship: A Liberal Theory of Minority Rights*. Oxford: Oxford University Press.

Lakoff, George. 2004. *Don't Think of an Elephant!: Know Your Values and Frame the Debate*. White River Junction: Chelsea Green Publishing.

Lakoff, George, and Mark Johnson. 1999. *Philosophy in the Flesh: The Embodied Mind and Its Challenge to Western Thought*. New York: Basic Books.

Lâm, Maivan Clech. 1994. "Feeling Foreign in Feminism." *Signs* 19, 4: 865–893.

Landes, Joan B. 1992. "Jurgen Habermas, The Structural Transformation of the Public Sphere: A Feminist Inquiry." *Praxis International* 12, 1: 106–127.

Langlois, Anthony J. 2001. *The Politics of Justice and Human Rights: Southeast Asia and Universalist Theory*. Cambridge: Cambridge University Press.

Laurent, Erick. 2005. "Sexuality and Human Rights: An Asian Perspective." *Journal of Homosexuality* 48, 3/4: 163–225.

Lennie, June, Caroline Hatcher, and Wendy Morgan. 2003. "Feminist Discourses of (Dis)Empowerment in an Action Research Project Involving Rural Women and Communication Technologies." *Action Research* 1, 1: 57–80.

Lentin, Alana. 2004. "Racial States, Anti-Racist Responses: Picking Holes in 'Culture' and 'Human Rights'." *European Journal of Social Theory* 7, 4: 427–443.

Li, Huey-Li. 2004. "Rethinking Silencing Silence." In *Democratic Dialogue in Education: Troubling Speech, Disturbing Silence*, ed. Megan Boler. New York: P. Lang, 69–86.

Liamputtong, Pranee, Susanha Yimyam, Sukanya Parisunyakul, Chavee Baosoung, and Nantaporn Sansiriphun. 2004. "When I Become a Mother!: Discourses of Motherhood among Thai Women in Northern Thailand." *Women's Studies International Forum* 27, 5–6: 589–601.

Lichter, Daniel, and Jensen Leif. 2002. "Rural America in Transition: Poverty and Welfare at the Turn of the Twenty-First Century." In *Rural Dimensions of Welfare Reform*, ed. Bruce A. Weber, Greg J. Duncan, and Leslie A. Whitener. Kalamazoo: W.E. Upjohn Institute for Employment Research, 77–110.

Linklater, Andrew. 1994. "Dialogue, Dialectic and Emancipation in International Relations at the End of the Post-War Age." *Millennium* 23, 1: 119–131.

Locke, John. [1688] 1988. "Two Treatises of Government." In *Cambridge Texts in the History of Political Thought*, ed. Peter Laslett. Cambridge: Cambridge University Press.

Lucas, Anne. 2004. "No Remedy for the Inuit: Accountability for Environmental Harms under US and International Law." In *New Perspectives on Environmental Justice: Gender, Sexuality, and Activism*, ed. Rachel Stein. New Brunswick: Rutgers University Press, 191–206.

Lugones, Maria C. 1990. "Structure/Antistructure and Agency under Oppression." *Journal of Philosophy* 87, 10: 500–507.

Lukes, Steven. 1993. "Five Fables About Human Rights." In *On Human Rights: The Oxford Amnesty Lectures*, ed. Stephen Shute and S. L. Hurley. New York: Basic Books, 19–40.

Lyons, David. 1972. "Rawls Versus Utilitarianism." *The Journal of Philosophy* 69, 18: 535–545.

MacDorman, Marian F., and Joanne O. Atkinson. 1999. Infant Mortality Statistics from the 1997 Period Linked Birth/Infant Death Data Set. National Vital Statistics Reports. Retrieved July 26, 2005, from www.Cdc.Gov/Nchs/Data/Nvsr/Nvsr47/Nvs47_23.Pdf.

MacIntyre, Alasdair C. [1981] 1984. *After Virtue: A Study in Moral Theory*. Notre Dame: University of Notre Dame Press.

Mackinnon, Catharine A. 1989. *Toward a Feminist Theory of the State*. Cambridge, MA: Harvard University Press.

1993. "Crimes of War, Crimes of Peace." In *On Human Rights: The Oxford Amnesty Lectures*, ed. Stephen Shute and Susan Hurley. New York: Basic Books, 83–109.

2006. *Are Women Human?: And Other International Dialogues*. Cambridge, MA: Belknap Press of Harvard University Press.

Madley, Benjamin. 2005. "From Africa to Auschwitz: How German South West Africa Incubated Ideas and Methods Adopted and Developed by the Nazis in Eastern Europe." *European History Quarterly* 35, 3: 429–464.

Maguire, Patricia, and University of Massachusetts at Amherst. 1987. *Doing Participatory Research: A Feminist Approach*. Amherst: Center for International Education, School of Education, University of Massachusetts.

Mamdani, Mahmood. 2001. *When Victims Become Killers: Colonialism, Nativism, and the Genocide in Rwanda*. Princeton: Princeton University Press.

Manderson, Lenore. 2004. "Local Rites and Body Politics: Tensions between Cultural Diversity and Human Rights." *International Feminist Journal of Politics* 6, 2: 285–307.

Manfredi, Christopher P. 1993. *Judicial Power and the Charter: Canada and the Paradox of Liberal Constitutionalism*. Norman: University of Oklahoma Press.

Manin, Bernard. 1987. "On Legitimacy and Political Deliberation," trans. Elly Stein and Jane Mansbridge. *Political Theory* 15, 3: 338–368.

Mansbridge, Jane. 1986. *Why We Lost the ERA*. Chicago: University of Chicago Press.

1993. "Feminism and Democratic Community." In *Democratic Community: NOMOS 35*, ed. John W. Chapman and Ian Shapiro. New York: New York University Press, 339–395.

Marais, Hein. 2001. *South Africa: Limits to Change: The Political Economy of Transition*. London: Zed Books.

Marcus, Sharon. 1992. "Fighting Bodies, Fighting Words: A Theory and Politics of Rape Prevention." In *Feminists Theorize the Political*, ed. Judith Butler and Joan Wallach Scott. New York: Routledge, 385–403.

Marglin, Stephen A. 1990. "Towards the Decolonization of the Mind." In *Dominating Knowledge: Development, Culture, and Resistance*, ed. Frédérique Apffel-Marglin. Oxford: Clarendon Press, 1–28.

Maritain, Jacques. 1949. "Introduction." In *Human Rights: Comments and Interpretations*. New York: Columbia University Press, 9–17.

Marx, Karl. [1843] 1967. "Letter to A. Ruge, September 1843." In *Writings of the Young Marx on Philosophy and Society*, ed. Loyd David Easton and Kurt H. Guddat. Garden City, NY: Doubleday, 211–215.

Matilal, Bimal Krishna. 1989. "Ethical Relativism and Confrontation of Cultures." In *Relativism: Interpretation and Confrontation*, ed. Michael Krausz. Notre Dame: University of Notre Dame Press, 339–362.

Mayer, Ann Elizabeth. 1995a. "Cultural Particularism as a Bar to Women's Rights: Reflections on the Middle Eastern Experience." In *Women's Rights, Human Rights: International Feminist Perspectives*, ed. Julie Peters and Andrea Wolper. New York: Routledge, 176–188.

1995b. *Islam and Human Rights: Tradition and Politics*. Boulder: Westview Press.

1995c. "Rhetorical Strategies and Official Policies on Women's Rights: The Merits and Drawbacks of the New World Hypocrisy." In *Faith and Freedom: Women's Human Rights in the Muslim World*. Syracuse: Syracuse University Press, 104–132.

[1991] 1999. *Islam and Human Rights: Tradition and Politics*. Boulder: Westview Press.

McAfee, Noëlle. 2000. *Habermas, Kristeva, and Citizenship*. Ithaca: Cornell University Press.

2004. "Three Models of Democratic Deliberation." *Journal of Speculative Philosophy* 18, 1: 44–59.

McCarthy, Thomas. 1990. "Private Irony and Public Decency: Richard Rorty's New Pragmatism." *Critical Inquiry* 16, Winter 1990: 355–370.

McIntosh, Peggy. 1988. "White Privilege and Male Privilege: A Personal Account of Coming to See Correspondences through Work in Women's Studies." Working Paper No. 189. Wellesley, MA: Wellesley Center for Women.

Messer, Ellen. 1993. "Anthropology and Human Rights." *Annual Review of Anthropology* 22: 221–249.

Mies, Maria. 1983. "Towards a Methodology for Feminist Research." In *Theories of Women's Studies*, ed. Gloria Bowles and Renate Klein. London: Routledge and Kegan Paul, 117–139.

Mill, John Stuart. [1859] 1989. "On Liberty." In *On Liberty and Other Writings*, ed. Stefan Collini. Cambridge: Cambridge University Press, 1–145.

[1869] 1998. "The Subjection of Women." In *On Liberty and Other Writings*, ed. Stefan Collini. Oxford: Oxford University Press, 117–217.

Mills, Charles W. forthcoming. "Contract and Domination." In *The Illusion of Consent*, ed. Dan O'Neill, Mary Shanley, and Iris Marion Young. University Park, PA: Pennsylvania State Press.

Mills, Charles W, and Carole Pateman. forthcoming. *The Domination Contract*.

Mills, Charles W. 1997. *The Racial Contract*. Ithaca: Cornell University Press.

2005. "'Ideal Theory' as Ideology." *Hypatia* 20, 3: 165–184.

Milner, Wesley T., Steven C. Poe, and David Leblang. 1999. "Security Rights, Subsistence Rights, and Liberties: A Theoretical Survey of the Empirical Landscape." *Human Rights Quarterly* 21, 2: 403–443.

Milwertz, Cecilia. 2003. "Activism against Domestic Violence in the People's Republic of China." *Violence Against Women* 9, 6: 630–654.

Misak, Cheryl. 2004. "Making Disagreement Matter: Pragmatism and Deliberative Democracy." *Journal of Speculative Philosophy* 18, 1: 9–22.

Mitchell, Michele. 1999. "Silences Broke, Silences Kept: Gender and Sexuality in African-American History." *Gender and History* 11, 3: 433–444.

Moghadam, Valentine M. 1994. *Identity Politics and Women: Cultural Reassertions and Feminisms in International Perspective*. Boulder: Westview Press.

2005. *Globalizing Women: Transnational Feminist Networks*. Baltimore: Johns Hopkins University Press.

Mohanty, Chandra Talpade. [1984] 1991. "Under Western Eyes: Feminist Scholarship and Colonial Discourses." In *Third World Women and the Politics of Feminism*, ed. Chandra Talpade Mohanty, Ann Russo, and Lourdes Torres. Bloomington: Indiana University Press, 51–80.

2003. *Feminism without Borders: Decolonizing Theory, Practicing Solidarity*. Durham: Duke University Press.

Mohanty, Chandra Talpade, Ann Russo, and Lourdes Torres. 1991. *Third World Women and the Politics of Feminism*. Bloomington: Indiana University Press.

Moody-Adams, Michele M. 1997. *Fieldwork in Familiar Places: Morality, Culture, and Philosophy*. Cambridge, MA: Harvard University Press.

1998. "The Virtues of Nussbaum's Essentialism." *Metaphilosophy* 29, 4: 263–272.

Moon, Katharine H. S. 1997. *Sex among Allies: Military Prostitution in US–Korea Relations*. New York: Columbia University Press.

Morgan, Jamie. 2003. "Addressing Human Wrongs: A Philosophy-of-Ontology Perspective." *Philosophy East and West* 53, 4: 575–587.

Mouffe, Chantal. 1995. "Feminism, Citizenship, and Radical Democratic Politics." In *Social Postmodernism: Beyond Identity Politics*, ed. Linda Nicholson and Steven Seidman. Cambridge: Cambridge University Press, 315–331.

2000. *The Democratic Paradox*. London: Verso.

Muse, Toby. 2006. "Colombia Loosens Strict Abortion Laws." *Associated Press*, 4:29 PM PDT, May 12, 2006.

Muzaffar, Chandra. 2002. *Rights, Religion, and Reform: Enhancing Human Dignity through Spiritual and Moral Transformation*. London: Routledge.

Mwenda, Kenneth K., Judge Florence N. M. Mumba, and Judith Mvula-Mwenda. 2005. "Property-Grabbing under African Customary Law: Repugnant to Natural Justice, Equity, and Good Conscience, Yet a Troubling Reality." *George Washington International Law Review* 37: 949–967.

Nagar, Richa. 2002. "Footloose Researchers, 'Traveling' Theories, and the Politics of Transnational Feminist Praxis." *Gender, Place and Culture* 9, 2: 179–186.

Nagel, Thomas. 1979. *Mortal Questions*. Cambridge: Cambridge University Press.

Naples, Nancy A. 2003. *Feminism and Method: Ethnography, Discourse Analysis, and Activist Research*. New York: Routledge.

Narayan, Deepa, Robert Chambers, Meera Kaul Shah, and Patti Petesch. 2000a. *Voices of the Poor: Crying out for Change*. New York: Oxford University Press.

Narayan, Deepa , Raj Patel, Kai Schafft, Anne Rademacher, and Sarah Koch-Schulte. 2000b. *Voices of the Poor: Can Anyone Hear Us?* New York: Oxford University Press.

Narayan, Uma. 1997. *Dislocating Cultures: Identities, Traditions, and Third-World Feminism*. New York: Routledge.

2003. "Coercing Women for Their Own Good: Women's Choices, Criminal Sanctions and the State." Paper presented at Investigating Identity and Experience: An Interdisciplinary Graduate Conference on Gender, Sexuality, and Cultural Politics, Vanderbilt University, Nashville, April 18.

Nash, Kate. 2002. "Human Rights for Women: An Argument for 'Deconstructive Equality'." *Economy and Society* 31, 3: 414–433.

2005. "Human Rights Culture: Solidarity, Diversity and the Right to be Different." *Citizenship Studies* 9, 4: 335–348.

Nelson, Cary, and Lawrence Grossberg, eds. 1988. *Marxism and the Interpretation of Culture*. Urbana: University of Illinois Press.

New Mexico Human Services Department. 2005. "Health Insurance Legislation Overwhelmingly Passes the House and Senate." Retrieved

August 27, 2005, from http://hpc.state.nm.us/news/Insure_NM!_Bills_passHouse%20andSenate.pdf.

*New York Times*. 2006. "Abortion Ruling in Colombia." Editorial, May 24.

Nicholson, Linda J., and Steven Seidman. 1995. *Social Postmodernism: Beyond Identity Politics*. Cambridge: Cambridge University Press.

Niebuhr, H. Richard. 1951. *Christ and Culture*. New York: Harper.

Nino, Carlos Santiago. 1991. *The Ethics of Human Rights*. Oxford: Oxford University Press.

Nord, Mark, Margaret Andrews, and Steven Carlson. 2004. "Household Food Security in the United States Food Assistance and Nutrition Research." Report No. (Fanrr42) 69, October. Retrieved August 27, 2005, from www.Ers.Usda.Gov/Publications/Fanrr42/.

Nozick, Robert. 1974. *Anarchy, State, and Utopia*. New York: Basic Books.

Nthabiseng, Motsemme. 2004. "The Mute Always Speak: On Women's Silences at the Truth and Reconciliation Commission." *Current Sociology* 52, 5: 909–932.

Nussbaum, Martha Craven. 1992. "Human Functioning and Social Justice: In Defense of Aristotelian Essentialism." *Political Theory* 20, 2: 202–246.

1993. "Non-Relative Virtues: An Aristotelian Approach." In *The Quality of Life*, ed. Amartya Kumar Sen. Oxford: Oxford University Press, 242–269.

1995a. "Aristotle on Human Nature and the Foundations of Ethics." In *World, Mind, and Ethics: Essays on the Ethical Philosophy of Bernard Williams*, ed. J. E. J. Altham and Ross Harrison. Cambridge: Cambridge University Press, 86–131.

1995b. "Human Capabilities, Female Human Beings." In *Women, Culture, and Development: A Study of Human Capabilities*, ed. Martha Craven Nussbaum, Jonathan Glover, and World Institute for Development Economics Research. Oxford: Clarendon Press, 61–105.

1997. "Human Rights Theory: Capabilities and Human Rights." *Fordham Law Review* 66: 273–300.

1998. "Political Animals: Luck, Love and Dignity." *Metaphilosophy* 29, 4: 273–287.

1999a. "Conversing with the Tradition: John Rawls and the History of Ethics." *Ethics* 109, 2: 424–430.

1999b. "A Plea for Difficulty." In *Is Multiculturalism Bad for Women?*, ed. Susan Moller Okin, Joshua Cohen, Matthew Howards, and Martha Craven Nussbaum. Princeton: Princeton University Press, 105–114.

1999c. "The Professor of Parody." *The New Republic* 220, 8: 37–45.

2000a. "Aristotle, Politics, and Human Capabilities: A Response to Antony, Arneson, Charlesworth, and Mulgan." *Ethics* 111, 1: 102–140.

2000b. *Women and Human Development: The Capabilities Approach*. Cambridge: Cambridge University Press.
2001. "Political Objectivity." *New Literary History* 32, 4: 883–906.
2003a. "Capabilities as Fundamental Entitlements: Sen and Social Justice." *Feminist Economics* 9, 2–3: 33–59.
2003b. "Women and the Law of Peoples." *Politics, Philosophy and Economics* 1, 3: 283–335.
2004. "Women's Education: A Global Challenge." *Signs* 29, 2: 325–355.
O'Hare, Ursula A. 1999. "Realizing Human Rights for Women." *Human Rights Quarterly* 21, 2: 364–402.
O'Neill, Onora. 1995. "Justice, Capabilities, and Vulnerabilities." In *Women, Culture, and Development: A Study of Human Capabilities*, ed. Martha Craven Nussbaum, Jonathan Glover, and World Institute for Development Economics Research. Oxford: Oxford University Press, 140–152.
1996. *Towards Justice and Virtue: A Constructive Account of Practical Reasoning*. Cambridge: Cambridge University Press.
2000. "Women's Rights: Whose Obligations?" In *Bounds of Justice*, ed. Onosa O'Neill. Cambridge: Cambridge University Press, 97–111.
Office of the High Commissioner for Human Rights. 1993. "Vienna Declaration and Programme of Action." World Conference on Human Rights, Vienna, Austria, June 14–25.
Okin, Susan Moller. 1979. *Women in Western Political Thought*. Princeton: Princeton University Press.
1989. *Justice, Gender, and the Family*. New York: Basic Books.
1994. "Gender Inequality and Cultural Differences." *Political Theory* 22, 1: 5–24.
1995. "Response to Jane Flax." *Political Theory* 23, 3: 511–516.
1998. "Feminism, Women's Human Rights, and Cultural Differences." *Hypatia* 13, 2: 32–52.
1999. "Is Multiculturalism Bad for Women?" In *Is Multiculturalism Bad for Women?*, ed. Joshua Cohen, Matthew Howard, and Martha Craven Nussbaum. Princeton: Princeton University Press, 7–24.
2003. "Poverty, Well-Being, and Gender: What Counts, Who's Heard?" *Philosophy and Public Affairs* 31, 3: 280–316.
Okin, Susan Moller, Joshua Cohen, Matthew Howard, and Martha Craven Nussbaum, eds. 1999. *Is Multiculturalism Bad for Women?* Princeton: Princeton University Press.
Oliveira, Victor, Elizabeth Racine, Jennifer lmsted, and Linda M. Ghelfi. 2002. The WIC Program: Background, Trends, and Issues. Food Assistance and Nutrition Research Report No. (Fanrr27) 44 pp, October. Retrieved August 8, 2005, from www.Ers.Usda.Gov/Publications/Fanrr27/.

Omang, Joanne. 2005. "US Withdraws Destructive Amendment to UN Declaration Reaffirming UN Platform for Action for Women." *Ms. Magazine Online*, March.

Orhant, Melanie. 2001. *Trafficking in Persons: Myths, Methods and Human Rights*. New York: Population Reference Bureau.

Oster, Emily. 2005. "Hepatitis B and the Case of the Missing Women." *Journal of Political Economy* 113, 6: 1163–1216.

Otto, Diane. 2001. "Defending Women's Economic and Social Rights: Some Thoughts on Indivisibility and a New Standard of Equality." In *Giving Meaning to Economic, Social, and Cultural Rights*, ed. Isfahan Merali and Valerie Oosterveld. Philadelphia: University of Pennsylvania Press, 52–67.

Palmer, Gary B. 2001. "Book review of: *Understanding Cultures through Their Key Words: English, Russian, Polish, German and Japanese and Semantics: Primes and Universals*." *Journal of Linguistic Anthropology* 10, 2: 279–284.

Panikkar, Raimundo. 1988. "What Is Comparative Philosophy Comparing?" In *Interpreting across Boundaries: New Essays in Comparative Philosophy*, ed. Gerald J. Larson and Eliot Deutsch. Princeton: Princeton University Press, 116–136.

Parpart, Jane L. 2000. "The Participatory Empowerment Approach to Gender and Development in Africa: Panacea or Illusion?" Occasional Paper, Center of African Studies, University of Copenhagen.

Pateman, Carole. 1988. *The Sexual Contract*. Stanford: Stanford University Press.

2002. "Self-Ownership and Property in the Person: Democratization and a Tale of Two Concepts." *The Journal of Political Philosophy* 10, 1: 20–53.

2004. "Democratizing Citizenship: Some Advantages of a Basic Income." *Politics and Society* 32, 1: 89–105.

Pearson, Ruth. 1998. "'Nimble Fingers' Revisited: Reflections on Women and Third World Industrialization in the Late Twentieth Century." In *Feminist Visions of Development: Gender Analysis and Policy*, ed. Cecile Jackson and Ruth Pearson. London: Routledge, 171–188.

Pence, Ellen, and Melanie Shepard. 1988. "Integrating Feminist Theory and Practice: The Challenge of the Battered Women's Movement." In *Feminist Perspectives on Wife Abuse*, ed. Kersti Yllo and Michele Louise Bograd. Newbury Park: Sage Publications, 282–298.

Perry, Michael J. 1998. *The Idea of Human Rights: Four Inquiries*. New York: Oxford University Press.

Pesce, Francesca. 1998. "End of Violence Working Group Posting."

Petchesky, Rosalind P. 2003. *Global Prescriptions: Gendering Health and Human Rights*. New York: Zed Books.

2006. "On the Unstable Marriage of Reproductive and Sexual Rights: The Case for a Trial Separation." *Conscience*. Retrieved January 15, 2007, from www.catholicsforchoice.org/conscience/default.asp.

Peters, Julie, and Andrea Wolper. 1995. *Women's Rights, Human Rights: International Feminist Perspectives*. New York: Routledge.

Peterson, V. Spike. 1990. "Whose Rights? A Critique of The 'Givens' In Human Rights Discourse." *Alternatives* XV: 303–344.

Pettit, Philip. 1997. *Republicanism: A Theory of Freedom and Government*. Oxford: Clarendon Press.

Phillips, Anne. 1993. *Democracy and Difference*. University Park: Pennsylvania State University Press.

1996. "Dealing with Difference: A Politics of Ideas, or A Politics of Presence?" In *Democracy and Difference: Contesting the Boundaries of the Political*, ed. Seyla Benhabib. Princeton: Princeton University Press, 139–152.

Poe, Steven C., Sabine C. Carey, and Tanya C. Vazquez. 2001. "How Are These Pictures Different? A Quantitative Comparison of the US State Department and Amnesty International Human Rights Reports, 1976–1995." *Human Rights Quarterly* 23, 3: 650–677.

Poe, Steven C., and C. Neal Tate. 1994. "Repression of Human Rights to Personal Integrity in the 1980s: A Global Analysis." *American Political Science Review* 88, 4: 853–872.

Poe, Steven C., C. Neal Tate, and Linda Camp Keith. 1999. "Repression of the Human Right to Personal Integrity Revisited: A Global Cross-National Study Covering the Years 1976–1993." *International Studies Quarterly* 43, 2: 291–313.

Poe, Steven C., Dierdre Wendel-Blunt, and Karl Ho. 1997. "Global Patterns in the Achievement of Women's Human Rights to Equality." *Human Rights Quarterly* 19, 4: 813–835.

Pollis, Adamantia. 2000. "A New Universalism." In *Human Rights: New Perspectives, New Realities*, ed. Adamantia Pollis and Peter Schwab. Boulder: Lynne Rienner Publishers, 9–30.

Pollis, Adamantia, and Peter Schwab. 1979. "Human Rights: A Western Construct with Limited Applicability." In *Human Rights: Cultural and Ideological Perspectives*, ed. Adamantia Pollis and Peter Schwab. New York: Praeger Publishers, 1–18.

2000. *Human Rights: New Perspectives, New Realities*. Boulder: Lynne Rienner Publishers.

Povey, Elaheh Rostami. 2001. "Feminist Contestations of Institutional Domains in Iran." *Feminist Review* 69, Winter: 44–72.

Power, Samantha. 2002. *"A Problem from Hell": America and the Age of Genocide*. New York: Basic Books.

Proctor, Bernadette, and Joseph Dalaker. 2001. "Poverty in the United States 2001." United States Census Bureau. Retrieved August 21, 2005, from www.census.gov/prod/2002pubs/p60-219.pdf.

Prügl, Elisabeth. 1999. *The Global Construction of Gender: Home-Based Work in the Political Economy of the 20th Century*. New York: Columbia University Press.

Puja, Kim. 2001. "Global Civil Society Remakes History: The Women's International War Crimes Tribunal 2000." *Positions: East Asia Cultures Critique* 9, 3: 611–620.

Putnam, Robert D. 2001. *Bowling Alone: The Collapse and Revival of American Community*. New York: Simon & Schuster.

2002. *Democracies in Flux: The Evolution of Social Capital in Contemporary Society*. Oxford: Oxford University Press.

Quisumbing, Agnes R., Ellen Payongayong, J. B. Aidoo, and Keijiro Otsuka. 2001. "Women's Land Rights in the Transition to Individualized Ownership: Implications for Tree-Resource Management in Western Ghana." *Economic Development and Cultural Change* 50, 1: 157–181.

Rahmani, Ladan. 2005. "The Politics of Gender in the United Nations Human Rights Treaty Bodies." Ph.D. Dissertation. University of Sydney, Australia.

Ramadan, Tariq. 2004. *Western Muslims and the Future of Islam*. Oxford: Oxford University Press.

Rao, Anupama. 2006. "Representing Dalit Selfhood." Dalit Perspectives: a symposium of the changing contours of Dalit politics, India, February.

Ratna, Kapur. 2000. "Too Hot to Handle: The Cultural Politics of Fire." *Feminist Review*, 64: 53–64.

Rawls, John. 1985. "Justice as Fairness: Political not Metaphysical." *Philosophy and Public Affairs* 14, 3: 223–51.

Rawls, John. 1987. "The Idea of an Overlapping Consensus." *Oxford Journal of Legal Studies* 7, 1: 1–25.

1993. *Political Liberalism*. New York: Columbia University Press.

1996. *Political Liberalism*. New York: Columbia University Press.

1999a. "The Idea of Public Reason Revisited." In *The Law of Peoples With "The Idea of Public Reason Revisited."* Cambridge, MA: Harvard University Press, 130–180.

1999b. "The Law of Peoples." In *The Law of Peoples with "The Idea of Public Reason Revisited."* Cambridge, MA: Harvard University Press, 3–128.

[1971] 1999. *A Theory of Justice*. Cambridge, MA: Belknap Press of Harvard University Press.

[1980] 1999. "Kantian Constructivism in Moral Theory." In *Collected Papers*, ed. Samuel Richard Freeman. Cambridge, MA: Harvard University Press, 303–358.

[1993] 1999. "The Law of Peoples." In *Collected Papers*, ed. Samuel Richard Freeman. Cambridge, MA: Harvard University Press, 529–564.

2001. *Justice as Fairness: A Restatement*. Cambridge, MA: Harvard University Press.

Rawls, John, and Erin Kelly. 2001. *Justice as Fairness: A Restatement*. Cambridge, MA: Harvard University Press.

Ray, Raka. 1999. *Fields of Protest: Women's Movements in India*. Minneapolis: University of Minnesota Press.

Reinharz, Shulamit. 1992. *Feminist Methods in Social Research*. New York: Oxford University Press.

Reyntjiens, Filip. 2004. "Rwanda, Ten Years On: From Genocide to Dictatorship." *African Affairs* 103, 411: 177–210.

Rich, Adrienne Cecile. 1979. *On Lies, Secrets, and Silence: Selected Prose, 1966–1978*. New York: Norton.

Richards, David L. 1999. "Perilous Proxy: Human Rights and the Presence of National Elections." *Social Science Quarterly* 80, 4: 648–665.

Riles, Annelise. 2002. "Rights inside Out: The Case of the Women's Human Rights Campaign." *Leiden Journal of International Law* 15, 2: 285–305.

Risman, Barbara J. 2004. "Gender as a Social Structure: Theory Wrestling with Activism." *Gender & Society* 18, 4: 429–450.

Robinson, Mary. 2005. "Justice Ruth Bader Ginsburg Distinguished Lecture on Women and the Law." Association of the Bar of the City of New York. Retrieved September 21, 2005, from www.realizingrights.org/images/stories/Ruth_Bader_Ginsburg_lecture.doc.

*Roe v. Wade*. 410 U.S. 113 (1973).

Rome Statute of the International Criminal Court. 1998. "Rome Statute of the International Criminal Court," Rome, June 17.

Rorty, Richard. 1991. *Objectivity, Relativism, and Truth*. Cambridge: Cambridge University Press.

1993. "Human Rights, Rationality, and Sentimentality." In *On Human Rights: The Oxford Amnesty Lectures*, ed. Stephen Shute and Susan Hurley. New York: Basic Books, 111–134.

Rosenberg, Shawn W. 2002. *The Not So Common Sense: Differences in How People Judge Social and Political Life*. New Haven: Yale University Press.

Rosenfeld, Michel. 1991. *Affirmative Action and Justice: A Philosophical and Constitutional Inquiry*. New Haven: Yale University Press.

Ross, Jen. 2005. "Women-Health: Brazil Begins Talking Openly About Abortion." Women's E-news. Retrieved August 10, 2005, from www.womensenews.org/article.cfm/dyn/aid/2296/context/archive.

Ross, Loretta J. 2005. "A Feminist Perspective on Katrina." *Collective Voices* 1, 3: 1–4.

Rothschild, Cynthia, Scott Long, and Susana T. Fried, eds. 2005. *Written Out: How Sexuality Is Used to Attack Women's Organizing*. New York: International Gay and Lesbian Human Rights Commission, and The Center for Women's Global Leadership.

Rowe, Mary P. 1990. "Barriers to Equality: The Power of Subtle Discrimination to Maintain Unequal Opportunity." *Employee Responsibilities and Rights Journal* 3, 3: 153–163.

Roy, Arundhati. 2004. *An Ordinary Person's Guide to Empire*. Cambridge, MA: South End Press.

Rubin, Edward L. 2005. *Beyond Camelot: Rethinking Politics and Law for the Modern State*. Princeton: Princeton University Press.

Runzo, Joseph, Nancy M. Martin, and Arvind Sharma, eds. 2003. *Human Rights and Responsibilities in the World Religions*. Oxford: Oneworld Publications.

Rusesabagina, Paul, and with Tom Zoellner. 2006. *An Ordinary Man: An Autobiography*. New York: Viking.

Safi, Louay. 2003. *Tensions and Transitions in the Muslim World*. Lanham: University Press of America.

Said, Edward W. [1978] 1979. *Orientalism*. New York: Vintage Books.

Sandel, Michael J. [1982] 1998. *Liberalism and the Limits of Justice*. Cambridge: Cambridge University Press.

Sander, Richard H., and E. Douglass Williams. 1997. "An Empirical Analysis of the Proposed Los Angeles Living Wage Ordinance – Final Report." City of Los Angeles.

Sander, Richard H., E. Douglass Williams, and Joseph Doherty. 2000. "An Economic Analysis of the Proposed Santa Monica Living Wage." Empirical Research Group, UCLA.

Sandoval, Chela. 2000. *Methodology of the Oppressed*. Minneapolis: University of Minnesota Press.

Sardá, Alejandra. 2007. "Resisting Kirchner's Recipe (Sometimes): 'LGBTTTI' Organizing in Argentina." *NACLA Report on the Americas* 40, 2: 30–32, 42–43.

Schaffer, Kay, and Sidonie Smith. 2004. *Human Rights and Narrated Lives: The Ethics of Recognition*. New York: Palgrave Macmillan.

Schama, Simon. 2006. *Rough Crossings: Britain, the Slaves, and the American Revolution*. New York: Ecco.

Schechter, Susan. 1988. "Building Bridges between Activists, Professionals, and Researchers." In *Feminist Perspectives on Wife Abuse*, ed. Kersti Yllo and Michele Louise Bograd. Newbury Park: Sage Publications, 299–312.

Scherrer, Christian P. 2002. *Genocide and Crisis in Central Africa: Conflict Roots, Mass Violence, and Regional War*. Westport: Praeger.

Schipper, Mineke. 2003. *Never Marry a Woman with Big Feet: Women in Proverbs from Around the World*. New Haven: Yale University Press.

Scott, David. 1999. *Refashioning Futures: Criticism after Postcoloniality*. Princeton: Princeton University Press.

Sedgwick, Eve Kosofsky. 1990. *Epistemology of the Closet*. Berkeley: University of California Press.

Semujanga, Josias. 2003. *Origins of Rwandan Genocide*. Amherst: Humanity Books.

Sen, Amartya K. 1990a. "Gender and Cooperative Conflicts." In *Persistent Inequalities: Women and World Development*, ed. Irene Tinker. New York: Oxford University Press, 123–149.

1990b. "Justice: Means Versus Freedom." *Philosophy and Public Affairs* 19, 2, Spring: 111–121.

1990c. "More Than 100 Million Women Are Missing." *The New York Review of Books* 37, 20: 61–66.

1999a. "Human Rights and Economic Achievements." In *The East Asian Challenge for Human Rights*, ed. Joanne R. Bauer and Daniel A. Bell. Cambridge: Cambridge University Press, 88–99.

1999b. *Development as Freedom*. New York: Oxford University Press.

2004. "Elements of a Theory of Human Rights." *Philosophy and Public Affairs* 32, 4: 315–356.

Sen, Gita, and Caren Grown. 1987. *Development, Crises, and Alternative Visions: Third World Women's Perspectives*. New York: Monthly Review Press.

Shachar, Ayelet. 2001. *Multicultural Jurisdictions: Cultural Differences and Women's Rights*. Cambridge: Cambridge University Press.

Shanley, Mary Lyndon, Joshua Cohen, and Deborah Chasman, eds. 2004. *Just Marriage*. Oxford: Oxford University Press.

Shapiro, Ian. 1986. *The Evolution of Rights in Liberal Theory*. Cambridge: Cambridge University Press.

1990. *Political Criticism*. Berkeley: University of California Press.

1999. *Democratic Justice*. New Haven: Yale University Press.

Shea, John B. 2003. "The Moral Status of In Vitro Fertilization (Ivf) Biology and Method." Retrieved August 25, 2005, from http://catholicinsight.com/online/church/vatican/article_475.shtml.

Shiffman, Gary. 2002. "Construing Disagreement: Consensus and Invective In 'Constitutional' Debate." *Political Theory* 30, 2: 175–203.

Shue, Henry. [1980] 1996. *Basic Rights: Subsistence, Affluence, and US Foreign Policy*. Princeton: Princeton University Press.

Silliman, Jael Miriam, and Ynestra King, eds. 1999. *Dangerous Intersections: Feminist Perspectives on Population, Environment, and Development*. Cambridge, MA: South End Press.

Singer, Peter. 1993. *Practical Ethics*. Cambridge: Cambridge University Press.

ed. 1994. *Ethics*. Oxford: Oxford University Press.

Skocpol, Theda. 2003. *Diminished Democracy: From Membership to Management in American Civic Life*. Norman: University of Oklahoma Press.

Skocpol, Theda, and Morris P. Fiorina. 1999. *Civic Engagement in American Democracy*. Washington, DC: Brookings Institution Press; Russell Sage Foundation.

Slingerland, Edward. 2004. "Conceptual Metaphor Theory as Methodology for Comparative Religion." *Journal of the American Academy of Religion* 72, 1: 1–31.

Smith, Dorothy E. 1974. "Women's Perspective as a Radical Critique of Society." *Sociological Inquiry* 44: 7–13.

1987. *The Everyday World as Problematic: A Feminist Sociology*. Boston: Northeastern University Press.

Smith, Linda Tuhiwai. 1999. *Decolonizing Methodologies: Research and Indigenous Peoples*. London: Zed Books.

Smith, Rogers M. 2003. *Stories of Peoplehood: The Politics and Morals of Political Membership*. Cambridge: Cambridge University Press.

Snyder, Margaret. 2006. "Unlikely Godmother: The United Nations and the Global Women's Movement." In *Global Feminism: Transnational Women's Activism, Organizing, and Human Rights*, ed. Myra Marx Ferree and Aili Mari Tripp. New York: New York University Press, 24–50.

Soares, Vera, Anna Alice Alcantrara Costa, Christina Maria Buarque, Denise Dourado Dora, and Wania Sant'anna. 1995. "Brazilian Feminism and Women's Movements: A Two-Way Street." In *The Challenge of Local Feminisms: Women's Movements in Global Perspective*, ed. Amrita Basu, C. Elizabeth McGrory, and Ford Foundation Women's Program Forum. Boulder: Westview Press, 302–323.

Sobrino SJ, Jon. 2001. "Human Rights and Oppressed Peoples: Historical-Theological Reflections." In *Truth and Memory: The Church and Human Rights in El Salvadore and Guatemala*, ed. Michael Hayes and David Tomb. Gloucester: Gracewing, 134–158.

Song, Sarah. 2005. "Majority Norms, Multiculturalism, and Gender Equality." *American Political Science Review* 99, 4: 473–489.

South and Southeast Asia Resource Center on Sexuality. 2005. Sexual Pleasure, Sexuality, and Rights, October 17 – December 27, 2005, Subtopic 3. Retrieved December 8, 2006, from www.asiasrc.org/eforum1/sexual_pleasure_and_rights.php.

South and Southeast Asia Resource Centre on Sexuality. 2006. *E-Discussion E-Forum #1: "Sexual Pleasure, Sexuality, and Rights."*

South Carolina Department of Education. 1998. "The State of Literacy in America: Estimates at the Local State and National Level." Retrieved August 12, 2005, from www.sclrc.org/NalsNarrative.htm.

Spelman, Elizabeth V. 1988a. *Inessential Woman: Problems of Exclusion in Feminist Thought*. Boston: Beacon Press.

1988b. "Who's Who in the Polis." In *Inessential Woman: Problems of Exclusion in Feminist Thought*. Boston: Beacon Press, 37–56.

Spickard, James V. 2002. "Human Rights through a Religious Lens: A Programmatic Argument." *Social Compass* 49, 2: 227–238.

Spinner-Halev, Jeff. 2000. *Surviving Diversity: Religion and Democratic Citizenship*. Baltimore: Johns Hopkins University Press.

Spivak, Gayatri Chakravorty. 1988. "Can the Subaltern Speak?" In *Marxism and the Interpretation of Culture*, ed. Cary Nelson and Lawrence Grossberg. Urbana: University of Illinois Press, 271–313.

2005. "Use and Abuse of Human Rights." *boundary* 2 32, 1: 131–189.

Staeheli, Lynn A., and Richa Nagar. 2002. "Feminists Talking Across Worlds." *Gender, Place and Culture* 9, 2: 167–172.

Stamatopoulou, Elissavet. 1995. "Women's Rights and the United Nations." In *Women's Rights, Human Rights: International Feminist Perspectives*, ed. Julie Peters and Andrea Wolper. New York: Routledge, 36–48.

State of Tennessee. [1974] 1998. "Rules of Tennessee," Department of Human Services.

Stern, Maria. 2005. *Naming Security – Constructing Identity: "Mayan Women" in Guatemala on the Eve of "Peace."* Manchester: Manchester University Press.

2006. "Racism, Sexism, Classism and Much More: Reading Security-Identity in Marginalized Sites." In *Feminist Methodologies for International Relations*, ed. Brooke Ackerly, Maria Stern, and Jacqui True. Cambridge: Cambridge University Press, 174–197.

Stiehm, Judith Hicks. 1983. "The Unit of Political Analysis: Our Aristotelian Hangover." In *Discovering Reality: Feminist Perspectives on Epistemology, Metaphysics, Methodology, and Philosophy of Science*, ed. Sandra G. Harding and Merrill B. Hintikka. Dordrecht: D. Reidel, 31–43.

Stokes, Susan. 1998. "Pathologies of Deliberation." In *Cambridge Studies in the Theory of Democracy*, ed. Jon Elster. Cambridge: Cambridge University Press, 123–139.

Stoller, Paul. 1997. *Sensuous Scholarship*. Philadelphia: University of Pennsylvania Press.

Suskind, Ron. 2004. "What Makes Bush's Presidency So Radical – Even to Some Republicans – Is His Preternatural, Faith-Infused Certainty in Uncertain Times. Without a Doubt." *The New York Times Magazine*: 44.

Suthrell, Charlotte A. 2004. *Unzipping Gender: Sex, Cross-Dressing and Culture*. Oxford: Berg.

Suu Kyi, Aung San. 1991. *Freedom from Fear: And Other Writings*. New York: Penguin Books.

Sylvester, Christine. 1994. *Feminist Theory and International Relations in a Postmodern Era*. Cambridge: Cambridge University Press.

Talbott, W. J. 2005. *Which Rights Should Be Universal?* New York: Oxford University Press.

Taylor, Charles. [1992]1994. "The Politics of Recognition." In *Multiculturalism: Examining the Politics of Recognition*, ed. Charles Taylor, Amy Gutmann, and Charles Taylor. Princeton: Princeton University Press, 25–74.

1999. "Conditions of an Unforced Consensus on Human Rights." In *The East Asian Challenge for Human Rights*, ed. Joanne R. Bauer and Daniel Bell. Cambridge: Cambridge University Press, 124–144.

Taylor, Charles, and Amy Gutmann, ed. [1992] 1994. *Multiculturalism: Examining the Politics of Recognition*. Princeton: Princeton University Press.

Taylor, Jill Mclean, Carol Gilligan, and Amy M. Sullivan. 1995. *Between Voice and Silence: Women and Girls, Race and Relationship*. Cambridge, MA: Harvard University Press.

Tenenbaum, David J. 1998. "Northern Overexposure." *Environmental Health Perspectives* 106, 2: A64–A69.

Thucydides. 1954. *The Peloponnesian War*, trans. Rex Warner. New York: Penguin Classics.

Tickner, J. Ann. 1992. *Gender in International Relations: Feminist Perspectives on Achieving Global Security*. New York: Columbia University Press.

1997. "You Just Don't Understand: Troubled Engagements Between Feminists and IR Theorists." *International Studies Quarterly* 41, 4: 611–632.

Tripp, Aili Mari. 2004. "Women's Movements, Customary Law, and Land Rights in Africa: The Case of Uganda." *African Studies Quarterly* 7, 4: 1–19.

Trowbridge, John. 2000. "Asian Values and Human Rights: A Confucian Communitarian Perspective." *Philosophy East and West* 50, 3: 465–468.

True, Jacqui. 2003. *Gender, Globalization, and Postsocialism: The Czech Republic after Communism*. New York: Columbia University Press.

True, Jacqui, and Michael Minstrom. 2001. "Transnational Networks and Policy Diffusion: The Case of Gender Mainstreaming." *International Studies Quarterly* 45: 27–57.

Tsing, Anna Lowenhaupt. 2005. *Friction: An Ethnography of Global Connection*. Princeton: Princeton University Press.

Twagilimana, Aimable. 2003. *The Debris of Ham: Ethnicity, Regionalism, and the 1994 Rwandan Genocide*. Lanham: University Press of America.

UNESCO (United Nations Economic and Social Council). 57th Session. Commission on Human Rights, Conclusions and Recommendations of the Special Representative of the UN Secretary General on Human Rights Defenders. E/CN.4/2001/94. Retrieved December 15, 2006, from www.ishr.ch/hrdo/secretariat/AnnualReportsCHR/2001.pdf.

UNIFEM (United Nations Development Fund for Women). 1999. *A World Free of Violence against Women*. Digital Generation Systems, Inc.

United Nations. 1975. "Proceedings of the First World Conference on Women," Mexico City, June 19–July 2.

1979. Division for the Advancement of Women. "Convention on the Elimination of All Forms of Discrimination against Women, Declarations, Reservations and Objections." Retrieved December 15, 2006, from www.un.org/womenwatch/daw/cedaw/text/econvention.htm.

1980. "Proceedings of the Second World Conference on Women," Copenhagen, July 14–30. Resolution 25/136.

1985. "Proceedings of the Third World Conference on Women," Nairobi, July 15–26.

1989. "Convention on the Rights of the Child." In *Annex GA Res. 44/25 Doc. A/Res/4425*. Adopted November 20, 1989.

1992. "Report of the UN Conference on Environment and Development, Earth Summit, Rio De Janeiro, Brazil." A/CONF.151/26 (Vol. 1). Retrieved December 20, 2006, from www.un.org/documents/ga/conf151/aconf15126-1annex1.htm.

1993. "World Conference on Human Rights, Vienna, Austria, June 14–25." A/CONF.157/24 (Part I). Retrieved December 20, 2006, from www.unhchr.ch/huridocda/huridoca.nsf/(Symbol)/A.CONF.157.24+(PART+I).En?OpenDocument.

1994. "International Conference on Population and Development." International Conference on Population and Development, Cairo, Egypt, September 5–13.

1995. "Fourth World Conference on Women, Beijing Platform for Action." In *United Nations Fourth World Conference on Women*. A/CONF.177/20/Rev.1. Retrieved December 20, 2006, from http://rih.stanford.edu/rosenfield/resources/FWCW%20Beijing%20Report%201995.pdf.

1996. "Conference on Human Settlements (Habitat II)." Istanbul, Turkey, June 3–14.

2000. "Security Council Resolution 1325." S/RES/1325. Retrieved December 20, 2006, from www.un.org/events/res_1325e.pdf.

2005. "49th Session of the Commission on the Status of Women." March 11.

Universal Declaration of Human Rights. 1948. In *G.A. Res. 217A(III), U.N. Doc. A/810*. www.unhchr.ch/udhr/lang/eng.htm.

US Department of State. 2006. *Country Reports on Human Rights Practices* 8, March 2006. Retrieved June 1, 2006, from www.state.gov/g/drl/rls/hrrpt/2005/61556.htm.

Uvin, Peter. 1998. *Aiding Violence: The Development Enterprise in Rwanda*. Bloomfield: Kumarian Press.

2004. *Human Rights and Development*. Bloomfield: Kumarian Press.

Vandenbergh, Michael P. 2001. "The Social Meaning of Environmental Command and Control." *Virginia Environmental Law Journal* 20, 191: 201–204.

2005. "Order without Social Norms: How Personal Norm Activation Can Protect the Environment." *Northwestern University Law Review* 99: 1101–1167.

Vickers, Jill. 2002. "Thinking About Violence." In *Gender, Race, and Nation: A Global Perspective*, ed. Vanaja Dhruvarajan and Jill Vickers. Toronto: University of Toronto Press, 222–246.

Vincent, R. J. 1986. *Human Rights and International Relations*. Cambridge: Cambridge University Press.

Volf, Miroslav. 1996. *Exclusion and Embrace: A Theological Exploration of Identity, Otherness, and Reconciliation*. Nashville: Abingdon Press.

Voting Rights Act. 1965. 42 U.S.C. § 1973–1973aa-6.

Waldron, Jeremy. 1999. *Law and Disagreement*. Oxford: Oxford University Press.

Walker, Scott, and Steven C. Poe. 2002. "Does Cultural Diversity Affect Countries' Respect for Human Rights?" *Human Rights Quarterly* 24, 1: 237–263.

Wallace, Michele. 1990. *Invisibility Blues: From Pop to Theory*. London: Verso.

Wallace-Sanders, Kimberly, ed. 2002. *Skin Deep, Spirit Strong: The Black Female Body in American Culture*. Ann Arbor: University of Michigan Press.

Waltz, Susan. 2001. "Universalizing Human Rights: The Role of Small States in the Construction of the Universal Declaration of Human Rights." *Human Rights Quarterly* 23, 1: 44–72.

Walzer, Michael. 1983. *Spheres of Justice: A Defense of Pluralism and Equality*. New York: Basic Books.

1984. "Liberalism and the Art of Separation." *Political Theory* 12, 3: 315–330.

1987. *Interpretation and Social Criticism*. Cambridge, MA: Harvard University Press.
1988. *The Company of Critics: Social Criticism and Political Commitment in the Twentieth Century*. New York: Basic Books.
1990. "The Communitarian Critique of Liberalism." *Political Theory* 18, 1: 6–23.
Warnke, Georgia. 1989–90. "Social Interpretation and Political Theory: Walzer and His Critics." *The Philosophical Forum* 21, 1–2: 204–226.
1993. *Justice and Interpretation*. Cambridge, MA: MIT Press.
Waters, Tony. 1997. "Conventional Wisdom and Rwanda's Genocide: An Opinion." *African Studies Quarterly*. Online journal available at http://web.africa.ufl.edu/asq/v1/3/10.htm.
Weatherley, Robert. 1999. *The Discourse of Human Rights in China: Historical and Ideological Perspectives*. New York: St. Martin's Press.
Weber, Max, and Introduction by Talcott Parsons, trans. A. M. Henderson and Talcott Parsons. 1947. *The Theory of Social and Economic Organization*. New York: Oxford University Press.
Weeks, Jeffrey, and Janet Holland. 1996. *Sexual Cultures: Communities, Values, and Intimacy*. New York: St. Martin's Press.
West, Robin. 1997. *Caring for Justice*. New York: New York University Press.
White, Sarah C. 1992. *Arguing with the Crocodile: Gender and Class in Bangladesh*. Atlantic Highlands: Zed Books.
White, Stephen K. 2000. *Sustaining Affirmation: The Strengths of Weak Ontology in Political Theory*. Princeton: Princeton University Press.
Whitworth, Sandra. 2001. "The Practice, and Praxis, of Feminist Research in International Relations." In *Critical Theory and World Politics*, ed. Richard Wyn Jones. Boulder: Lynne Rienner Publishers, 149–160.
Wierzbicka, Anna. 1996. *Semantics – Primes and Universals*. Oxford: Oxford University Press.
2005. "Empirical Universals of Language as a Basis for the Study of Other Human Universals and as a Tool for Exploring Cross-Cultural Differences." *Ethos* 33, 2: 256–291.
Williams, Brackette. 1996. "Skinfolk, Not Kinfolk: Comparative Reflection on the Identity of Participant-Observation in Two Field Situations." In *Feminist Dilemmas in Fieldwork*, ed. Diane L. Wolf. Boulder: Westview Press, 72–95.
Williams, Patricia. 1993. *The Alchemy of Race and Rights*. London: Virago Press.
Wilson, Ara. 1996. "Lesbian Visibility and Sexual Rights at Beijing." *Signs* 22, 1: 214–218.
Winstanley, Gerrard. 1652. *The Law of Freedom in a Platform: Or, True Magistracy Restored*. London: printed by J.M. for the author.

Winstanley, Gerrard, and George Holland Sabine. 1941. *The Works of Gerrard Winstanley*. Ithaca: Cornell University Press.

Wolf, Diane L., ed. 1996. *Feminist Dilemmas in Fieldwork*. Boulder: Westview Press.

Wolf, Margery. 1992. *A Thrice-Told Tale: Feminism, Postmodernism, and Ethnographic Responsibility*. Stanford: Stanford University Press.

Wolfensohn, James. 2005. "Conversation: James Wolfensohn." In *The News Hour with Jim Lehrer*. US: National Public Television.

Wollstonecraft, Mary. 1792[1985]. *A Vindication of the Rights of Woman*. London: Penguin.

Women for Women's Human Rights (WWHR) Istanbul, Turkey. *End-of-Violence Working Group* 1998 [cited November 10].

Women's World Congress. 2005. "Women's Worlds 2005." Seoul, Korea, June 19–24.

Wood, Neal. 1984. *John Locke and Agrarian Capitalism*. Berkeley: University of California Press.

World Social Forum Panel. 2004. "Overcoming Gender-Based Violence in the Private Sphere." In *World Social Forum, Bread for the World*, Mumbai, India, January 16–21.

Xiaorong, Li. 1998. "'Asian Values' And the Universality of Human Rights." *Business and Society Review* 102/103: 81–87.

Yasuaki, Onuma. 1999. "Toward an Intercivilizational Approach to Human Rights." In *The East Asian Challenge for Human Rights*, ed. Joanne R. Bauer and Daniel A. Bell. Cambridge: Cambridge University Press, 103–123.

Young, Iris Marion. 1989. "Polity and Group Difference: A Critique of the Ideal of Universal Citizenship." *Ethics* 99, 2: 250–274.

1990. *Justice and the Politics of Difference*. Princeton: Princeton University Press.

1997a. "Difference as a Resource for Democratic Communication." In *Deliberative Democracy: Essays on Reason and Politics*, ed. James Bohman and William Rehg. Cambridge, MA: MIT Press, 383–406.

1997b. "Unruly Categories: A Critique of Nancy Fraser's Dual Systems Theory." *New Left Review* 222, March–April: 147–160.

2000. *Inclusion and Democracy*. Oxford: Oxford University Press.

2001a. "Activist Challenges to Deliberative Democracy." *Political Theory* 29, 5: 670–690.

2001b. "Political Theory and Feminist Social Criticism." *American Political Science Review* 95, 3: 713.

2006. "Taking the Basic Structure Seriously." *Perspectives on Politics* 4, 1: 91–97.

Yu, Anthony C. 2000. "Which Values? Whose Perspective?" *The Journal of Religion* 80, 2: 299–304.

Zalewski, Marysia. 2000. *Feminism after Postmodernism: Theorising through Practice*. New York: Routledge.

Zerilli, Linda. 2002. "Contingency, Hegemony, Universality: Contemporary Dialogues on the Left." *Political Theory* 30, 1: 167–170.

2005. *Feminism and the Abyss of Freedom*. Chicago: University of Chicago Press.

# *Interviews*

I1. 2004. Gender and development expert from Guinea-Bissau. Interview conducted in French: World Social Forum, Mumbai, India, January 21.

I2. 2004. Activist with the World March of Women from Burkina Faso. Interview conducted in French: World Social Forum, Mumbai, India, January 21.

I3. 2004. Activist with the World March of Women from Burkina Faso. Interview conducted in French: World Social Forum, Mumbai, India, January 21.

I4. 2004. Director of Activist Organization in Rajasthan (India). Interview conducted in English: World Social Forum, Mumbai, India, January 19.

I5. 2004. Jayati Ghosh, Professor of Economics at J. Nehru University in New Delhi. Interview conducted in English: World Social Forum, Mumbai, India, January 20.

I9. 2004. Sonalini Sapra, Research Assistant, Trade and Labour Rights Department, Centre for Education and Communication, New Delhi. Interview conducted in English: World Social Forum, Mumbai, India, February 19.

I10. 2004. Leading activist for women in India. Interview conducted in English: World Social Forum, Mumbai, India, January 20.

I12. 2004. Anonymous South Asian queer rights activist. Interview conducted in English: World Social Forum, Mumbai, India, January 20.

I14. 2004. Nilofar Sakhi, a women's activist from Afghanistan. Women Activities and Social Services Association (WASSA). Email interview conducted in English: February 22.

I17. 2004. Anonymous South African LGBT rights activist. Interview conducted in English: World Social Forum, Mumbai, India, January 20.

I18. 2004. American scholar-activist in the field of women's human rights. Interview conducted in English: World Social Forum, Mumbai, India, January 18.

IB1. 2005. Joanna Kerr, Executive Director, Association of Women's Rights and Development, Canada. Interview conducted in English: Feminist Dialogues, Porto Alegre, January 23–25.

IB2. 2005. Pramada Menon, Director Programs, Creating Resources for Empowerment in Action, India. Interview conducted in English: Feminist Dialogues, Porto Alegre, January 23–25.

IB3. 2005. Svati P. Shah, activist for lesbian/gay/bisexual/transgender-rights organizations in the queer/people of color community in New York and in India. Interview conducted in English: Feminist Dialogues, Porto Alegre, January 23–25.

IB5. 2005. Natalia Flores. Part of the coordinating group of young Chilean feminists. Interview conducted in Spanish: Feminist Dialogues, Porto Alegre, January 23–25.

IB6. 2005. "Carolina," Network coordinator for women in Paraguay. Interview conducted in Spanish: Feminist Dialogues, Porto Alegre, January 23–25.

IB7. 2005. An activist with Articulacao das Mulheres Brasileiras, Brazil. Interview conducted in Portuguese: Feminist Dialogues, Porto Alegre, January 23–25.

IB8. 2005. "Elizabeth," activist with a member organization of REDLAC, which is a Latin American and Caribbean network of youth for sexual and reproductive rights. Interview conducted in Spanish: Feminist Dialogues, Porto Alegre, January 23–25.

IB9. 2005. "Maria." Interview conducted in Spanish: Feminist Dialogues, Porto Alegre, January 23–25.

IB10. 2005. Dieuwertje, feminist activist from The Netherlands. Interview conducted in English: Feminist Dialogues, Porto Alegre, January 23–25.

IB11. 2005. "Ana." Interview conducted in Portuguese: Feminist Dialogues, Porto Alegre, January 23–25.

IB12. 2005. An activist from Turkey whose organization works locally and transnationally within the Middle East and North Africa Region. Interview conducted in English: World Social Forum, Porto Alegre, January 26–31.

IB13. 2005. Loretta Ross, founder the National Center for Human Rights Education, Atlanta, Georgia and co-founder Sister Song, Women of Color for Reproductive Health. Interview conducted in English: World Social Forum, Porto Alegre, January 26–31.

IB14. 2005. A feminist activist for Asian women. World Social Forum, Porto Alegre, January 26–31.

IB17. 2005. Activist from Kenya. Interview conducted in English: World Social Forum, Porto Alegre, January 26–31.

IB18. 2005. Peace activist from El Salvador. Interview conducted in English: World Social Forum, Porto Alegre, January 26–31.

IB19. 2005. Female economist working with ecumenical churches, Philippines. Interview conducted in English: World Social Forum, Porto Alegre, January 26–31.

ID6. 2004. Annemarie Reerink, Gender and Development scholar in the Asia-Pacific Region: Australia, February 9.

ID7. 2004. Erica Lewis, National Policy and Research Officer, YWCA of Australia: Australia, February 4.

ID13. 2004. Anonymous feminist researcher working on indigenous property rights: Australia, February 11.

ID16. 2004. Burmese women's human rights activist, working on trafficking of women and children in the Asia-Pacific Region: Australia, February 20.

ID23. 2004. Scholar–activist with Development Alternatives with Women for a New Era (DAWN). Email interview, March 8.

IS3. 2005. Poonam Arora, Associate Professor of English and Film Studies, Chair, Department of Humanities, University of Michigan, Dearborn. Feminist Dialogues, Porto Alegre, January 23–25.

IS5. 2005. Nang Lao Liang Won. Activist for women and refugees from minority communities in Southeast Asia. Feminist Dialogues, Porto Alegre, January 23–25.

# Index